SELECTIONS FROM MEDIEVAL PHILOSOPHERS

II

ROGER BACON TO WILLIAM OF OCKHAM

SELECTIONS FROM MEDIEVAL PHILOSOPHERS

II
ROGER BACON TO WILLIAM OF OCKHAM

EDITED AND TRANSLATED, WITH INTRODUCTORY
NOTES AND GLOSSARY BY

RICHARD McKEON

PROFESSOR OF PHILOSOPHY AND GREEK
UNIVERSITY OF CHICAGO

CHARLES SCRIBNER'S SONS

NEW YORK

CONTENTS

GENERAL INTRODUCTION

The study of philosophy has as end, Thomas Aquinas said, not the knowledge of what others have thought, but objective truth. The method and practice of medieval philosophers, working upon the writings of past philosophers, are adapted to the determination of truth from their statements. There is little in the scholastic method that conforms to the outlook and approach of modern philosophy. It is historical, but the history involved has been shown to be bad history: works as patently neoplatonic as the *Book of Causes* and the *Theology of Aristotle* were long thought to have been written by Aristotle. It is authoritarian, whereas the way to truth, the scientific method, according to the dicta which positivistic science has insinuated into philosophy, is by facts, not by what men have said.

By these circumstances the middle ages were for a long time closed and kept from influencing openly the progress of modern thought. Philosophers continued to read their predecessors, not only as historians, but to find hints for the discovery of truth. Only occasionally, however, did a logician or a metaphysician go for suggestions to the middle ages. To be sure, many doctrines and many lines of influence have continued uninterrupted though constantly modified from the middle ages to the present, and our language and ideology is strewn with vestiges confusing and difficult to explain in their modern guise alone. In part, in the beginnings of the middle ages, a difference separates philosophers from those of the present in the spirit and the enterprise, common then but unfamiliar to philosophic concerns to day, of faith engaged in understanding itself; in part, in the height of the thirteenth and fourteenth centuries, there is a difference less in spirit than in terminology. When philosophy became the handmaiden of science instead of theology, when Aristotle fell into disrepute, the philosophic labors of the middle ages were locked tight in a double prejudice, grown from its purpose and its language. This prejudice did not prevent vast borrowings of what was condemned in other terms, but with the passing centuries the discredit of medieval thought was fortified by a growing ignorance of what had been discredited and why.

None the less, translation is not impossible of medieval discussions into terms that are at the very center of the problems of the new metaphysics and method, which have lately been constructed for science. True, much of the discussion comes to conclusions other than those currently held, but then, it was the conviction of medieval philosophers that conclusions are safe only if they have been fortified by examination of conclusions dialectically opposed to them. In the evolution of philosophy from Augustine through the debates of the fourteenth century it was important always to consider what opponents had said or might say in opposition to the doctrine: for that reason philosophers had grown learned in authorities and adept in the manipulation of arguments. But seldom, save where philosophic arguments require it, are authorities to be followed unsupported by reason. The method encounters dangers: to one unfamiliar with the terms it has the sound of a logomachy; to one concerned with the practical it is tenuously speculative. But the opposed method encounters evils even worse: if one forgets the old distinctions, one is very apt to repeat the old sophisms; what was supposed to be practical is found on examination to be threaded and bolstered with fragments and wisps of the speculative, dangerous now, not because they are speculative, but because they are unexamined.

The citation of authorities for the discovery of truth may go on without great concern for historical niceties of doctrine. Men were learned in the history of philosophy during the middle ages, and there were among them many notable scholars even by the standards of a later age. Philosophy was studied, however, not in the fashion of the innumerable *Lives of the Philosophers* of the hellenistic times and the late Roman Empire, with an emphasis on the idiosyncrasies and careers of philosophers and schools, nor in the modern fashion of determining precisely who first said what and by what circumstances he was determined (and though texts showed more philological variations then, they were more apt to be intelligible philosophically), but the history of philosophy is used in the works of Thomas Aquinas and Roger Bacon as Plato and, more systematically, Aristotle had been adept in it, stating doctrines of preceding philosophers and criticising them before going to a statement of the position they were themselves to advance. Criticism was employed, but most usually it was criticism of a single doctrine, by which to interpret it, often away from its original intent, or refute it. It is not important that platonic doctrines are quoted against platonic doctrines, aristotelian doctrines against aristotelian. There have been and still are unnumbered platonisms and many fragmentary doctrines of a persisting aristotelianism, and even with our improved methods of critical scholarship and our surer texts, it is difficult to decide, for example, whether the aristotelianism of Averroes is closer to Aristotle than the aristotelianism of Thomas Aquinas. Rather more interesting is the difference in the fate of the two philosophies, that which stemmed from Plato and that which stemmed from Aristotle, during the middle ages. In Augustine's writings christian philosophy had already taken the neoplatonic ordering which it was to continue, one God, three persons, eternal ideas and numbers, contingent things, among the latter of which rational souls were uppermost and turned to the contemplation of eternal things. The philosophy of Aristotle, progressively rediscovered, contributed first a logic, then a metaphysics, a physics, a psychology, an ethics, a politics, but without altering the outlines of the philosophy. In the case of Aristotle it is frequently a matter of dispute whether or not he held that the world is eternal, that the soul is immortal, that the active intellect is a faculty of the human soul. Chiefly he was the source of doctrines and distinctions. Plato, however, entered the middle ages by way of neoplatonisms that had taken some of his analyses literally and had found a religion in his myths. An ordering hierarchy, so derived, early became part of christian dogma, and the analogical method proper to the philosophy was free to play within that framework. As some point in the analogy becomes literal doctrine, a new platonism emerges, so that it might be said that there are many platonisms in the middle ages but only one aristotelianism, often incomplete, often subject to dispute on a given question, but for the most part a body of terms, distinctions, doctrines, used almost universally and precisely understood.

It was easy therefore for the two to merge, and the spectacle of the middle ages reconciling Plato and Aristotle is not so fantastic as a later age, thinking only of its critical editions, has imagined. The order of the world, the structure of eternal things is the dogma drawn from Plato; the language, logic, and order of sciences is the doctrine drawn from Aristotle. Plato spoke the language of wisdom; Aristotle the language of science;

Augustine, illumined by the Holy Ghost and lighting in turn the whole line of christian philosophers, the language of both. There are, therefore, as many augustinisms in the thirteenth century, as there were platonisms before; and as Augustine had constructed a platonism, little related to the *Dialogues*, for all the doctrinal continuities that might be pointed out, so each of the writers of the thirteenth and fourteenth centuries (and therefore each of the six who appear in translation in this volume), since each quotes Augustine and finds in his works "authorities" for doctrines, constructs an augustinism, one differing from the other, each differently related to the doctrine Augustine himself expounded. Matthew of Aquasparta finds, quoting Augustine for authority, that divine illumination is necessary for the explanation of knowledge; Duns Scotus finds, with the same authority, that the natural power of the intellect suffices. According to Matthew the principles of philosophy can not alone explain knowledge, but must be supplemented by the principles of theology; according to Thomas, that authority of Augustine holds for the knowledge of God, but for the knowledge of things, the activity of the active intellect is sufficient. Bonaventura finds authority in Augustine for the doctrine that intellectual excellence presupposes moral excellence; Duns Scotus can find no statement in him that the good have greater wisdom, but only that they have greater love of God. Aristotle enters similarly with Augustine into the interplay of authorities. Roger Bacon can (thus) quote him for support of the augustinian position that virtue is needed for knowledge.[1] For the argument proceeds by reason even when authorities are quoted: what Augustine said is like the theory according to which the scientist works; it is proper that

[1] See below, p. 76.

his saying should have some additional or some other
meaning after the discussion.

The evolution of thought down the middle ages might
be described in terms of a shift of interest or in terms of
a change of method. In Augustine the preoccupation had
been the discovery of God as the basis of all things and
the inspiration of all activities; philosophy had been
turned to the conversion of all knowledge and energy to
the knowledge and love of God and to human salvation.
The source of being, the object of love, the ground of
truth were the same, and therefore the way to God by
love and understanding was undifferentiated: one can
not know the good without loving it, one can not love
God without knowing him, at least partially and to the
extent of one's powers. For later discussions the one,
the true, and the good are still (by the authority of
Aristotle as well as Augustine) convertible, that is to say,
whatever is true is good, whatever is good is true. But
though all truths are from the first truth, it is possible to
differentiate truths from each other as well as to see in
them their common truth. Short of the recognition of
God behind truths, there are the practises of logic to examine consequences and oppositions, truths and falsities;
short of the recognition of God behind goods, there are
the distinctions of the virtues and the habits, the speculative and the practical. From the consideration of truth as
the reflection of divine things, philosophy passed to the
consideration of the truth of things situated between God
and man, deriving their truth still from God, but causing
truth in the human mind. Such a step between the works
of Augustine and Thomas does not make it necessary
that the former be contradicted in the works of the latter,
but it does explain why the augustinism of Thomas differs from that found in Augustine himself or in (say)
Bonaventura. In that step philosophy had become some-

what other than faith knowing itself, and thereafter it
can play another role than that set by the inspiration of
the theology: theology can concern itself with the domain
of things as they are related to God, and there remains
for philosophy the domain of things in their relations to
things and to man. The next step, that taken by the
scotists and the ockhamites, is in the enlarging and ex-
ploring of the subjects so revealed, of logic, physics, and
metaphysics.

Corresponding to the steps of this transition of interest, the methods employed underwent shifts and alterations. For the exploration of the variety of things to
discover an identical Truth and Good at their basis, the
medieval philosophers found the analogical method of
Plato to their hands. To be sure, the method could not
be carried to its extreme, as Plato might have been
tempted to carry it, for the data on which it was employed are accepted by faith; the triune God, omnipotent
creator of the world, may be submitted to dialectical
examination, but in his case one must guard against
literal statements, save those made in the dogmas of religion. Within the dogmas the translation from the doctrine of the philosophers to the philosophic truth is
made easy. For as Bacon observed,[2] using the method,
the temple of God was constructed by the servants of
Solomon and the servants of Hiram, that is, by the wisdom of the apostles and the wisdom of the philosophers
and wise men of the gentiles. When the problem is to
show forth a doctrine perspicuously or to lead the mind
to the contemplation of a truth too lofty for statement
and beyond demonstration, on which, however, demonstrations depend and by which the meanings of things are
possible, the method of analogy is peculiarly effective.
The aristotelian method, on the other hand, is a method

[2] See below, p. 27.

of demonstration, proceeding by syllogism from principles stated. The one is a method for the presentation of a truth immediately and perspicuously; the other a method for guaranteeing a truth by showing its dependence on stated principles. The difficulty of the one is that it can only lead to and present; if the truth in question is seen, that must be sufficient, for there are no reasons why it is so, and one who does not see may easily question it. The difficulty of the other is that the truth of a doctrine is richer and fuller than the principles on which it is based; to state only the principles is to impoverish it save in the eyes of a trained philosopher who (as a mathematician can see the system of a mathematical discipline in its postulates) can see the deductive consequences which follow from the principles. The scholastic method is in one sense a device for remedying this defect of a body of philosophic truth stated in propositions: by setting down in each of a variety of questions, besides the conclusions, the diversity of opinions which might be opposed to the conclusion, it places the doctrine in its intellectual setting. But the usual device of the medieval philosopher was to supplement one of the methods with the other: to present the doctrine and lay its broad outlines by analogy, and to analyze its consequences and search out the principles on which it depends by means of the aristotelian syllogism. There remains room for wide diversity in the use of the methods, as wide as the difference between the analogical method of Bonaventura which is designed to present the way that leads back to God that he may be known and loved, and the demonstrative method of Thomas which is concerned to prove by natural reason whatever falls properly within the domain of philosophy, so that even the existence of God, who exceeds reason, is demonstrated *a posteriori* since it can not be demonstrated *a priori*.

The criticism that the middle ages were lost in wordy contentions and in irrational invocations of authority is based only on the surface of the medieval disputes: the distinctions were precise, but they were subtle to a nicety, and therefore since they have grown unfamiliar, they seem often too meticulous and sharp; the erudition required to enter into the rational dispute of authorities grew finally too massive, and since we have forgotten the ancient authorities (while constituting new authorities of our own) we lose the illumination that may come from the expert use of citations and see only the heavy weight of unfamiliar texts. We use authorities and distinctions much as the medieval philosophers did, yet on one point there may still seem an important difference: we appeal more frequently to facts and experience, whereas they may seem lost in the unfounded inferences of rationalism or the unexamined preferences of voluntarism. Certainly augustinism, turned to eternal things, and even aristotelianism, finding the bases of truths in first principles, for all the origin of knowledge in experience, are faced in the opposite direction to empiricism and positivism. But it was not ignorance of "facts", but a precise estimation of their place in the scheme of knowledge, which determined the orientation of these philosophies, in the direction that Plato and Aristotle had faced, toward eternal things and eternal truths in terms of which contingent things may be known. It is the recognition that any proposition may be false, though established carefully on experience and though the senses are unerring, and the recognition on the other hand that absolute truth would be possible, though all the senses were erring. It is recognition that the bases of truth must be in principles of knowledge and that any appeal beyond them must use them. What those principles are is discussed variously and the doctrinal differences are important. It is worth going to the philosophers themselves for those discourses, but they can be read sympathetically and understood, only if it is seen that the cause they are arguing is far from lost. Even if it could be decided however that they are in error, the distinctions they made ought not to be forgotten. They constructed a powerful, precise language, the remnants of which, blunted, dulled, and broadened by long and varied usage, are still the center of the philosophic idiom. That language has been reproduced as carefully as possible in the present translations, and the glossary appended should make clear the precise sense in which words grown vague are used. For if the terminology is made clear, and with it the distinctions it was designed to express, the discussions of the middle ages have much that is relevant to problems still current, and in time the outstanding philosophers of that period may be studied, not only for the historical end of knowing the work of an important period of thinkers, but for the philosophic end of knowing the truth.

RICHARD MCKEON.

SELECTIONS FROM MEDIEVAL PHILOSOPHERS

II

ROGER BACON TO WILLIAM OF OCKHAM

ROGER BACON (1210 or 1215 – 1294)

The philosophic attitude of Roger Bacon is in agreement in most respects with the augustinian movements of the thirteenth century. On the questions of seminal reasons, of spiritual matter, of the plurality of substantial forms, and other doctrines which had come to be the mark of augustinian thought, he had nothing to say distinct from what Bonaventura and other franciscans had held. Moreover, the enthusiasm for experimental science which marked him apart from his contemporaries, far from standing in contradiction with this conservative attitude, flowed naturally from it. For if on the one hand he could insist that the whole intention of philosophy is to evolve the natures and properties of things, that insistence can be understood properly only if it is balanced by his repeated statement that there is but one wisdom, found in the divine scriptures, which philosophy develops in doctrine and action.

Knowledge may be had in three manners, by authority, by reason, and by experience; but authority is insufficient without reason, and reason is not tranquil in the possession of truth if its data are not confirmed by experience. Experience is therefore the one source of certitude. But experience is of two sorts, external and internal; the former the work of the exterior senses, aided by instruments, formulating its conclusions with the precision of mathematics; the latter the interior knowledge consequent to divine inspirations and consummated in seven stages. Significantly, the mystical knowledge of these internal experiences is of the same type and efficacy as experimental knowledge, for the doctrine of the unity of knowledge is a fundamental doctrine in his philosophy, and consequently no science will pursue only an end of its own, but all will unite their utilities in the service of theology. Science for Bacon is a neglected and more efficacious instrument by which to attain, by acquiring a knowledge of his handiwork, to the augustinian ideal of knowledge of God. The ecstatic or mystic way will rise to a knowledge of all human sciences, not only of spiritual, but of corporeal things, and of the various sciences of philosophy.

Bacon, it must be remembered, was an unusually able and well informed scientist. He wrote with distinction on the natural sciences, mathematics, perspective, optics, geography, astronomy, alchemy, and philology. In many of these he conducted inquiries and formulated theories at variance with those commonly pursued or held in his times: there is evidence that he may have had a telescope and a microscope; we have his cipher formula for gunpowder and a few chemical processes and medical remedies as well as unciphered statements scattered through his major writings; his work on the calendar prepared for the gregorian reform; his work in geography influenced the men who furnished the geographic notions by which the explorations of two and a half centuries later were guided; and it is impossible to say whether or not there are further items of practical discovery and research hidden in the libraries of Europe, since Bacon's sage counsel was to encipher all such bits of information. His doctrine of knowledge, therefore, is not formulated in ignorance of the possibilities of experimental science, for experience enjoys all prerogatives over other ways of knowledge—it can discover the secrets of nature; it alone can reach complete certitude. Even more, Bacon rose not infrequently to a prophetic fury: through ignorance of this method the age was coming to desuetude; abstract superfluous questions abounded to the neglect of useful, necessary, and fruitful knowledge; philosophy was dying and the world was filled with books of futilities and puerilities.

Much of Bacon's work was conceived and planned as outline for the reform of learning, and therefore superficially there is much in his attitude and manner that reminds one of his later namesake and in general of the seventeenth century. It is in fulfillment rather than in contradiction of these plans that experimental knowledge of the world is crowned by an experimental knowledge that turns inward. For all knowledge is a *species*, that is, an action of the thing known upon the knower, and ultimately it must be clear that the action of no particular thing can stop in itself; knowledge leads back definitely from any information to God. The light pouring through a window is attributed to the sun, and the knowledge present in the mind similarly is due to the action of God. The great discoveries of the sciences and the arts would have been impossible to man without the revelation of God; in effect, God revealed all philosophy to man in the beginning, and the history of thought since has been the cyclical rediscovery, after periods of sin, of a wisdom the patriarchs received. Of course, the primitive revelation had to be filled by the details of science (that was why the patriarchs lived three hundred years), and Bacon therefore strikes the double posture of the prophet who heralds the return to the ancient truths and of the scientist who possesses new and strange truths with which to revivify the ancient doctrine. Wisdom is one, but items of information may be added to build it out and substantiate it without altering its outlines. Experimental knowledge is to accomplish this, and its procedure will be to work either with the things without the mind or the things within; God is present in both; indeed, God is the active intellect. The study of Bacon is chiefly the study of this theory of knowledge and of the details of reform to which knowledge of languages and of the various sciences is to be subjected.

ROGER BACON

THE OPUS MAJUS[1]

THE FIRST PART[2]
OF THIS DEMONSTRATION

THE CAUSES OF ERROR

*In which the four universal causes of all human igno-
rance are removed. There are four distinctions in
this part, and in the first distinction there are four chapters. In the first chapter, after the intention of the
whole demonstration has been stated, these four causes
are criticized in general.*

CHAPTER I.

The perfect consideration of wisdom consists in two
things, namely, in perceiving what is required for wisdom that it may be known best, and then, in perceiving
how wisdom should be related to all things that they
may be directed by it in proper ways. For by the light
of wisdom (1) the Church of God is directed; (2) the
commonwealth of the faithful is disposed; (3) the conversion of unbelievers is procured; and (4) by the excellence of wisdom those who are obstinate in evil can be
curbed that they may be thrust far from the bounds of

[1] *The Opus Majus of Roger Bacon*, ed. by J. H. Bridges.
London: Williams and Norgate, 1900, 3 vols.
[2] Vol. I, pp. 1-8, and vol. III, pp. 1-8.

the Church more effectively than by the shedding of
christian blood. All matters, in fact, which need the
guidance of wisdom are reduced to the above four,
nor can wisdom be related to more. Wherefore, that this
wisdom be known not only relatively but absolutely, I
shall try here to present to Your Holiness, following the
tenor of your recent letter, whatever I can at the present
time in a probable demonstration, until a more certain
and fuller writing is completed. But, since the subjects
under consideration are weighty and uncommon, they
demand for human frailty, grace and favor. For according to the Philosopher in the seventh book of the
Metaphysics, those things which are of greatest understanding in themselves are of least apprehension to us.
Indeed, enveloped truth is concealed in the depths and
deposited in the abyss, as Seneca says in the seventh
book on Favors and in the fourth of Natural questions;
and Cicero says in the Hortensius that all our understanding is obstructed by many difficulties, since our understanding is related to what is most manifest in its
own nature, as the eye of the owl and the eye of the
bat are to the light of the sun (as the Philosopher says
in the second book of the Metaphysics[3]) and as one deaf
from birth is related to harmonic delights, as Avicenna
says in the ninth book of the Metaphysics. Wherefore
we are sufficiently impressed with the weakness of our
own intellect in the investigation of truth, to want to
remove, as much as possible, extraneous causes and oc-
casions of error from the imperfection of our perception.

  There are, indeed, four chief hindrances to the understanding of truth, which stand in the way of every man,
however wise, and permit hardly any to arrive at the
true title of wisdom; to wit, (1) the example of frail
and unsuited authority, (2) the long duration of custom,

  [3] ARISTOTLE, *Met.* II, 1, 993^{b}9-11.

(3) the opinion of the unlearned crowd, and (4) the concealment of one's own ignorance in the display of apparent wisdom. Every man is involved in these difficulties, every condition of man is held by them. For every one in all the acts of life and study and every occupation uses three of the worst arguments to the same conclusion; namely, (1) this has been exemplified by our ancestors, (2) this is the custom, (3) this is the common belief: therefore, it must be held. But the opposite to the conclusion follows far better from the premises, as I shall prove in many instances by authority and experience and reason. But if these three arguments are sometimes refuted by the splendid power of reason, the fourth is always before the eyes or on the lips of every one to excuse his own ignorance; and although he knows nothing worth knowing, nevertheless what he knows he magnifies shamelessly so that he overwhelms and shatters the truth in the consolation of his unhappy stupidity. Moreover, all the evils of the human race come from these deadly plagues; for the most useful and the greatest and most beautiful instances of wisdom and the secrets of all the sciences and arts are ignored; but what is even worse, men blinded by the mist of these four arguments do not perceive their own ignorance, but cover and conceal it with all caution so that they find no remedy for it; and finally, what is worst of all, they think they are in the full light of truth when they are in the densest shadows of error; because of this they hold the most true to be in the bounds of falsity, the best to be of no value, the greatest to possess neither weight nor worth; and on the contrary they honor the most false praise the worst, extol the most vile, blind to the truth that all the brightness of wisdom is other than these, disdainful of what they can attain with great ease; and because of the greatness of their stupidity they spend

most considerable labors, consume much time, pour out
vast expenditures on things which are of no utility or
little and of no merit in the judgment of the wise man.
Hence it is necessary that the violence and harm of these
four causes of all evils be known in the beginning and
be condemned and put off far from the consideration of
wisdom.   For where the first three of these causes dominate, no reason moves; no right judges; no law binds;
the injunctions of religion have no place; the dictates
of nature perish; the face of things is changed; order
is confounded; vice prevails; virtue is extinguished;
falsity reigns; truth is puffed away. And therefore nothing is more necessary to this consideration than the sure
condemnation of these four causes of error by chosen
arguments of wise men which shall not possibly be contradicted.

Since moreover the wise bring the first three together
and condemn them at the same time and since the fourth
requires a separate investigation because of its special
stupidity, therefore, I shall try first to disclose the harm
of the three.   But although authority is one of them,
I speak in no wise of the solid and true authority which
is bestowed by the judgment of God on the Church or
which arises from the merit and dignity of some one
among the saints and perfect philosophers and other
wise men who are expert to the full measure of human
possibility in the cultivation of wisdom; but I speak of
that authority which many men seize upon violently in
this world without the help of God, not from the merit
of their wisdom, but because of their own presumption
and their desire for fame; and I speak of the authority
which the unlearned multitude grants (to its own destruction in the just judgment of God) to many. For according to the Scripture the hypocrite often rules because
of the sins of the people; I speak, in fact, of those

sophistical authorities of the insensate multitude which
are authorities in an equivocal sense, as a stone eye or a
painted eye has the name of eye but not its power.

CHAPTER II.

The sacred Scripture, moreover, reproves these three
causes of error; the holy doctors condemn them; canon
law forbids them; philosophy reprehends them. But
for reasons touched upon before with reference to philosophic treatments and because the opinions of philosophers concerning these three are very little known,
I shall treat principally of the philosophic opinions.
Seneca, of course, in the second book of his Letters
(near the end) condemns all three of these banes in a
single phrase. He says, *Among the causes of our ills
is that we live according to model; we are not regulated
by reason but are carried along by custom; that which
we would not care to imitate if few were to do it, we
do when many begin to do it rather because it is more
frequent than because it is more honorable: and error
holds the place of right among us when it has been
made general.*[4] The Philosopher moreover, attacking
throughout his philosophy unworthy authority, asserts
in the second book of the Metaphysics that the principal causes of human error are custom and the influence of the masses.[5] And again Seneca in the book
on the Happy Life says, *No man errs for himself alone,
but he is the cause and author of another's error, and
error transmitted from one to another turns us aside and
throws us down and we perish by the examples of other
men.*[6] And in the second book on Anger, *Because of*

[4] SENECA, *lib.* XX, *Ep.* 8, ed. Haase.
[5] *Meta.* II, 3, 995a 3-6.
[6] SENECA, *Dialog.* VII, 1.

the evil of custom, he says, *vices which have grown with us are removed with difficulty.*[7] And in the book on the Happiness of Life he contends against the opinion of the crowd,

> Nothing implicates us in greater evils than that we adapt ourselves to rumor and think those things best which have been received with great approval; nor do we live according to reason but according to likeness and precedent. Thence is that great heaping together of men rushing upon other men. For this befalls man in a great massacre, since people so press upon one another that no one falls without drawing another with him, and the first are the cause of destruction to those who follow. You may see this happen in every life.

And again he says in the same book, *The people, defenders of their own evil, stand against reason*; and further on, *Human affairs are not so well ordered that the better pleases most*; and then follows, *The crowd is the worst argument.*[8] And Cicero in the third of the Tusculan questions says, *When we have been handed over to school masters, we are so filled with a variety of errors, that truth yields to vanity, and nature itself yields to established opinion.*[9] And he says in the Lucullus, *Some, having accommodated themselves to a friend or having been captivated by only the speech of some one whom they have heard, judge of unknown things, and into whatever art or discipline they are borne as by a tempest, they hold fast to that judgment as to a rock; most would rather err and defend the opinion which*

[7] SENECA, *Dial.* IV, 18.

[8] Seneca, *Dial.* VII, 1 and 2.

[9] CICERO, *Tus. Disput.* III, 1, 2.

they had liked, than investigate without obstinacy what they say most surely.[10] And because of the depravity of custom he asks in the first book on Divine Nature, *Does it not shame him who speculates on nature to seek from minds steeped in custom the testimony of truth?*[11] And against the opinion of the mob, he says in the introduction to the second book of Disputations, *Philosophy is content with few judges, fleeing the multitude deliberately, and suspected and detested by it,*[12] and in the same second book he says, *All things which are done without publicity seem to me the more praiseworthy.*[13] But other authors take up these three errors separately. For in the book of Natural Questions of Adalardus [Adelard of Bath], the question is raised concerning frail authority: *What else is authority of this sort than a halter? For surely as brute animals are led by any halter, and see neither whither nor why they are led, so this very authority leads not a few into danger, taken and bound in bestial credulity.* And in the book on the Eternity of the World it is said, *He who has chosen one side of a question because of love of custom can not rightly distinguish true opinion.* And Averroes at the end of the second book of the Physics says,

> Custom is the greatest cause in keeping us from many manifest things. Just as certain actions, although they are harmful, will be easy to the man accustomed to them and as, for that reason, he believes that they are useful, so when one has been accustomed to believe certain false statements from boyhood, that custom will be the cause of denying the truth, as some people

[10] CICERO, *Academ. Prior.* II, 3.
[11] *De Deorum Natura* I, 30.
[12] *Tusc. Disp.* II, 1, 4.
[13] *Ibid.* II, 26, 64.

have been so accustomed to eating poison that
it has become a food for them.

And Averroes likewise holds in the second book of the
Metaphysics, *When the opposites to principles have be-*
come well-known, they are more readily received by the
multitude and by those following the testimony of the
many than the principles themselves. And Jerome in the
Prologue to the fifth book on Jeremiah asserts that truth
is content with few, and it is not terrified by a multitude
of enemies. John Chrysostom says likewise in his commentary on Matthew, that they have professed themselves stripped of truth who have armed themselves with
multitude.

CHAPTER III.

Whatever has been proved by authorities is determined even more certainly from the experience of
any man. For we find in ourselves and in others that
these three practices, embracing evils as they do in most
instances, adhere very frequently to what is false. But,
if occasionally they are found in connection with good
and true things, they are almost always imperfect, and
they contain but a weak degree of wisdom. As normally
the daughter follows the deeds of the mother, the son
those of the father, the slave those of the master, the
subject those of the king, the subordinate those of the
prelate, the disciple those of the master. Because it
is customary for the sons of Adam to claim authority
and to scatter their examples in the light. For all men,
according to Aristotle in the fourth book of the Ethics,
love their own deeds, as parents love their children, poets
their measures, and so with the others. And for this
reason many have used too much freedom in writing,
and have not hesitated even to insinuate to depraved

and bestial men the thought, Why do you not fill up pages of paper? And why do you not write on the back of the sheet? These men are like a lame and purblind shepherd with many sheep which they are neither able nor know how to recall from wandering in the byways of falsity to the healthier pasturage of wisdom, and they are like birds who wish to fly without wings, presuming to the master's place before they are proficient in the grade of good disciple. They fall necessarily into so many errors that idlers comparing themselves to them [these bad workers] deem themselves happy, as, when many run a race, he whom hopelessness will not permit to run notwithstanding that the prize seems precious to him, nevertheless counts himself happy in comparison to him who while racing falls into an unseen pit. And for that reason we see with en- lightened faith that for one example of truth, in knowl- edge as in life, there are more than a thousand examples of falsity. The world indeed is full of examples of this sort, and one example of true perfection easily finds ten thousand imperfect. Nature, in fact, has formed for us in numbers the fitting illustration of perfection and imperfection. For a number is said to be perfect[14] the sum of whose divisors, added, equal the number itself, and there is only one such number beneath ten, namely six, and one between 10 and 100, namely 28, and one between 100 and 1000, namely 496, and one between 1,000 and 10,000, namely 8,128, and so on; and would that it were thus with men and that this was accorded to the human race! But this never was the case, neither in life nor in knowledge, nor will it ever be, even to the final destruction of sin, since not only is there the scarcity of those who are perfect in

[14] If $2^n - 1$ is a prime number, then $(2^n - 1) (2^{n-1})$ is a perfect number, as 6, 28, 496, 8,128, etc.

all virtue and knowledge, but of those who have arrived
at the perfection of one virtue or knowledge. The first
are and will be and have always been very rare. For
they are the truly perfect, but of 10,000 men not one
is found so perfect in either condition of life or profession of wisdom; would that there were of the second
class of perfect men one in the first ten and so on, that
the perfection of numbers might be preserved in men!
But it is not thus, indeed it is found to be far otherwise. In the same way with respect to custom we prove
by experience in our acts what has now been stated in
examples of individuals. Let any one go over his life
from his infancy, and he will find that in a great many
of his acts he very easily transformed evils and falsenesses into custom. For in goods and in truths identity
is mother of satiety for human frailty, and unfortunate
man is delighted in the variety of useful things, according to the opinion of the authorities whom I brought
forward in the beginning. But the contrary is true in
the case of evils and falsenesses and things harmful to
himself and others, for in most actions, except where
special grace and divine privilege intervene in some
perfect men, human corruption preserves carefully the
things which are contrary to truth and salvation; nor
is it affected with weariness in the continuance of sin,
nor does it easily find loathing in things that are vain.
But if one be devoted from youth to the truth of life
and of knowledge, such an one retains imperfection in
a great many of his actions and he is pleased in imperfection; perfection indeed saddens him more frequently, for it delights extremely few and most of all
in the plenitude of virtues and science, and so it happens
that youth seldom guards against error, and old age
with the greatest difficulty ascends to perfection in any
thing. Of the crowd moreover the judgment is the

same. For the multitude of the human race has always
erred in the truth of God, and only the small group of
christians has received it; and we know that the great
mass of christians is imperfect, for the paucity of the
saints shows that. Similarly in the case of philosophical
doctrine, for the crowd has always lacked the wisdom
of philosophy. The slight number of philosophers, in
fact, declares that. And the ordinary run of those who
philosophize has always remained imperfect. For of
famous philosophers only Aristotle, together with his
followers, has been called philosopher in the judgment
of all wise men, since he ordered all the parts of philosophy so far as it was possible in his times, but still
he did not come to the limit of wisdom, as will be made
sufficiently manifest below. . . .

THE SECOND PART
OF THIS DEMONSTRATION[15]

THE AFFINITY OF PHILOSOPHY WITH
THEOLOGY

CHAPTER I.

Having banished to infernal regions, then, the four
general causes of all human ignorance and having removed them completely from this demonstration, I want
in this second distinction to show that one wisdom is
perfect and that it is contained in sacred letters; all
truth has grown from the roots of this wisdom. I say,
then, that either there is one science the mistress of
the others, namely theology (to which the rest are entirely necessary; and without the others it can not attain
to its effect; their excellence it claims as its right; the

[15] O. c., vol. I, pp. 33-44, and vol. III, pp. 36-53.

rest of the sciences obey its nod and authority), or better, there is only one perfect wisdom which is contained
wholly in the sacred Scriptures, to be explained by
canon law and philosophy. Indeed, the exposition of
the divine truth is had through these sciences. For,
although it is spread out by sciences as if in the palm
of the hand, yet of itself it brings all wisdom together
in the grasp of the fist, for all wisdom was given by one
God and to one world and for one end. Wherefore this
wisdom divides unity by its triple comparison. The
way of salvation is one, although there may be many
steps; but wisdom is the way to salvation. Indeed,
every consideration of man which is not of salvation is
full of blindness and leads to the final gloom of hell;
for which reason many wise men, famous in this world,
have been damned, because they did not have the true
wisdom but an apparent and false one, whence holding
themselves wise they were made fools according to the
Scripture. Augustine speaking of the sacred Scripture
says in the second book on Christian Doctrine, *If there
is truth elsewhere, it is found here; if there is evil, it is
condemned here.* And he wishes the christian, wheresoever he may have found the truth, to understand it to
be of his Lord, as was said in the beginning. The truth
of Jesus Christ is the wisdom of the sacred Scriptures.
Therefore there is no truth elsewhere except the truth
contained in that knowledge. Ambrose on the Epistle
to the Colossians says, *All reason of celestial knowledge
and of terrestrial creature is in him who is the head and
author, so that he who knows him should seek nothing
beyond, because he is perfect virtue and wisdom. Whatever is sought elsewhere, is found here perfectly.* Since,
therefore, the sacred Scriptures give us this wisdom,
which is of Christ, it is manifest that all truth is included here. But if wisdom is so called elsewhere and

if it is contrary to this, it will be erroneous, nor will it have anything save the name of wisdom; or if it is not said to be contrary, it is nevertheless diverse. But diversity, although it does not induce contrariety elsewhere, does here, as is evident from evangelical authority, *He who is not with me, is against me.* So it is true of this wisdom that what is not bound to it, is proved to be against it, and therefore to be avoided by the christian.

CHAPTER II.

This moreover appears more clearly to one considering the division of the sciences. For if we attempt to separate the sciences one from the other we can not say that theology is not both the science of canon law and philosophy. For under one division of philosophy, namely moral science, which Aristotle called civil, is contained civil law, as will be noted below. Canon law, moreover, is named from the canonical Scriptures, not from others, as the name itself reveals. The books of the Old Testament are referred to as these canonical books, as is done many times in the ninth distinction of the first part of the Decreta and elsewhere. Or else canon law is called canonical, from that same word, namely canon; for *canon* in greek is translated by *regula* in latin, and canon law as well as divine law is acknowledged to transmit the mode of living according to rule. But canon law is founded wholly on the authority of Scripture and on its expositors, as is clearly evident throughout the whole body of the Decretum and the Decretals: for either the authorities of the expositors of sacred Scriptures, such as Augustine, Jerome, Gregory, Ambrose, Isidore, Cyprian, Hilary and others are cited in support of the ordinances of the canons, or the holy and supreme pontiffs bring forward authorities and examples of the New and Old Testaments in support of their decrees; and therefore this law is only the explication of the will of God in the Scriptures. Again, canon law is called ecclesiastical law, by which the church of God is ruled in spiritual matters, as well in its head as in its members. But Scripture gives utterance to nothing other than this guidance of the Church. Furthermore, the natural law is contained in the sacred Scripture, as is taught in the beginning of the Decretum; but whatever has been accepted in customs or comprehended in writings, if it should be contrary to natural law, must be held to be vain and invalid, as is stated in the first part, eighth section. Canon laws can not be different from divine law; indeed, they must be derived from the fountains of divine law; and common law is either divine or human. It is divine if it was proclaimed to the world by the understanding and spirit of God in his Scripture; human if it was devised by the understanding of man. But it is clear that the church is ruled by the divine understanding and spirit and therefore by the divine law which is included in the sacred writings, and it is certain that the church is ruled by canon law. Wherefore this law is divine and must be drawn from the treasury of the sacred Scriptures. And this is manifest to one considering the divisions of canon law. For it orders the degrees of ecclesiastical offices, or it determines the sacraments of God, or it discusses the questions of conscience, or it decides ecclesiastical cases. But the roots of all these matters and the upright trunk itself are to be found in the sacred Scriptures; the branches moreover are in the expositors of the Scriptures; but the leaves, flowers, and salvation-bringing fruit are to be found in the body of the canon. For the delightful embellishment of canonic discourse is likened to leaves according to the Scriptures, but the utility of flowers and fruit comprehends in its own metaphor the four above-stated parts. And therefore the canons are only the golden shoots of corn, and the sprigs, and the ripeness of grapes by virtue of their presentation of the Scripture. Since, therefore, things are so, canon law is contained in one body under the authority of the Scripture, as the body of a single tree is composed of roots and trunk, branches, flowers, and fruits.

CHAPTER III.

It must be shown, however, both in general and in particular that the power of philosophy is not foreign to the wisdom of God, but is included in it. After this has been shown by authorities and examples and common reasons, it will then be explained more fully by taking up the four or five parts of philosophy within the range of each of the sciences and arts. For if christians ought to seize from the philosophers as from unlawful possessors the useful things which are contained in their books, as I showed in the beginning by the opinion of Augustine, it is obvious that philosophy is wholly worthy of and proper to sacred truth. Augustine says again in the same book [namely in the eighth book on Christian Doctrine] that the philosophers did not themselves originate the gold and silver of philosophers, but that it was drawn, as it were, from certain metals of divine providence which are spread out everywhere; which he shows to have been prefigured, saying,

> As the egyptians had vessels and ornaments
> of gold and silver and clothing which that people departing from Egypt appropriated to it-

self as to a better use, so the doctrines of the
gentiles contain liberal disciplines better suited
to the use of truth and contain more useful
moral precepts; and some points are found in
these philosophers concerning even the worship
of God himself; which gold, as it were, and
silver of theirs, the christian should take from
them for good use in preaching the gospel.

And he explains this in all things subject to human
treatment, which are moral, or historical, or artificial,
or natural, or logical and grammatical. For as regards
morals he says, *The clothing likewise of those men
(that is certain institutions of men), if accommodated
to human society which we can not dispense with in
this life, properly have to be converted to christian use.*
He says of the *historical,*

The history of the gentiles helps us greatly in
the understanding of the sacred books. For
many things are sought by us, and frequently,
by means both of the Olympiads and the names
of the consuls; and ignorance of the consulship
under which our Lord suffered causes many to
err in thinking that our Lord suffered in the
forty-sixth year of his life, because it was said
by the jews that the temple was built in that
number of years and because it was symbol-
ically representative of the Lord's body.

And this is manifest in almost innumerable places in
the New and Old Testament. Moreover, of other human
considerations, as well of the *arts* as of *nature* he says,
*Of the other arts, however, by which something is manu-
factured or remains after the operation, as for example,
a house, bench, vessel, and other objects of this sort, or*

medicine, or agriculture, and navigation, or of those arts whose only effect is the action, as of jumping, running, wrestling: knowledge of these must be used in judgment lest we be wholly ignorant of what the Scripture would teach when it uses some figures from these arts, and we may take the *natural sciences* broadly that medical matters may be included under them and what belongs to agriculture. For these latter sciences are based on natural things and are two of the eight principal natural sciences, as will be explained below. But in general he says of all the natural sciences, *That man would indeed perform a worthy task for the sacred Scripture who would bring together the characteristics of times and of places, of stones and other inanimate things, of plants and animals.* And in regard to the *logical* sciences he says, in the first book, that discipline of disputation is most valuable for all kinds of questions which must be examined and solved in the sacred writings. And elsewhere in the same book he says that there is a difference in the case of logic from that of the other sciences. For certain things which are necessary and very important for theology can be found in these latter sciences, but I do not see, he says, whether this can be done in the case of logic, since it is to be found, like nerves, throughout the whole text of the Scriptures. And in the third book, on the order of discipline, he says that no one should approach the sacred science without knowledge of the power of logic. Almost all of the second, third, and fourth books exhort us concerning the application of *grammatical* sciences to sacred things. And Jerome in his commentary on the Epistle to Titus, speaking of the utility of grammatical science in respect to theology, which is beyond that of many other sciences, says, *The doctrine of the grammarians can benefit life provided it be applied to better uses,* concerning which many and important things must be said in what follows. But of *mathematics* Cassiodorus says in his book on that science,

> When we turn over these four sciences, geometry, arithmetic, astronomy, music, with a careful mind, they whet perception, they cleanse away the filth of ignorance, and they lead, God granting, to that speculative contemplation; the holy fathers rightly urge that these four be read, since by them the appetite is in large part withdrawn from carnal things, and they make us desire that which we can contemplate with heart alone, the understanding aiding.

But these things will be shown abundantly in their proper place. And if such is the case in these sciences, much more forcefully are the *metaphysical* sciences in accord with divine utterances. For metaphysics occupies the place of one part of theology for philosophers, and it is called by them, together with moral philosophy, the divine science and physical theology, as is clear from the first and eleventh books of the Metaphysics of Aristotle and from the ninth and tenth books of the Metaphysics of Avicenna. For metaphysics takes up many things concerning God and the angels and divine subjects of this sort, and thus it is clear that the sacred Scripture claims the power of all wisdom. But not only does Augustine teach the above doctrines but he brings to mind that many saints have done this when he asks, *Do we not see with how much gold Cyprian, most delectable doctor and most blessed martyr, went enriched out of Egypt, and Lactantius and Victorinus, Optatus, Hilary (to say nothing of those still living) and innumerable greeks, as indeed Moses him-*

self, the most faithful servant of God had done before, of whom it was written that he was learned in all the wisdom of the egyptians?

CHAPTER IV.

Not only the blessed Augustine but also other saints assert the same thing, and they show likewise that it was expressed figuratively, and they testify that the saints acted accordingly. For I think that Jerome should be called to be our great spokesman in the present instance, for he says,

> But do you ask the reason that we sometimes place in our works examples drawn from secular literature and pollute the purity of the Church with the filth of the pagans? You are easily answered. You would never ask this if Cicero did not possess you wholly; you would never ask it if you read the sacred Scriptures, or if you pondered the commentators on them, with the exception of Vulcatius. For who does not know that in Moses and in the books of the prophets certain things are taken over from the books of the gentiles, and that Solomon proposed some questions to the philosophers of Tyre and answered some? Wherefore he admonishes us at the beginning of the Proverbs to understand the discourses of wisdom and the subtleties of words, parables and obscure speech, the sayings of wise men, and the enigmas which belong properly to dialecticians and philosophers. But even the Apostle Paul used a verse of the poet Epimenides when he wrote to Titus, *Cretans are always liars, evil*

beasts, idle bellies.[16] In another letter likewise
he sets down the verse of Menander, *Evil
companionships corrupt good morals.*[17] Moreover, disputing before the Athenians on the
hill of Mars, he calls Aratus to witness, *For
we too are his offspring;*[18] which is the close
in greek of an heroic verse. And lest that
should be too little, the leader of the christian
army, and invincible orator advancing the cause
for Christ, turns even a chance inscription
artfully into an argument of the faith. He
had, indeed, learned from the true David to
wrench the sword from the hands of the foe
and to cut off the head of the very haughty
Goliath with his own sword. He had read
moreover in Deuteronomy a precept given in
the speech of the Lord, that the head of the
woman captive must be shaved, the eyebrows,
all the hair and nails of her body must be cut
off, and thus must she be taken in marriage.
Why then is it strange if I too wish to make
secular wisdom, because of its charm of speech
and beauty of words, an israelite, from a handmaiden and slave? And if I cut and shave off
whatever there is dead in her of idolatry,
pleasure, error, lusts, and if united to her most
pure body I beget of her servants to the Lord
of Sabaoth, my labor is profitable in the house-
hold of Christ. Julian Augustus vomited forth
on his parthian expedition seven books against
Christ; if I shall attempt to write against him,
am I to think that you will forbid me to beat

[16] *Epistle of Paul to Titus* 1:11.
[17] *I Corinthians* 15:33.
[18] *Acts* 17:28.

> back the mad dog with the doctrines of the
> philosophers and of the stoics, that is to say,
> with the club of Hercules?

And he [Jerome] brings to the proof of this the prophets
themselves and all the famous doctors from the beginning of the Church who by the doctrines of the
philosophers have urged on the princes and unbelievers
the faith of Christ and have strengthened the faith
in many ways. And Bede, in his commentary on the
book of Kings, says that it is proper for christians to
take over to divine science as their own whatever is
useful in the liberal sciences. Otherwise Moses and
Daniel would not have suffered themselves to be instructed in the wisdom and letters of the egyptians
and the chaldeans. Again he says in his book on the
building of the temple that Solomon with his servants
symbolize Christ, and Hiram with his servants symbolize the philosophers and wise men of the gentiles,
so that the temple of God, that is the Church, was constructed not only by the apostolic wisdom but by the
wisdom of the philosophers. And the Scripture says,
*The servants of Hiram were more skillful in hewing
wood than the servants of Solomon.* Because, as Bede
says in reference to this, the gentiles, when they had
been converted from error and transformed to the truth
of the Gospels, knew the errors of the gentiles better,
and the more certainly they knew them, the more skill-
fully they learned to refute and dislodge them. Paul
knew the Gospel, which he had learned by revelation,
better; but Dionysius was better able to refute the false
dogmas of Athens, the arguments of which, as well as
similar errors, he had known from boyhood; and
therefore Solomon says, *For you know that there is
no man in my people who knows how to hew wood like*

the sidonians. These and many statements of this sort
the Venerable Bede recounts and many other writers
too, but let these suffice now.

CHAPTER V.

The causes can be given why the saints state thus the
point which we seek, and why they declare that it was
prefigured, and why they announce that it was seized
upon in effect by the saints. First, because the truth,
wheresoever it be found, is judged to be of Christ, according to the opinions and authorities of Augustine
mentioned above. In the second place, although the
truth of philosophy is said in one manner to belong to
philosophers, nevertheless that they might have this
[the philosophic] truth, the divine light first poured
into their minds and illumined them with additional
light. For it lighteth every man that cometh into this
world, as the Scripture says; with which opinions the
philosophers themselves agree. For they maintain that
there is an active and possible intellect. The human
soul is called possible by them, because of itself it is
in potentiality with respect to the sciences and virtues,
and receives them from another source. That which
flows into our minds, illuminating them to knowledge
and virtue, is called the active intellect, because although
the possible intellect may be called active from the act
of understanding, still if the active intellect be taken
as they take it, it is the intellect which flows upon and
illumines the possible intellect to knowledge of truth
that is called the active intellect. And thus the active
intellect, according to the ancient philosophers, is not
a part of the soul, but is an intellective substance other
than and separated in essence from the possible in-

tellect. And since this point is necessary to the demonstration of my proposition, which is that philosophy
exists through the influence of divine illumination, I
wish to prove it conclusively; particularly since a great
error has taken possession of the general run of philosophers in this matter, and likewise of the great mass of
theologians, since what a man is in philosophy, that he
is proved to be in theology. Alfarabi in fact says in
his book on the Understanding and the Understood that
the active intellect, which Aristotle spoke of in his third
treatise on the soul, is not matter, but is a separated
substance. And Avicenna teaches the same doctrine in
the fifth book on the Soul and the ninth of the Metaphysics. Likewise the Philosopher himself says that
the active intellect is separate from the possible, and
unmixed. Again he holds that the active intellect is
incorruptible with respect to being and substance, since
he says that it differs from the possible in the possession of incorruption; but the possible is incorruptible
with respect to substance and corruptible with respect
to being, because of its separation. Therefore the active
intellect will be incorruptible with respect to being and
substance; wherefore it will not be part of the soul,
since then it would be corrupted in respect to its being
in body, when it was separated from the body; and
he says that it is related to the possible as the artisan
to his material and as the light of the sun to colors.
The artisan, however, is outside the material in which he
works and is separated from it in essence; in the same
way the light of the sun expelling shadows from colors
and other things, is separated from them in essence and
comes from without. He says also that the active intellect knows all things, and is always in actuality,
which is true neither of the rational soul nor of the

angel, but of God alone. Again if it were part of the soul, the soul would then know the same thing through something active [*agens*] and be ignorant of it through something possible because the active is in actuality what the possible is in potentiality, as Aristotle maintains. Again a thing should be denominated rather from its more worthy part, therefore the soul should be spoken of rather as knowing by the active intellect than as ignoring by the possible intellect before discovery and learning. If it be said that the active intellect, although it is part of the soul, is still not the actuality and form of the body as the possible intellect is, and that therefore man has the functions of the possible and not of the active intellect, this is contrary to the definition of the soul, in which it is stated that the soul is the actuality of the physical body. For if one part of the soul only is actuality because it is the form of the body, then it is wrongly made to differ from the whole soul both absolutely and simply through the actuality of the body, and therefore that part which is the actuality of the body should then be excluded, as Aristotle himself (when, in the beginning of the second book, he states that some parts of the soul are not only the actuality of the whole body, but of its parts, such as the sensitive and vegetative parts of the soul) excludes the intellect which he says is not the actuality and perfection of a part of the body, because it is not attached to an organ like the other parts of the soul. Again, to state this more expressly, Aristotle says that the intellect is in the body as a sailor is in a ship, since it is not bound to any part any more than the sailor is bound to the ship, although it is the actuality and perfection of the whole. The sailor however is not the perfection of the ship but only the mover. Moreover, the soul would then be composed of a separated substance and of a conjunct substance; but this is impossible. For the Intelligence or angel and the soul differ in species as unible or not unible, and therefore the soul is not composed of something which is the actuality of the body and of something which is not. For one species is not composed of something of another opposite species. Since therefore the opinion stated here is in agreement with truth, and since the text of the Philosopher indicates it clearly, and since his greatest expositors state it in this form, and since these words *active* and *possible* have been taken from the Philosopher, not from the saints, it is far better, in accordance with the opinion of the Philosopher, to speak of the active intellect as a substance separated from the soul in essence. No one learned in philosophy, to be sure, is doubtful that this is his opinion; and in this, all the wise and learned men of the past are in agreement. For I twice saw and heard, at convocations of the University of Paris, the venerable priest, Master William, bishop of Paris, of blessed memory, declare in the presence of all, that the active intellect can not be part of the soul; and Master Robert, bishop of Lincoln, and brother Adam of the Marsh and elders of this sort supported this same opinion. How possible objections to this may be refuted will be made clear in the principal work, when natural questions are taken up. But lest some caviller arise on the side, alleging the doctrine by which the mass is deceived, I reply that although the following words are attributed to Aristotle, *But since in every nature there is something which acts and something else which suffers, so it is in the soul,*[19] this has been translated falsely many times and even more

[19] *De An.* III, c. 5, 430a 10-15.

often obscurely. For although it is said in the third book on the Heavens and the World that the circle and the orbicular figure fill space, the statement is false, as those expert in the natural and geometrical sciences know, as Averroes demonstrates in the same place. And the statement made in the third book of the Meteorologics that the rainbow of the moon occurs only twice in fifty years, is false too. For experience teaches that whenever the moon is full, and there is rain, and the moon is not covered with clouds, the rainbow appears. And so many other things have been translated falsely, the cause of which will appear in the third part of this work when the question of faults of translators will be taken up; but a great many more passages have been translated obscurely and unintelligibly, so that any one of them might contradict some other. And in this place both faults occur or at least the second one, which I shall prove by Aristotle himself. For he says in the second book of the Physics, that matter does not coexist with the other causes in any single thing [i.e. a thing which is the same in number]: therefore in no nature are there at the same time active cause and matter; therefore not in the soul. If, therefore, the badly translated text be held to the letter, then it is wholly false and contrary to Aristotle elsewhere, and so great an author does not contradict himself. And however that may be, his statement in the second book of the Physics is true and conceded by all; therefore his statement in the third book on the Soul is falsely translated or is in need of exposition. For he intends nothing other than that two things, to wit, agent and matter, are required in the soul and in the operation of the soul, as in all nature. That is, in every operation of nature two things are needed, namely, an efficient cause and

matter, and this is true, but the agent is always different than matter and outside it as regards substance,
although it operates in it. Moreover, we can relieve
this passage in still another way. For Aristotle in the
fourth book of the Physics says that there are eight
modes of being in anything, one of which is as the mover
is in the moved, because the moving principle or the
agent is in the matter moved with respect to its power,
although not with respect to substance. And thus the
agent is in every nature in which it operates and so it
is in the soul. And thus in no manner does it follow
that the active intellect is part of the soul as the run
of people imagines; and this opinion is completely in
accordance with the faith and confirmed by the saints,
for all theologians know that Augustine says in the
Soliloquies and elsewhere that the rational soul is subject to God alone in illuminations and in all important
influences. And, although the angels may purify our
minds and illumine them and stir them in many ways,
and although they may be to our souls as stars are to
the corporeal eye, nevertheless Augustine ascribes to
God the principal influence, just as the flow of light
falling through the window is ascribed to the sun, and
the angel is compared to one opening a window, according to Augustine in his gloss on the Psalm, *Give me
understanding*.[20] And what is more he holds in many
places that we know no truth except in the uncreated
truth and in the eternal laws, and this must be understood to mean at least effectively and by influence, although Augustine not only maintains this but intimates
something else in his words, for which reason some
have believed that he is thinking here of greater things,
as is commonly known. All these things are evidence

[20] *Psalms* 119:34, 73, 125, 144, 169.

that the active principle illuminating and influencing the possible intellect is a separated substance, that is, God himself. Since, therefore, God has illumined the souls of those men in perceiving the truths of philosophy, it is manifest that their labor is not unrelated to divine wisdom.

CHAPTER VI.

The third cause by which the wisdom of philosophy is reduced to divine wisdom, is not only that God enlightened their minds to acquire a knowledge of wisdom, but that they had wisdom from him and he has revealed, presented, and given it to them. For all wisdom is from the Lord God, as the authority of the Scripture holds, because, as the apostle says, *That which is known of God is manifest in them, for God manifested it unto them.*[21] And Augustine says in the commentary on John, that God is warrant to them for wisdom, and the greatest philosopher, Aristotle, in the Book of Secrets, asserts that all philosophy was manifestly given and revealed by God; and one of the greatest of philosophers, namely Cicero, asks in the first book of the Tusculan questions, *What is philosophy except, as Plato says, a gift and, as I believe, a discovery of God?* Whence he says also that even the poet does not pour forth a grave and full song without some heavenly instinct of mind. And Augustine in the eighth book of the City of God teaches and approves of what Socrates, the father of great philosophers, affirmed, that man can not know the causes of things except in the divine light and by the divine gift; and any one can prove for himself that nothing which is of the power of philosophy

[21] *Romans* 1:19.

is discovered by man first. And I set down a very minor example: that although Porphyry's universals are explained almost sufficiently by him and are expounded elsewhere sufficiently in logic, and metaphysics, and natural philosophy, and perspective, nevertheless there is not a man so well prepared that it is not essential that he have teachers of many sorts, and that he listen and study for a long time before he knows the whole truth about universals. And almost no one learns sufficiently about them before death howsoever many doctors he have, which is evident by the discord of all in this subject, since some hold that universals are only in the soul, others only outside, others that they are in things with respect to being, but that in their status as universal they are in the soul. Avicenna shows in his commentary on Porphyry that Porphyry lacked the sixth universal [i.e. a sixth predicable] and that he made many false statements. If therefore every man is ignorant of these things, even though he study throughout his whole life in the books of the philosophers, and though he have illustrious teachers, he will much the more be ignorant of them and never discover the truth about them for himself without books and teachers. Wherefore it is necessary that the truth of philosophers was revealed to man from the beginning. If moreover any one, knowing howsoever much concerning universals, had delivered the book of Porphyry to oblivion as well as all things that are necessary for knowing universals, and if he were not able to have either books or teachers, it would be impossible for him ever to explain the truth of universals. I speak of universals with respect to their true being, as a metaphysician must consider them, not merely with respect to the childish doctrine of Porphyry and the considerations of logic. Wherefore any one can judge for himself that revelation is necessary in this part; and since these are childish and very slight matters, it will be much more evident in the whole wisdom of philosophy.   But what is from God and what was revealed, set forth, and given, must be wholly in conformity with his wisdom.

CHAPTER VII.

For the rest, the whole aim of philosophy consists in this, that through the knowledge of his creature, the creator be known, who is served on account of the reverence due his majesty and the benefits of creation and conservation and future felicity, in honorific worship and in beauty of morals and in honor of useful laws, that men may live in peace and justice in this life. For speculative philosophy rises to the knowledge of the creator from his creatures, and moral philosophy sets up the honor of morals, just laws, and the cult of God, and is usefully and magnificently persuasive concerning the future felicity so far as that is possible to philosophy.   These things are certain to any one who runs through all the principal parts of philosophy, as that which follows will show.   Since, therefore, these are all absolutely necessary to christians and are wholly consonant with the wisdom of God, it is manifest that philosophy is necessary to the divine law and to the faithful who glory in it.

CHAPTER VIII.

Again, all the saints and all the ancient wise men in their expositions take a literal sense from the natures of things and from their properties, that they may bring forth spiritual senses by appropriate adaptations and likenesses. Augustine declares this in the second book on Christian Doctrine, adducing an example from the word of the Lord speaking to his Apostles, *Be ye wise as serpents and harmless as doves.*[22] For the Lord intended by this, that the apostles and the apostolic men, like the serpent exposing its whole body in defense of its head, give themselves and theirs for Christ, who is their head, and for his faith. And for this reason every creature is placed in the Scripture either in itself or in its like, either in universal or in particular, from the heights of the heavens to their very ends, for, as God made creatures and Scripture, so he wished to place in the Scripture the things themselves which he had made for the understanding of its literal as well as its spiritual sense. But the whole intention of philosophy is only to work out the natures and properties of things. Wherefore the power of all philosophy is contained in the sacred writings; and this is especially apparent in that the Scripture deals with creatures far more surely and far better and more truly than philosophic labor is able to work out. This may be shown, out of infinite examples, for the present in the rainbow. The Philosopher Aristotle disturbs us with his obscurities, nor are we able to understand through him anything that is proper; nor is that surprising since Avicenna, his chief imitator, the prince and leader of philosophy after him, confesses (as the Commentator says in connection with Aristotle's chapter on the rainbow in the third book of the Meteors) that he does not understand the nature of the rainbow very well. The cause of this is that the philosophers did not know the final cause of the rainbow; and having ignored the end, they do not

[22] *Matthew* 10:16.

know the things which lead to the end, because the end imposes a necessity on those things which are ordered to the end, as Aristotle holds in the second book of the Physics. But the final cause of the rainbow is the dissipation of aqueous vapor, as is manifest in the book of Genesis, whence in the apparition of the rainbow there is always a resolution of clouds into an infinity of drops. And the aqueous vapors are consumed in the air and in the sea and in the land, for one part of the rainbow falls into the spheres of water and earth. Moreover, the consumption of the aqueous vapor can not be through the rainbow except as the rays of the sun accomplish it, for by various reflections and refractions an infinity of rays are congregated, and the congregation of rays is the cause of the resolution and consumption of the waters, and for that reason the rainbow is generated by multiple reflections. For the rays can not be congregated except by fraction and reflection, as will be shown later in its proper place. From the Scripture, then, when it is said in Genesis, I shall set my bow in the clouds of heaven, that there may no more be a deluge over the earth,[23] the final cause of the rainbow itself is given, from which can be investigated the efficient cause and the mode of generating the rainbow. This mode was not known sufficiently to philosophers, as their books make manifest to us. And so it is with every creature. In fact, it is impossible for man to know the ultimate truth of the creature as it is employed in the Scripture, unless he shall have been especially illuminated by God. For creatures are employed there to bring forth the truths of grace and of glory, concerning which philosophers were ignorant, and therefore they did not attain to the most exalted power of

[23] *Genesis* 9:13-15.

the wisdom of creatures, such as the sacred Scripture
contains in its bowels. Whence all the excellence of
philosophy reposes in the literal sense ornamented with
the sacred mysteries of grace and of glory, as if
wreathed in a manner of paintings and of most noble
colors. . . .

[THE THIRD PART,

THE KNOWLEDGE OF LANGUAGES—

takes up the study of grammar which is the first of the
five divisions of philosophy. The study of grammar, not
only of latin but of the languages from which latin is
derived, is important for eight reasons which Bacon
discusses in detail—

1. The quality of one language can never be reproduced perfectly in translation in another.

2. Latin lacks many of the necessary words for things
described by foreign authors.

3. The translator must be perfectly acquainted not
only with his subject but with the two languages with
which he deals.

4. There are vast omissions, as well as confused and
corrupt passages, in the texts now possessed.

5. Allusions to foreign languages in writings of antiquity are not otherwise to be understood.

6. The latin text of the Scriptures is extremely corrupt and is becoming more so.

7. When the text is correct there is often obscurity
in its interpretation.

8. Confusion arises from the circumstances that latin
grammar is formed on the model of greek and hebrew
grammar.]

THE FOURTH PART
OF THIS DEMONSTRATION[24]

THE UTILITY OF MATHEMATICS

*In which the power of mathematics in the sciences and
in things and in the occupations of this world is shown.*

FIRST DISTINCTION

*The utility of mathematics in the physical arts and sci-
ences; having three chapters.*

CHAPTER I.

Now that it has been shown that many very famous
roots of wisdom are dependent on the power of languages and that through them there is entry into the
wisdom of the latins, I wish to examine the foundations
of that same wisdom as found in the great sciences in
which there is special power with respect to other
sciences and the things of this world.   There are four
great sciences, without which the other sciences can not
be known nor a knowledge of things be had: if they
are known, any one can advance in power of wisdom
gloriously, without difficulty and labor, not only in human sciences but in divine.   And the virtue of each one
of them will be touched on, not only because of wisdom
absolutely, but in respect to the other sciences mentioned above.   The door and key of these sciences is
mathematics, which the saints discovered at the beginning of the world as I shall show, and which has always

[24] O. c., vol. I, pp. 97-111, and vol. III, p. 129.

been in the use of all the saints and wise men before all the other sciences. The neglect of it now for thirty or forty years has wiped out all learning among the latins. Since he who ignores it can not know the other sciences nor the things of this world, as I shall prove. And what is worse, men who are ignorant of it do not perceive their own ignorance, and therefore seek no remedy for it. And on the contrary, knowledge of this science prepares the mind and elevates it to a certified knowledge of all things, so that if one learns the roots of wisdom given in relation to it, and if one applies those roots rightly to the notions of the other sciences and of things, then one will be able to know all things which follow without error and without doubt and easily and powerfully. Without these roots of wisdom, on the other hand, neither the precedents nor the consequences can be known; whence they perfect and regulate things prior, as the end perfects and regulates the things which are related to the end, and they dispose and open the way to things that follow. To this I plan now to refer by authority and reason; and first in respect to human sciences and the things of this world, then in respect to divine science, and finally as they are related to the Church and the other three sciences.

Chapter II.

In which it is proved by authority that every science requires mathematics.

As regards authority I proceed thus. Boethius says in the second prologue to the Arithmetic that, *If the inquirer lacks the four parts of mathematics, he can in no wise discover truth.* And again, *Without this specula-*

tion of truth no one is rightly trained. And even more he says, *Who spurns these paths of wisdom, I declare to him he does not rightly philosophize.* And once again, *It is known that whosoever has neglected these, has lost the doctrine of all wisdom.* He likewise confirms this by the opinion of all men of importance, saying, *Among all the men of early authority, who have flourished, with Pythagoras as leader, in the purer reason of the mind, it is held to be manifest that almost no one comes to the height of perfection in the disciplines of philosophy except only him to whom such nobility of knowledge is discovered by something like the quadrivium.* And this is shown in particular by Ptolemy and by Boethius himself. Since, in fact, there are three essential modes of philosophy, as Aristotle says in the sixth book of the Metaphysics, mathematical, natural, and divine, the mathematical is of no little value for the understanding of the other two modes of knowledge, as Ptolemy teaches in the first chapter of the Almagest and which he himself shows there. And since the divine science is twofold, as is evident from the first book of the Metaphysics, namely, the first philosophy, which shows that God is, whose high properties it investigates, and civil science, which sets up the divine cult and expounds many things concerning God to the extent of the possibility of man, the same Ptolemy asserts and declares that mathematics is of great value to both of these. Whence Boethius at the end of the Arithmetic insists that mathematical means are to be found in civil affairs. He says, in fact, that

the arithmetical mean is to be compared to a commonwealth which is ruled by a few, for this reason, that its greater proportion is in its lesser terms, and he says that the musical mean is a commonwealth of aristocrats, in that the greater proportionality is found in the greater terms. The geometrical mean is in a certain sense of the equalized democratic state: for its people are compounded in equal proportionality of all, whether in the lesser or in the greater terms. For there is among all a certain parity of mean conserving a proportional right of equality.

And Aristotle and his expositors teach in several places in morals that without proportional evaluations the commonwealth can not be ruled. But these means will be expounded when they are to be applied to the divine truths. Since, moreover, all the essential modes of philosophy, which make up more than forty sciences distinct one from the other, are reduced to these three: the authorities already cited are sufficient to be convincing of the worth of mathematics in respect to the essential modes of philosophy.

Further, the accidental modes of philosophy are grammar and logic. And that these sciences can not be known without mathematics is evident from Alfarabi in the book on the Sciences. For although grammar supplies to children that which pertains to speech and its properties in prose and meter and rhythm, none the less it does it childishly, and by the way of narration, not by causes nor by reasons. For it is the function of another science to give the causes for these things, namely, of that science which has to consider fully the nature of speech and that is music alone, of which the species and parts are many. For one deals with prose, and a second with meter, and a third is rhythmical, and a fourth is lyrical in singing. And there are more parts besides these. The prosaic part teaches the causes of all the elevations of speech in prose, with reference to differences of accents, and with reference to colons and commas and periods and others of this sort. The metrical part teaches all the reasons and causes of feet and meters. The rhythmical treats of every modulation and pleasing proportion of rhythms, because all these are certain kinds of song, although they are not as in the ordinary song. For *accentus* is spoken of as if *accantus,* derived from *accino, accinis.* Whence they pertain to music as Cassiodorus teaches in his Music, and Censorinus in his book on Accent, and so too with the other topics. Moreover, authors of music and books on that science testify to this. And Alfarabi agrees with them in the book on the Division of the Sciences. Therefore grammar depends causally on music.

In the same way logic. For the end of logic is the composition of arguments which move the practical intellect to belief and to love of virtue and of future felicity, as has been shown before; and these are treated in the books of Aristotle on these arguments, as has been stated. But these arguments should have to do with the end of beauty, that the mind of man may be pulled to salubrious truths suddenly and without prevision, as is taught in those books. And Alfarabi teaches this most of all in relation to poetic argument, the words of which should be sublime and beautiful, and therefore with prose and metric and unusual rhythmic adornments, such as are suitable to the place and time and persons and material with which the demonstration is concerned. And thus Aristotle taught in his book on poetic argument [i.e. the Poetics] which the translator Hermann did not dare to turn into latin because of the difficulty of the meters, which he did not understand, as he himself says in the prologue to the commentary of Averroes on that book. And, therefore, the end of logic depends on music. But the end is the most noble aspect in the thing, and it imposes necessity on whatever is related to the end, as Aristotle says in the second book of the Physics; nor do things which are ordered naturally to their end have their utility, except when they are related to their end, as is evident in each individual thing. And consequently the whole utility of logic arises from the relation of all logical arguments to arguments of this sort, and therefore since they depend on musical arguments, it is necessary that logic depend on the power of music. All these things are according to the opinion of Alfarabi in the book on the Sciences, and they are made clear similarly by Aristotle and Averroes in their books, although the latins do not have the use of them. But the knowledge of logic depends on mathematics not only because of its end but because of its middle and heart, which is the book of the Posterior [Analytics], for that book teaches the art of demonstration. But the principles of demonstration can not be learned nor the conclusions nor the demonstration as a whole, nor can they be shown except in mathematical things, because there alone is demonstration true and forceful, as all know and as will be expounded later. Wherefore it is necessary that logic depend on mathematics.

Likewise because of its beginning as well as because of its middle and its end. For the book of the Categories is the first book of logic according to Aristotle. But it is obvious that the category of quantity can not be known without mathematics. For only mathematics is constituted for the understanding of quantity. The categories of when and where, moreover, are related to quantity. For when pertains to time and where arises from place. The category of condition [*habitus*] can not be known without the category of where, as Averroes teaches in the fifth book of the Metaphysics. The greater part, moreover, of the category of quality contains affections and properties of quantities, because all things that are in the fourth class of quality are called qualities in quantities. And all the affections of these [quantities] which are due absolutely to them are the qualities from which the great part of geometry and arithmetic is constituted, such as right and curved and others which are due to line and triangulation and every other figuration, which are assigned to surface and body; and the prime and unfactorable in numbers, as Aristotle teaches in the fifth book of the Metaphysics, and other essential affections of numbers. Whatever, moreover, is worthy of consideration in the category of relation is the property of quantity, such as proportions and proportionalities, and geometrical, arithmetical, and musical means, and the kinds of greater and lesser inequality. Spiritual substances, moreover, are not known by philosophy except by means of corporeal substances and, most of all, supercelestial substances, according to what Aristotle teaches in the eleventh book of the Metaphysics. Inferior things are not known except through superior things, because the celestial substances are the causes of inferior substances. But the celestial substances are not known except through quantity, as is evident from astronomy. And thence all categories depend on a knowledge of quantity, concerning which mathematics treats, and therefore the whole excellence of logic depends on mathematics.

Chapter III.

In which it is proved by reason that every science requires mathematics.

Moreover, what has been shown by authority concerning mathematics as a whole, can now be shown likewise by reason. And in the first place because the other sciences use mathematical examples; but examples are given to clarify the things of which the sciences treat: wherefore, if the examples are not understood, the things for the understanding of which they were adduced are not understood. Since, for example, alteration [i.e. change of quality] is not found without augmentation and diminution [i.e. change of quantity] in any natural phenomena whatsoever, and since augmentation and diminution are not found without alteration, Aristotle could not show by any natural example the difference between augmentation and alteration in their purity, because they always accompanied each other in some way; for which reason he gave the mathematical example of the quadrilateral which, when a gnomon is added, increases and is not altered. This example can not be understood before the twenty-second proposition of the sixth book of the Elements. For in that proposition of the sixth book, it is proved that the smaller quadrilateral is similar in every particular to the larger one. And therefore the smaller is not altered, although the larger is made of the lesser by the addition of the gnomon.

In the second place because the knowledge of mathematical things is, as it were, innate in us. For when Socrates questioned a little boy concerning geometry, as Cicero mentions in the first of the Tusculan questions, the boy replied as if he had learned geometry. And

this is often found to be the case in many instances,
which does not happen in other sciences, as will be more
manifest in what follows. Wherefore, since this knowledge is as if innate, and as if preceding discovery and instruction, or at least requiring them less than other
sciences, it will be first among the sciences and will
precede the others, disposing us to them, since things
which are innate or almost innate dispose to what are
acquired.

In the third place because this science was found first
of all the parts of philosophy. For at the beginning of
the human race this was first found. Since it was known
before the flood and then later by the sons of Adam and
by Noah and his sons, as is evident from the prologue
to the Construction of the Astrolabe according to Ptolemy and from Albumazar in the larger Introduction to
Astronomy, and from the first book of Antiquities; and
this is true as regards all the parts of mathematics, to
wit, geometry, arithmetic, music, astronomy. That, however, would not have been the case except that this science is prior to the others and naturally precedes them.
Wherefore it is manifest that it should be known first
that we may be advanced by it to all the later sciences.

In the fourth place because the natural way for us is
from the easier to the more difficult. But this science is
the easiest. This is manifest in that mathematics is not
beyond the understanding of any one. In fact, the lay
and the wholly illiterate know how to figure and compute
and to sing, and these are mathematical operations. But
one must begin first with things which are common to
lay and learned; and not only is it most hurtful to the
clergy, but absolutely disgraceful and abominable, that
they are ignorant of what the laity knows profitably and
beautifully. In the fifth place we see that the clergy,
even the most unlettered, are able to understand things

mathematical, even though they are not able to attain
to the other sciences. Besides, a man can learn more
about mathematics certainly and truly without error by
listening once or twice than he can by listening ten times
about other parts of philosophy, as is evident to one who
tries. In the sixth place because the natural way for us
is from the things which are proper to the state and
ability of the child, for children begin by learning the
things which are better known to us and to be acquired
first. But mathematics is of this sort since children are
taught first to sing, and in that same manner they can
grasp the method of figuring and counting, and it would
be far easier, and it would even be necessary, for them
to know about numbers before singing; because in the
proportions of numbers the whole rationality of number
is explained in examples, as authors of music teach, as
well in ecclesiastical music as in philosophical. But the
rationality of numbers depends on figures, because linear
numbers and superficial and corporeal and square and
cubic and pentagonal and hexagonal and the others are
known from lines and figures and angles. It has been
found, indeed, that children learn mathematical truths
better and more quickly, as is manifest in singing, and
besides we know from experience that children learn
and grasp mathematical truths better than the other
parts of philosophy. For Aristotle says in the sixth
book of the Ethics that youths can comprehend mathematical truths quickly, but not so with natural nor metaphysical nor moral truths. Wherefore the mind must
be trained by this science before it is trained by the
others.

In the seventh place when the things known to us and
the things intelligible by nature are not the same, the
natural way for us is from the things better known to
us to those better known in nature or absolutely. And

we know the things which are better known to us very easily, and we arrive with great difficulty at those which are better known in nature. And those known in nature are poorly and imperfectly known to us, because our understanding is disposed to things which are so manifest in nature as the eye of the bat to the light of the sun, as Aristotle maintains in the second book of the Metaphysics; among these particularly are God and the angels and the future life and heavenly things and creatures more noble than the others, because the more noble they are the less they are known to us. And these are called things known in nature and absolutely. Therefore, on the contrary when the same things are known to us and in nature, we advance a great deal in regard to things known in nature and in regard to all things which are there included, and we can attain to a perfect knowledge of them. But in mathematics only, as Averroes says in the first book of the Physics and in the seventh of the Metaphysics and in his commentary on the third book of the Heavens and the World, things known to us and in nature or absolutely are the same. Therefore as we attain completely in mathematics to those things which are known to us, so we attain to those which are known in nature and absolutely. Wherefore we can arrive absolutely at the innermost parts of that science. Since, therefore, we are not able to do this in the other sciences, it is manifest that mathematics is better known. Wherefore the beginning of our knowledge is from the acquisition of it.

Again in the eighth place because all doubt is made clear by that which is certain, and every error is wiped out by unshaken truth. But in mathematics we can come to the full truth without error and to a certitude of all points involved without doubt, since in mathematics demonstration must be made through proper and necessary

cause. And demonstration makes truth to be known.
And in the same way in mathematics a sensible example
may be had for all things, and a sensible test in figuring
and counting, so that all may be made clear to the sense;
because of this there can be no doubt in mathematics.
But in the other sciences, once the aid of mathematics
has been excluded there are so many doubts, so many
opinions, so many errors on the part of man, that the
sciences can not be developed, as is manifest, since the
demonstration by a proper and necessary cause does not
exist in them by their own power, because there is no
necessity in natural things because of generation and
corruption of proper causes as also of effects. In metaphysics a demonstration can not be made except by effect [i.e. *a posteriori*], because spiritual things are
discovered by corporeal effects and the creator by his
creature, as is made evident in that science. In morals,
demonstrations can not be from proper causes, as Aristotle teaches. And in the same way there can not be
very cogent demonstrations in logical and grammatical
subjects, as is plain, because of the weakness of the
matter of which these sciences treat. And therefore, in
mathematics alone are there most cogent demonstrations
by a necessary cause. And, therefore, there alone can
man come to truth by the power of that science. Similarly in the other sciences there are doubts and opinions
and contrarieties on our part, so that there is hardly
agreement in even one most insignificant question or in
a single sophism; for the experiments of figurations and
numerations are not in these sciences from their own
nature, by which all must be certified. And therefore
in mathematics alone is there certitude without doubt.

Wherefore it is evident that if we ought to come to
certitude without doubt and to truth without error in the
other sciences, it is necessary that we place the founda-

tions of knowledge in mathematics, in so far as, disposed
by it, we can attain to certitude in other sciences and to
truth by the exclusion of error. And this reason can
be made clearer by comparison, and the principal proposition, in fact, is in the ninth book of Euclid. Just as,
indeed, the knowledge of the conclusion is so related to
the knowledge of the premises that if there be error and
doubt in the premises, truth can not be had through them
in the conclusion, nor certitude, for doubt is not made
certain through doubt, nor is truth proved by falsity,
although truth can be syllogized from false premises
(the syllogism in that case inferring but not proving);
so it is with all the sciences, that those in which there
are violent and numerous doubts and opinions and errors
(I speak at least from our part) should have doubts of
this sort and falsities removed by some science certain
to us and in which we neither doubt nor err. Since indeed conclusions and principles proper to them are parts
of the whole of the sciences, therefore just as part is
related to part, as conclusion is related to premises, so
science is related to science, so that, obviously, the science which is full of doubts and bestrewn with opinions
and obscurities, can not be made certain or clear nor
be verified except by some other science known and
verified and certain to us and plain, as is the case with a
conclusion from premises. But only mathematics, as
has been advanced before, remains certain to us and
verified with the utmost certitude and verification.
Wherefore it is necessary that all the other sciences be
known and certified by it.

And since it has been shown already by the property
of that science, that mathematics is prior to the other
sciences and is useful and necessary to them, the same
thing may be shown now by reasons taken from its subject matter. And first this, that the natural way for

us is from sense to understanding, because if a sense is lacking, the science which is related to that sense is lacking also, as is pointed out in the first book of the Posterior [Analytics], since in the degree that sense advances, human understanding advances. But quantity is in the highest degree sensible, because it pertains to the common sense and is perceived by the other senses, and nothing can be perceived without quantity, for which reason the understanding is able to advance most of all in what relates to quantity. Secondly, because the very act of understanding is not accomplished in itself without continuous quantity, since Aristotle says in the book on Memory and Reminiscence that all our understanding is concerned with the continuous and with time. Whence we understand quantities and bodies by the consideration of the understanding, because their species are present in the understanding. But the species of incorporeal things are not received thus in our understanding; or if they are produced in it, according to what Avicenna says in the third book of the Metaphysics, we still do not perceive that, because of the more vigorous occupation of our understanding with bodies and quantities. And, therefore, we investigate the notion of incorporeal things by way of argumentation and concern with corporeal things and quantities, as Aristotle does in the eleventh book of the Metaphysics. For which reason the understanding will make most progress with quantity itself, in that quantities and bodies, so far as they are such, are appropriated to the human understanding according to the common status of understanding. Each and every thing is because of some thing, and that thing is in a higher degree.

However the final reason for complete confirmation can be drawn from the experience of the wise men; for all the wise men of antiquity worked in mathematics that they might know all things, as we have seen in the case of some of our own times and as we have heard in the case of others who learned all knowledge through mathematics, which they knew well. For very famous men have been found, like Bishop Robert of Lincoln and Brother Adam of the Marsh, and many others, who knew how to explain the causes of all things through the power of mathematics and to explain sufficiently things human and divine. The certainty of this thing, moreover, is evident in the writings of these men, as on impressions, such as on the rainbow and on comets, and on the generation of heat, and the investigation of the places of the world, and on celestial things and others, of which theology as well as philosophy make use. Wherefore it is manifest that mathematics is absolutely necessary and useful to the other sciences.

These reasons are universal, but it can be shown in particular, by going through all parts of philosophy, how all things are known by the application of mathematics. And this is nothing other than to show that the other sciences should not be known by means of the dialectical and sophistical arguments which are introduced commonly, but by mathematical demonstrations descending to the truths and the works of the other sciences and regulating them, without which they can not be understood, nor manifested, nor taught, nor learned. If any one, moreover, should descend to the particular by applying the power of mathematics to the separate sciences, he would see that nothing magnificent in the sciences can be known without mathematics. This however would be nothing other than to establish sure methods of all the sciences and to verify all things which are necessary to the other sciences by the ways of mathe-

matics.   But that does not fall within the **present**
speculation.

Second Distinction

*In which it is shown that the things of this world require
mathematics; in three chapters.*

Chapter I.

*In the first chapter is taught in general that heavenly
things and things below require mathematics.*

What has just been shown in regard to the sciences
can be made clear in regard to things.   For the things
of this world can not be known unless mathematics is
known.   Of heavenly objects, to be sure, that is certain
to all, seeing that two great mathematical sciences treat
of them, namely, speculative astrology and practical astrology.   The first considers the quantities of all things
that are included among the celestial and all things
which are reduced to quantity, as well discrete as continuous quantity.   For it certifies the number of the
heavens and of the stars, whose quantity can be measured by instruments, and the shapes of all and the magnitudes and altitudes from the earth and the thicknesses
and the number and magnitude and smallness, the rising
and setting of the constellations, and the motion as well
of the heavens as of the stars, and the quantities and
varieties of eclipses.   Again, it takes up the quantity and
shape of the habitable world and of all the great divisions of it which are called climates, and it shows the
diversity of the horizons and of the days and nights in
every climate.   These things, then, are determined in

speculative astrology and many others connected with
them.   Practical astrology on the other hand treats of
this, that we know at every hour the positions of the
planets and the stars and their combinations and all
things which occur in celestial things; and it treats of
those things which happen in the air, such as comets
and rainbows and other things that occur there, that we
may know their positions and altitudes and magnitudes
and shapes and many things which must be considered in
them.   And all these things are done by instruments
suitable to them and by tables and canons, that is, rules
invented to certify these things so that a way may be
prepared for the judgments [i.e. horoscopes] that can
be formed within the power of philosophy, not only in
natural things, but in those which take their tendency
from nature and follow freely the heavenly disposition;
and not only for judgments [horoscopes] of things present, past, and future, but for wondrous works that all
the fortunate circumstances of this world may be advanced and the adverse be held in check, usefully and
magnificently.   Nor are these matters doubtful.   For the
patriarchs and prophets from the beginning of the world
have certified these as they have other matters.   And
Aristotle renewed the certification of the ancients and
brought it out into the light.   And all who are wise in
great things agree in this, and experience teaches it.
But exposition will be made of these matters in the
proper place.

It is plain, therefore, that heavenly things are known
by means of mathematics and that the way is prepared
by it to things below.   That, moreover, those things
below can not be learned without mathematics is evident
first by this, that we know things only through causes,
if science be taken properly, as Aristotle says.   But

heavenly things are the causes of the things below. Therefore, these inferior things will not be known unless the heavenly things are known, and they can not be known without mathematics. Therefore, the knowledge of these inferior things depends on the same science. In the second place, we can see from their properties that no one of these lower or higher things can be known without the power of mathematics. For every natural thing is produced in being by an efficient cause and by the matter in which it operates, for these two concur first. The agent, indeed, by its force moves and transmutes the matter that the thing may be made. But the force of the efficient cause and of the matter can not be known without the great power of mathematics, as is the case with the force of the effect produced. There are therefore these three, the efficient cause, the matter, and the effect. And in celestial things there is set up a mutual influence of forces as of light and of other agents, and there is alteration in them, but not toward corruption. And so, too, it can be shown that nothing can be known in things without the power of geometry. We hold by this argument that the other parts of mathematics are necessary in the same way: for what applies to geometry applies likewise to them, except that it applies much more because they are nobler. If, therefore, what was proposed is shown in geometrical things, it is not necessary to speak in this demonstration of the others.

In the first place, I show therefore what was proposed concerning geometry from the point of the efficient cause. For every efficient cause acts by its own force which it produces in the subject matter, as the light of the sun produces its own force in the air, which force is illumination [*lumen*] diffused through all the world by the solar light [*lux*]. And this force is called a likeness and image and species, and by many names; and it is produced by substance as well as accident and by spiritual as well as corporeal substance. And by substance more than by accident, and by spiritual more than by corporeal. And this species produces every operation in this world, for it operates on sense, on understanding, and on all the matter of the world for the generation of things, because one and the same thing is done by a natural agent on whatsoever it operates, seeing that it does not have freedom of choice; and therefore it produces the same thing, whatever may occur to it. But if it acts on the sense and the understanding, a species is formed, as all know. Therefore, it acts in the same way on that which is contrary to these, and a species is made in matter. And in beings that have reason and understanding, although they do many things by deliberation and freedom of the will, still this operation which is the generation of species, is natural in them as in other things. Whence the substance of the soul multiplies its own force in the body and outside the body, and every body produces its own force outside itself, and angels move the world by forces of this sort. But God produces forces out of nothing, which he multiplies in things; created agents do not act so, but in another manner, of which there need be no concern at the present time. Forces of agents of this sort, therefore, produce every operation in this world. But now two things need be considered concerning them: one is the multiplication itself of species and of force in the place of their generation; and the other is the varied operation in this world due to the generation and corruption of things. The second can not be known without the first. And therefore it is necessary that the multiplication itself be described first. . . .

The Fifth Part
of This Demonstration[25]

ON THE SCIENCE OF PERSPECTIVE; HAVING THREE PARTS:

The first part is concerning matters common to the other two parts; the second descends to special matters, principally to direct vision; the third to reflected and refracted vision. The first part has twelve distinctions.

First Distinction

This distinction is concerned with the properties of this science and with the parts of the mind and the brain and with the organs of seeing; having five chapters.

Chapter I.

On the properties of this science.

Having propounded the roots of wisdom, as well divine as human, which are found in the languages from which the sciences of the latins have been translated and likewise the roots of wisdom which are in the power of mathematics, I wish now to discuss some roots which arise from the power of perspective. And, if the consideration which has already been stated is noble and delectable, the present one is by far more noble and more delectable, since our peculiar delight is in vision; and light and color have a special beauty beyond any which are brought to our senses; and not only beauty shines forth, but utility and a greater necessity arise

[25] O. c., vol. II, pp. 1-12, and vol. III, p. 136.

For Aristotle says in the first book of the Metaphysics that vision alone shows us the differences of things: by it, in fact, we seek out the sure experiences of all things which are in the heavens and on earth. For those things which are in the heavens are considered by visual instruments, as Ptolemy and other astronomers teach. And similarly too, those which are generated in the air, as comets, and rainbows, and others of this sort. For their altitude above the horizon, and their magnitude, and shape and number, and all qualities which are in them, are made certain by methods of seeing with instruments. Moreover, the things which are here on the earth we find by vision, in that the blind man is able to discover nothing of this world that is worthwhile. Hearing makes us believe because we believe what we have learned, but we can not discover what we learn except by sight. If, moreover, we should adduce taste and touch and smell, then we assume a bestial wisdom. For the brutes are conversant with gustibles and tangibles, and they exercise their sense of smell for taste and touch, but the things which these senses certify are of trifling value and few in number and common to us and to brutes and, therefore, they do not rise to the dignity of human wisdom. But sciences are constituted in view of necessity and utility and difficulty, because art is of the difficult and the good, as Aristotle says in the second book of the Ethics. For if what is sought is easy, there is no need that a science be constituted. In the same way, even though something is difficult and still not useful no science is made of it, because the labor would be stupid and inane. Furthermore, if it were not exceedingly useful and had not many and outstanding truths, it should not have a separate science set up, but it suffices that it be marked out in some part of a book or chapter together with other subjects in the common science. But of vision alone is a separate science formed among philosophers, namely perspective, and not of any other sense. Wherefore, through vision there must be a special utility to wisdom, which is not found in the other senses. And what I have already touched on in general, I wish to show in particular by going over the roots of this most beautiful science. To be sure some other science may be more useful, but no other science has such delightfulness and beauty of utility. And therefore it is the flower of all philosophy and that by which the other sciences can be learned and without which they can not be acquired. It should be known, moreover, that Aristotle first found this science, of which he speaks in the second book of the Physics, because the matter is a sub-topic of that book, and in the book on Sense and the Sensed, and he confuted Democritus because he did not mention the reflections and the refractions of vision of the optic nerves and the concave visual nerves; this has been translated into latin. After him Alhazen expounds the subject fully in a book which is also to be had. Likewise Alkindi composed some things more fully and also authors of books on vision and mirrors.

CHAPTER II.

On the internal faculties of the sensitive soul, which are imagination and the common sense.

Since the optic nerves, that is, the concave nerves causing sight, have their origin in the brain and since writers on perspective ascribe the formation of judgments on twenty species of visible things to a distinguishing faculty with vision mediating, which twenty will be touched on later, and since it is not known whether that distinguishing faculty is among the faculties of the soul, the organs of which are distinct in the brain, and since many other things, which will be treated below, underlie the determination of the faculties of the sensitive soul, therefore, it is necessary to begin with the parts of the brain and the faculties of the soul that we may discover those things which are necessary to sight. And writers on perspective furnish us the way to this, showing how the visual nerves descend from the membranes of the brain and from the lining of the cranium; but no one explains all the details that are necessary to this part. I say therefore, that, as all natural and medical and perspective philosophers agree, the brain is wrapped in a double membrane of which one is called the *pia mater*, which is the one containing the brain immediately; and the other is called the *dura mater*, which adheres to the concavity of the bone of the head, which is called the cranium. For the latter is harder that it may resist the bone, and the former is softer and smoother because of the pliability of the brain, the substance of which is medullar and unctuous, and phlegm is the chief constituent, and it has three distinctions which are called chambers, and cellules, and parts, and divisions. In the first cell there are two faculties: and one is the common sense located in the anterior part, as Avicenna says in the first book on the Soul, which is like a fountain with respect to the particular senses and like a center with respect to the lines extending from the same point to the circumference, according to Aristotle in the second book on the Soul;[26] the common sense judges of individual sensible particulars. For judgment concerning the visible is not completed before the species comes to the common sense; and it is so too with the audible and the others, as is evident from the end of the work on Sense and the

[26] The reference should be to the third book.

Sensed and from the second book on the Soul, and the common sense judges of the diversity of sensibles, as that in milk the whiteness is other than the sweetness, which sight could not do, nor taste, in that they do not distinguish extremes, as Aristotle holds in the second book on the Soul. And it judges of the operations of the particular senses, for sight does not perceive itself see, nor does hearing perceive itself hear, but another faculty which is the common sense does, as Aristotle holds in the second book on Sleep and Waking. The final operation of the common sense, however, is to receive the species coming from the particular senses and to complete judgment on them. But it does not retain them, owing to the excessive slipperiness of its organ, according to what Avicenna holds in the first book on the Soul. And therefore it is necessary that there be another faculty of the soul in the back part of the first cellule, the function of which is to retain the species coming from the particular senses because of its temperate moistness and dryness, which is called the imagination and is the treasury and repository of the common sense, according to Avicenna who uses the example of a seal, the image of which water receives well but does not retain because of its superfluous moistness: but wax retains the image well because of its moistness tempered with dryness. Whence he says that it is one thing to receive and another to retain, as appears in these examples. So it is in the case of the organ of the common sense and of the imagination. Nevertheless, the whole faculty compounded of these faculties, that is, that which occupies the whole first cellule, is called phantasy or the phantastical faculty. For it is evident from the second book on the Soul and from the book on Sleep and Waking and from the book on Sense and the Sensed that phantasy and common sense are the same in respect

to subject and different in respect to being, as Aristotle
says, and that phantasy and imagination are the same
in respect to subject and different in respect to being.
Wherefore phantasy comprehends both faculties and
does not differ from them except as the whole from the
part. And, therefore, when the common sense receives
the species and the imagination retains it, there follows
a complete judgment of the thing, which judgment phantasy forms.

CHAPTER III.

*Concerning sensibles which are perceived by the senses
proper and by the common sense and by imagination.*

It must be noted that imagination and common sense
and the particular sense judge by themselves only of
twenty-nine sensibles; as sight of light and color; touch
of heat and cold, moist and dry; hearing of sound; smell
of odor; taste of savor. These are the nine proper sensibles which are appropriated, as I have named them,
to their senses; of which no other particular sense can
form a judgment. There are, however, twenty other
sensibles, namely, distance, situation, corporeity, figure,
magnitude, continuity, discreteness or separation, number, motion, rest, roughness, smoothness, transparency,
thickness, shadow, obscurity, beauty, ugliness, and also
likeness and difference in all these sensibles and in all
things compounded from them. And besides these there
are others which are placed under some one or
more of them, as ordination under situation, and writing
and painting under ordination and figure; and as
straightness and curvedness, and concavity and convex-
ity, which are placed under figure; and multitude and

paucity, which are placed under number; and as equality and augmentation and diminution which are placed under likeness and diversity; and as liveliness and laughter and sadness, which are comprehended from the figure and form of the face; and as weeping which is comprehended from the figure of the face with the motion of tears; and as moistness and dryness which are placed under motion and rest, since moistness is not comprehended by the sense of sight except from the liquidity of the moist body and from the motion of one part of it before another, and since dryness is comprehended from the retention of the part of the dry thing and from the privation of liquidity. This, however, must be considered, which Aristotle maintains in the second book on Generation, that moist and dry are, in one manner, primary qualities inherent naturally in the elements, and because of them moistness and dryness in the things compounded of the elements[27] are reduced to the first and are caused by them. Concerning the primary qualities, therefore, it has been said that they are proper sensibles and perceptible by touch alone. Of the others the following statement is made. The primary moistness is, in fact, that which passes easily into all figures which are terminable of themselves with difficulty and readily terminable by the limit of something else, as in the case of air in the highest degree and then in the case of water. Dryness is the contrary and dryness is most of all in earth and secondarily in fire. Moreover, moistness is here used in the sense of liquid and slippery, and dry in the sense of arid and coagulated. And it is thus too with many others which are reduced to the species and principal modes of the visible objects enumerated above. And all these things are apparent from the first

[27] The text reads *inelementales*; it is interpreted here as *in elementatis*.

book of Ptolemy on Optics and from the second book of
Alhazen on Appearances and from other authors on perspective.   There are also the common sensibles, some
of which Aristotle exemplifies in the second book on the
Soul and in the beginning of his work on Sense and the
Sensed, as of magnitude and figure, motion, rest, and
number; but not only these are common sensibles but
all those mentioned above, although the run of natural
philosophers do not take that up because they are not
expert in the science of perspective.   For the common
sensibles are not so called because they are perceived
by the common sense, but because they are determined
in common by all the particular senses or by several,
and most of all by sight and touch, since Ptolemy says
in the second book on Perspective that touch and sight
share in all the above twenty.   And these twenty-nine,
together with those which are reduced to them, are perceived by the particular senses and by common sense and
imagination; and these faculties of the soul can not
judge by themselves of other sensibles except by
accident.

CHAPTER IV.

*On the investigation of the estimative faculty and the
memorative and the cogitative faculties.*

There are however other sensibles *per se,* for brute
animals use only sense because they do not have understanding.   The sheep, even if he has never seen a wolf,
flees from it at once, and every animal is terrified at the
roar of a lion, even though it may never have heard or
seen a lion before, and the same is true in the case of
many things which are hurtful and contrary to the constitution of animals.   And in the same way in the case

of the useful and agreeable. For even if a lamb has never seen another lamb, it runs to one and stays willingly with it and so with other animals. Brutes, therefore, perceive something in advantageous and in hurtful things. Therefore, there is something there sensibly besides the twenty-nine sensibles enumerated above and besides those which are reduced to them. For there must be something more active and alterative of the sentient body than light and color, because it leads not only to comprehension but to the affection of fear or love or flight or tarrying. And this thing is the quality of the constitution of each thing in which the natural kinship of different individuals of the same species or genus is grounded and in consequence of which they are drawn together and strengthened and fortified by each other, or by which they differ and are opposed and made hurtful to each other. Whence not only do light and color make their species and powers, but even more the qualities of the constitutions make them, and indeed the substantial natures themselves of things, agreeing with each other or contrary, make strong species which modify the sensitive soul strongly, that it is moved by the affections of fear and of horror and of flight or the contraries. And these species or virtues coming from the things, although they modify and alter the particular senses and the common sense and the imagination, just as they do the air through which they pass, nevertheless, none of these faculties of the soul judge of them, but it is necessary that there be a faculty of the sensitive soul far nobler and more powerful, and this is called estimation or the estimative faculty, as Avicenna says in the first book on the Soul, which he says perceives the unperceived forms connected with sensible matter. That is called sensible matter here which is known by the particular senses and the common sense, such as the

twenty-nine enumerated above. And that is called the
unperceived form which is not perceived by those senses
of themselves, since they are commonly called senses,
although other faculties of the sensitive soul could be
called senses equally well, should we wish to call them
so, since they are parts of the sensitive soul. For each
part of the sensitive soul can be called a sense because
it is in truth a sense and a sensitive faculty. When it
is said, therefore, that the constitutional qualities are
not perceived by the sense, it must be understood that
they are not perceived by the particular sense and the
common sense and the imagination; but they can very
well be perceived by estimation, which although it is not
called a sense, is nevertheless a part of the sensitive soul.

But estimation does not retain a species although it
receives it, as does the common sense, and therefore
there is needed another faculty in the last part of the
posterior cellule to retain the species of the estimative
faculty and to be the treasury and repository of it, as
imagination is the treasury of the common sense, and
this is the memorative faculty, and Avicenna says this
in the first book on the Soul. But judgment, or the
cogitative faculty, is in the middle cellule; it is the mistress of the sensitive faculty and takes the place of
reason in brutes, and therefore it is called logistic, that
is, rational, not because it uses reason, but because it is
the ultimate perfection of brutes, as reason is of man,
and because the rational soul in men is united directly
to it. By virtue of it the spider weaves its geometrical
web and the bee its hexagonal house, choosing one from
the figures which fill space, and the swallow its nest and
so with all the works of brutes which are similar to
human art. Man sees wonders in dreams by that faculty, and all the faculties of the sensitive soul serve
and obey it, as well the posterior as the anterior, since

all of them are because of it. For the species which are in the imagination multiply themselves in cogitation, although in the imagination they are according to their first being because of phantasy which makes use of those species; but the cogitative faculty contains these species in a more noble way, and the species of the estimative and the memorative faculties acquire in the cogitative faculty a being which is nobler than the one it has in them, and therefore the cogitative faculty uses all the other faculties as its instruments. In man the rational soul comes above these from without and by creation, and it is united first and immediately to the cogitative faculty, and it uses that principally as its special instrument, and species are formed in the rational soul by it. Whence, when this faculty is injured, the judgment of reason is perverted to the highest degree, and when it is sound, then the understanding operates well and rationally.

CHAPTER V.

On the exposition of opposed authorities concerning the aforesaid faculties.

But the latin text of Aristotle does not disclose to us this division, for no mention is made expressly except of the common sense and imagination and memory. However, since the text of Aristotle can not be understood in these places, as elsewhere, because of perversity of the translation, and since Avicenna was almost everywhere the perfect imitator and expositor of Aristotle and the leader and prince of philosophy after him, as the Commentator says in the commentary on the chapter on the Rainbow, for this reason the opinion of Avicenna which is clear and perfect, must be followed. And, al-

though the translators of the books of Avicenna, as in
that book on the Soul and in the book on Animals and
in the books on medicine, have translated them differently and have changed words, so that the intention of
Avicenna is not everywhere translated in the same way,
since in the book on Animals of Avicenna it is found that
the estimation is in the place of reason in brutes, and so
sometimes there is found elsewhere a contrariety in
respect of the things said above, still it is not important
that different interpreters make differences in words and
sometimes have even some difference on the part of the
thing; but his opinion in the book on the Soul must be
held to because he there discusses the faculties of the
soul as his principal intention, whereas elsewhere he
rather makes mention of them incidentally. Furthermore, that book is better translated by far than the
others; which is evident in that it has few or no words
of other languages, while his other books have an infinite
number of them. If, moreover, any one should consider
what has been said above, he must assume three altogether diverse faculties distributed in three cellules.
For a diversity of objects shows us a diversity of
faculties. There are, in fact, two kinds of sensibles, to
wit one exterior, such as the twenty-nine stated above,
another internal unknown to the exterior sense, as the
quality of a hurtful or useful constitution, or rather the
useful or the hurtful substantial nature itself. Therefore it follows necessarily that there be, as a consequence of this cause, two kinds of senses: namely, one
which contains the particular senses and the common
sense and the imagination, which are moved by the
first kind of sensibles; and the other which contains estimation and memory, which are referred to the second
class of sensibles. But because of the nobility of the
operations which the cogitative faculty has, compared

with the other faculties, the cogitative faculty is distinguished from the others. In the generally accepted translation of Aristotle, therefore, every faculty is called memory which has the power of retaining species and, therefore, as well the storehouse of common sense as the storehouse of estimation, is called memory. And, therefore, what is here called imagination is comprehended under memory in the translation of Aristotle which is in common use. But it is necessary without doubt, then, that memory is double and of very different parts, so that one will be the storehouse of common sense and the other of estimation; and they will differ according to species and according to subject and organ and operation. Moreover, although these faculties have now been located in the brain, it must be understood that the medullar substance of the brain does not perceive as Avicenna teaches in the tenth book on Animals; and in this he corrects Aristotle with pious and reverent interpretation.[28]

For the marrow in other places of the body does not have sense, and therefore it does not here. But it is a receptacle and treasury of sensitive faculties containing subtle nerves in which sense and sensible species are located. But that all doubt may be removed, it must be considered that the sensitive soul has a twofold instrument or subject: one is basic and original like a well-spring, and this is the heart according to Aristotle and Avicenna in their books on animals; the other is that which is first modified by the species of the sensibles and in which the operations of the senses are made more

---

[28] Bridges points out that a passage in *De Animalibus*, III, c. 19, makes it clear that Aristotle was aware that the substance of the brain was not sensitive; the reference is doubtless to the discussion of marrow in the *Historia Animalium* III, 20, 521[b] 4-17.

manifest and are distinguished, and this is the brain. For if the head be injured we clearly see that a lesion of the sensitive faculties follows, and head lesions are more easily discerned by us and they occur more frequently than heart lesions, and therefore, because of [these more frequent and] more obvious manifestations [of connections as revealed by lesions] we locate the sensitive faculties in the head; and this is the opinion of physicians who do not think that the wellspring and origin of faculties is in the heart. But Avicenna says in the first book of the Art of Medicine, that although the opinion of the physicians is the more manifest to the sense, nevertheless, the opinion of the Philosopher is the truer, since all the nerves and veins and all the faculties of the soul arise from the heart first and principally, as Aristotle demonstrates in the twelfth book on Animals, and Avicenna in the third book on Animals. . . .

THE SIXTH PART
OF THIS DEMONSTRATION[29]

AND THE SIXTH PART OF THE OPUS MAJUS IS ON EXPERIMENTAL SCIENCE

CHAPTER I.

Having laid down the roots of the wisdom of the latins so far as they are found in languages and mathematics and perspective, I wish now to take up the roots of experimental science, because without experience nothing can be known sufficiently. There are, in fact, two ways of knowing, namely, by argumentation and experience. Argumentation concludes and makes us grant the conclusion, but does not make certain nor

[29] O. c., vol. II, pp. 167-174, and vol. III, p. 141.

remove doubt that the mind may be quiet in the contemplation of truth, unless it finds truth by the way of experience; many, because they have arguments for the knowable but do not have experience, neglect the arguments and neither avoid the hurtful nor follow the good. For if a man who has never seen fire should prove by sufficient argument that fire burns and that it injures things and destroys them, the mind of one hearing it would never be satisfied by that nor would a hearer avoid fire until he had put a hand or a combustible object into the fire that he might prove by experience what argument had taught. But once he has had experience of combustion, his mind is made sure and rests in the brightness of truth. Therefore, argumentation does not suffice but experience does.

This is evident too in mathematics, where demonstration is most convincing. But the mind of one who has a most convincing demonstration of the equilateral triangle will never adhere to the conclusion without experience nor will such an one trouble about it, but will neglect it until experience is offered him by the intersection of two circles, from the intersection of which are drawn two lines to the extremities of the given line; but then the man accepts the conclusion with full repose. What Aristotle says therefore to the effect that the demonstration is a syllogism that makes us know, is to be understood if the experience of it accompanies the demonstration, and it is not to be understood of the bare demonstration. What he says, likewise, in the first book of the Metaphysics, that those who have the reason and the cause are wiser than those who are experienced, is said of experienced men who know only the bare truth without the cause. But I speak here of the man of experience who knows the reason and cause by experience. These men are perfect in wisdom, as Aristotle

holds in the sixth book of the Ethics,[30a] and their simple
statements must be believed as if they offered demonstration, as he states in the same place.

He, therefore, who wishes to enjoy without doubt[30b]
the truths of things, should know how to devote his
time to experiment; this is evident in examples. For
authors write of and the people maintain many doctrines
by arguments which they fashion without experiment
and which are wholly false. For it is commonly believed that the diamond can not be broken except by
goat's blood, and philosophers and theologians misuse
this opinion. But no certainty has been arrived at yet
concerning fraction by blood of this sort although an
attempt has been made at it; and without goat's blood
the diamond can be broken easily. For I have seen it
with my own eyes; and it is necessary, because gems
can not be carved except with fragments of this stone.
In the same way, it is held generally that the follicles
[of beavers], which physicians use, are the testicles of
the male animal. But that is not true because the beaver
has them under its breast, and both the male and the
female produce testicles of this sort. And besides these
follicles the male has his proper testicles in their natural
place; and therefore, what is added to this is a horrible
lie, namely, that when hunters are tracking the beaver,
he, knowing what they seek, tears off the follicles with
his teeth. Moreover, it has come to be held generally
that hot water congeals in vessels more quickly than
cold, and it is argued as basis for this that contrary is
excited by contrary, as enemies resist each other. But
it is certain that cold water congeals more quickly, to
any one who makes the experiment. People read this

[30a] *Eth. Nic.* VI, 2, 6.

[30b] The text reads *sine demonstratione*; it is interpreted as an
error for *sine dubitatione*.

into Aristotle in the second book of the Meteorologics[31] but he certainly does not say that, but he does affirm something like it, by which they have been deceived, namely, that if cold and hot water be poured into a cold place, as upon ice, the hot water is congealed more quickly, and this is true. But if cold and hot water be placed in two vessels, the cold will be congealed more quickly. It is necessary, therefore, that all things be certified by the way of experience.

But experience is double: one is by means of the exterior senses, and such are those experiences which show things that are in the heavens through instruments made for these experiments and those things that we find below by visual ascertainments. We know things which are not present in the places in which we are, through other wise men who have experienced them. Just as Aristotle sent, by the authority of Alexander, two thousand men to various places of the world to learn of all things which are on the surface of the earth, as Pliny testifies in the Natural History. This experience is human and philosophical, as much as man can do in accordance with the grace given him; but this experience does not suffice man, in that it does not certify fully concerning corporeal things because of its difficulty, and it touches on nothing at all of spiritual things. Therefore, it is necessary that the understanding of man be aided otherwise, and therefore the holy patriarchs and prophets, who first gave the sciences to the world, received interior illuminations and were not dependent only on sense. In the same way in the case of many of the faithful since the time of Christ. For the grace of faith illumines greatly and divine inspirations likewise, not only in spiritual but in corporeal things and in the sciences of philosophy, according to what Ptolemy says

[31] Reference probably to *Meteor.* I, 13, 18.

in the Centilogium, that the way to come to a knowledge
of things is twofold, one by the experience of philosophy,
the other by divine inspiration, which is far the better,
as he says.

There are seven grades of this interior knowledge.
The first by purely scientific illuminations. The second
grade consists in the virtues. For the evil man is ignorant, as Aristotle says in the second book of the
Ethics. And Algazeli says in his Logic that the soul
which is cast down by sins is like a rusty mirror, in
which the species of things can not be seen well; but
the soul adorned with virtues is like a well-polished
mirror, in which the forms of things are clearly seen.
For this reason true philosophers have labored the more
in morals for the integrity of virtue, concluding among
themselves that they can not see the causes of things
unless they have souls free from sins. Saint Augustine
recounts this of Socrates in the eighth book of the City
of God in the third chapter. For this reason the Scripture says, *Wisdom will not enter into an ill-disposed
soul.*[32] For it is impossible that the soul repose in the
light of truth while it is stained with sins, but it will
recite like a parrot or a magpie the words of another
which it learned by long practice. And the test of this
is that beauty of a cognized truth attracts men by its
refulgence to love it, but the proof of love is the exhibition of work. And, therefore, he who acts contrary to
the truth, must necessarily be ignorant of it, although
he may know how to put together very elegant phrases
and to quote the opinions of others, like a brute animal
that imitates human voices or like a monkey who at-
tempts to perform the actions of men, although it does
not understand the reason of them. Virtue, therefore,
clarifies the mind that man may understand more easily

[32] *Book of Wisdom* 1:4.

not only moral things, but scientific things. And I have tested this carefully in many fine youths, who because of innocence of soul advanced to greater knowledge than can be stated when they have had sound counsel on their study. Of this number is the bearer of the present writings, whose foundations very few of the latins acquire. Since, indeed, he is very young, that is, about twenty years of age, and extremely poor, he could not have masters, nor has he devoted the time of one year to learning the great things which he knows, nor is he of great genius or of great memory, so that there can be no other cause than the grace of God which gave him, because of the purity of his soul, that which it has refused to give to almost all students. For he has gone from me an uncorrupted virgin nor have I been able to find in him any kind of mortal sin although I have searched out carefully, and therefore he has a soul so clear and perspicuous that he learned with little instruction more than can be judged. And I have done what I could to bring about that these two youths should be useful vessels in the Church of God to the end that they may rectify by the grace of God all the studies of the latins.

The third step consists in the seven gifts of the Holy Spirit which Isaiah enumerates. The fourth consists in the beatitudes, which the Lord defines in the Gospels.[33] The fifth consists in the spiritual senses. The sixth is in fruits among which is the peace of the Lord which exceeds all understanding. The seventh consists in raptures [*raptus*] and the modes of them, according to which different men are seized differently to see many things of which it is not given to man to speak. And he who is carefully disciplined in these experiences or in several of them, can assure himself and others not

[33] See *Matthew* 5:3-11; *Luke* 6:20-22.

only as regards spiritual things but as regards all
human sciences. Therefore, since all parts of speculative philosophy proceed by arguments which are based
either on grounds of authority or on other grounds of
argumentation, except this part which I am now investigating, that science is necessary to us which is called
experimental. And I want to explain it, as it is useful
not only to philosophy but to the wisdom of God and
to the guidance of the whole world, as I have shown in
the case of languages and sciences above in relation to
their end, which is divine wisdom by which all things
are disposed.

Chapter II.

And because this Experimental Science is wholly ignored by the general run of students, for that reason
I can not convince people of its utility unless I show at
the same time its excellence and its property. This
science alone, then, knows how to test perfectly by experience what can be done by nature, what by the industry of art, what by imposture; what the incantations,
conjurations, invocations, deprecations, sacrifices (which
are magical devices) seek and dream of; and what is
done in them, so that all falsity may be removed and
that only the truth of art and nature be retained. This
science alone teaches one to consider all the insanities
of magicians, not that they may be confirmed but that
they may be avoided, just as logic considers sophistical
argument.

This experimental science has three great prerogatives with respect to the other sciences. The first is
that it investigates by experiment the noble conclusions
of all of the sciences. For the other sciences know
how to discover their principles by experiments, but

their conclusions are reached by arguments based on
the discovered principles. But if they must have particular and complete experience of their conclusions,
then it is necessary that they have it by the aid of this
noble science. It is true, indeed, that mathematics has
universal experiences concerning its conclusions in figuring and numbering, which are applied likewise to all the
sciences and to this experimental science, because no
science can be known without mathematics. But if we
turn our attention to the experiences which are particular and complete and certified wholly in their own discipline, it is necessary to go by way of the considerations
of this science which is called experimental autonymically. I use the example of the rainbow and of the
phenomena connected with it, of which sort are the
circle around the sun and the stars, likewise the rod
[*virga*] lying at the side of the sun or of a star which
appears to the eye in a straight line and is called by
Aristotle, in the third book of the Meteorologics, the
perpendicular, but is called the rod by Seneca, and the
circle is called the corona, which often has the colors
of the rainbow. The natural philosopher, to be sure,
holds discussions concerning these things and the per-
spectivist has many things to add which pertain to the
mode of seeing, which is very necessary in this case. But
neither Aristotle nor Avicenna, in their Natural His-
tories, has given us knowledge of things of this sort, nor
has Seneca, who composed a special book on them. But
Experimental Science makes certain of them.

The experimenter, then, should first examine visible
things to discover colors ordered as in the above mentioned things and in the same figure. Let him, indeed,
take the hexagonal stones of Ireland or India, which
are called iris stones in Solinus on the Wonders of the
World, and let him hold them in the solar ray falling

through a window so that he may find in the shadow
near the ray all the colors of the rainbow and ordered
as in it. And further let the same experimenter betake
himself to any shady place, and let him place the stone
to his eye, almost closed, and he will see the colors of
the rainbow clearly ordered as in the rainbow. And
since many who use these stones think that it is because
of a special virtue of the stones and because of their
hexagonal figure, for that reason let the same experimenter proceed further and he will find this property in
crystalline stones which are properly shaped and in
other clear stones. Moreover not only in white stones
like the irish, but in black stones, as is evident in the
dark crystal and in all stones of similar transparency.
He will find it, too, in another figure than the hexagonal,
provided the surfaces are corrugated like the irish stone
and neither altogether polished nor more rough than
they are, and provided they are such property of surface as nature produces in the irish. For the diversity
of wrinkles produces a diversity of colors. And after
that, [the experimenter] considers rowers and he finds
the same colors in the falling drops dripping from the
raised oars when the solar rays penetrate drops of this
sort. It is the same with waters falling from the wheels
of a mill; and when a man sees the drops of dew in
summer of a morning lying on the grass in the meadow
or the field, he will see the colors. And in the same
way when it rains, if he stands in a shady place and if
the rays beyond it pass through dripping moisture, then
the colors will appear in the shadow nearby; and very
frequently of a night colors appear around the wax-
candle. Moreover, if a man in summer, when he rises
from sleep and while his eyes are yet only partly
opened, looks suddenly toward an aperture through
which a ray of the sun enters, he will see colors. And

if, while seated beyond the sun, he extend his hat before his eyes, he will see colors; and in the same way if he closes his eye, the same thing happens under the shade of the eyebrow; and again, the same phenomenon occurs through a glass vessel filled with water, placed in the rays of the sun. Or similarly if any one holding water in his mouth sprinkles it vigorously into the rays and stands to the side of the rays; and if rays in the proper position pass through an oil lamp hanging in the air, so that the light falls on the surface of the oil, colors will be produced. And so in an infinite number of ways, as well natural as artificial, colors of this sort appear, as the careful experimenter is able to discover. . . .

THE SEVENTH PART
OF THIS DEMONSTRATION[34]

MORAL PHILOSOPHY

FIRST PART

I have shown in the preceding parts that the knowledge of languages, and mathematics, and perspective as well as experimental science are extremely useful and particularly necessary in the pursuit of wisdom. Without them no one can advance as he should in wisdom, taken not only absolutely but relatively to the Church of God and to the other three sciences described above. Now I wish likewise to go over the roots of the fourth science which is better and more noble than all those previously mentioned; and it is the practical one among them all, that is, the operative one, and it consists of our actions in this life and in the other life. In fact, all other sciences are called speculative. For although cer-

[34] O. c., vol. II, pp. 223-232, and vol. III, p. 144.

tain of them are active and operative, nevertheless, they
are concerned with artificial and natural actions, not
with moral actions, and they consider the truths of
things and of scientific activities which have reference
to the speculative intellect, and they are not related to
things pertaining to the practical intellect; and it is
called practical because it directs *praxis*, that is, the
operation of good and evil. Whence the term practical
is taken here in a restricted sense as applying to the
activities of morality in accordance with which we are
good or evil; although if practical is taken in a broad
sense for all operative science, many other things are
practical; but this is called practical autonymically because of the chief operations of man which are related
to virtues and vices, and to the felicity and misery of
the other life.

This practical science, then, is called moral and civil
science, which places man in his proper order to God
and to his neighbor and to himself, and tests these orders
and invites and moves us to them efficaciously. For this
science is concerned with the salvation of man in fulfillment of virtue and felicity; and this science aspires to
that salvation so far as philosophy can. From these
things, it appears in general that this science is more
noble than all the other parts of philosophy. For since
it is the inward end of human wisdom and since the end
is the most noble aspect in anything, this science must
of necessity be the most noble. In the same way, this
science alone or in the highest degree treats of the
same questions as theology, because theology considers
nothing except the five subjects mentioned above, although in another manner, namely, in the faith of
Christ. This science contains many outstanding testi-
monies for the same faith; and it scents from afar the
principal articles for the great aid of the christian

faith, as what follows will declare. But theology is the
most noble of the sciences; therefore, this which agrees
in the highest degree with it, is more noble than
the others. But that the very great utility of this science may be apparent, its parts must be investigated to
the end that what we wish may be drawn from the parts
and from the whole.

Moreover, since moral philosophy is the end of all
the parts of philosophy, the conclusions of the other sciences must be the principles in it in accordance with
the relation of preceding sciences to those that follow,
because the conclusions of the preceding are naturally
assumed in those that follow. And therefore, it is
fitting that they be carefully proved and certified in the
preceding sciences, that they may be worthy of acceptance in the sciences which follow, as is evident from
metaphysics. Therefore, the principles of moral philosophy are certified in the preceding sciences; and for
that reason these principles should be drawn from other
sciences, not because they belong to those sciences, but
because these sciences have prepared them for their
mistress. Whence, wheresoever they may be found they
must be ascribed to moral philosophy, since in substance
they are moral. And, although they may be repeated
in other sciences, it is by the grace of moral philosophy.
Wherefore, all things of this sort must be reckoned as
moral philosophy and ascribed to it. Therefore, if we
wish to use them according to their natural right, they
must be brought together in moral science from all the
other sciences. Nor is it strange if philosophers have
spread moral philosophy through all speculative philosophy: because they knew that it is of the salvation of
man; and therefore, they have mixed beautiful doctrines
in all the sciences that men might always be directed to
the good of salvation, and that all might know that the

other sciences are to be sought after only for this one
science which is the mistress of human wisdom. Therefore, if I adduce authorities from other places than those
which are contained in the books on morals, it must be
considered that they should properly be placed in this
science; nor can we say that they have not been written
in the books of this science, since we do not have except
in part in latin the philosophy of Aristotle, Avicenna,
and Averroes, who are the principal authors in moral
science. For just as theology understands that salvation-bringing truths belong to it, wheresoever they be
found, as was stated in the beginning and touched on
later, so too moral philosophy vindicates as its own
whatever it finds written elsewhere on things of this sort.
Moreover, this moral science is called by Aristotle and
by others civil science, because it shows the rights of
citizens and of states. And since it was ordinary that
states dominate regions as Rome ruled the world, for
that reason this science is called civil from the state
[*civitas*], although it is formed to construct the laws of
the Kingdom and the Empire.

This science, moreover, teaches in the first place to
draw up the laws and the rights of living; secondly, it
teaches that these rights are to be believed and approved
and that men are to be urged to act and live according
to these laws. The first part is divided into three sec-
tions; for first comes naturally the relation of man to
God and in respect to the angelic substance; secondly,
his relation to his neighbor; thirdly, to himself, as the
Scripture states. For in the first place in the books of
Moses are the commands and laws concerning God and
divine worship. In the second place concerning the
relation of man to his neighbor in the same books and
those that follow. In the third place there are instruc-
tions concerning customs, as in the books of Solomon.

In the same way in the New Testament, these three alone are contained. For man can not assume other relations.

Not only because of the first but because of all those which follow, it is necessary that the principles of this science, by which the others are verified, be set forth in the beginning. Of these principles, however, there are some which are purely principles and are capable of being stated only metaphysically. Others, although they are principles with respect to the sciences which follow, are nevertheless either first conclusions of this science [i.e. morals], or else, although they enjoy some of the privilege of a principle, still because of their extreme difficulty, and that they may meet with less contradiction, and because of their excellent utility in respect to the sciences which follow, they should be demonstrated sufficiently: as Aristotle in the beginning of his natural philosophy proves the first principle of that science, namely, that there is motion, against those who suppose only the one immovable being.[35] It should be noted, however, that metaphysics and moral philosophy agree with each other to the highest degree; for both have to do with God and angels and eternal life and with many subjects of this sort although in different ways. For metaphysics investigates metaphysically by means of the common properties of all the sciences: and it investigates spiritual things by way of the corporeal: and through created things it finds the Creator: and through the present life it treats of the future: and it sets forth many preambles to moral philosophy. Metaphysics investigates these subjects because of civil science, so that it is right to join this science with metaphysics, lest (since principles are assumed in this science, which have to be proved in metaphysics) I

[35] The reference is to the *Physics* I, 2, 184[b] 27 ff.

should confuse different sciences with each other, by trying to prove in this science principles which are proper to metaphysics.

I state therefore, that God must be, just as he must be shown to be in metaphysics: second, that all men know naturally that God is: and third, that God is of infinite power and of infinite goodness, and together with that, that he is of infinite substance and essence, so that it follows thus that he is best, wisest, and most powerful. In the fourth place, that God is one in essence and not many. Fifth, that not only is he one in essence but three in another manner, which has to be explained in general by metaphysicians, but here it must be explained in the discipline itself. Sixth, that he has created all things and governs them in the being of Nature. Seventh, that besides corporeal things he has formed spiritual substances which we call Intelligences and Angels; for intelligence is the name of a nature, and angel is the name of a function; and how many they are and what their activities are, as it pertains to metaphysics, as far as it is possible for them to be known by human reason. Eighth, that besides angels he made other spiritual substances which are the rational souls in men. Ninth, that he made them immortal. Tenth, that the felicity of the other life is the highest good. Eleventh, that man is capable of this felicity. Twelfth, that God governs the human race in the way of morals just as he governs other things in the being of nature. Thirteenth, that God promises future felicity to those who live rightly in accordance with the governance of God, as Avicenna teaches in the tenth book of the Metaphysics, and that a horrible future infelicity is due those who live evilly. Fourteenth, that worship is due God with all reverence and devotion. Fifteenth, that as man is ordered naturally to God through the reverence due him, so he is ordered to his neighbor by justice and peace, and to himself by honorableness of life. Sixteenth, that man can not know by his own effort how to please God with the worship due him, nor how he should stand in relation to his neighbor nor to himself, but he needs the revelation of truth in these things. Seventeenth, that the revelation must be made to one only; that he must be the mediator of God and men and the vicar of God on earth, to whom is subjected the whole human race, and in whom one must believe without contradiction when it has been proved with certitude that he is such as I have just described him; and he is the lawgiver and the high priest who has the plentitude of power as if God on earth in temporal and in spiritual things, as Avicenna says in the tenth book of the Metaphysics, whom it is proper to adore after God.

By these principles metaphysics is continuous with moral philosophy and approaches it as its end; thus Avicenna joins them beautifully at the end of his Metaphysics. The other principles, however, are peculiar to this science and are not to be explained in metaphysics, although Avicenna adds a number of them. But in the beginning of his volume he gives the reason for this, that he had not constructed a moral philosophy and he did not know whether he would complete one; and therefore he mixed with these metaphysical principles many which are nevertheless proper to moral philosophy, as is evident to the inquirer. And once these have been considered, the legislator should then at the beginning take up the properties of God in particular, and of angels, and the felicity and the misery of the other life, and the immortality of bodies after the resurrection, and things of this sort to which the metaphysician could not aspire. For the metaphysician treats in all these principally of the question of whether the thing is; because it is proper for him to take up that question in regard to all things, in that he considers that which is and being in their common properties. But the other sciences take up other questions involved in things: namely, what each one is, and of what kind, and how much, and other questions of this sort, in accordance with the ten categories. The moral philosopher, however, does not have to explain all the secrets of God and of the angels and of others; but he must explain those which are necessary to the multitude, in which all men should agree, lest they fall into questions and heresies, as Avicenna teaches in the Principles of Moral Philosophy.

I say, therefore, that moral philosophy explains first the trinity in relation to God, which truth the legislator has by revelation rather than by reason. The reason, indeed, why philosophers have said a great deal concerning divine things in particular which exceed human reason and fall under revelation, was touched on before in mathematics. For there it was shown how they could have many noble truths concerning God which were had through revelation made to them, as the Apostle says, for God revealed these things. But rather to the patriarchs and the prophets who, it is known, had revelation and from whom the philosophers learned all things, as was proved clearly above. For the patriarchs and the prophets not only treated divine things theologically or prophetically but also philosophically, because they devised all philosophy as was proved in the second part of this work. The metaphysician, however, was able to teach sufficiently that God is, and that he is known naturally, and that he is of infinite power, and that he is one, and that he is three. But how the Trinity is, he could not there explain to the full; and, therefore, that must be shown here.

There is, then, the blessed Trinity, the Father and the Son and the Holy Ghost. For Claudius, one of the expositors of the sacred Scripture, in the book in which he combats the following heresy, that God feels nothing with a sense of passion but with an affect of compassion, brings forward this argument, *Plato with praiseworthy daring, admirable skill, unchangeable purpose, sought, found, and proclaimed three persons in the Divinity: God the Father, also the paternal mind, art, or counsel, and the love of the two for each other.* He taught thus not only that we must believe in one supreme equitrinal undivided Divinity, but he demonstrated that he must be thus. These things are clear from his book on Divine Things. Porphyry, as Augustine says in the tenth book of the City of God, chapter twenty-nine, spoke of the Father and his Son whom he called the paternal intellect and mind, and the medium of them whom, as Augustine says, we think he called the Holy Spirit; and following his manner he calls them three Gods, where although he uses words loosely, he sees nevertheless what should be maintained. Augustine, in the same book in the thirty-second chapter,[36] recounts that a certain platonic philosopher, whose name he does not give, stated the beginning of the Gospel according to John as far as the incarnation of Christ, in which the distinction of the divine persons is stated clearly. Augustine, also in the tenth book of the City of God in the thirty-sixth and the thirty-seventh[37] chapters, insists that Porphyry says in the first book on the Return of the Soul that sins can not be purged except by the Son of God. And Aristotle says in the beginning of the Heavens and the World that in divine wor-

[36] *De Civit. Dei*, X, 29.   [37] *De Civit. Dei*, X, 32.

ship we exercise ourselves to magnify the one God by the number three, which is prominent in the properties of the things which are created. And therefore, since every creature, as is evident from the Metaphysics, is a trace and imprint of the Trinity, there must be the Trinity in the Creator. And since Aristotle completed the philosophy of his predecessors to the limit of the possibility of his times, he had to feel far more certainly concerning the blessed Trinity of persons that he might confess the Father and the Son and the Holy Spirit. For this reason there were three sacrifices in the law of Aristotle and three prayers, as Averroes says in his commentary on the beginning of the Heavens and the World: and this is manifest from the politics of Aristotle, which is the Book of Laws. Avicenna, moreover, the most outstanding expositor of Aristotle, assumes the Holy Spirit in the principles of moral philosophy.

But he [i.e. Aristotle] could perceive the truth of the Father and the Son far better, because it is more difficult to understand the procession of the Holy Spirit from two distinct persons than the generation of one of them from the other. For this reason philosophers failed more in the comprehension of the Holy Spirit than in the knowledge of the Father and the Son. And therefore they who were able to have a knowledge of the Holy Spirit, had far more knowledge of the other persons. The philosopher Ethicus in his book on divine and human and natural things, which he wrote in the hebrew, the greek, and the latin languages, because of the greatness of the secrets, places in God, the Father, and the Word of the Father, and the Holy Spirit, and maintains that there are three persons, namely, the Father and the Son and the Holy Spirit. This must also be held by reason. This reasoning, nevertheless, could not have been given before the things which have

to be expressed of God in particular nor before the
authorities of the great philosophers, which are introduced to this same end in this science as in the place
appropriate to them.

I say, therefore, that God is of infinite power; and
infinite power is powerful of infinite operation; therefore, something infinite can be made by God, but not
something infinite in essence, because then there could
be several Gods; the contrary of which has been shown
in the section on mathematics. Therefore, that which
is begotten of God must be God since it has the essence
of its progenitor; but it is different in person. And
since this which is begotten has infinite power, and since
it is infinite good, it can bring forth something infinite:
therefore it is able to bring forth another person.
Either, then, the Father brings forth the same person,
and then the Holy Spirit will proceed from both of
them; or he will be brought forth from the Son only,
and in that case he will not pertain to the Father and
the relationship will not be full and there will not be
complete agreement in the divine persons, which is contrary to reason. Further, there can not be parity of love
according to this view, because the Father would love
the Son more than the Holy Spirit, because he begets
the Son and does not bring forth the Holy Spirit. But
since the Holy Spirit is God, because he has the divine
essence, an infinite love must be due him; and therefore,
the Father will love him with an infinite love as he does
the Son. And likewise because the love of the Father
can not be other than infinite, because his love is in
accordance with his power, it remains, therefore, that
the love of the Father for the Holy Spirit will be as
great as the love of the Son for the Holy Spirit. Wherefore, the Holy Spirit as well as the Son must be brought
forth from the Father. That, however, there are not

and can not be more persons, can not and should not
be explained here, but must be assumed until it is proved
in the fourth part of this science [of morals], to which
the full measure of the demonstration will be assigned.
But it was necessary that the trinity of persons, namely,
of the Father and the Son and the Holy Spirit be
proved and expounded here because it is the radical
foundation of this science for establishing divine worship and for many other things.   Nor should it be alleged in opposition that no science has to prove its
principles.   For how that is to be understood has been
shown above.   But other things which can be inquired
concerning God and in which there should be probable
doubt, are conclusions of the fourth part and, therefore,
will be determined there. . . .

THE SECOND PART OF MORAL PHILOSOPHY[38]

CHAPTER I.

On observance of the laws of matrimony and of the
commonwealth.

The second part treats of the laws and statutes of
the relations of men to each other.   In the first place,
the welfare of the human species is considered in the
line of propagation, to bind people by laws in their increase.   Therefore laws of marriage are given and how
marriages must be made is determined and how impedi-
ments are to be removed; and most of all, that fornica-
tors and sodomites be excluded from states, who are
inimical to the construction of the state, since they
draw men away from that which is better in states,
namely, from marriage, as Avicenna and others maintain.

[38] O. c., vol. II, pp. 250-255, and vol. III, p. 145.

Next, laws are given in accordance with which subjects are ordered in respect to prelates and princes, and contrariwise, and servants to masters according to every type of servitude and mastership; and laws are given in accordance with which the fathers of families must live in guiding their offspring and family, and the master is ordered in respect to his disciples. Next, the doctors and the skilled in each of the sciences and arts are appointed; and those best suited to engage in studies and duties of this sort are chosen according to the advice of the wise men from the youths who are to be instructed; and the rest are deputed to the military service to execute justice and to check malefactors. And it is necessary, as Avicenna says, that this be the first intention in instituting the law, namely, to order the state in three parts, that is, into disposers, ministers, and those learned in the law, and that in each of them some one in charge be appointed. After him, other officials inferior to him should be appointed, and after these still others, until few remain; to the end that no one be useless in the state and not have some praiseworthy function, and that some utility to the state may be derived from each one. Whence, in Plato, that state is held to be most justly ordered in which each one knows his own condition. Therefore, as Avicenna says, the prince of the state should prohibit idleness and disoccupation. Those, moreover, who can not be curbed should be expelled from the state, unless the cause is infirmity or old age; and then a place should be set apart in which people of that sort should remain and have a procurator allotted to them. It is necessary, moreover, that there be in the state a certain place for the moneys of the commonwealth, which should be derived partly from the law governing contracts, partly from fines which are inflicted for punishment, partly from the estates and spoil of rebels, partly from other sources; and to the end that this public fund be available partly for those who can not acquire money for themselves because of infirmity and old age and partly for teachers of law and medicine, and partly for public uses.

And then, the legislator instructs men to make patrimonies and inheritances and testaments, because Avicenna says that the substance necessary for life is partly the branch and is partly the root. But the root is the patrimony and anything bequeathed and given by testament, of which three roots the most secure is patrimony. The branch of substance, however, comes from gains derived from kinds of business. Then laws should be published concerning contracts in all sorts of business, in buying, selling, leasing, hiring, borrowing, lending, paying, saving and the like, that whatever can do harm in contracts may be removed, as Avicenna says.

Then, laws must be framed in accordance with which it may be shown in all lawsuits and in all cases what rights and wrongs are, and according to which legal processes may be terminated that peace and justice may be fostered among the citizens. Later, as Avicenna says, activities by which inheritances and fortunes are lost and by which the peace and concord of citizens are disturbed, must be prohibited; and those who set up and practise these pursuits are people who wish to win for the sake of some gain, such as the wrestler, the dice player, and others of this sort. In the same way, activities should be prohibited which lead to things contrary to the utilities, such as he exemplified in his teaching concerning stealing and plundering and other acts of this sort.

And further ordinances should be made, as Avicenna says, that men aid and defend each other, and that they be unanimous against the enemies of the law even to subduing them by violence. If, however, there be another commonwealth and another regimen of good constitutions and laws, this is not opposed to the first unless the time should come when there must be no other law than this one, the establishment of which, since it is the best, must then be extended throughout the whole world. And in this statement the christian law is signified, as will be explained below. If, however, there should be some among those who are at variance with the law, they should first be corrected that they may return to their senses; but if they do not wish to do that, they should be put to death.

CHAPTER II.

The last point that is required here is that the legislator set up a successor to himself. This is done, according to Avicenna, in the following manner. For he should do it with the consensus of the nobles and of the people; and he should choose such an one as can rule well and be prudent and be of good morals, brave, kind, skilled in governing and learned in the law, than whom none is more learned, and this should be manifest to all. But if thereafter they should so disagree that they wish to choose another, they have in that denied God, and therefore the legislator should interpose in his law enactments to the effect that the entire state should fall unanimously upon any one who should wish to intrude himself by power or money and should kill him. But if they shall be able to do this and shall not have done it, they have in that contradicted God, and he is not guilty of blood who has killed one of this sort provided, however, it is previously known to the people. If, on the other hand, he who should be made successor is not worthy and has been so proved, another should be appointed.

And so in a summary way the intention and aims of the fundamental parts [the roots] of this second section [of moral philosophy] and of those matters that proceed from such fundamentals have been brought to a close. In this part is comprehended the civil law, which is now in use among the latins, as is manifest from the roots of this part. Moreover it is certain that the latins have derived their rights and laws from the greeks; that is, from the books of Aristotle and Theophrastus, his successor, as well as the laws of the twelve tables which were taken first from the laws of Solon the athenian.

The Third Part of Moral Philosophy

Chapter I.

On the guidance of man relative to himself.

The third part of moral and civil science is concerned with the practices of each person relative to himself, that everyone may have honorableness of life and may pass over the foulness of vices because of future felicity and the horror of eternal punishment. That this should be the third part appears evidently, since it is plain that that part which contains the worship of God is first, as has been declared. The common good, moreover, is set before the private good, as Aristotle says in the first book of the Metaphysics. But the preceding part has to do with the common good; whereas this part advances the private good. For charity is the greatest virtue, and it is ordered with reference to the common good, and peace and justice attend it, which virtues go beyond the morals of individual persons. For man is a social animal and it is one of his properties, as Avicenna says in the fifth book on the Soul, that he should not live alone like the brute animal which in its life suffices to itself alone. Therefore the laws which order men to their neighbor are the more important.

According to Aristotle and Averroes, in the tenth book of the Metaphysics, the hermit man who is not part of the state, but is concerned with himself alone, is not good nor is he evil. And Cicero, in the book on Duties, quoting the words of Plato says that Plato wrote very truly that we are not born for ourselves alone. Our native land claims part of our origin; our friends part; and as the stoics are pleased to believe that all things are created for the use of men, men are generated for the sake of men, that they may be able to aid one another. As Cicero himself, in the fifth book of the Academics, says, *Nothing is so noble as the communication of benefits*. It is, in fact, innate in man that he have something of the civil and the popular, which something the greeks call *politicon*. Whence, in the book on the Happy Life, Seneca says, *This word is required of man that he aid all, if he is able to, or many; if he is less able, a few; if still less, his neighbors; if less, himself*. Wherefore, the second principal part of moral philosophy must be concerned with public laws, as has been stated; and the third will be on the life and the honor which each one should pursue. This, moreover, is true according to the order of the dignity of nature and absolutely speaking, although Aristotle does not adopt this manner in his books, for he proceeds according to the way of investigation and therefore goes from the things which are better known to us and not from those better known to nature. But since we have already made certain through him and others what the power of this science requires, therefore, we can arrange its parts according to the order which the dignity of nature demands.

And here the philosophers have said wondrous things concerning virtues and vices; so that every christian may be confounded when we conceive that unbelieving men had such sublimities of virtues and we seem to fall ignominiously from the glory of virtues. For the rest, we should be greatly encouraged to aspire to the apex of virtue, and stirred by noble examples we should give forth more noble fruits of the virtues, since we have greater aid in life than those philosophers, and since we are assured we shall receive greater aids beyond comparison by the grace of God. I shall first quote certain phrases relating to virtues and vices in general: secondly, I shall pass on to particulars. . . .

THE FOURTH PART OF MORAL PHILOSOPHY[39]

CHAPTER I.

I have dwelt on this third part of Moral Philosophy at length because of the beauty and utility of moral sentiments and because the books from which I have gathered these roots, flowers, and fruits of morals, are rarely found. Now, however, I wish to go on to the fourth part of this science [of morals] which, although it is not so copious and so pregnant as the third, is nevertheless more wonderful and more worthy, not only than that part, but than all the parts of the science, since it consists in the elucidation of the belief, and the love, and the proof by works, of the religion of the faithful which the human race should accept. Nor is there anything of philosophy more necessary for man or of so great utility or dignity. For it is especially on

[39] O. c., vol. II, pp. 366-68, and vol. III, pp. 149-150.

account of this part [of morals] that all the sciences are subordinate to moral philosophy. In fact, all wisdom is ordered with a view to knowing the salvation of the human race; and this salvation consists in the perception of the things which lead man to the felicity of the other life. Avicenna says of this felicity that it is such as eye has not seen nor ear heard, as has been touched on above. And since this fourth part of philosophy purposes to investigate this salvation and to attract men to it, therefore, all the sciences, arts, and functions, and whatever falls under the consideration of man, are bound to this most noble part of civil science; and this is the goal of human consideration.

For this reason it is most useful to consider the intention of this part; and it is fitting that every christian do so for the confirmation of his profession and that he may have wherewith to correct those who have wandered astray. Assuredly, God can never deny to the human race a knowledge of the way of salvation, since he wishes all men to be saved according to the Apostle. And his goodness is infinite, wherefore he has always left men means by which they may be enlightened to know the ways of truth. Aristotle indeed in his Politics takes up the different kinds of religions, and says that he wishes to consider the religions and the laws of four or five simple commonwealths and to see what laws corrupt commonwealths and kingdoms, and what laws do not. He says, moreover, that there are four or five simple corrupt religions, intending that the religion or law be called simple because of a simple end and composite because of a composite end, since every religion varies according to the condition of the end, as Alfarabi teaches in the book on the Sciences, expounding the view of Aristotle concerning religions. And these simple ends, according to Alfarabi, but more clearly according to

Boethius in the third book of the Consolation of Philosophy, are: pleasure, riches, honor, power, fame or glory of name.

And now I shall tell of the principal nations among which are varied throughout the world, the religions which still continue, and they are, saracens, tartars, pagans, idolaters, jews, christians. For there are no more principal religions, nor can there be until the religion of the Anti-Christ. But religions are compounded from all these, or from some four, or three, or two, according to various combinations.

But besides the ends enumerated, there is another, namely, the felicity of the other life, which different religions seek and strain toward in different ways, because some place it in the delights of the body, some in the delights of the soul, some in the delights of both. In addition there are religions compounded of this felicity and all the other ends, or from several, and this in diverse manners. For although they seek after a future felicity, nevertheless many men give themselves up to pleasures, and others strive eagerly after riches, and some aspire after honors, and some after the power of dominion, and some after the glory of fame. I shall touch, however, on the three divisions of the religions first, that the end to which they tend may be clear. Then I shall deal with the choice of the religion of the faithful, which alone should be spread throughout the world. . . .

CHAPTER I (continued)[40]

Having set forth these principal religions in respect to the use of peoples as well as in respect to the ways of astronomy and in respect to the diversities of their ends,

[40] O. c., vol. II, pp. 372-79, and vol. III, p. 150.

the consideration proceeds to the means of persuading
men of the truth of religion. It was said above in the
section on mathematics, in relation to the conversion
of unbelievers, that the persuasion of the religious truth
which is contained in the christian religion alone, is
brought about in a twofold manner, since it is either by
miracles which are beyond us and beyond unbelievers,
and concerning this way no man can presume; or else
it is by a way, common to unbelievers and to us, which
is in our power and which they can not deny, because
it proceeds along the ways of human reason and by the
ways of philosophy. Philosophy belongs especially to
unbelievers, since we have derived the whole of philosophy from them, and not without the greatest reason,
that we may have confirmation of our faith for ourselves, and that we may pray efficaciously for the salvation of unbelievers. Nor should the statement of
Gregory be urged in objection, that faith has no place
where human reason lends proof. For this statement
must be understood of the christian man who would
lean only or principally on human reason. But this
should not be done: on the contrary, he must believe
in the Church and the Scripture and the Saints and
the Catholic doctors, and that he should do principally.

But for the solace of human frailty, that it may avoid
the attacks of error, it is useful for the christian to
have effective reasons for the things which he believes,
and he should have a reason for his faith for any occasion that requires it, as the blessed Peter teaches in
his first Epistle, saying,[41] *But sanctify in your hearts
Christ as Lord; being ready always to give answer to
every man that asketh you a reason concerning the faith
and hope that is in you.* But we can not argue this by
quoting our law, nor the authorities of the saints, be-

[41] *First Epistle of Peter* 3:15.

cause unbelievers deny the Lord Christ and his law
and saints. Wherefore it is necessary to seek reasons
in another way, and this way is common to us and to
unbelievers, namely, philosophy. But the power of
philosophy in this part accords in the highest degree
with the wisdom of God; indeed, it is the trace and
imprint of the divine wisdom given by God to man,
that by this trace man may be moved to divine truths.
Nor are these things proper to philosophy, but are
common to theology and philosophy, to believers and
unbelievers, given by God and revealed to philosophers,
to the end that the human race might be prepared for
special divine truths. And the reasons of which I speak
are not unrelated to faith nor outside the principles of
faith, but are dug from its roots, as will be manifest
from only stating them.

I could, of course, set forth the simple and crude
methods suited to the mass of unbelievers, but that is
not worth while. For the crowd is too imperfect, and
therefore the conviction of faith which the crowd must
have is crude and confused and unworthy of wise men.
I wish, therefore, to go higher and give a demonstration
of which wise men must judge. For in every nation
there are some men who are assiduous and apt to wisdom, who are open to rational conviction; so that once
they have been informed, persuasion through them of
the crowd is made easier.

I assume in the beginning, of course, that there are
three kinds of knowledge; one is in the effort of personal discovery through experience. Another is by the
learning of others. The third precedes these, and is
the way to them, called natural knowledge; and it is
so named because it is common to all. That, in fact, is
natural which is common to all members of the same
species, as burning is natural to fire, according to the

example of Aristotle in the fifth book of the Ethics; and Cicero says this same thing in the first of the Tusculan Questions, and we see it in an infinite number of examples. For we say the cries of brutes have a natural significance, because they are common to the individuals of their species; and things are known naturally by us of the sort in which we all agree, as that every whole is greater than its part, and others of this sort, as well simple as complex. We know likewise that the rational soul is formed to learn the truth and to love it, and the proof of this love is the exhibition of action, according to Gregory and all the saints and philosophers. There are some, however, who think that there are two distinct parts in the soul, or two faculties, so that there is one by which the soul knows the truth, another by which it wishes to seize on[42] the truth when learned. On the other hand some believe that there is one substance of the soul which performs both functions, because its acts are coordinated to each other, in that the knowledge of truth exists on account of the love for it; for it is one and the same faculty. According to them the soul first apprehends the truth and then loves it when known and completes it in action. Whence Aristotle holds in the third book on the Soul,[43] that the speculative intellect is made practical by the extension of knowledge of truth to the love of it. Nor does he ever make a specific difference between the speculative intellect and the practical as he does between the intellect and the sense and the vegetative soul. For he argues, in the second book on the Soul that these three are diverse in species, because their operations are diverse in species, that is, understanding, perceiving and vegetating; nor are they

[42] *Audire* in the text has been interpreted as erroneous, probably, for *adpetere*.

[43] *De An.* III, 7, 431a 10-20.

ordered in relation to each other. But the knowledge of
truth is ordered toward the love of it, and it is formed
because of it; and therefore there is one faculty, or
nature, or substance of the rational soul which knows
truth and loves it. Whence in the third book on the
Soul,[44] Aristotle begins thus: *However, concerning the
part of the soul with which it knows and judges, I must
now speak*; meaning that it is the same part which has
both functions; just as it is in the sensitive part; because it is the same faculty which perceives and desires,
as is evident in every sense. For the sense of touch
knows the hot and desires it; and the sense of taste
knows flavors and desires them, and so with others.

But it is not of great moment how we may speak of
these matters. For we know that the rational soul is
formed to know and to love the truth. But the truth
of religion is perceived only so far as the knowledge
of God overflows in one, for every religion is referred
to God; and therefore he who wishes to come to a certain knowledge of religion must begin with God. But
the knowledge of God, so far as concerns the question
of whether he is, is known to all naturally, as Cicero
teaches in his book on the Immortality of the Soul.
And he proves it saying, *No nation is so savage and
monstrous that its mind has not been imbued with an
opinion of God nor is there a people that does not show
some form of divine worship.*[45] But if Avicenna says
in the first book of the Metaphysics[46] that this science
seeks to prove the being of God, it must be said that
this is true as regards full certitude. For the natural
knowledge which every one has of God is weak, and
it is weakened by the sins which are numerous in every

[44] *De An.* III, 4, 429a 10.
[45] Probably from *De Nat. Deorum* I, 16 and 23.
[46] *Met.* I, 1.

one. For sin obscures the soul and most of all in what concerns the divine.

Therefore, it is necessary that this knowledge be aided by argument and faith. But the knowledge of the unity of God, and of what God is, and how, and of what sort, is not known naturally. For in these matters men are always in disaccord, some maintaining several gods, others considering that the stars are gods, others, things here below, as, for example, the pure pagans and the idolaters. And so they must err in religion. All others who say that there is one God do not understand other points which are true of God. And therefore one who advances a religion must know in the beginning how to present the attributes which are required in general of God. However, it is not necessary that he go into all the particular truths in the beginning; but he should proceed little by little and he should begin with the easier questions in this way. For as the geometer sets down his definitions that the things he deals with may be known in respect to what they are and what they are called, so one must proceed here: because unless one knows what it is that is meant by a name, there will be no demonstration.

God, therefore, is the first cause antecedent to which there is no other, and which did not emerge into being, nor will it be possible for it not to be, of infinite power, wisdom, and goodness, Creator of everything and director of everything, according to the susceptibility of the nature of individual things. And in this definition tartars, saracens, jews, and christians agree. The wise men also of the idolaters and the pagans, when they have been given the reason for this, can not contradict it; nor consequently can the multitude over whom the wise men stand as directors and leaders. For two ways of arguing to this end will be presented for them: one by

the consensus of all other nations and religions and of
all the rest of the human race. But the lesser should
conform itself to the greater part; and that part is
disgraceful which does not accord with its whole. It is
well known that there are wiser men in the other religions; and the pagans and the idolaters are not ignorant
of this. For when a meeting is arranged with them
they are convinced easily, and they perceive their own
ignorance clearly; as appeared in the case of the em-
peror of the Tartars who summoned before him christians, saracens, and idolaters to confer on the truth of
religion; and forthwith the idolaters were confounded
and convinced. This fact appears in the book on the
Practices of the Tartars addressed to our Lord the
present King of France. And when christians confer
with pagans, like the Prusceni and the other adjoining
nations, they yield easily and see that they are held
by errors. The proof of this is that they wished most
willingly to be made christians if the Church were willing to permit them to retain their freedom and to enjoy
their goods in peace. But the christian princes who
labor for their conversion, and most of all the brothers
of the Teutonic house, wish to reduce them to servitude,
as is known to the dominicans and franciscans and other
good men throughout Germany and Poland. And, therefore, they offer opposition; whence, they stand against
oppression, not against the arguments of a better religion.

Further, one who advocates the religion of the faithful
has from the part of Metaphysics and of this moral
science another manner by which he may proceed in
arguing. This I wish only to indicate until such a time
as the treatise which Your Highness demands will be
completed. And, indeed, it can be set down as a postu-
late for the man who is assiduous and amenable to the

efficacy of reason, that causes do not go back *in infinitum,* since an infinite number of causes can not be nor be understood. For all things which are and which are understood are comprehended in some number, as Aristotle says in the third book of the Physics. There is not therefore cause preceding cause *in infinitum.* Therefore we must stop at some first cause which does not have a cause before it, and all the multitude is reduced to unity. And in every genus there is one first to which the others are reduced. But if this be the first cause, with no other cause antecedent to it, it is manifest that it did not come forth into being through a cause; nor is anything else the cause of its being; nor does it make itself to be after not being, because it would have to be when it was not, that it might make itself be. For everything which causes something else to be after not being, has being while it does this: therefore, nothing is cause of its own being. Wherefore, this first cause never had non-being: therefore, it always was. But if that is the case, then it will always be, since there are many things which will always be, and nevertheless have not always been, as angels and souls and the heavens and the earth and others of this sort. And, therefore, that which never had non-being will conserve its being far more easily in eternity. Furthermore, that which never had non-being is removed infinitely from non-being; and therefore it is impossible that it fall into non-being. Some things, in fact, which have come forth into being are able not to be, because they are not infinitely removed from non-being, for at one time they were not: therefore, since non-being is removed *in infinitum* from that which always was, there is no proportion between it and this other. And therefore such a thing will not be able not to be: and this is more acceptable than any of the doctrines which have been spoken of here, and therefore it is rather conceivable than in need of proof.

It is evident, however, that the thing which always was and will be is of infinite power. Because if it is of finite power, then its power is imperfect, since something can be added to all finite things, and every imperfect thing is naturally subject to change; but it is not possible to assume any change unless the first be assumed. For the first is naturally prior to the posterior. And therefore since the first change is in respect to being and non-being, it must be possible in that which has finite power. But this change does not occur in that which always was and always will be: wherefore, neither does finitude in power pertain to it.

Further, Philosophy argues in the third book of the Consolation[47] in this fashion. In every genus in which the imperfect is found, it is natural that the perfect be found. And therefore in the genus of power a perfect power must be found after we find an imperfect one. But the perfect is that from which nothing is lacking, nor can anything be added, according to Aristotle in the third book of the Physics and the fifth of the Metaphysics. And that to which nothing can be added is infinite; because an addition can be made to every finite thing in so far as it is such, and something else can be understood beyond it. It is necessary, therefore, that the perfect power be infinite. But there is no perfect and infinite power in things other than this cause which we seek: therefore, in this cause there will be such power. But if its power is infinite, then its essence is infinite; because power does not exceed essence. For essence is either equal to power or greater. And demonstrations have already been given for this in the observations which were made concerning mat-

47 *Consol. Phil.* III, prosa 10.

ter. It is manifest, therefore, that the essence of the first cause is infinite.

And certainly if its essence and power are infinite, its goodness must be infinite, since a thing whose essence is finite has finite goodness. Therefore the infinite will have infinite goodness; and otherwise there is no proportion of goodness to essence in this cause; which can not be in so great majesty. And if its goodness were finite, it would be imperfect, and something could be added to it and taken from it, and thus it could be subjected to transmutation; and therefore it would be natural for it to have non-being, as was argued previously of power. Nor is it possible that that which has infinite majesty in essence and power and goodness, should lack knowledge, because a thing which is of this sort [i.e. deficient] has a lowliness[48] and can not be related to the infinity of majesty, as is the case with elements and stones and vegetables.

Moreover, we see that things lacking infinite power, as animals and men and angels, have knowledge because of the nobility of their nature: therefore, since the nature of the cause which is now sought is infinitely more noble than anything of this sort, it will have the power of knowing. But since all other things which are in it are found to be infinite, this cause has infinite wisdom. Again, if it were finite, it would be imperfect and subject naturally to transmutation into greater and lesser, as is clear in the case of other things that know, as in every imperfect thing. And therefore the first mutation which is in respect to being and non-being could be discovered here, as was shown above. It is necessary, therefore, that there be infinite wisdom in this cause;

[48] The text reads *utilitatem*; this has been interpreted as an error for *vilitatem*; an interpretation which is reinforced by the contrast below to *nobilitas*, i.e. *nobilis*=*non vilis*.

but if its power is infinite it is able to produce this world, and its infinite wisdom knows how to order it best, and its goodness requires that that be done, because it is the property of the best to do the best and to communicate its goodness to others, so far as goodness is adaptable to them. Therefore this cause has necessarily produced the world. . . .

SAINT BONAVENTURA (1221–1274)

Whether platonism and aristotelianism are expressions of an identical philosophical attitude, or whether they are different but reconcilable positions, or finally whether they are totally contradictory, is a question, which notwithstanding that it was long agitated in the middle ages, submits to no simple answer. Modern historians of philosophy have not been much concerned with such questions, though the reiteration of changes on the aphorism that one is born either a platonist or an aristotelian, might be supposed to indicate that one answer to the question is currently assumed. Yet according as it is decided that Plato and Aristotle can or can not be reconciled, the philosophers of the thirteenth century will appear devoted to the placable development of a single philosophy or engaged in acrimonious debate concerning the fundamentals of philosophy.

It is not easy to state even the manner in which the thirteenth century worked out its affiliations to the two philosophies, for legend and evidence are at crucial variance. There is, for example, the inescapable tradition (though its history does not bear examination) that Bonaventura and Thomas Aquinas were close friends; it is equally certain that a bitter debate is to be read between the lines of their works wherever they wrote on the doctrines of the possible eternity of the world or the unity of substantial forms. There is the notion, too, that christianity in the thirteenth century developed a single christian philosophy. It has been questioned, therefore, whether any differences can be found to indicate a departure from the fundamental principles of augustinism. If the augustinian tradition can harbor such diverse philosophers as Alexander of Hales, John of la Rochelle, Saint Bonaventura, Roger Bacon, Matthew of Aquasparta, Duns Scotus in the thirteenth century, the addition of the names of Albert the Great and Thomas Aquinas does not seem to stretch the limits of the philosophy much further. Albert the Great and Thomas seem to have treated the tradition of augustinism, which in their time had been for centuries the philosophy of christendom, as their own; where they could not follow it, they ignored it or modified it; they seldom refuted it in any point; and the modifications they introduced into the aristotelian philosophy, the doctrines of exemplarism, of creation, of providence, of immortality, were augustinian doctrines. Viewed point by point, platonism and aristotelianism are too inter-mingled in the thirteenth century to permit facile gen-eralization concerning them: Bonaventura could make the aristotelian doctrine of abstraction fit the augustin-ian doctrine of illumination; and Thomas Aquinas could make use of the same elements: divine illumination caps and actuates the process of abstraction by which the mind knows things. None the less, in the total doctrines composed of these elements and the debates they engendered, are to be found nice specifications of the problems of philosophy. And, apart from the dif-ficulties which attended the introduction of Aristotle into the west and apart from the consequent debates concerning averroism, the differences are those between platonism and aristotelianism. In the century in which Albert and Thomas labored to free the aristotelian phi-losophy from the averroistic interpretation which rendered it dangerous to orthodoxy, Bonaventura saw in aristotelianism a fundamental opposition to christianity; where Albert and Thomas were concerned with the superiority of the aristotelian physics and natural philosophy to any previous science, acknowledging none the less that the metaphysics lacked proper doctrines of creation and immortality, Bonaventura turned his attention to finding eternal reasons behind the processes of knowledge which he was content to describe in aristotelian terms.

The source of Aristotle's error, then, was to have rejected the platonic doctrine of ideas, but Bonaventura saw no difficulty in making the aristotelian analysis of knowledge serve as the groundwork to the platonic. The augustinian doctrine of illumination, which has by even Augustine's admission important affiliations with the platonic doctrine of ideas, was once more in the history of thought to be pitted against and reconciled with the aristotelian doctrine of abstraction. Knowledge is to be explained by the presence in us of a weakened ray of divine light. The source of our knowledge is the eternal ideas; not only by them but in them we see truth. We do not, however, attain to the eternal reasons or ideas as they are in the divine mind; rather we know confused reflections of them. But except by the created principles placed in us by God, we can have no certain and clear knowledge of things. Such statement is insufficient, however, if it is supposed that the mind knows only the influence of eternal truths and not the eternal truths: the mind in its sure knowledge must be regulated by immutable and eternal rules, not as if by the conditions of the mind itself, but as if through the things to which it is turned and which are above it in the eternal truth. Our intellect is conjoined to the eternal truth, and for certain knowledge an eternal reason which is regulative and motive, must be granted to be present, not only in its own status and transcendent clarity, but in its conformity to the lower human status and as perceived by created reason. Before the original sin, man enjoyed full knowledge in the contemplation of God, but in his present state there is a defect in man's understanding: God is supremely knowable in himself, but he is not supremely knowable to man. The consequence is that man may approach the principles by which he may have a knowledge of things without veils, but his knowledge will never be complete, for the eternal reasons on which the principles are based will escape him. In this life and in time he can know nothing with full knowledge.

The true way of knowledge, therefore, was expressed by neither Plato nor Aristotle, but by Augustine; Aristotle spoke the language of science; Plato, the language of wisdom; Augustine, illumined by the Holy Spirit, the language of both. To follow either Plato or Aristotle is to neglect the double aspect of knowledge which Augustine stated; it is to forget that man is situated between God and things, nearer to things than to God; that he can consider truth in things or in himself or in God; that when he contemplates things by sensation and the inferior part of his soul he receives a relative certitude from below, whereas when his soul is turned from things to God, he receives an absolute certitude from above. Man's ways of knowing, moreover, are diversified according to the objects of knowledge to which he turns himself. Corporeal things he perceives by the senses; the active intellect abstracts intelligibles from the data amassed in sensation and stored in memory. The arts and the sciences are composed of universals so abstracted from particulars, for the senses are necessary if the intellect is to understand anything other than itself. Without sensation the mechanical arts and knowledge of natural objects would be impossible. It is not difficult to recognize the aristotelian elements in this description of the growth of science from sensation, memory, and experience; and Bonaventura does not hesitate to employ the entire aristotelian apparatus of the active intellect abstracting species from the phantasms of sensation, which in turn convert the possible intellect and are judged by it. The exterior senses, of course, are insufficient when the soul passes from natural objects to a knowledge of itself and of God; an interior light is needed; by it man perceives the principles of science and the natural truths innate in him. This is not to say that man is born with innate ideas; like Aristotle, like Thomas, like most of the medievals, Bonaventura held that the mind of man prior to experience contains no ideas. But he further held that all ideas are not abstracted from the experience of external objects, but certain ideas are infused in the mind; the latter are perceived in the mind by no exterior light but by a light present to the mind alone. The first principles of knowledge are known in virtue of no experience save the mind's experience of itself, of its nature, and constitution, and of the things that are in it.

The direction philosophy must take in its development is determined by this orientation of man among the things and truths present to him. He possesses an imperfect but very certain knowledge of the supreme object toward which he tends, for he is made to perceive an infinite Good. No other knowledge is so certain as the knowledge of the supreme Good which is known by the light within us and since that knowledge carries to a faith in revealed truth, it is not improper, Bonaventura argues, to make faith the source of philosophic speculation. For some objects are too high for reason,

but by love, an act of faith may be made, and thereafter he who believes by love, may seek also to have
reasons for his belief; thence philosophy follows after
faith. Historically, moreover, this is proper, since prior
to the fall, man contemplated God, but now, to an intelligence blinded by sin, the universe and things can not
be made intelligible by the effort of natural reason un-
aided. The way to the rehabilitation of the senses is
illuminative. God is the supreme good and the supreme
transcendent truth, in relation to whom all things are
true: the things of the universe are to God like signs
to their significations.

The philosophy of St. Bonaventura is properly, therefore, the detailed working out of the journey projected
in the title of one of his works, the *Itinerary of the
Mind to God*, and his interest in other knowledge than
that of God is properly temporary and such as is
implicated in the title of another of his works, the
Reduction of the Arts to Theology. By knowledge and
by things man may be led back to God whom things
and ideas express; but to remain in the contemplation
of creatures is to be condemned to error. From the
nature of the problem, the exposition which Bonaventura undertakes must follow a peculiar turn: God is not
to be demonstrated by the things of the world, but rather
men are to be recalled from things of the world to
the love of the author. The steps of the ascension to
God are worked out in detail repeatedly in the works of
Bonaventura, and the contour of the ascent is present
behind each of the particular doctrines he expounds.
First the shadow of God is found in the sensible world,
for the splendors of things reveal God so insistently
that they would wake us even if we were deaf. There
is no technical elaboration of the traditional proofs of
God, but God is to be perceived directly in the order,

movement, measure, beauty, and disposition of things. The contemplation of the shadows of God in things, however, is only preliminary to the second step, the contemplation of the traces of God in the soul; the unity, truth, and goodness of the traces in the soul require an efficient, a formal, and a final cause (there is no material cause) in God; the trinity of properties in the soul can be explained only by the Trinity in God. The third and final step consists in turning to God and contemplating him not only as cause but as object. For the intellect is joined naturally to God; he is most present to the soul and knowable to the soul by a certain likeness not abstracted but impressed, inferior to God, because it is in an inferior nature, yet superior to the soul because it makes the soul better. Without that knowledge of God, knowledge of things and of truths would be impossible since the principle of things and knowledge would be lacking; he in turn is known directly without exterior senses, as the soul knows itself and its own operations. The knowledge of him is in the interior of ourselves, and if he seems to need demonstration, it is not because of his nature but because of our nature, since the veils of concupiscence sometimes blind us and since we sometimes fail to reflect. Philosophy becomes an aid to the attainment of the end to life recognized by faith and love. The love of God is the end, and the science which works the accomplishment of that end, theology, must perforce be an affective science: the end of the itinerary of life is given by faith, the route is illuminative, and the pilgrimage is adhered to by love of the end; philosophy is to be engaged in the understanding of the stages by which progress may be made along the route.

SAINT BONAVENTURA

COMMENTARY ON THE FOUR BOOKS OF SENTENCES OF PETER LOMBARD[1]

COMMENTARY ON BOOK I. DISTINCTION III[2]

PART I

ON THE KNOWLEDGE OF GOD BY DISTANT LIKENESSES

For the Apostle says that the invisible things of God[3] *etc.*

DIVISION OF THE TEXT

The Master treated above of the sacred *Trinity* and *Unity* in so far as it is a matter of belief. In this

[1] DOCTORIS SERAPHICI S. BONAVENTURAE, *Commentaria in Quatuor Libros Sententiarum Magistri Petri Lombardi.* Ad Aquas Claras (Quaracchi): Ex Typographia Collegii S. Bonaventurae, 1882, tom. I, pp. 66-80.

[2] The scholastic method, since it is primarily a method for the orderly and effective presentation of arguments, is not likely to prove sympathetic to the modern reader in his first encounter with it. The interest of the reader and the thinker has changed since the middle ages: philosophy and science are read primarily for conclusions, and a mechanism, therefore, for presenting the arguments on which the conclusions are based and for considering meticulously the variety of arguments that might be advanced against these, must impress the reader today, engrossed in practical concerns, as sophistical, hairsplitting, impertinent. He will, however, find the questions more easily intelligible, if he reads the exposi-

second part he treats of it, in so far as it is a matter of understanding. And this part is divided into three parts. In the first of these he adduces appropriate likenesses and reasons for the understanding of the Trinity. In the second he resolves the doubts which arise at the beginning of the fourth distinction: *Here arises a question which is necessary enough. For it is known*[4] etc. In the third, having resolved these doubts, he determines the properties and conditions of the Trinity and Unity in the eighth distinction: *Now the question of the truth or the property and immutability and simplicity of the divine nature or substance or essence must be taken up*[5] etc.

The first part again has two parts. In the first he brings forward distant likenesses; in the second, close or express likenesses, which are considered in the image, in the following place: *Now, however, let us proceed to the consideration.*[6]

Again the first part has two parts. In the first he shows the Unity, in the second he shows the Trinity, in

---

tion in a slightly different order: first looking through the division of the text, proceeding from the statement of the question directly to the conclusion, then reading the arguments numbered at the beginning of the article together with the replies to them which follow the conclusion, argument 1 then reply 1, argument 2 then reply 2, (these arguments are always those contrary to the position the writer will himself take, and therefore in the order of presentation the reader would come first on the positions contrary to that of the writer); finally there will remain the *arguments to the contrary* which, since they usually supplement and confirm the author's position, seldom require refutation.

[3] *The Book of Sentences* I, d. 3, ch. 1; see above vol. I, p. 189.

[4] *The Book of Sentences* I, d. 4, ch. 1.

[5] *The Book of Sentences* I, d. 8, ch. 1.

[6] *The Book of Sentences* I, d. 3, ch. 2; see above vol. I, p. 193.

the following place: *It remains now to show whether
any vestige or slight trace of the Trinity could be had
through things which have been made*[7] etc. The first
part has four subdivisions. In the first he proves by the
authority of the Apostle in the first chapter of the
Epistle to the Romans,[8] that God is knowable through
the creature. In the second he takes up the various
modes and reasons of knowing, in the following place:
For as Ambrose says.[9] In the third he says that these
modes are involved in the statement of the Apostle, in
the following place: *Therefore, the truth of God could
be known in a great many ways*.[10] In the fourth he
touches on what can be proved by the aforesaid reasons,
namely, the unity of essence, not the trinity, in the
following place: *But all these relate to revealing the
unity of Deity*.[11]

It remains now to show whether[12] etc. The Master
showed above the unity or entity of the divine essence
by reasons. In this second part he shows the Trinity
by the distant likeness which is considered in its trace,
and this chapter has four subdivisions. In the first the
Master shows the nature [*ratio*] of the trace in the
creature. In the second he shows what corresponds to
the trace in the creator, since there is a trinity of appropriated aspects, that is, of origin, of beauty, and of love,
so that each of them corresponds to each, in the following place: *For in that Trinity is the supreme origin*.[13]

[7] *The Book of Sentences* I, d. 3, ch. 1; see above vol. I, p. 191.
[8] Vers. 20.
[9] *The Book of Sentences* I, d. 3, ch. 1; see above vol. I,
p. 190.
[10] *The Book of Sentences* I, d. 3, ch. 1; see above vol. I,
p. 191.
[11] *The Book of Sentences* I, d. 3, ch. 1; see above vol. I,
p. 191.
[12] See above, note 7.
[13] *The Book of Sentences* I, d. 3, ch. 1; see above vol. I,
p. 192.

In the third he teaches that the trinity is to be contemplated in God through the consideration of the trace in the creature, in the following place: *From the consideration of creatures therefore,*[14] etc. where he shows a trinity of things appropriated in God both with respect to the act of creation and with respect to the act of reformation. In the fourth subdivision he shows that the consideration of the Trinity by its trace is not sufficient, but distant, in the following place: *It has been shown, then, how in creatures.*[15]

Now, however, let us proceed to the consideration.[16] This is the second part of this distinction, in which the Master proves the Trinity and Unity by *close* and express likeness; *image* is of this sort. And this part is divided into two parts; in the first he shows the trinity and unity in the creator by the trinity and unity considered in the powers of the soul; in the second in the habits or conditions [*habitus*], in the following place: *Furthermore the Trinity can be distinguished in another way and by other names.*[17]

The first part of this part again has four subdivisions. In the first of these he shows where the image is to be sought in the soul, that is, in the higher part of it and in its three powers, namely, memory, understanding, and will. In the second he touches the conditions [*conditio*] of the image, which are trinity, unity, and equality, in the following place: *"These three, therefore," as Augustine says.*[18] In the third he takes up and resolves the

[14] *The Book of Sentences* I, d. 3, ch. 1; see above vol. I, p. 193.

[15] *The Book of Sentences* I, d. 3, ch. 1; see above vol. I, p. 193.

[16] See above, note 6.

[17] *The Book of Sentences* I, d. 3, ch. 3; see above vol. I, p. 199.

[18] *The Book of Sentences* I, d. 3, ch. 2; see above vol. I, p. 194.

doubt which arises from the aforesaid contentions,
namely, whether the soul is its own powers, in the following place: *In what sense that which has been stated
above should be taken, must be considered very ear-
nestly here.*[19] In the fourth place he teaches one to avoid
the error which could be caused by or could arise from
the exhibition of the created trinity, that it should be a
likeness in all detail to the uncreated; he shows there
that there is the greatest unlikeness of the image to God,
in the following place: *"Nevertheless he should take
care."*[20] *Furthermore the trinity can be distinguished in
another way and by other names*[21] etc.   This is the
second part of the second part of this distinction, in
which the Master purposes to investigate the image in
the habits or conditions [*habitus*] of the soul, so far as
that is possible, and this part is divided into four subdivisions.   For in the first he takes up those things in
which the image of the Trinity is considered, which are
mind, knowledge, and love.   In the second, having
treated of those things, he shows that the image is considered in them because of consubstantiality, order, and
equality, in the following place: *These three, however,
although they are*[22] etc.   In the *third* he shows how the
rational mind advances in the contemplation of the
created trinity to seeing and knowing the uncreated Trinity in Unity, in the following place: *Consequently, the
rational mind considering these three.*[23]   In the *fourth*

[19] *The Book of Sentences* I, d. 3, ch. 2; see above vol. I,
p. 196.
[20] *The Book of Sentences* I, d. 3, ch. 2; see above vol. I,
p. 197.
[21] *The Book of Sentences* I, d. 3, ch. 3; see above vol. I,
p. 199.
[22] *The Book of Sentences* I, d. 3, ch. 3; see above vol. I,
p. 199.
[23]. *The Book of Sentences* I, d. 3, ch. 3; see above vol. I,
p. 200.

he brings together briefly the things which have been demonstrated above, in the following place: *Wherefore, in accordance with that consideration.*[24]

TREATMENT OF THE QUESTIONS

Four inquiries are made for the understanding of the points which are touched on in this first part of the present distinction.

The first is, whether God is knowable by the creature.

The second is, whether he is knowable through the creature.

The third is, whether the mode of knowing through the creature is proper to man in respect to every state, namely, the state of innocence, the state of fallen nature, the state of glorified nature.

The fourth is, what is knowable concerning God through the creature.

ONE ARTICLE
ON THE KNOWABILITY OF GOD

QUESTION I.

WHETHER GOD IS KNOWABLE BY THE CREATURE

As regards the first, that God is not knowable by the creature is shown,

1. By the *authority* of Dionysius *on Divine Names*:[25] *It is possible neither to speak of nor to understand God.*

2. Again it is shown by *reason* by means of the four-fold supposition which is necessarily in knowledge,

[24] *The Book of Sentences* I, d. 3, ch. 4; see above vol. I, p. 200.

[25] Ch. 1, about the middle.

namely, *proportion, union* or reception, *judgment,* and *information* [i.e. endowment of form]. For the understanding understands only that which is proportional to it, and that which is united to it in some way, and that of which it judges, and that by which the vision of its understanding is informed [i.e. is endowed with form].

From the *first* supposition it is argued thus: it is necessary that there be a proportion of knower to knowable: but there is no proportion of God to the understanding, because God is infinite and the understanding finite: therefore etc. Moreover, if there is some proportion, it is seen that it is not sufficient, for the uncreated truth is further removed from the human understanding than any created intelligible is from the sense. But sense, which is perceptive of the sensible, is never elevated to knowledge of the created intelligible: therefore, neither will the understanding ever be elevated to knowledge of the uncreated intelligible.

3. Again, from the *second* supposition, thus: it is necessary that there be a union of the knowable to the knower, so that the one be in the other; however, the knower is not in the knowable, but conversely; but it is impossible that the infinite be grasped by the finite: therefore, it is impossible that the infinite be in the finite: therefore, it is impossible for God to be in the understanding, since he is infinite.

4. Again, from the *third* supposition, thus: it is necessary for knowledge that there be in the knower a judgment of the known; but every one who judges must have power over the judged; but a finite being does not have power over an infinite: therefore, a finite being does not judge an infinite; but judgment was required for knowledge: therefore, the finite understanding does not know the infinite God over whom it has no power.

5. Again, from the *fourth*, thus: it is necessary that

the understanding be informed, when it knows, by that
which is known; but everything which informs another,
informs it either by *essence* or by *likeness*; but God does
not inform by essence, for he is united to nothing as
form, nor by abstracted likeness, for an abstracted likeness is more spiritual than that from which it is abstracted; nothing, however, is nor can be more spiritual
than God: therefore etc.

TO THE CONTRARY: 1. The rational soul is formed
to the image of God. But as Augustine says in the book
on the Trinity, and as is stated in the text of the present
distinction: *The mind is the image of God in that by
which it is capable* [i.e. receptive] *of God and by which
it can be partaker of him.*[26] However, to be capable is
not according to substance or essence, because he is thus
in all creatures: therefore, by knowledge and love: therefore, God can be known by the creature.

2. Again, it is shown by *reason*, thus: all spiritual
knowledge is made by reason of light and by reason of
uncreated light, as Augustine says in the *Soliloquies*;[27]
but light is in the highest degree knowable, and God is
the greatest light: and therefore he is in the highest
degree knowable to the soul itself: therefore etc.

3. Again, since knowledge of some things is by their
presence, and knowledge of some by their likeness, those
are known more truly which are known by presence, as
Augustine says;[28] but God is united to the soul itself by
presence: therefore, God is known more truly than other
things which are known by likeness.

4. Again, as the supreme goodness is related to love,

---

[26] AUGUSTINUS, *De Trinit.* XIV, c. 8, n. 11. Cp. *The Book
of Sentences*, I, d. 3, ch. 2; see above vol. I, p. 194.

[27] AUGUSTINUS, *Soliloq.* I, c. 8.

[28] AUGUSTINUS, *De Trinit.* X, c. 8-11.

so the supreme truth is related to knowledge; but the supreme goodness is supremely lovable by the affect: therefore, the supreme truth is supremely knowable by the understanding.

5. Again, each thing has power more efficaciously toward that to which it is ordered naturally; but our understanding is ordered naturally to the knowledge of the supreme light: therefore, the supreme light is knowable to it in the highest degree.

CONCLUSION

God, knowable in the highest degree in himself, would be in the highest degree knowable to us too, if there were no defect on the part of our understanding.

I REPLY: it must be said that God in himself as supreme light is in the highest degree knowable; and that, as light fulfilling our understanding in the highest degree and as far as he is of himself, he would be supremely knowable to us too, if there were not some defect on the part of the power knowing, which is not removed perfectly except through the deiformity of glory. Therefore, the reasons must be granted, which prove that God is knowable by the creature and likewise most clearly knowable as far as he is of himself, if there were not something impeding or something deficient on the part of the understanding, as will be clear later.[29]

1. To the objections to the contrary it must be said that there is knowledge by *comprehension* and knowledge by *apprehension*. Knowledge by apprehension consists in the manifestation of the truth of the thing known; but

[29] In the two questions which follow, also Book II, d. 23, a. 2, q. 3.

knowledge by comprehension consists in the inclusion
of the totality.   To the first knowledge a proportion of
agreement is required; and there is such knowledge in
the soul in respect to God, because *the soul is in a certain manner all things*,[30] by assimilation to all, for it is
formed naturally to know all things, and it is in the
highest degree capable of God by assimilation, for it is
the image and likeness of God.   As regards knowledge
by *comprehension,* a proportion of equality and equivalence is required; and there is no such proportion in the
soul in respect to God, because the soul is finite, but
God is infinite; and therefore it does not have this knowledge; and Dionysius meant this knowledge, and the
objection holds concerning it, but not concerning the
other.

2. To the objection which is raised concerning the
distance of the intelligible and the sensible, it must be
said that there is distance according to the relation
[*ratio*] of *being* and according to the relation of *knowable* [i.e. there is a distance in so far as you consider
them as beings and another in so far as you consider
them as objects of knowledge].   In the first manner the
distance is greater; in the second manner it is not, because both are intelligible, namely, God and the soul.
It is not thus in the case of the understanding and sense,
because sense is a determined power, but the understanding is not.

3. To the objection that the infinite is not grasped
by the finite, some say that grasping the infinite is to be
taken in two ways, namely, with respect to *essence,* and
thus it is grasped; and with respect to *power,* and thus
it is not grasped, just as a point is wholly determined by
the line with respect to substance, but not totally with
respect to power.   But this solution does not seem to

[30] ARISTOTLE, *on the Soul* III, 8, 431^b 21.

solve, because in God essence is the same as power, and both are infinite.

Therefore, it must be said that infinity is to be taken in two senses: one, which is constituted by opposition to the simple; and such an infinite is not grasped by the finite, such as infinite mass; there is another which has infinity together with simplicity, such as God; and such an infinite, because it is *simple*, is everywhere whole; because it is *infinite*, it is in nothing in such wise that it is not outside it. It is to be understood thus in the case of the knowledge of God. And therefore it does not follow, although he is known whole, that he is comprehended, because the understanding does not include the totality of him, as the creature does not include his immensity.

4. To the objection which was raised: the one judging has power, etc., it must be said that judging of anything is in two ways: in the first way by *distinguishing*, whether it is or is not; and in this way judgment is proper to every understanding, when it knows, in respect to every object; in another way by *approving* or reproving, that it should be thus; and thus it does not judge of truth, but it judges according to it of other things, as Augustine says *on True Religion*[31] that *the judge does not judge of the law, but he judges of other things according to the law*. And in this way what Augustine says is true, that *no one judges of that truth, yet no one judges without it*. And in this second way that which is stated in opposition is true, that the one who judges has power over that which is judged; but in the first way it is not true, that he has power over it; still he can be guided as toward the object by the help of it [i.e. the truth].

5. To the objection which was raised last concerning

[31] Ch. 31, n. 58.

information [endowing with form], it must be said that
God is present to the soul itself and to every understanding by way of truth: therefore, it is not necessary
that a likeness be abstracted from him, by which he may
be known; yet none the less, when he is known by the
understanding, the understanding is informed by a certain idea, which is, as it were, a certain likeness, not
abstracted but impressed, inferior to God, because it is
in an inferior nature, yet superior to the soul, because
it makes the soul better. And Augustine says this in
book IX *on the Trinity*, chapter eleven:[32] *As, when we
learn bodies by the senses of bodies, some likeness of
them is made in our mind: so when we know God, some
likeness of God is made; that idea, however, is inferior,
because it is in an inferior nature.*

QUESTION II.

WHETHER GOD IS KNOWABLE THROUGH CREATURES

In the second place it is inquired whether God is knowable through creatures. And it seems that he is not.

1. For the way to error is not the way to knowledge;
but knowledge through the creature is the way of error:
therefore etc. The proof of the minor premiss: in the
Book of Wisdom, chapter fourteen:[33] *The creatures of
God are for deception and hatred and as a trap to the
feet of fools.* Moreover, Augustine, *on the Free Will*,[34]
speaks of those who are occupied with creatures: *turning their back to you, they are fastened firmly in corporeal work as in their own shadows.*

2. Again, the way to know the luminous or the light
is not darkness or the dark; but the creature is darkness,

---

[32] n. 16.   [33] Vers. 11.
[34] Book II, ch. 16, n. 43; see above vol. I, p. 61.

whereas God is light: therefore, God is not knowable through the creature.

3. Again, the medium by which something is known or proved of an end term, must have something in common with that for which it must be known; but the Creator and the creature have nothing in common: therefore, God is not known through creatures.

4. Again, every medium by which one ascends to an end term is distant from it by finite steps; but every creature, howsoever noble, is distant from God by infinite steps, because however so many times it may be doubled, the creature will never attain to the nobility of God: therefore, by the creature one does not ascend to the knowledge of God.

To the contrary: 1. In the thirteenth chapter of the *Book of Wisdom*[35] it is said: *From the greatness of the species and the creation it will be possible that the Creator of them be seen in knowledge.* Wherefore Isidore *on the Highest Good*[36] says: *From the beauty of the circumscribed creature God makes his beauty, which can not be circumscribed, to be understood.*

2. Again, it is shown by *reason*, thus: not only may the effect be known by the cause, but also the cause by the effect: therefore, if God is the cause operating according to his nobility, and the creature the effect, it will be possible that God be known through the creature.

3. Again, the sensible is the way of knowing the intelligible; but the creature is sensible, God intelligible: therefore, the way to come to the knowledge of the Creator is through the creature.

4. Again, like may be known through like; but every creature is like God, either as trace or as image: there-

[35] Vers. 5.　　　　　　　　[36] Or *Sentences* I, c. 4.

fore, it comes about that through every creature God is known.

It is inquired, then, what difference there is between a trace and an image; and since there is in every creature a trace, it is inquired, why not in like manner an image, and in accordance with what the trace is so considered.

CONCLUSION

God can be known through creatures in the natural light of reason.

I REPLY: it must be said that as the cause shines forth in the effect, and as the wisdom of the artificer is manifested in his work, so God, who is the artificer and cause of the creature, is known through it.

And the reason for this is double, one is because of *agreement*, the other because of *need*: because of agreement, for every creature leads to God more than to anything else; because of need, for, since God as the supremely spiritual light could not be known in his spirituality by the understanding, which is almost material, the soul needs to know him through the creature.

1. To the objection which is raised that knowledge of the creature is the way to error, it must be said that the creature may be known in two ways: either with respect to *special properties*, which are of imperfection, or with respect to *general conditions*, which are of completion; but if with respect to special conditions and of imperfection: either by *attributing* them to God or by denying them. In the first fashion is the way of error, in the second the way of knowledge; and thus God is known by denial.

But if he be known with respect to the conditions of *perfection*, this can be in two ways, as a picture is known in two ways: either as *picture* or as *image*: whence, either one rests in the beauty of the creature or by that one tends to something else. If in the first way, then it is the way which leads astray; wherefore Augustine in the book *on the Free Will*:[37] *Alas, for those who love, instead of you, your beckonings, and who stray among your traces [instead of rising from them to you], and who abandon you as leader.* If in the second way, as it is the way to something else, so it is the reason of knowing by superexcellence, for every noble quality in the creature must be attributed to God in the highest degree; and thus that is clear.

2. To the objection which is raised, that the dark medium is not the way for knowing light, it must be said that there is the well-disposed eye and the bleared eye. Of the well-disposed eye this is true, but not of the bleared eye, to which the overcasting cloud or the land receiving the clarity of the light is the medium for seeing the sun; thus for our understanding, which is like the eye of the owl to the things most manifest of nature, [the dark or the creature is the medium for knowing the light or God].

3. To the objection which is raised concerning the lack of community, it must be said that it is not common by *univocation*, but it is common by *analogy*, which names the relation of *two to two*, as in the sailor and the doctor, or of *one to one* as of the exemplar to the exemplified.

4. To the objection which is raised that there are always infinite steps, it must be said that the ascent to God can be in two ways: either with respect to the *sight of the presence*; and in that way every creature is formed

[37] Book II, ch. 16, n. 43; see above vol. I, p. 60.

naturally to lead to God, nor are there infinite steps that way; or with respect to *equality of equivalence*; and in that way it is true that there are infinite steps, for the created good, howsoever much it be doubled, is never equal to the uncreated.

The *first* step, however, in respect to the ascent to the sight of the presence is in the consideration of visible things, the *second* in the consideration of invisible things, as of the soul or of another spiritual substance; the *third* is from the soul to God, because *the image is formed by truth itself and is joined immediately to God.*[38]

To the inquiry which was made last *concerning the difference of trace and image*, some make this difference, that the trace is in sensible things, the image in spiritual. But this distinction and position does not hold, because the trace is also in spiritual things. For unity, truth, goodness, in which there is a trace, are conditions in the highest degree universal and intelligible.

Others say that the trace is so called because it represents in respect to the part, but the image in respect to the whole. But this difference again does not hold because, as God is simple, he has no representative in respect to part; again since he is infinite, he can be represented with respect to the whole by absolutely no creature, not even by the whole world.

And therefore it must be understood that since the creature leads to the knowledge of God by the mode of *shadow*, by the mode of *trace*, and by the mode of *image*, the better known difference of these modes by which likewise they are named, is taken from the *mode of representing*. For *shadow* is spoken of in so far as it represents in a certain removal and confusion; *trace* in so far as it represents in removal but distinction; but *image* in so far as it represents in nearness and distinction.

[38] Cp. AUGUSTINUS, *LXXXIII Quaestiones*, quaestio 51, n. 2.

From this difference is gathered a *second* which is in the conditions in which the three are found. For creatures are called a *shadow* with reference to properties which look to God in some kind of cause according to an undetermined relation [*ratio*]; a trace with reference to a property which looks to God under the relation of the triple cause, efficient, formal, and final, as one, true, and good; an *image* with reference to conditions which look to God not only in the relation of cause, but also of object; these are memory, understanding, and will.

From these, *two other differences are concluded*: with respect to the things to which they *lead*; for the creature as shadow leads to the knowledge of *common things* as *common*; as trace to knowledge of *common things* as *appropriated*; as image to knowledge of *properties* as *proper*.

Another difference is in the things in which these [three modes] are *discovered*. For as every creature is compared to God both in the relation of cause and in the relation of triple cause, so every creature is shadow or trace. But as only the rational creature is related to God as to its object, because he alone is capable of God by knowledge and love: so he alone is image.

QUESTION III.

WHETHER MAN IN EVERY STATE KNOWS GOD THROUGH CREATURES

In the third place it is inquired whether the knowledge of God through creatures is proper to man in respect to every state. That it is proper to man in respect to *his first state* is shown thus:

1. Man in the state of innocence did not know God

face to face: therefore, if he knew God, he knew him through an effect, therefore through a trace, therefore through a creature.

2. Again, in man in the state of innocence sensible knowledge was not an impediment but an aid to intellective knowledge; but the intellective knowledge, for which man was made, is knowledge of God: therefore, all sensible knowledge in the first man was ordered to that end; but knowledge of God through the aid of sensibles is knowledge through the creature: therefore etc.

Again, that it is proper to man with respect to *the state of blessedness* is seen:

1. Because the Blessed know the creature, but do not remain in the creature, but return to God: therefore, they know God through the creature.

2. Again, the blessed souls praise God through creatures; but to praise God through creatures is to know through creatures: therefore etc.

But to the contrary: that it is not proper to man *as he was created* is shown thus.

1. Knowledge by trace is knowledge by a medium; but *the mind* as Augustine says,[39] *is formed by truth itself immediately*: therefore, such knowledge is not suited to human nature with respect to that state, nor likewise with respect to any other.

2. Again, that is not the right order which goes to the end which is nearer, by a medium which is more distant; but man in his first state was nearer to God than to any other creatures: therefore, it was not fitting that he come to the knowledge of God by way of other creatures.

Again, that such knowledge is not proper to man with respect to the state of *blessedness* is seen.

[39] See above note 37.

1. Because knowledge by way of a trace is knowled r : by manuduction: therefore, it is not perfect knowledge, therefore, it is from the part: therefore, it does not remain in the Blessed, because in them, that which is from the part will be laid aside.

2. Again, the trace or creature is like a ladder for ascending to, or like a road for arriving at, God; but when one has arrived at the end, there is no further use for the way: therefore similarly, when man is high up, he does not need a ladder; but the knowledge of the Blessed is immediately in God: therefore, it is not through creatures.

Conclusion

God is known in creatures perfectly by those who comprehend, half-fully by those on their way, but through creatures he is known properly by those on their way, in one way, however, before, and in another after the fall.

I reply: for the understanding of the aforesaid questions it must be noted that it is one thing to know God *in* the creature, another to know him *through* the creature. To know God *in* the creature is to know his presence and influence in the creature. And this is proper half-fully to those on their way, but perfectly to those who comprehend; whence Augustine says at the end of the book *on the City of God*[40], that God will then be seen expressly, when God will be all in all. To know God *through* the creature, however, is to be elevated from knowledge of the creature to knowledge of God as by the means of an intermediate ladder. And this is properly the possession of those on their way, as Bernard says to Eugenius.[41]

[40] Book XXII, c. 30, n. 4.
[41] *De Consideratione* V, c. 1.

Yet it is suited to man in different ways in the state of nature as created and in the state of fallen nature: because in the first state man knew God through the creature as *through a clear mirror*; but after the fall he knew him as *through a mirror and enigma,* as the Apostle says in the thirteenth chapter[42] of the *First Epistle to the Corinthians,* because of the overclouding of the understanding and the deterioration of things.

To the objection which is raised, therefore, concerning the state of *blessedness,* it must be said that, as has been said, it is not proper to the Blessed to know *through* creatures, but rather *in* creatures. And the reasons which seem to prove the contrary do not prove it, but rather that he is known by them *in* creatures.

1. To the objection which is raised concerning the state of *innocence,* that the mind is formed immediately, etc., it must be said that the medium is double, namely, *efficient* and *disposing.* What Augustine said should be understood of the first medium, but not of the second, since God is the efficient medium and the object of the mind itself. That argument, however, Augustine directs against the philosophers whose opinion was that the mind was not joined to the first principle immediately, but with some intelligence mediating.

2. To the objection which is raised that that is not the right order, it must be said that man can be considered in two ways: either as that which is *in himself* or as that which is *outside himself.* In the first manner he does not attain through creatures from himself to God, but that which is outside himself is gathered through knowledge of creatures into himself and is raised up above himself.

Or it must be said that other creatures can be con-

42 Vers. 12.

sidered as things or as signs. In the *first* way they are inferior to man, in the *second* manner they are media in becoming or on the way, not at the end, because they do not reach to the end, but through them man reaches God, having left them behind him.

QUESTION IV.

WHETHER THE TRINITY OF PERSONS TOGETHER WITH THE UNITY OF ESSENCE CAN BE KNOWN NATURALLY THROUGH CREATURES

In the fourth and last place it is inquired what is knowable of God through creatures. And the Apostle says[43] *the everlasting power and divinity.* And it is inquired whether the plurality of persons can be known through creatures. And it seems that it can.

1. Because philosophers had no knowledge of God except through creatures, and they knew the Trinity: therefore etc. The minor premiss is clear by Augustine *on the City of God*:[44] *Philosophers say that philosophy is tripartite,* in which there is knowledge of the Trinity.

2. Again, the magicians failed in the third sign, according to the eighth book of *Exodus*;[45] and it is expounded that they failed in knowledge of the third person; either therefore with respect to *properties* or with respect to *appropriated qualities.* Not with respect to appropriated qualities, because goodness shines forth to us in the creature: therefore, with respect to properties: therefore, they knew at least two persons.

3. Again, this same conclusion appears through *reason*: for the trace, since it names a distinction, is a reason of knowing God distinctively or in distinction; but there is in God only a distinction of persons: therefore,

[43] *Rom.* 1:20.   [44] Book XI, c. 25.   [45] Vers. 18.

through the trace they could know the distinction of persons.

4. Again, there is knowledge of the Trinity by image with respect to order, distinction, and equality; but knowledge by image is knowledge through creature: therefore, they could know the Trinity through the creature.

5. Again, knowledge of the hidden properties of a creature is more difficult than knowledge of the plurality of persons, because the former is grasped only by great and subtle minds, whereas the latter is grasped even by the untutored and by fools: therefore, if they have been able to arrive by way of the visible properties of creatures at invisible things, all the more are they able to arrive at the knowledge that the persons are many. And it is this that is said in the thirteenth chapter[46] of the *Book of Wisdom*: *For if they have been able to know so much that they are able to estimate the world, how have they not more easily found the Lord of it?*

TO THE CONTRARY: 1. Knowledge of the Trinity is knowledge of faith; but knowledge of faith is of those things which are above reason; and the things which are above reason can not be known through creatures: therefore etc.

2. Again, knowledge of God through creatures is had in only two ways, either by affirming what is in the creature or the like, or else by denying it; but the Trinity is not known through denial, but by affirmation; but in no creature is there found a plurality of supposita together with a unity of essence: therefore etc.

3. Again, the written law is above the law of nature, or the book of the sacred Scripture above the book of the mundane creation; but no one lacking faith comes to

[46] Vers. 9.

knowledge of the plurality of persons through the sacred Scripture: therefore, much the less through the book of mundane creation.

CONCLUSION

The Trinity of persons is not knowable through crea-
tures, but only the trinity of qualities appropriated,
namely, unity, truth, goodness.

I REPLY: that it must be said that the plurality of persons together with a unity of essence is the property of the divine nature alone, the like of which is not found in the creature nor can be found nor can be thought rationally: therefore, in no wise is the trinity of persons knowable through the creature by ascending rationally from the creature to God. But although it has absolutely no like, it has nevertheless in some way that which *is believed* to be like in the creature. Whence I say that the philosophers never knew the trinity of persons by reason, nor even the plurality of persons, unless they had some condition of faith, such as some heretics have; whence the things which they said, either were spoken without their understanding them, or else they were illumined by the ray of faith.

There is another trinity of qualities appropriated, namely, of unity, truth, and goodness, and they knew this trinity, because it has a like.

1. To that objection which is raised, therefore, that the philosophers knew the Trinity by way of tripartite philosophy, it must be said that it is true that by this and by other means they came to a knowledge of appropriated qualities, but those who believe come to a knowledge of both trinities.

2. To the objection which is raised concerning the third sign, it is said and well said, that the wise men are said to have failed thus in the third sign, because they failed in knowledge of the most potent effect of goodness, namely, of redemption.

3. To another it must be said that a trace indicates a distinction of essential properties, and to this corresponds the trinity of appropriated qualities, not the trinity of properties or of persons.

4. To the objection which is raised concerning image, it must be said that knowing the soul is either according to that which it *is*; and this knowledge is of reason; or else it is according to that of which it is *image*; and that knowledge is of faith alone.

5. To the objection which is raised finally, that it is more difficult to know the world, it must be said that this is to be understood, when divine aid has been added; but speaking absolutely it is false. For man would be disposed to faith more quickly than he would acquire a knowledge of philosophy. Our understanding, nevertheless, has more power in the knowledge of mundane things than of the Trinity, for the Trinity is above reason, and our intellect sees the contrary of the trinity in sense; and therefore it needs new elevation, such as knowledge by infusion.

Doubts Concerning the Text of the Master

Doubt I

In this part there are the doubts concerning the text relative to those arguments which the Master states with respect to the purpose [*ratio*] of proving and the strength of inferring, because they all seem either not to hold or to rest on doubtful grounds.

For the first argument is the following. He who can do what no creature can do, is above every creature; but he who made this world, made that which no creature could make: therefore, he is not a creature, but above every creature. And this reason begins at this point: *For as Ambrose says, "That God"*[47] etc. In this argument two doubtful points seem to be assumed, namely, that this world has been made, and that the creature could not make it, both of which are extremely doubtful.

The second argument is the following: He who made corporeal things and mutable spirits, is above all corporeal and mutable things: therefore, he is spiritual and immutable. Here in the same way a doubtful point seems to be supposed, that God made spirits. And again, it does not follow from this, even if he made mutable things, that he is immutable, but rather the opposite seems to follow, namely, that he is mutable.

The third argument is the following. He who made the good and the better is the best; but God made corporeal things which are good, and spiritual things which are better: therefore, God is the best. This argument similarly seems to have no cogency, because then in the same way every craftsman who makes good and better, would be best, which is false.

The fourth argument is the following. He who made beautiful and more beautiful things, is beauty itself or the species and that is most handsome [*speciosissimus*]; but we see that corporeal things are handsome, and spiritual things are more handsome: therefore, he who made them is most handsome. It is seen in the same way that the argument stated does hold because of the instance stated above.

Again inquiry is made concerning the difference of

[47] *The Book of Sentences* I, d. 3, ch. 1; see above vol. I, p. 190.

these arguments and how they are distinguished. *If you say*, as some say, that the arguments are four according to the four genera of causes, this is nothing, because the genus of material cause does not fall in God. *If you say* that the arguments are according to the modes of knowing, on the *contrary*: there are only three, that is, in the relation of cause, denial, and excellence.

I REPLY: it must be said that all these arguments for the purpose of proving and inferring suppose something certain. For the first argument supposes that the *production* of a thing out of nothing can be only by an infinite power. If this is supposed, since it is certain that no creature has infinite power, it follows that the act of the production of things out of nothing is his who is above every creature. And thus from this act, as from a property, God is known omnipotent, immense.—In the other three arguments a *state* is supposed, just as in all philosophy a state is supposed in causes; and therefore everything mutable is reduced to the immutable, because in the mutable there is no state [i.e., one can pause at no point in the regress] in the class of the efficient except among movers, not among the moved: for everything which is moved is moved by something else. In the same way, the good and better are reduced to the best, because there is no state in the genus of end except in the best. In the same way, the beautiful and the more beautiful in relation to the most beautiful, because there is no state in the genus of species and form, except in that which is itself species by essence.

To the objection which is raised concerning the distinction of the arguments, the answer is now clear from what has been said. For they can not be distinguished according to the genus of causes only, nor according to the modes of knowing only, but according to both. For

the first argument is taken according to the relation of
cause; the others are taken according to the relation of
cause and of excellence, because they consider order,
and they are distinguished according to order into a
triple class of causes, efficient or moving, ending, and
exemplar.

Doubt II

Again, inquiry is made concerning that which the
Master says later, that *the eternal Author is understood
from the perpetuity of creatures.*[48] For the following
argument does not hold: the effect is perpetual, therefore
the efficient is eternal.

Again, it is inquired similarly concerning this which
he says: *the omnipotent Author from the magnitude of
creatures.*[49] For the following does not hold: he made
great things, therefore he is omnipotent or could make
all things.

I reply: to this some say that it is only a kind of
persuasion by sign, not a necessary argument. For they
say that omnipotence and eternity, since they are infinite,
can not be proved sufficiently by creatures which are
finite.[50]—In another way, however, it can be said that
although it does not follow in any efficient whatsoever,
still it follows necessarily in the first efficient and perpetuating cause. For it is impossible that the creature
have being and great being and have this whole from
some one who does not have power in the whole; and
for this reason it is in this whole and in each thing. In

[48] *The Book of Sentences* I, d. 3, ch. 1; see above vol. I,
p. 191.
[49] *Ibid.*
[50] Cp. Duns Scotus *Sent.* I, d. 2, q. 3, n. 6, and d. 42, q. unic.

the same way, if there is a first perpetuating cause, it is absolutely in actuality and not at all in potentiality; and if this is so, since it could make something else endure infinitely, it is itself actually infinite in duration: therefore eternal.

Doubt III

Again, inquiry is made concerning the following statement which he makes: *All things which have been made by the divine art, show in themselves a certain unity and species and order.*[51] For he seems first to state that which is false, because if this is so, since these three qualities have been made, then they have *unity, species,* and *order,* and so with the others: therefore, if it is to stand, then some things are fashioned, which do not have these.

Again he seems to enumerate badly, because Augustine stated the following three: *mode, species,* and *order,* and the following three others: *unity, truth,* and *goodness.* It is inquired therefore, concerning the different modes of enumerating, whence they come.

I REPLY: to this some say that it is understood of perfect creatures, or if it is understood of all, then those three are not called conditions in the created thing, but in the uncreated exemplar.—Nevertheless it can be said that in the first and general intentions there is the reflection and therefore the state, nor need one proceed further.

To the inquiry which is made concerning the enumeration of those three, which does not seem proper, it must be said that the created thing has to be considered

[51] *The Book of Sentences* I, d. 3, ch. 1; see above vol. I, p. 192.

in three ways: in itself, or in comparison to other creatures, or in comparison to the first cause. And according
to all these modes the trinity may be found in two ways.

For if the thing were considered in so far as it is in
itself or as it is in respect to itself, that is, either with
respect to the *substance of the principles*, there is
thus that trinity: matter, form, composition, which is
stated in the book *on the Rule of the Faith*;[52] or with
respect to the *conditions* [*habitudo*] there is thus that
trinity in the eleventh chapter of the *Book of Wisdom*:[53]
*You have disposed all things in number, weight, and
measure*. For in *number* is understood the distinction of
principles, in *weight* the proper inclination of principles,
in *measure* the proportion of principles to each other.

Again, if one creature were considered *in comparison
to other creatures*, this could be either in so far as it
performs a *natural* action; and thus that trinity of
Dionysius is taken, *substance*, *power*, and *operation*;
or in so far as it performs a spiritual action; and thus
that trinity of Augustine, *on LXXXIII Questions*,[54] *of
what it determines, with what it agrees, by what it distinguishes*, and the last is referred to the soul.

If, however, creatures were considered in *comparison
to God*, this can be in two ways: in so far as they are
referred only; and thus there is the former trinity, *mode,
species*, and *order*; or in so far as they are referred and
assimilated; and thus there is the latter trinity, *unity,
truth*, and *goodness*.

Since therefore a trace is considered in comparison to
God properly, therefore the trace is taken properly in
these last conditions. And because there is a great agreement among these comparisons, therefore the Master
mixes them with each other because of the great agree-

---

[52] ALANUS AB INSULIS, *De arte seu articules catholicas fidei*,
art. 24.   [53] Vers. 21.   [54] Quaest. 18.

ment and correspondence; because *unity* corresponds to *mode*, which considers God as efficient cause; *truth* to *species*, which considers him as exemplar; *goodness* to *order*, which considers God as end.

Doubt IV

Again, inquiry is made concerning the fact that he appropriates *truth* to the Son saying: *The most perfect beauty is understood as the Son, that is, the truth of the Father.*[55] But on the contrary Augustine says in the *Soliloquies*:[56] *Truth is that which is*; but being is appropriated to no person: therefore, neither is truth.

Again, he seems to appropriate *order* to the holy Spirit incorrectly, because he says in the preceding chapter that from order the wise man understands; but *wisdom* is appropriated to the Son: therefore *order* too.

I REPLY: it must be said that truth can be considered in two ways, just as color can. For in one way color is considered according to *that in which it is*; and thus it is defined in the book *on Sense and the Sensed*:[57] *Color is the extremity of the perspicuous, terminated in body.* In another manner in comparison *to sight* which it moves; and thus it is defined in the book *on the Soul*:[58] *Color is the motive of sight according to the act of the lucid body.*

In the same way *truth* can be considered in comparison to that *in which it is*; and thus the true is that which is; in another manner by comparison to *the understanding* which it moves; and thus truth, as the philosopher says in the second book of the *Metaphys-*

[55] *The Book of Sentences* I, d. 3, ch. 1; see above vol. I, p. 192.   [56] Book II, c. 5.   [57] Chapter 3.
[58] Book II, 7, 418^a 31–418^{b}2.

ics,[59] *is the end of speculative understanding*. According to the first manner Anselm says: *The truth of the Father is the essence of the Father*. With respect to the second manner Hilary says[60] that *truth is declarative being*. And since the Son proceeds as the Word, to which is appropriated the reason of declaring, therefore, the reason of exemplar is appropriated to him, and consequently the reason of truth, with respect to the second mode of truth; the Master himself, however, takes the first mode.

To the objection which is raised concerning *order*, it must be said that there is an order of things in the universe; and this is appropriated to wisdom; and there is an order of things to an end; and this is appropriated to goodness; and thus it is clear that there is no contrariety.

[59] *Met.* II, 1, 993^b 20.
[60] Cp. *on the Trinity* V, n. 3 ff.

SAINT THOMAS AQUINAS (1225–1274)

Following after the philosophic projects of his master,
Albert the Great, Thomas Aquinas devoted himself to
the detailed statement of a christian aristotelianism.
The project won him, during his own lifetime, determined opposition both within and outside the Dominican
Order; after his death many of his doctrines were pro-
scribed at Paris, despite the efforts of the aged Albert,
who traveled from Cologne to defend his dead disciple,
and the same doctrines were condemned again a short
time later at Oxford, notwithstanding that Bishop Robert Kilwardby was a dominican. For half a century,
even the reading of his works was prohibited in the
Franciscan Order, and the *correctoria* and refutations
with which the franciscans notably assailed the philosophy are indication that philosophers who came after
Thomas continued to read what his contemporaries had
considered doctrinal novelties as departures from the
true philosophy.

The condemnations and the attempted condemnations
of thomism were usually worked into pronouncements
that purported to be directed against averroism; there
is, moreover, direct evidence that some points of the
aristotelianism of Thomas seemed as suspect as the
aristotelianism of the averroists. Two doctrines were
particularly object of criticism: the doctrine of the possible eternity of the world and the doctrine of the
unity of substantial forms. In the one, Thomas had held,
not that the world was eternal, but that it could not be
shown by reason to be eternal or created in time; since

the question transcended the powers of reason, the
revelation of faith that the world was created should be
followed. In the other, Thomas argued that there was
no need of intermediate forms between the soul and matter, that the soul could be joined directly to the matter
of its body without the preliminary preparation of
matter by inferior forms. Significantly, both these doctrines are combatted most strenuously by franciscan
philosophers: Bonaventura gives beautifully detailed
arguments to show by reason that the eternity of the
world is impossible (most of them restated among the
arguments Thomas undertakes to refute in his resolution of the question), and Bonaventura too, among many
franciscans, urges that the denial of the plurality of
substantial forms endangers the immortality of the soul
(for the soul will be without matter between death and
resurrection) and the identity of angels (for since angels
have no matter, there will be nothing to distinguish two
angels of the same species from each other). There can
be no mistaking the debate, therefore, nor the parties
to the debate; when Thomas wrote his treatises *on Separated Substances* and *on the Eternity of the World
Against Those Who Murmur Against It*, the adversaries,
those who murmured against him, are the continuators of
the augustinism which the Franciscan Order professed.

In the problems of knowledge and truth the traces
of this debate are not always easily revealed. Yet if
the detail of the difference is not detected, the problems
and the interests among which Thomas and, say, Bonaventura work in their treatments of the question of
truth are starkly and totally different; it is a difference
of temper, not only in two philosophers, but in two
philosophies. For Bonaventura (impressed by the shadows and traces of God in things and the images of God
in thought) the divine illumination and the way to return

from things illumined to the source of light are objects
of constant preoccupation. The idea of God implies the
existence of God; and by its omnipresence in all creation, the most intelligible thing is also best known, to
such extent, even, that if our physical forces were like
our intellectual powers, we should more easily move the
largest mountain than the smallest pebble. Thomas concedes that the proposition, God is, is in itself self-
evident, for its predicate is contained in its subject; but
it is not self-evident to us. We begin with sense-experi-
ence; from it we derive data least evident in nature but
most evident to us; from that data we work to that
which is most evident in nature. That which is most
intelligible is least known to us; God who is supremely
intelligible is inconceivable to deficient creatures; in the
presence of intelligibles our minds are like the eyes of
bats or owls; we are blinded by the full light of truth,
and we can perceive only in partial light.

There is radical opposition between the two doctrines in that one is turned to the contemplation of
the infinite intelligibility from which all knowledge proceeds, while the other is turned to the problems of a
finite intellect working among the finite effects of a cause
that exceeds its understanding. The treatment which
the doctrines of Augustine and Anselm receive in Aquinas's resolution of the problems of knowledge is the
symptom of the place of the augustinian doctrine in the
thomist philosophy: what Augustine and Anselm said
of the eternal truth is often listed among the doctrines
to be refuted or restated, and it turns out in each case
that what Augustine or Anselm said is true of one part
or of one manner of the objects of the question. For
Thomas Aquinas carried perhaps further than any philosopher the medieval conviction that the opinions of past
philosophers were not held without reason; his refuta-

tions of philosophic doctrines are usually prefaced by an examination of what in the nature of things the doctrine attempted to express, and doubtless for this reason his philosophy is more than usually full of distinctions: before truth or being or substance can be considered it must be noted that truth or being or substance can be understood in two, three, four, or more ways; if preceding philosophers have erred, their error can usually be accounted for by accommodating their doctrine to one of the possible senses, and their solution is censured, if at all, for supposing that that meaning is the only possible.

The philosophy of Thomas Aquinas, then, considers in turn the relativity of our truths and the changeless eternal truth of which the discovery of even a tentative truth is indicative. We proceed by definitions in which we attempt to express the quiddities of things; then we make judgments by compounding and dividing concepts. Our definitions by genus and difference seek to state the real, yet the real is not constituted of genus and species. From the very beginning of knowledge, therefore, we are doomed to fall short of absolute truth. The hunt for definitions expressing essence (*venare quod quid est*) is never at end. There are many differences of things which are unknown to us; we are often obliged to classify and name things according to their accidents; our schemae, therefore, of knowledge are relative. Moreover, even when difference is known, one does not penetrate the essence of things. The definition of man as a rational animal does not exhaust the reality of man nor even express it; if an accident is added to the description, say, biped, the accidental difference will reinforce the essential. Sometimes, as in the case of the immaterial substances, we do not know accidents, and therefore our knowledge of the immaterial substances is very limited.

Truth properly speaking, however, does not enter in the activities of the understanding seeking the quiddities of things. A definition is false only in two senses: either the definition is applied to the wrong thing or the definition states an impossible combination of concepts, such as immortal animal, for no animal can be immortal. Truth is first in the human understanding when the understanding adds something which is proper to itself and not in the thing it understands, but which none the less corresponds to the thing. The quiddities of things are only likenesses of things, similar in this to the images of sensation. But the understanding adds judgment, and judgments are true or false dependent on whether or not that which is understood is adequated to that which is. Judgment is the activity of the understanding compounding and dividing concepts; in judgment we consider that which is (*ens*). Strictly speaking we do not perceive the thing which is; we perceive its accidents; but we can nevertheless conceive that which is, and notwithstanding that it does not enter in sensation, it is that which the intellect seizes as best known. The universality of the entity of things in being and in understanding, indeed, convinced Aristotle of the impossibility of making being or that which is a genus.

The metaphysics of the relation of what a thing is and what a thing is known as, is worked explicitly and subtly into the basis of the theory of knowledge in the thomist philosophy. That which is (*ens*) is known first, and all conceptions of the mind are resolved into it, since all other conceptions are arrived at by addition to it. Taking that which is (*ens*) in its essential meaning, it can be distinguished from its affirmative and negative consequences, that is, from thing (*res*) which is the affirmative consequence expressing the quiddity or essence of that which is and from one (*unum*) which is the negative consequence expressing the indivision of each thing that is. Relative to other things, that which is may be considered divided from other things: then it is called something (*aliquid*); or it may be considered in its conformity to some other thing—that last consideration would be impossible if there were not something which can be conformed to all things; this is the soul which is the measure of all things. But there are two faculties to be considered in the soul: cognitive and appetitive. *Good* expresses the conformity of that which is to appetite; *true* the conformity of that which is to understanding. The true and that which is, are, therefore, convertible; the true adds over and above that which is an adequation of it to the understanding; the true is that which is in the fashion in which it enters understanding; it is the intention of that which is. If the true is to be defined, therefore, it is possible to define it in three ways: it may be considered as that which is; it may be considered as perfective of the adequation of thing and understanding; it may be considered as the effect which results in the mind from that adequation. Much of the discussion concerning the nature of truth has followed from the failure to realize that all three are compossible; indeed, all three are necessarily implied in any one of the definitions.

Truth in created things, therefore, includes the entity of the thing and the adequation of the thing to the understanding. Truth is in creatures in two ways: in the things themselves and in the understanding. Natural things have their peculiar status in knowledge as consequence of the fact that they stand between two understandings, the divine understanding and the human understanding. If our relative genera can be applied even approximately to things, it is because things are constituted on a scheme of intelligibility; the truth of things constituted in the adequation of things to the divine understanding is guarantee of our truths even though we can not penetrate to it. The ideas of God are creative of all that is; our ideas are effective from that which is; fundamentally the laws of thought and the laws of nature are the same. Moreover, by this relation of divine and human understandings to things, what Augustine and Anselm had said concerning the relation of all truths to one eternal truth is reconcilable with what Aristotle said concerning the activity of the active intellect abstracting forms. The eternal ideas of God and the changing ideas of man meet in the forms of things by virtue of which they are and are known.

By ideas are understood the forms of some things, existing outside the things themselves. The form of anything, however, existing outside the thing itself, can serve a double purpose: either to be exemplar of that of which it is called the form, or to be the principle of knowledge according to which the forms of knowable things are said to be in the knower. —And with respect to either purpose it is necessary to posit ideas. For in all things which are not generated by chance, it is necessary that the form be the end of any generation whatsoever. The agent, however, can not act in view of a form except in so far as the likeness of the form is in it. That however can happen in two ways. For in certain agents the form of the thing to be made preexists according to its natural being [*secundum esse naturale*], as in those things which act by nature, as man generates man, and fire fire. But in certain agents the form of the thing to be made preexists according to its intelligible being [*secundum esse intelligibile*], as in those things which act by understanding, as the likeness of a house preexists in the mind of the builder. And this can be called the *idea of the house,* because the artificer intends the house to assimilate the form which he conceived in his mind. Because, therefore, the world was not made by chance but was made by God acting by understanding, it is necessary that there be in the divine mind a form to the likeness of which the world was made. And in that consists the reason of idea.[1]

When therefore the question is raised whether there is one truth by which all things are true, with the authority of Anselm heavily on the affirmative side of the question, the answer may be governed by the consideration that truth in the divine understanding is one; but truths in things are many; the truth in the divine understanding is necessary; but truth in the human understanding, accidental. The divine understanding is a measure, but it is not measured, things are measured by the divine understanding, and things in turn measure the human understanding; our understanding, however, is measured by things, but it measures no natural things, only artificial things projected and made by it. Finally, the motions of changeable things among truths and falsities may be understood if it is remembered that things are denominated true according to an intrinsic truth in them and an extrinsic truth in God.

The questions whether or not things can be true or false, whether or not sensation can be true or false, whether or not understanding can be true or false, are

[1] *Summa Theologica* I. q. 15, a. 1 concl.

solved once these distinctions have been made; that truth or falsity is not in things nor in sense properly, but only in some certain respect (*secundum quid*) has consequences in the question, how the understanding knows truth. For the understanding knows truth as it reflects on itself. Truth is in the understanding in two ways, as a consequence to its activity and as known by the understanding. Therein lies the difference between understanding and sensation; for truth is in sensation only as a consequence to its activity; sense does not know the truth by which it judges truly, and so it does not know the nature of its act or the relation of its act to the thing; therefore, it does not know truth. The understanding, being among the most perfect of the things which are, returns to its essence with a complete return. It proceeds outside itself when it knows that which is, and begins to return to itself, because the act of cognition is medium between knower and known; the return is completed when the understanding knows its own essence; knowing its own essence it returns with a complete return. The senses can not make such a return, for although the interior sense perceives sense perceiving, still sense does not know its own nature, but its action is like that of fire which does not know its own heating.

The search for truth by this analysis may turn from metaphysics to the contemplation of the source of truth; that is the injuncture of religion; but there is besides that pious inference the suggestion that the examination of that which is, be conducted with the aid of logic. For the metaphysics is excellent statement of the proposition that the ways in which that which is can determine itself are as many as the ways in which a thing can be declared to be. Our knowledge is of things that are and as they are: the categories of logic are the categories of things, but without the needless supposition, which is usually insinuated into the doctrine for purposes of refutation, that things as they are and things as they are in the mind are in any sense identical, or that the classifications of things in the mind must represent externally constituted groupings. The true and that which is are convertible, but for that very reason they can not be identical. The impossible test of a comparison of idea to thing known is not necessary for the perception of truth. Truth is based in the principles of the understanding itself. These principles the understanding perceives in perceiving itself; they are known of and through themselves, not by comparison to any experience, for they did not originate in experience, nor on the other hand as innate in the mind; rather the understanding from its observation of its own operations knows at once that they are true. The concept of being, thus, is included in everything that man thinks; from that alone the first principle is known that the same thing can not be affirmed and denied at the same time. This first principle is the condition of all other principles, yet it is itself indemonstrable; all truths depend in demonstration on the principles which the mind knows in knowing itself. The thomist doctrine of knowledge is comfortable in the conviction that truth may be relative in human minds, without rendering certainties impossible, and that truths which are neither exhaustive of all possible statements concerning the thing, nor exclusive of all possible alternatives, may nevertheless be adequate in judgment of that which is.

THOMAS AQUINAS

THE DISPUTED QUESTIONS ON TRUTH[1]

QUESTION I.

ON TRUTH

(Divided into twelve articles)

It is inquired, 1st, what is truth; 2nd, whether truth is found principally in the understanding or in things; 3rd, whether truth is only in the understanding compounding and dividing; 4th, whether there is only one truth by which all things are true; 5th, whether some other truth beside the first truth is eternal; 6th, whether created truth is immutable; 7th, whether truth is predicated of divine things essentially or personally; 8th, whether all truth is from the first truth; 9th, whether truth is in sense; 10th, whether any thing is false; 11th, whether falsity is in sense; 12th, whether falsity is in the understanding.

ARTICLE I.

What is truth?[2]

The question is concerning truth and it is inquired first what truth is. Now it seems that truth is abso-

---

[1] SANCTI THOMAE AQUINATIS, *Quaestiones Disputatae*, in *Opera Omnia*, ed. S. E. Fretté. Paris: Vives, 1875, vol. XIV, pp. 315-341.　　　[2] Cp. *Summa Theologica* I, q. 16, a. 3.

lutely the same as the thing which is [*ens*], for Augustine says in the book of *Soliloquies*, chapter V, that *the true is that which is*. But that which is, is nothing but the thing which is. Therefore the true signifies absolutely the same as the thing which is.

2. Replying to this, it was said that the true and that which is are the same with respect to subjects [*suppositum*] but that they differ with respect to reason [*ratio*].—But on the other hand, the reason of anything is that which is signified by its definition. But that which is, is given by Augustine as the definition of the true after he had rejected certain other definitions. Since, therefore, the true and the thing which is agree with respect to that which is, it seems that they are the same in reason.

3. Moreover, things which differ in reason are so constituted that one of them can be understood without the other, wherefore Boethius says in his book *De hebdomadibus*[3] that the divine being [*Deus esse*] can be understood if God's goodness be abstracted for a time by the understanding. The thing which is, however, can in no wise be understood if the true be taken away: for it is understood by the fact that it is true. Therefore, the true and the thing which is do not differ in reason.

4. Moreover, if the true is not the same as that which is, it must be a disposition of that which is. But it can not be a disposition of that which is. For

[3] The reference is to the sevenfold division in which Boethius is supposed to have classified his shorter works, as well as to the philosophic group, which met weekly, before which they were probably read. The work in which the difficulties in the *Hebdomads* are expounded (cited here) is *How substances, in that they are, are good, although they are not substantial goods*; for the passage quoted, see p. 44, 92–93 (Loeb Classical Library).

it is not a totally corrupting disposition, otherwise it would follow: this is true, therefore it is that which is not, just as it follows: the man is dead, therefore he is not man. Similarly, the true is not a diminishing disposition, otherwise it would not follow: this is true, therefore it is, just as it does not follow: this person is white with respect to teeth, therefore he is white. Similarly, the true does not constrain or specify the thing that is, since it would not then be converted with that which is. Therefore, the true and that which is are wholly the same.

5. Moreover, things whose disposition is the same are the same. But the disposition of the true and of that which is is the same. Therefore, they are the same. For it is said in the IInd book of the *Metaphysics*: *The disposition of a thing in being is the same as its disposition in truth*. Therefore, the true and the thing that is are entirely the same.

6. Moreover, things which are not the same, differ in some manner. But the true and the thing that is [*ens*] differ in no manner, for they do not differ in essence [*essentia*] since the thing that is is true by its essence, nor on the other hand do they differ by other differences, for it would be necessary that they should agree in some genus. Therefore, they are wholly the same.

7. Moreover, if they are not absolutely the same, the true must add something to the thing that is. But the true adds nothing to the thing that is, since it would then be more than that which is. This is stated clearly by the Philosopher when he says in the IVth book of the *Metaphysics*: *Defining the true we say that that which is is or that that which is not is not*, and so the true includes that which is and that which is not.

Therefore, the true does not add to that which is and so it seems to be entirely the same as that which is.

1. BUT TO THE CONTRARY, nonsense is useless repetition. If, therefore, the true were the same as the thing that is, it would be nonsense to say true being; this is false: therefore, they are not the same.

2. Moreover, that which is and that which is good are convertible. But the true is not convertible with the good, for a thing may be true which is not good, as that this man commits fornication. Therefore, that which is true is not converted with that which is.

3. Moreover, Boethius says in the book *De hebdomadibus: In all creatures being* [esse] *and that which is* [quod est] *are diverse.* But the true follows from the being of things. Therefore, the true is diverse from that which is in creatures. But that which is [*quod est*] is the same as the thing that is [*ens*]. Therefore, the true in creatures is diverse from the thing that is.

4. Moreover, things which bear the relation to each other of prior and posterior must be diverse. But that which is true and the thing that is are of such sort that, as is said in the book *on Causes,* the first of created things is being; and the Commentator says, commenting on that book, *all other things are predicated as informing the thing that is,* and thus they are posterior to that which is. Therefore, the true and that which is are diverse.

5. Moreover, those things which are predicated in common of a cause and of things which are caused, are one in the cause rather than in the things caused; and particularly in God rather than in creatures. But in God the following four, being, one, truth, and good, are so appropriated that *being* [ens] pertains to essence [*essentia*], *one* to the person of the Father,

truth to the person of the Son, *good* to the person
of the holy Spirit. But the divine persons are distinguished not only according to reason but according
to fact: therefore, they are not predicated of each other.
Consequently, in creatures these must all the more
surely differ more than in reason.

I REPLY that it must be said that, just as in demon-
strables there must be a reduction to some principles
known through themselves to the understanding, so
too in investigating what anything is; otherwise one
would in either case go on *in infinitum*; and thus science
and the knowledge of things would perish utterly. That,
however, which the understanding conceives first as
best known, and in which it resolves all conceptions,
is that which is, as Avicenna says in the beginning of
his *Metaphysics,* book I, chapter 9. Therefore, all
other conceptions of the understanding must be arrived
at by an addition to that which is. But something can
not be added to that which is as an extraneous nature,
in the fashion that a difference is added to a genus or
an accident to a subject, for every nature is essentially
that which is, and therefore the Philosopher in the IIIrd
book of the *Metaphysics* proves likewise that that which
is cannot be a genus. But some things are said to be
added over and above that which is so far as they express
a mode of it which is not expressed by the name of
that itself which is. This is possible in two ways:
in one way so that the mode expressed be some special
mode of that which is. For there are diverse grades
of entity according to which diverse modes of being
are taken on, and in accordance with these modes,
diverse genera of things are taken on. For substance
does not add over and above that which is, any difference
which signifies some nature superadded to that which

is, but rather a certain special mode of being is expressed by the word substance, namely, that which is through itself [*per se ens*]; and so it is in the other genera. *In a second way,* so that the mode expressed is a mode generally consequent to each thing that is, and this mode can be taken in two ways, in one way as that which follows each thing that is, in itself; in another way as that which follows each thing that is, in its relation to some other thing. If in the first way, it is said to express something affirmative or negative in the thing that is. But nothing affirmative is found predicated absolutely which can be taken in each thing that is except its essence according to which it is said to be; and thus the word *thing* [*res*] is imposed, which according to Avicenna in the beginning of his *Metaphysics* differs from the thing which is [*ens*] in this, that the thing which is is derived from the act of being, but the name *thing* expresses the quiddity or essence of the thing which is. The negation, moreover, which is the consequent absolutely to each thing that is, is indivision, and the word *one* expresses this, for *one* is nothing else than an undivided thing which is. If, however, the mode of being is taken in the second way, that is, according to the order of one thing to another, this can be in two ways. In one according to the division of one thing from the other, and this is expressed by the word *something*, for it is called *something* as if *some other thing*;[4] and therefore as that which is is called *one* in so far as it is undivided in itself, so it is called *something* in so far as it is divided from others. In a second way, according to the conformity of one thing that is to anything else, and this can not be unless there is given something which is formed to accord with all things

---

[4] That is, *aliquid = aliud quid.*

that are. But this is the soul, which is in a measure all things, as is said in the IIIrd book *on the Soul*. There is in the soul, however, a cognitive power and an appetitive power. Consequently, the word *good* expresses the conformity of the thing which is to appetite, as is stated in the beginning of the *Ethics: the good is what all desire*. Clearly the word *true* expresses the conformity of the thing which is to understanding. But all knowledge is perfected by the assimilation of the knower to the thing known, so that that assimilation is said to be the cause of the knowledge, just as sight knows color through the fact that it is disposed by the species of color. Consequently, the first comparison of the thing which is to understanding is that the thing which is correspond to the understanding, which correspondence is called the adequation of the thing and the understanding; and the principle [*ratio*] of truth is perfected formally in this. It is this, consequently, which the true adds over and above that which is: namely, conformity or adequation of thing and understanding, and to this conformity, as has been said, the knowledge of the thing follows. Thus, therefore, the entity of the thing precedes the reason of truth, but knowledge is a certain effect of truth. According to this, therefore, it is found that truth and the true are to be defined in three ways. In one way, according to that which precedes the principle of truth and in which the true is founded, and thus Augustine defines it in the book of *Soliloquies*, chapter V, *The true is that which is*, and Avicenna in the IInd book of the *Metaphysics*, chapter XII, *The truth of any thing is the property of its being which is the stabilition of the thing*, and a certain other philosopher, *Truth is the indivision of being and that of it which is* [eius quod est]. And in another way truth is defined according to that which perfects formally the principle of the true, and thus Isaac says that *Truth is the adequation of thing and understanding*; and Anselm in the book *on Truth*, chapter XI,[5] *Truth is rightness perceptible to the mind alone.* For this rightness is so called from a certain adequation according to which the Philosopher in the IVth book of the *Metaphysics* says, that defining the true we say that that which is is or that that which is not is not. And in a third way, the true is defined according to the effect which results; and Hilary defines it thus, that *Truth is manifestive and declarative being*, and Augustine in the book *on True Religion*, chapter XXXVI, *Truth is that by which that which is is shown*, and in the same book, chapter XXXI: *Truth is that according to which we judge concerning inferior things.*

To the first, therefore, it is replied that this definition of Augustine is given of the true according to that which it has as foundation in the thing and not according to that which the reason of the true fulfills in the adequation of thing to understanding. Or it must be added that, when it is said, *the true is that which is*, it is not taken there as it signifies the act of being but rather as it is the name of the composite understanding, that is, as it signifies the affirmation of a proposition, so that the sense is: the true is that which is, that is, when it is said of anything which is that it is; so that the definition of Augustine comes to the same as the definition of the Philosopher introduced above.

The answer to the second is obvious from what has just been said.

To the third it must be replied that for something

[5] See above, vol. I, page 172.

to be understood without something else, can be taken in two ways. In one way as follows, that something is understood when the other thing is not understood; and thus those things which differ in reason are so constituted that one can be understood without the other. For something to be understood without something else can be taken in another way, in which the one is understood when the other does not exist, and thus that which is can not be understood without the true, because that which is can not be understood without that which corresponds or is adequated to the understanding. But it is not necessary that whosoever understands the reason of the thing which is, understand the reason of the true, just as not any one at all understands the active intellect, and yet without the active intellect man can understand nothing.

To the fourth it must be said that the true is a disposition of the thing that is, not as adding some nature nor as expressing some special mode of that which is, but something which is generally found in that which is but which is not expressed by the expression, the thing which is. Therefore, it is not necessary that it be a disposition corrupting or diminishing or contracting into part.

To the fifth it must be said that disposition is not taken there in the respect that it is in the genus of quality, but in the respect that it imports a certain order. For since those things which are the cause of the being of others, are in the highest degree things that are, and those which are the cause of the truth of others are in the highest degree true, the Philosopher concludes that the order of any thing is the same in being and in truth, in such wise that where that is found which is in the highest degree a thing which is, that is found which is in the highest degree true. Nor is this so because that which is and the true are the same in their reason, but because a thing is naturally equated to the understanding by the circumstance that it has something of entity; and thus the reason of the true follows the reason of that which is.

To the sixth it must be said that the true and that which is differ in reason by the fact that there is something in the reason of the true which is not in the reason of that which is. But they do not so differ that there is something in the reason of that which is, which is not in the reason of the true. Nor do they differ in essence, nor are they distinguished from each other by opposed differences.

To the seventh it must be said that the true is not something more than the thing which is. For the thing which is, taken in a certain way, is predicated of that which is not, according as that which is not is apprehended by the understanding. Therefore, in the IVth book of the *Metaphysics*, the Philosopher says that negation or privation of being is in one sense called being. So, too, Avicenna says in the beginning of his *Metaphysics*, that discourse can not be formed except of that which is, because that concerning which the proposition is formed must be apprehended by the understanding; from this it is obvious that each true thing is in a certain sense a thing that is.

To the first of the objections to the contrary it must be said that it is not nonsense to speak of true being, because something is expressed by the word true which is not expressed by the word being; not because they differ in fact.

To the second it must be said that although he who commits fornication is evil, nevertheless, according as he has something of entity, he is made to be conformed to the understanding, and the reason of the true follows according to that, and thus it is evident that the true does not exceed nor is it exceeded by that which is.

To the third it must be replied that when it is said, *being and that which is are diverse,* the act of being is distinguished from that to which the act of being conforms. The reason of that which is, however, is derived from the act of being, not from that to which the act of being conforms, and therefore the reasoning does not follow.

To the fourth it must be said that the true is posterior to that which is, in this respect, that the reason of the true differs from the reason of that which is in the manner stated above.

To the fifth it must be said that this reasoning is defective in three respects. First, that although the three divine persons are distinguished in fact, nevertheless, the persons do not differ by their appropriated fact, but by reason. Second, that although the persons are distinguished from each other really, still they are not distinguished really from being, and therefore neither is the true which is appropriated to the person of the Son distinguished from being which is maintained on the part of essence. Third, that although that which is, the true, the one, and the good are united more in God than in created things, nevertheless, it does not follow necessarily from the fact that they are distinguished in God by reason that they are distinguished really in created things. For this happens in the case of those things which do not have unity in fact from their nature, such as wisdom and power, which although they are one in God, are really distinguished in creatures. But that which is, the true, the one, and the good have unity according to their nature; wherefore, wheresoever they are found, they are really one, although the unity of the thing by which they are united in God is more perfect than the unity of that by which they are united in creatures.

ARTICLE II.

*Whether truth is found principally in the understand-
ing rather than in things*

Second, it is inquired whether truth is found principally in the understanding rather than in things. And
it seems that it is not. For the true, as has been said,
is convertible with the thing that is. But that which
is, is found principally outside the mind. Therefore
the true also.

2. Moreover, things are not in the mind by their
essence but by their species, as is pointed out in the
IIIrd book *on the Soul*. If, therefore, truth is found
principally in the mind, truth will not be the essence
of the thing, but the likeness or species of it; and the
true will be the species of a thing existing outside the
mind. But the species of a thing existing within
the mind is not predicated of the thing which is outside
the mind, as likewise it is not convertible with it.
Therefore, neither is the true convertible with the thing
that is; which is false.

3. Moreover, all that which is in anything follows
that in which it is. If, therefore, truth is principally
in the mind, the judgment of truth is according to
the estimation of the mind; and thus will return the
error of the philosophers of antiquity, who said that
all that which any one believes, is true, and that two
contradictories are true at the same time; which is
absurd.

4. Moreover, if truth is principally in the understanding, it is necessary that something which pertains

to the understanding of truth be posited in the definition of truth. But Augustine in his book of *Soliloquies,* book II, chapters 4 and 5, condemns definitions of such sort as the following, *That is true which is as it is seen,* because according to this, that would not be true which is not seen, which is obviously false in the case of the deeply hidden stones which are in the bowels of the earth. Similarly he rejects the following, *That is true which is as it appears to a knower who is willing and able to know,* because according to this, a thing would not be true unless a knower wished to and could know it. And therefore, there would be the same reason against any other definitions in which something pertaining to the understanding was placed. Therefore, truth is not principally in the understanding.

BUT TO THE CONTRARY, the Philosopher says in the VIth book of the *Metaphysics, There is no true or false except in the mind.*

Moreover, truth is the adequation of thing and understanding. But this adequation can not be save in the understanding. Therefore, neither is truth save in the understanding.

I REPLY that it must be said that in those things which are predicated of many things by priority and posteriority, it is not always necessary that that receive by priority the predication of common which is as the cause of the others, but rather that in which the principle of that which is common is first found completed. Thus, healthy is predicated by priority of animal in which the principle of health is first found perfected, although medicine is called healthy as effective of health. And therefore, when true is predicated of many things by priority and posteriority, it is necessary that it be predicated as prior of that in which is found the perfect principle of truth. The complement, however, of every motion or operation is in its end. But the motion of the cognitive faculty is terminated in the soul. For a thing must be known in the knower according to the mode of the knower. But the motion of the appetitive faculty is terminated in the thing, and thence it is that the Philosopher, in the IIIrd book *on the Soul,* places a kind of circle in the actions of the mind, that is, according to which a thing which is outside the mind moves the understanding, and the thing understood moves the appetite, and the appetite, then, brings it about that it attain to the thing from which the motion started. And because, as was pointed out in the preceding article, the order to the appetite is called good, but the order to the understanding true, thence it is that the Philosopher says in the VIth book of the *Metaphysics* that good and evil are in things, and true and false are in the mind. But a thing is not called true except as it is adequated to the understanding, and therefore true is found posterior in things and prior in the understanding. But it must be borne in mind that a thing is compared in one fashion to the practical intellect and in another to the speculative. For the practical intellect causes things, and therefore, it is the measure of things which are made by it; but the speculative intellect, since it is receptive of things, is in a certain measure a motion from things themselves; and so things measure it. From this it is obvious that natural things from which our understanding receives its knowledge, measure our understanding, as is said in the Xth book of the *Metaphysics*; but they are measured by the divine understanding in which all created things are, as all artificial things are in the understanding of the artisan. Thus therefore, the divine understanding measures but is not meas-

ured; natural things measure and are measured; but
our understanding is measured, and it does not measure
natural things but only artificial things. A natural
thing, therefore, set up between two understandings,
is said to be true by an adequation to both; for according to the adequation to the divine understanding
it is said to be true in so far as it fulfills that to which
it is ordered by the divine understanding, as is made
evident by Anselm in the book *on Truth,* chapter VII,[6]
and in Augustine in the book *on True Religion,* chapter
XXXI, and in Avicenna in the definition quoted above,
namely, *the truth of any thing is the property of its
being which is the stabilition of the thing.* On the other
hand, according to the adequation to the human understanding, a thing is said to be true in so far as it is
constituted to form a true estimation of itself, just as,
on the contrary, things are said to be false which are
constituted to seem what they are not or as they are not,
as is said in the Vth book of the *Metaphysics.* However,
the first principle of truth is present in the thing prior
to the second, because the comparison to the divine
understanding is prior to the human, so that even if
the human understanding were not, things would still
thus far be said to be true in their order to the divine
understanding. But if both understandings were understood to be removed, which is impossible, the principle of truth would in no wise remain.

To the first it must be said, therefore, that as is
obvious from what has been said, true is predicated
of the understanding as prior and of the thing which
is adequated to it as posterior; and in both ways it is
convertible with the thing which is but in diverse man-

ners, for as it is predicated of things it is converted by predication with the thing which is. For every thing that is, is adequated to the divine understanding and is able to adequate the human understanding to it, and conversely. But if true is taken as predicated of the understanding, it is converted with the thing which is outside the mind, not by predication but by conformity, in that it is necessary that some thing which is, respond to every understanding, and conversely.

And from this the solution to the second is clear.

To the third it must be said that that which is in something, does not follow that in which it is, except when it is caused by the principles of that thing; whence the light which is caused in the air by something extrinsic, namely, by the sun, follows the motion of the sun rather than the air. Similarly, truth which is caused in the mind by things, does not follow the estimation of the mind, but the existence of the things. For from the fact that the thing is or is not, speech is said to be true or false, and understanding likewise.

To the fourth it must be said that Augustine speaks of the vision of the human understanding on which the truth of the thing does not depend. For there are many things which are not known to our understanding; but there is no thing which the divine understanding does not know in actuality and the human understanding does not know in potentiality, since the active intellect is described as that whose function it is to make all things, and the possible intellect as that whose function it is to be made all things. And therefore, vision in the actuality of the divine understanding can be posited in the definition of the true thing, but not the vision of the human understanding except in potentiality, as appears from what has been said.

Article III.

Whether truth is in the understanding compounding and dividing[7]

In the third place, it is inquired whether truth is only in the understanding compounding and dividing. And it seems that it is not. For truth is said to be according to the comparison of the thing that is to the understanding. But the operation by which the understanding is first compared to the thing is that by which the understanding forms the quiddities of things by conceiving their definitions. Therefore, truth is found principally and more properly in that operation of the understanding.

2. Moreover, truth is the adequation of thing and understanding. But just as the understanding compounding and dividing can be adequated to things, so too the understanding when it understands the quiddities of things. Therefore, truth is not only in the understanding compounding and dividing.

To THE CONTRARY, in the VIth book of the *Metaphysics* it is said, *True and false are not in things but in the mind.*

Moreover, in the IIIrd book *on the Soul* it is said that the understanding of indivisibles is in those things in which there is no true and false.

I REPLY that it must be said that just as the true is found prior in understanding than in things, so too it is found prior in the act of the understanding compounding and dividing than in the act of the understanding forming the quiddities of things. For the

7 Cp. *Summa Theologica* I, q. 16, a. 2.

principle of truth consists in the adequation of thing
and understanding; the same thing, however, is not
adequated to itself, but equality is of diverse things;
and therefore, the principle of truth is found first in
the understanding when the understanding first begins
to have something proper to itself which the thing outside the mind does not have, but something corresponding to the thing. Adequation can be looked for between
these. But the understanding forming quiddities has
only the likeness of the thing existing outside the mind,
as sense has in so far as it receives the species of the
sensible thing. When, however, it begins to judge concerning the thing apprehended, then the very judgment
of the understanding is something proper to it which
is not found outside in the thing. But when it is adequated to that which is outside in the thing, the judgment is said to be true. The understanding, then,
judges of the thing apprehended, when it says that
something is or is not, which is the result of the understanding compounding and dividing; and therefore
the Philosopher says in the VIth book of the *Metaphysics,* that composition and division are in the understanding and not in things. And thence it is that
truth is found prior in the composition and division
of the understanding; and it is said to be secondarily
and posterior in the understanding forming definitions.
Consequently, a definition is said to be true or false
by reason of a true or false composition, as when a
definition is said to be of that of which it is not,
as if, for example, the definition of a circle be assigned
to a triangle; or again when the parts of a definition
can not be compounded with each other, as if the definition of some thing were given as *an insensible animal,*
for this composition which is implied, namely, that
some animal is insensible, is false. And so a definition

is not said to be true or false except in relation to composition, just as a thing is said to be true in relation to the understanding. It is evident, therefore, from what has been said, that truth is predicated of the composition or division of the understanding as prior; secondly, of the definitions of things so far as true or false composition is implicated in them; thirdly, of things as they are adequated to the divine understanding or are constituted apt to be adequated to the human understanding; fourthly, of man who is selective of his words, true or false, or who makes a true or false estimation of himself or of others by that which he says or does. Words in this same way receive the predication of truth, as do the meanings which they signify.

To the first, therefore, it must be said that although the formation of the quiddity is the first operation of the understanding, nevertheless, through it the understanding does not have something else proper to itself which could be adequated to the thing; and therefore truth is not properly there.

And by this the solution to the second is evident.

Article IV.

Whether there is only one truth by which all things are true[8]

In the fourth place it is inquired whether there is only one truth by which all things are true. And it seems that there is. For Anselm in his book *on Truth*, chapter XIII toward the end,[9] says that as time is

---

[8] Cp. *Summa Theologica* I, q. 16, a. 6.

[9] See above, vol. I, p. 184.

related to all temporal things, so truth is related to all
true things. But time is so related to all temporal
things that there is only one time. Therefore, truth
will be so related to all true things that there will be
only one truth.

2. But it must be said that truth is spoken of in
two ways. In one way as it is the same as the entity
of the thing, as Augustine defines it in his book of
Soliloquies, chapter V, *The true is that which is*; and
so there must be many truths according as there are
many essences of things. In another way it is spoken
of as it expresses itself in the understanding, as Hilary
defines it, *The true is declarative being*; and in this way,
since nothing can manifest anything to the understanding except according to the power of the first divine
truth, all truths are in a certain manner one in moving
the understanding, just as all colors are one in moving
the sight, in so far as they move it in the relation of
one thing, namely, of light.—On the other hand, the
time of all temporal things is one in number. If, therefore, truth is related to true things as time to temporal
things, the truth of all true things ought to be one in
number; nor does it suffice that all truths are one in
moving or are one in exemplar.

3. Moreover, Anselm in the book *on Truth*, chapter
XIII,[10] argues thus: if there are many truths of many
true things, truths ought to vary according to the variation of true things. But truths do not vary through
the variations of true things, since if true and right
things are destroyed, there still remains the truth and
rightness according to which they are true and right.
Therefore, there is only one truth. He proves the
minor premiss from the fact that, if that which is signified is destroyed, there still remains the rightness of

[10] See above, vol. 1, pp. 180-182.

the signification, since it is right that that be signified which that sign signified; and for the same reason, if anything whatsoever which is true or right be destroyed, its rightness and truth remains.

4. Moreover, in created things, no truth is that of which it is the truth; just as the truth of man is not man, and the truth of flesh is not flesh. But every created thing is true. Therefore, no created thing is truth: therefore, all truth is something uncreated, and there is only one truth.

5. Moreover, in creatures there is nothing greater than the human mind except God, as Augustine says. But truth, as Augustine proves in the book of *Soliloquies*, chapters II and III, is greater than the human mind, since it can not be said that it is less, for then the human mind would have to judge to truth, which is false; for it does not judge of it but according to it, just as a judge does not judge of the law but according to the law, as he himself says in the book *on True Religion*, chapter XXXI. In the same way it can not be said that the human mind is equal to truth, because the soul judges all things according to truth, but it does not judge all things according to itself. Therefore, there is no truth except God, and thus there is only one truth.

6. Moreover, Augustine in the book of *LXXXIII Questions*, question 9 toward the beginning, proves in the following fashion that truth is not perceived by the sense of the body: nothing except the mutable is perceived by the sense of the body; but truth is immutable. Therefore, it is not perceived by sense. In the same way it can be argued: every created thing is mutable. Truth is not mutable. Therefore, it is not a creature: therefore, it is an uncreated thing: therefore, there is only one truth.

7. Moreover, Augustine argues in the same place for the same conclusion in this fashion: there is no sensible thing which does not have something like to the false, so that it can not be distinguished, for, to pass over other points, in sleep or in madness, we suffer the images of all things which we perceive through the body, even when they are not present to the senses, as if they were directly present. But truth does not have anything like to the false. Therefore, it is not perceived by sense. It can be argued in the same way: every created thing has something like to the false, in so far as it has something of defect. Therefore, no created thing is truth, and thus there is only one truth.

1. To the contrary, Augustine in the book *on True Religion,* chapter XXXVI, about the middle, says: *Just as likeness is the form of like things, so truth is the form of true things.* But there are many likenesses of many like things. Therefore, there are many truths of many true things.

2. Moreover, just as every created truth is derived from the uncreated truth and has its power from it; so all intelligible illumination is derived from the first light as from an exemplar and has its strength of manifesting from it. But there are said to be many intelligible lights, as is manifest in Dionysius *on Mystic Theology,* chapter I, paragraph 3. Therefore it must be conceded in the same way that there are many truths.

3. Moreover, colors, although they move the sight by virtue of light, are nevertheless said to be many and different absolutely, and they can not be said to be one except in some one respect [*secundum quid*]. Therefore, although all created truths express themselves in the understanding by virtue of a first truth, still they could not because of that be called one truth, except in some one respect [*secundum quid*].

4. Moreover, just as created truth can manifest itself in the understanding only by virtue of an uncreated truth, so no created power can do anything except by virtue of an uncreated power. But we can in no way say that there is one power of all things which have power. Therefore, it must in no way be said that there is one truth of all true things.

5. Moreover, God is compared to things in the condition [*habitudo*] of a triple cause, namely, efficient, exemplary, and final; and the entity of things according to a certain appropriation is referred to God as to the efficient cause, the truth as to the exemplary cause, and the goodness as to the final cause, although each can be referred to each of the others according to the property of speech. But in no fashion of speech do we say that there is one goodness of all good things or one entity of all things that are. Therefore, neither should we say there is one truth of all true things.

6. Moreover, although there is one uncreated truth from which all created truths are extracted, still they are not extracted from it in the same way, for although it is related to all things in the same way, still all things are not related to it in the same way, as it is said in the book *on Causes*, proposition 22: therefore, the truth of necessary and of contingent things is extracted from it in different manners. But the different manner of imitating the divine exemplar makes the diversification in created things. Therefore, in the same way there are many created truths.

7. Moreover, truth is the adequation of thing and understanding. But of things diverse in species there can not be one adequation of thing to understanding. Therefore, since true things are diverse in species, there can not be one truth of all true things.

8. Moreover, Augustine says in book XI *on the Trin-*

ity, chapter XV toward the beginning: *It must be believed that the nature of the human mind is so joined to
intelligible things that it perceives all things which it
knows in a certain light of its own genus* [sui generis].
But the light according to which the mind knows all
things is truth. Therefore, truth is of the genus of
the soul itself; and therefore, truth must be a created
thing; and therefore, there will be diverse truths in
diverse creatures.

I REPLY that it must be said that, as is evident from
what has been said above in article 2, truth is found
properly in the human or in the divine understanding,
just as health is found properly in animal. Truth,
however, is found in other things through their relation
to the understanding, just as health is predicated of
certain other things in so far as they are effective or
conservative of the health of the animal. Therefore,
truth is properly and first in the divine understanding; it is properly and secondarily in the human understanding; but in things it is improperly and secondarily,
since it is only in respect to one or the other of the
two truths. Therefore, the truth of the divine understanding is only one, from which many truths are
derived in the human understanding, just as many
likenesses result from the face of one man in a mirror,
as the *Gloss* [of Augustine] says concerning that statement of the Psalmist:[11] *Truths fail from among the
children of men.* The truths, however, which are in
things are as many as there are entities of things. But
the truth which is predicated of things in comparison
with the human understanding, is in a certain manner
accidental to the things; since if it were supposed that

[11] *Psal.* 11 (or 12): 1. Some translations render *veritates,
the faithful* or *faithfulness.*

the human understanding was not and could not be, the things would still continue in their essence. But the truth which is predicated of them in comparison to the divine understanding, is communicated to them insepa- rably; for they can not subsist except by the divine understanding producing them in being. Truth, there- fore, is in the thing by comparison to the divine un- derstanding prior to comparison to the human: since it is compared to the divine understanding as to its cause, but to the human understanding it is compared as if to its effect in a certain fashion, in so far as the understanding takes its knowledge from things. Thus, therefore, something is said to be true principally in its order to the truth of the divine understanding rather than in its order to the truth of the human un- derstanding. If, therefore, truth properly speaking is taken in the sense according to which principally all things are true, then all things are true by one truth, that is, by the truth of the divine understanding; and Anselm speaks thus of truth in the book *on Truth*, chapters VII and X.[12] If, however, truth properly speaking is taken in the sense according to which things are said to be true secondarily, then there are many truths of many true things in different minds. If, however, truth is taken improperly in the sense accord- ing to which all things are said to be true, then there are many truths of many true things; but there is only one truth of one thing. Things, however, are denomi- nated true from the truth which is in the divine under- standing or in the human understanding, as food is denominated healthy from the health which is in the ani- mal, and not as by an inherent form; but [they are denominated true] by the truth which is in the thing it- self (which is nothing other than the entity adequated

[12] See above, vol. I, pp. 163, 170.

to the understanding or adequating the understanding to itself) as by an inherent form, as food is denominated healthy by its quality by which it is called healthy.

To the first it must be said, therefore, that time is compared to temporal things as a measure to that which is measured, and consequently, it is evident that Anselm speaks of that truth which is only a measure of all true things and that truth is only one, as time is one, as is concluded in the second argument. But the truth which is in the human understanding or in things themselves is not compared to things as an extrinsic measure and common to things which are measured; but either it is compared as that which is measured to its measure, as is the case of the truth of the human understanding, and so it must be varied according to the variation of things, or else as an intrinsic measure, as is the case of the truth which is in things themselves, and these measures must be increased according to the number of things measured, just as the dimensions of diverse bodies are diverse.

The second we concede.

To the third it must be said that the truth which remains when things have been destroyed is the truth of the divine understanding; and this is one in number absolutely. The truth, however, which is in things or in the soul is varied according to the variety of things.

To the fourth it must be said that when the statement is made: no thing is its own truth, it is understood of things which have their being complete in nature; just as, when the statement is made: no thing is its own being; and nevertheless, the being of a thing is something created [and in the same way the truth of a thing is something created].

To the fifth it must be said that the truth according

to which the soul judges of all things, is the first truth. For just as from the truth of the divine understanding, the innate species of things flow into the angelic understanding, according to which the angelic understanding knows all things, so too from the truth of the divine understanding, the truth of the first principles proceeds, in the manner of an exemplar, into our understanding, and according to that truth we judge of all things. And since we can not judge by means of it except as it is the likeness of the first truth, therefore, we are said to judge of all things according to the first truth.

To the sixth it must be said that that immutable truth is the first truth; and it is neither perceived by the sense nor is it something created.

To the seventh it must be said that the created truth does not itself have something like to the false, even though some creature or other may have something like to the false. For in so far as a creature has some thing like to the false, to that degree it is deficient. But truth does not follow from a creature in that part in which it is deficient, but according as, having been conformed to the first truth, it recedes from defect.

To the first of the objections which are raised to the contrary it must be said that likeness is found properly in both of the like things, but truth, since it is a certain agreement of the understanding and the thing, is not found properly in both, but in the understanding. Consequently, since there is one understanding, namely the divine understanding, according to conformity with which all things are said to be true, all things ought to be true according to one truth, although there are many different likenesses in many like things.

To the second it must be said that although the intelligible light is patterned from the divine light, nevertheless, that light is spoken of properly, too, in regard to created intelligible lights. The truth, however, is not properly predicated of things properly patterned from the divine understanding; and therefore we do not say one light as we say one truth.

And in the same way it must be said to the third in regard to colors, since colors are properly called visible, although they are not seen except by means of light.

And in the same way it must be said to the fourth in regard to power and to the fifth in regard to entity.

To the sixth it must be said that although things are patterned in deformation [*difformiter*] from the divine truth, nevertheless, it is not impossible because of this, that things be true by one truth and not by many, properly speaking, since that which is received in diverse fashion in the patterned things is not properly called truth, as truth is spoken of properly in the pattern.

To the seventh it must be said that although those things which are diverse in species from the standpoint of things, are not adequated in one adequation to the divine understanding, nevertheless, the divine understanding to which all things are adequated is one; and from the standpoint of it there is one adequation to all things, although all things are not adequated in the same manner; and therefore, in the manner spoken of above there is one truth of all things.

To the eighth it must be said that Augustine speaks of truth patterned in our mind from the divine mind itself, just as the likeness of a face results in a mirror, and truths of this sort resulting in our souls from the first truth, are many, as has been said. Either it must be said that the first truth is in a certain manner of the genus of the soul, taking genus in a broad sense as all intelligibles. or else incorporeal things are said

to be of one genus, in the fashion in which it is said in
Acts 18: 28, *For we are his genus*.[13]

Article V.

Whether any other truth besides the first truth is eternal

In the fifth place it is inquired whether any other
truth besides the first truth is eternal. And it seems
that there is another. For Anselm says in the *Monologium*, chapter XVIII toward the end,[14] speaking of
the truth of things subject to statement in propositions
[*enuntiabilia*]: *Whether truth be said to have, or
whether it be understood not to have, beginning or end,
truth can be limited by no beginning or end.* But all
truth is understood either to have a beginning or an
end or not to have a beginning or an end. Therefore,
no truth is limited by a beginning or an end. But
everything which is of this sort is eternal. Therefore,
all truth is eternal.

2. Moreover, all that of which the being follows on
the destruction of its being, is eternal, since, whether
it is predicated to be or whether it is predicated not
to be, it follows that it will be, and it is necessary to
predicate of each thing in reference to each time that
it is or that it is not. But on the destruction of truth
it follows that truth is, since if truth is not, it is true
that truth is not, and nothing can be true except by
truth. Therefore, truth is eternal.

3. Moreover, if the truth of propositions is not eternal,
then it will be possible to assign a time when there
will not be a truth of propositions. But then, the

[13] English translations of the *Acts* usually render *genus,*
offspring.
[14] Cp. above, vol. I, p. 172.

following proposition is true, that there is no truth of propositions. Therefore, the truth of propositions is; which is contrary to that which was granted. Therefore, it can not be said that the truth of propositions is not eternal.

4. Moreover, the Philosopher proves in book I of the *Physics* that matter is eternal (although this is false) by the fact that it remains after its own corruption and that it is prior to its own generation, since if it is corrupted, it is corrupted in something, and if it is generated, it is generated out of something; that, however, out of which something is generated and that into which it is corrupted is matter. But if, similarly, truth is supposed to be corrupted or generated, it follows that it is prior to its generation and after its corruption, since if it is generated, it has been changed from non-being to being, and if it is corrupted, it has been changed from being to non-being. However, when there is no truth, it is true to say that truth is not, which surely can not be unless truth is. Therefore, truth is eternal.

5. Moreover, whatever can not be understood not to be is eternal, since whatsoever is able not to be, can be understood not to be. But the truth of propositions can not be understood not to be, since the understanding can not understand anything unless it understand that it is true. Therefore, the truth of propositions is eternal.

6. Moreover, Anselm argues thus in the *Monologium*, chapter XVIII toward the middle: *Let him who can, think of a time when it began to be true and when it was not true.*[15]

7. Moreover, that which is future always has been future and that which is past always will be past. But the proposition concerning the future is true for this reason, that there is something future, and the proposi-

[15] Cp. above, vol. I, p. 151.

tion concerning the past is true for this reason, that there is something past. Therefore, the truth of the proposition concerning the future always has been, as the truth of the proposition concerning the past always will be, and so not only the first truth is eternal, but many others.

8. Moreover, Augustine says in the book *on Free Will*[16] that nothing is more eternal than the reason of a circle and that two plus three equals five. But the truth of these is a created truth. Therefore, another truth besides the first truth is eternal.

9. Moreover, it is not required for the truth of discourse that anything be said actually, but it suffices that there be that concerning which discourse can be formed. But before the world was, there was something concerning which discourse was possible even besides God. Therefore, before the world was made, there was a truth of discourse. But whatsoever was before the world is eternal. Therefore, the truth of discourse is eternal, and so it is the same as above. Proof of the middle premiss: the world was made of nothing, that is, after nothing. Therefore, before the world was, there was non-being. But a true statement is formed, not only concerning that which is, but also concerning that which is not, for just as it is possible for that which is to be stated truly to be, so it is possible for that which is not to be stated truly not to be, as it is held in book I of the *on Interpretation*. Therefore, before the world was, there was that whence a true statement could be formed.

10. Moreover, all that is known is true while it is known. But God knows from eternity all things possible in discourse. Therefore, the truth of all discourse is from eternity, and so, many truths are eternal.

[16] Cp. above, vol. I, p. 35.

11. But it must be said that it does not follow from this that those things are true in themselves but in the divine understanding.—But to the contrary, they must be true according as they are known. But all things are known by God from eternity, not only as they are in his mind, but existing in their proper nature. *All things were known to our Lord God before they were created just as he knows all things after their perfection;*[17] and so he knows things after they were made not otherwise than he knew them before. Therefore, there were many truths from eternity not only in the divine understanding but also in themselves.

12. Moreover, something is said to be absolutely, according to what is in its complement. But the principle [*ratio*] of truth is fulfilled in the understanding. If, therefore, there were in the divine understanding from eternity many truths absolutely, it must be conceded that there are many eternal truths.

13. Moreover, it is said in the *Book of Wisdom* 1:15, *Justice is perpetual and immortal.* But truth is part of justice, as Cicero says in the *Rhetoric*, book II, *on Invention.* Therefore, truth is perpetual and immortal.

14. Moreover, universals are perpetual and incorruptible. But the true is in the highest degree universal, because it is converted with that which is. Therefore, truth is perpetual and incorruptible.

15. But it must be said that the universal is not corrupted through itself [*per se*] but it is accidentally [*per accidens*].—But on the contrary, a thing must be denominated more by that which agrees with it through itself than by that which agrees with it by accident. If, therefore, speaking of truth through itself, truth is perpetual and incorruptible, and if it is not corrupted or

[17] *Ecclesiasticus* 23:29.

generated except by accident, it must be conceded absolutely that truth spoken of universally is eternal.

16. Moreover, God was from eternity prior to the world. Therefore, the relation of priority in God was from eternity. But having posited one of the relatives, it is necessary to posit the other also. Therefore, the posterity of the world to God was from eternity. Therefore, in some manner there was something besides God from eternity, with which truth coincides, and so it is the same as above.

17. But it must be said that that relation of priority and posteriority is not something in the nature of things but in reason only.—To the contrary, as Boethius says in the end of the *Consolation of Philosophy*, book V, last prose section, God is prior in nature to the world, even if the world always was. Therefore, that relation of priority is a relation of nature and not of reason only.

18. Moreover, truth of signification is rightness of signification. But from eternity it has been right that something be signified. Therefore, truth of signification has been from eternity.

19. Moreover, it was true from eternity that the Father begat the Son and that the Holy Spirit proceeded from both. But these are many. Therefore, there have been many truths from eternity.

20. But it must be said that these are true by one truth; whence it does not follow that there are many truths from eternity.—But to the contrary, in one way the Father is the Father and he begets the Son; in another the Son is the Son and inspires the Holy Spirit. But by that by which the Father is the Father, it is true that the Father begets the Son or that the Father is the Father; and on the other hand, by that by which the Son is the Son, it is true that the Son was begotten

of the Father. Therefore, propositions of this sort are not true by one truth.

21. Moreover, although man and risible are convertible, nevertheless, the truth of these two propositions is not the same, *Man is man*, and *Man is risible*, because the property which the word, *man*, predicates and the property which the word, *risible*, predicates are not the same. In the same way, the property which the word, *Father*, and the property which the word, *Son*, convey, are not the same. Therefore, there is not one same truth of the propositions quoted.

22. But it must be said that these propositions were not from eternity.—But on the other hand, whensoever there is an understanding which can state discursively, there can be discourse. But there was from eternity the divine understanding which was the understanding that the Father is the Father and the Son is the Son, and so there was the stating or the saying, since, according to Anselm, in the *Monologium*, chapter XXXII toward the middle, it is the same for the supreme spirit to say and to understand. Therefore, the above mentioned statements were from eternity.

BUT TO THE CONTRARY, no created thing is eternal. All truth except the first truth is created. Therefore, the first truth alone is eternal.

Moreover, the thing that is and the true are converted. But only one being is eternal. Therefore, only one truth is eternal.

I REPLY that it must be said that, as was said above in article 3 of this question, truth conveys a certain adequation and commensuration: therefore, a thing is denominated true in the same way as a thing is denominated of a common measure [*commensuratum*]. However, body is measured by an intrinsic measure, as by line or surface or depth, and by an extrinsic measure, as a stationary object [*locatum*] by place, and motion by time, and cloth by an ell. Whence, too, a thing can be denominated true in two ways: in one way by an inherent truth; in another way by an extrinsic truth; and in the latter way all true things are denominated true by the first truth, and since the truth which is in the understanding is measured by the things themselves, it follows that not only the truth of the thing but also the truth of the understanding or of discourse, which signifies the understanding, is denominated by the first truth. In this adequation or commensuration of understanding and thing, however, it is not required that both of the extremes be in actuality. For our understanding can be adequated now to things which will be in the future, but which are not now; otherwise the following statement would not be true: the Antichrist will arise. Whence this is denominated true by a truth which is in the understanding only, even when the thing itself is not. Similarly, too, the divine understanding could be adequated from eternity with things which were not from eternity but were made in time; and thus, those things which are in time can be denominated true from eternity by an eternal truth. If, however, we take truth for the truth of created truths which inhere in these and which we find in things and in created understanding, then truth is not eternal, neither the truth of things nor of statements, since the things themselves or the understanding in which truths inhere are not from eternity. If, however, the truth of created truths is taken in the sense by which all things are denominated true as by an extrinsic measure which is the first truth, then the truth of all, of things and of statements and of understandings, is eternal, and Augustine sought after the eternity of truth of this sort in the book of *Soliloquies*, book III chapters 3 and 4, and Anselm in the *Monologium*; whence Anselm says in the book *on Truth*, chapter X:[18] *You can understand how I proved by the truth of discourse in my Monologium that the supreme truth has no beginning or end.* This first truth, however, can not be of all things unless it is one. For in our understanding, truth is diversified in only two ways: in one way because of a diversity of knowers, from whom it has diverse conceptions which lead to diverse truths in the soul; in another way from a diverse manner of understanding. So the running of Socrates is one thing, but the mind which, by compounding and dividing, understands time with it, as is pointed out in book III *on the Soul*, understands the running of Socrates in diverse manners, as past, present, and future; and in accordance with that it forms diverse conceptions in which diverse truths are found. However, neither of these modes of diversity can be found in the divine cognition. For God does not have diverse cognitions of diverse things, but by one cognition he knows all, since he knows through one thing, namely through his own essence, not introducing his cognition in single things, as Dionysius says in the book *on Divine Names*, chapter VII toward the middle. In the same way his cognition does not concern any time because it is measured by eternity, which is abstracted from all time since it contains all time. Whence it remains that there are not many truths from eternity but only one.

To the first, therefore, it must be said, that, as Anselm expounds himself in the book *on Truth*, he said that the truth of discourse is not confined by a beginning and an end, not because speech was without a beginning, but because no time can be conceived when that speech

[18] See above, vol. I, p. 170.

was and truth was absent from it; that speech, namely, of which it was a question, by which is signified truly that something will be. Whence it is apparent by this that he did not wish to add that the truth inhering in the created thing or that speech is without beginning or end, but the first truth, by which as by an extrinsic measure, discourse is said to be true.

To the second it must be said that outside the soul we find two things, namely, the thing itself and the privations and negations of the thing; which two are not related in the same way to truth, since they are not related in the same way to the understanding. For, by the species which it has, the thing itself is adequated to the divine understanding, as the artificial is to the art; and by virtue of that same species it is brought about that the thing adequates itself to our understanding, to the extent that, by the likeness of itself received in the soul, it forms a notion of itself. But when that which is not, outside the soul, is considered, it has not anything by which it may be adequated to the divine understanding nor anything by which it may form a notion of itself in our understanding. Whence that which is equated to any understanding whatsoever, is not of that which itself is not, but [it is] of the understanding itself which does not receive in itself the reason [of that which is not]. The thing, however, which is something positive outside the soul, has something in itself by which it can be called true. It is not thus, however, with the non-being of the thing, but whatsoever is attributed to it is from the part of the understanding. When he says, therefore, it is true that truth is not, since the truth which is signified here is a truth concerning that which is not, it has nothing save in the understanding. Whence nothing follows from the destruction of the truth which is in the thing, except the being of the truth which is in the

understanding. And so it is evident that nothing can
be concluded from this except the truth which is in the
understanding and which is eternal; and it must certainly
be in the eternal understanding; and this is the eternal
truth. Whence for the abovementioned reason, it is
shown that only the first truth is eternal.

And by this the solution to the third and to the fourth
is evident.

To the fifth it must be said that it can not be conceived that truth absolutely is not; but it can be conceived that no created truth be, just as it can be
conceived that there be no creature. For the understanding can understand itself not to be and not to
understand, even though it does not understand without
being or understanding. For it is not necessary that
the understanding understand by understanding whatsoever it has by understanding, since it does not always
reflect upon itself, and therefore, there is no contradiction if it understand that the created truth, without
which it can not understand, is not.

To the sixth and the seventh it must be said that that
which is future, in so far as it is future, is not; and
similarly the past in so far as it is of this sort. Therefore, the principle is the same in respect to the truth of
the past and of the future, and the same too in respect
to the truth of that which is not. From which fact the
eternity of no truth except the first truth can be concluded, as has been said in the body of the article.

To the eighth it must be said that the word of Augustine must either be understood that they are eternal
according as they are in the divine mind or else the word
eternal must be taken for perpetual.

To the ninth it must be said that although true discourse is formed concerning the thing which is and the
thing which is not, nevertheless, the thing which is and

the thing which is not are not related in the same way to truth, as is evident from what has been said in the solution to the second argument; from which is evident, further, the solution of the objection which is raised.

To the tenth it must be said that God knew from eternity many things capable of statement [*enuntiabilia*], but still he knew those many things by one cognition. Whence from eternity there was only one truth by which the divine cognition was true concerning many things future in time.

To the eleventh it must be said that, as is evident from what has been said above in the body of the article, the understanding is not adequated only to those things which are actually, but also to those which are not actually; particularly the divine understanding to which past and future are the same. Whence, although things were not from eternity in their own nature, nevertheless, the divine understanding was adequated to things, in their own nature, future in time, and for that reason it had true knowledge from eternity of things even in their own nature although the truths of the things were not from eternity.

To the twelfth it must be said that although the principle of truth is fulfilled in the understanding, still the principle of the thing is not fulfilled in the understanding. Whence, although it is conceded absolutely that the truth of all things was from eternity by the fact that it was in the divine understanding, still it can not be conceded absolutely that true things were from eternity by the fact that they were in the divine understanding.

To the thirteenth it must be said that that is understood of divine justice; or if it is understood of human justice, then it is said to be perpetual, as natural things are said to be perpetual, as we say that fire is always moved upward because of an inclination of nature unless it is impeded: and since, as Cicero says, in book II *on Rhetorical Invention*, virtue is a condition or habit [*habitus*] in a mode of nature, agreeing with reason: so far as it is of the nature of virtue, it has an unfailing inclination to its act although it is sometimes impeded; and therefore in the beginning of the *Digests*[19] too it is said that justice is *a constant and perpetual will to yield to each one his right.* And yet the truth concerning which we speak now is not a part of justice; but the truth which is in confessions to be made in judicial investigation is a part of justice.

To the fourteenth it must be said that Avicenna expounds in two ways that which is said, that the universal is perpetual and incorruptible: in one way to say that it is perpetual and incorruptible by reason of particular things which never began and will never cease according to those who believe in the eternity of the world; for generation is to the following end according to the Philosopher, that that which in the individual can not be preserved, be preserved perpetual in the species. In another way, to say that the universal is perpetual because it is not corrupted through itself but accidentally on the corruption of the individual.

To the fifteenth it must be said that something is attributed to anything through itself in two ways. In one way positively, as it is attributed to fire to be borne upward: and a thing is denominated more by such an attribution through itself than by that which it is accidentally; for, we say that fire is borne upward and that it is of those things which are borne upward rather than of those which are borne downward, although accidentally fire is sometimes borne downward, as is evident in heated iron. Sometimes an attribution is made through itself by reason of removal or denial,

[19] In the old *Digest*, book I, title I, law 10.

that is, by the fact that those things are removed from it which are formed to induce the contrary disposition. Whence, if some one of them should advene accidentally, that contrary disposition will be stated absolutely; as unity is attributed to first matter through itself, not through the imposition of some form of unity, but through the removal of diversifying forms. Therefore, when the forms distinguishing matter advene, we say absolutely that there are many matters rather than one. And so it is in what was stated above; for the universal is not said to be incorruptible as if it possesses some form of incorruption, but because the material dispositions which are the causes of corruption in individuals do not accord with it according to itself, and therefore the universal existing in things is said absolutely to be corrupted in this and in that.

To the sixteenth it must be said that although all other genera, in so far as they are of this sort, posit something in the nature of things, for quantity, from the very fact that it is quantity, states that something is; relation alone does not have, from the fact that it is a genus of this sort, the property of positing something in the nature of things, because it does not predicate something, but is relative to something. Whence, certain relations are found which posit nothing in the nature of things but only in reason; and this happens in four different ways as can be gathered from the sayings of the Philosopher and of Avicenna. In one way when something is referred to itself, as when we relate the same to the same. For if this relation were to posit in the nature of things something added to that which is called the same, there would be a regress *in infinitum* in relations, since that very relation through which any thing was said to be the same, would be the same with itself through another relation and thus *in infinitum*. In a second way, in the case when the relation itself is referred to something. For it can not be said that paternity is referred to its subject through another intermediate relation, since that intermediate relation too would need another intermediate relation and so *in infinitum*. Whence that relation which is signified in the comparison of paternity to its subject is not said to be in the nature of things but in reason only. In a third way, in the case when one of the relatives depends on the other and not conversely, as knowledge depends on the knowable and not conversely; whence the relation of knowledge to the knowable is something in the nature of things: the relation of the knowable to knowledge is not, but only in reason. In a fourth way, in the case when a thing which is, is compared with a thing which is not, as when we say that we are prior to things which will be after us; otherwise, it would follow that there could be infinite relations in the same thing, if the generation *in infinitum* should proceed into the future. From these two last, therefore, it appears that that relation of priority posits nothing in the nature of things but only in the understanding, as much because God does not depend on creatures as because such priority affirms a comparison of the thing which is to the thing which is not. Whence it would not follow from this that there is any other eternal truth besides that in the divine understanding which alone is eternal; and that is the first truth.

To the seventeenth it must be said that although God is prior in nature to all creatures, still it does not follow that that is a relation of nature, but that it is understood from a consideration of the nature of that which is called prior and of that which is called posterior; and so also the knowable is said to be prior in nature to knowledge, although the relation of knowable to knowledge is not in the nature of things.

To the eighteenth it must be said that when the statement is made: it is right that something be signified by a non-existent signification, it is true according to the ordination of things existing in the divine understanding, just as even while a chest does not exist, it is right for the chest to have a cover according to the ordination of the art in the artificer. Whence it can not be held from this fact that another truth besides the first truth is eternal.

To the nineteenth it must be said that the reason of the true is founded on that which is. Although, therefore, many persons or properties are posited in the divine, nevertheless, there is only one being posited there, because being is said to be in divine things only essentially: and there is of all the following statements, that the Father is or begets, that the Son is or was begotten, one truth in so far as they are referred to the thing, which is the first truth and eternal.

To the twentieth it must be said that although it is by one thing that the Father is the Father and the Son is the Son, because the former is by paternity and the latter by filiation, nevertheless, that by which the Father is and that by which the Son is, is the same, for each is by the divine essence which is one. The principle of truth, however, is not founded on the principle of paternity and filiation is so far as they are of this sort, but on the principle of entity; but paternity and filiation are one essence, and therefore, there is one truth of both.

To the twenty-first it must be said that the properties which this word, *man*, and this word, *risible*, predicate, are not the same by essence nor do they have one being, as is the case with paternity and filiation; and therefore it is not similar.

To the twenty-second it must be said that the divine understanding does not know, except by one cognition, things howsoever diverse, which nevertheless have in themselves diverse truths. Whence, all the more it does not know except by one cognition all things of this sort which are understood of persons. Whence, likewise, there is only one truth of all of them.

ARTICLE VI.

Whether created truth is immutable[20]

In the sixth place it is inquired whether created truth is immutable. And it seems that it is immutable. For Anselm, in the book *on Truth*, chapter XIV,[21] says: *I see that it has been proved by this argument that truth remains immobile*. But the reason advanced was concerning truth of signification, as is apparent from what has been said above in article 5. Therefore the truth of discourse is immutable and, for the same reason, the truth of the thing.

2. Moreover, if the truth of discourse is changed it is changed most of all with the change of the thing. But after the thing has been changed, the truth of the proposition remains. Therefore, the truth of discourse is immutable. Proof of the middle premiss. Truth according to Anselm, in the book *on Truth*, chapter VII,[22] is *a certain rightness in so far as it fulfills that for which it was formed in the divine mind*. But this proposition, Socrates sits, was formed in the divine mind to signify the sitting of Socrates, which it signifies even when Socrates is not sitting. Therefore, too, even while

[20] Cp. *Summa Theologica* I, q. 16, a. 1.
[21] See above, vol. I, p. 182.
[22] Cp. above, vol. I, p. 164.

Socrates is not sitting the truth remains in it, and thus the truth of the said proposition is not changed even if the thing is changed.

3. Moreover, if truth is changed, it can not be unless those things in which truth is, have changed, just as forms are not said to be changed unless their subjects have changed. But truth is not changed with the mutation of true things, since truth still remains after true things have been destroyed, as Augustine and Anselm, in the book *on Truth*, chapter X,[23] prove. Therefore, truth is absolutely immutable.

4. Moreover, the truth of the thing is the cause of the truth of the proposition; for from the fact that a thing is or is not, speech is said to be true or false. But the truth of the thing is immutable. Therefore, the truth of the proposition, too. Proof of the middle premiss. Anselm in the book *on Truth*, chapter XIII,[24] proves that the truth of discourse remains immobile as it fulfills that for which it was formed in the divine mind. But singly every thing fulfills that which it was formed in the divine mind to have. Therefore, the truth of every thing is immutable.

5. Moreover, that which remains after every mutation has been made, never changes; for in the alteration of colors we do not say that the surface is changed, because that remains in the thing whatever mutation of the colors is made. But truth remains in the thing whatever mutation of the thing is made, because that which is and the true are convertible. Therefore, truth is immutable.

6. Moreover, when the cause is the same, the effect also is the same. But the cause of the truth of the following three propositions, Socrates sits, Socrates will

[23] See above, vol. I, pp. 170-171.
[24] Cp. above, vol. I, p. 183.

sit, Socrates sat, is the same, namely, the sitting of
Socrates. Therefore, the truth is the same. But if one
of the three aforesaid propositions is true, one of the
other two must in the same way be true; in fact, if it
is ever true that Socrates sits, it always was true and
always will be true either that Socrates sat or that he
will sit. Therefore, the truth of one of the three propositions always maintains itself in one manner, and so it
is immutable and the same reason applies to every other
truth.

But to the contrary, when causes have been
changed the effects are changed. But the things which
are the cause of the truth of a proposition are changed.
Therefore, the truth of propositions is changed too.

I reply that it must be said that something is said to
be changed in two ways. In one way because it is the
subject of mutation, as we say that body is mutable;
and no form is mutable in this way, and so it is said
that form is the remaining in invariable essence; wherefore, since truth is signified by the way of form, the
present question is not whether truth is immutable in
this manner. A thing is said to be changed in another
way in that the mutation is made according to it, as we
say that whiteness is changed because the body is altered
according to whiteness, and in this sense it is inquired
concerning truth whether it is mutable.

As evidence of this, it must be known that that according to which mutation takes place is sometimes said
to be changed and sometimes not. For when it is inherent in that which is changed according to it, then it
too is said to be changed, as whiteness or quantity are
said to be changed when something is changed according to them, in that they themselves succeed to themselves in the subject according to this mutation. When,

however, that according to which something is said to be changed is extrinsic, then it is not changed in that mutation, [but perseveres immobile, just as place is not said to be moved] when something is moved with respect to place. Wherefore in the IVth book of the *Physics* it is said that place is the immutable bound [*terminus*] of that containing, in that, by local motion it is not meant that there is a succession of places in one thing which is in place, but rather a succession of things placed in one place. There is, however, a double mode of mutation of inherent forms which are said to change with the change of the subject: for in one way general forms are said to be changed and in another, special forms. For the special form does not remain the same after mutation either according to being or according to reason, as whiteness, once the alteration is made, remains in no manner. But the general form remains the same according to reason after the mutation has been made, but not according to being, as when the mutation has been made from white to black the color remains the same according to the common reason of color, but it is not the same species of color. It has been said above, however, in the preceding article, that some thing is denominated true by the first truth as by an extrinsic measure, but by the inhering truth as by an intrinsic measure. Wherefore, created things are varied in the participation of the first truth, but the first truth itself according to which they are called true, is changed in no manner, and this is what Augustine says in the book *on the Free Will*, part II, chapter VIII not far from the beginning:[25] *Our minds sometimes see more, sometimes less of the truth itself, but it, enduring in itself, neither advances nor declines.* If, however, we take

[25] Cp. above vol. I, p. 35.

truth as inhering in things, then, truth is said to be
changed as some things are changed in respect to truth.
Therefore, as was said above in article 2 of this question, truth is found in creatures in two ways: in the
things themselves and in the understanding; for truth
of action is comprehended under the truth of the thing,
as truth of discourse is comprehended under the truth
of understanding which it signifies. But a thing is said
to be true by comparison to the divine and the human
understanding.

If, therefore, the truth of a thing is taken in its order
to the divine understanding, then the truth of a mutable
thing is changed into another truth, not into falsity. For
truth is most of all a general form, since the true and
the thing which is are converted: therefore, just as the
thing remains that which is, after any mutation whatsoever has been made, even though it be according to some
other form by which it has being, so it always remains
true, but by another truth, because whatsoever form or
even privation it acquires by mutation, it is conformed
according to it to the divine understanding, which knows
it as it is according to any disposition whatsoever. If,
however, the truth of a thing were considered in its
order to the human understanding or conversely, then
mutation is sometimes made from truth to falsity, and
sometimes from one truth to another. For, since truth
is the adequation of thing and understanding, if equals
be removed from equals, equals still remain, although
not in the same quantity. In the same way it is necessary that when the understanding and the thing are
changed, truth remain, though another truth, as, if Socrates be understood to be seated when Socrates is sitting,
and then later when he is not sitting he be understood
not to sit. But since, if something be removed from one

of the equals and nothing from the other or if unequals
be removed from both, it is necessary that inequality
appear which is related to falsity as equality is to
truth, therefore it is that, if the thing is changed while
the understanding still exists, but understanding is not
changed, or conversely, or both are changed but not
similarly, falsity appears; and so there will be a mutation from truth to falsity, as, if Socrates is understood
to be white while he exists white, the understanding is
true; but if later Socrates is understood to be black,
while he remains white, or if conversely when Socrates
is changed to blackness, he is still understood to be
white, or when he has been changed to pallor he is understood to be ruddy, there will be falsity in the understanding. And thus appears how truth is changed and
how it is not changed.

To the first, therefore, it must be said that Anselm
speaks of truth as all things are said to be true according
to it as by an extrinsic measure.

To the second it must be said that since the understanding is bent inward upon itself and understands
itself as it understands other things, as is said in the
IIIrd book *on the Soul*, therefore, those things which
pertain to the understanding according as it regards the
reason of truth, can be considered in two ways. In one
way as they are certain things and thus truth is predicated of them in the same way as of other things, so that,
just as a thing is said to be true because it fulfills that
for which it was formed in the divine understanding by
retaining its nature, so discourse is said to be true by
retaining its own nature which was dispensed to it in the
divine mind; nor can that be removed from it, while the
discourse itself remains. In another manner, as they

are compared to the things understood, and so a state-ment is called true when it is adequated to the thing, and such a truth of thing is changed, as has been said in the body of the article.

To the third it must be said that the truth which re-mains after the true things have been destroyed is the first truth, which is not changed even when the things have been changed.

To the fourth it must be said that, while the thing continues, no change can be made about it in regard to those things which belong to it essentially, just as it is essential to a statement that it signify that which it was instituted to signify. Wherefore, it does not follow that the truth of the thing is in no way mutable, but that it is immutable as regards things essential to the thing, so long as the thing continues. In those things, however, in which mutation of the thing occurs through corruption with respect to accidents, mutation can occur while the thing still remains, and so with respect to the accidentals, mutation of the truth of the thing can be made.

To the fifth it must be said that after all mutation has been made, truth remains, but not the same truth, as is evident from what has been said above in the body of the article.

To the sixth it must be said that the identity of truth depends not only on the identity of the thing but also on the identity of the understanding, as the identity of the effect depends on the identity of agent and patient. Although that which is signified in these three proposi-tions is the same thing, nevertheless the understanding of the propositions is not the same, because time is added in the composition of the understanding: there-fore, according to the variation of time there are differ-ent understandings.

ARTICLE VII.

Whether truth is predicated in divine things personally or essentially

In the seventh place it is inquired whether truth in divine things is predicated essentially or personally. And it seems that it is predicated personally. For whatever introduces in divine things the relation of principle, is spoken of personally. But truth is of this sort, as is evident in Augustine in the book *on True Religion*, chapter 36, where he says that divine truth is the supreme likeness of the principle without any unlikeness from which falsity arises. Therefore, truth is spoken of personally in divine things.

2. Moreover, as nothing is like to itself, so nothing is equal to itself. But likeness in divine things imports a distinction of persons, according to Hilary, *on Synods*, paragraph 72, from the fact that nothing is like to itself. Therefore, for the same reason the same is true of equality. But truth is a certain equality. Therefore, it imports a personal distinction in divine things.

3. Moreover, all that which in divine things imports an emanation is spoken of personally. But truth imports a certain emanation because it signifies a conception of the understanding, as does the Word. Therefore, just as the Word is spoken of personally, so too truth.

BUT TO THE CONTRARY *there is one truth of the three persons*, as Augustine says in book VIII *on the Trinity*, chapter 1. Therefore, it is essential and not personal.

I REPLY that it must be said that truth in divine things can be taken in two ways: in one way properly, in the other way as if metaphorically. For if truth be taken

properly, then it will import an equality of the divine
understanding and the thing. And since the divine understanding understands first the thing which is its
essence, through which it understands all other things, so
too truth in God imports principally the equality of the
divine understanding and the thing which is its essence,
and consequently the equality of the divine understanding to created things. However, the divine understanding and its essence are not adequated as that which
measures to that which is measured, since one is not the
principle [*principium*] of the other, but they are absolutely the same: therefore, the truth resulting from such
an equality introduces no relation of principle, whether
it be taken from the part of the essence or from the part
of the understanding, which are one and the same there;
for as that which understands and the thing understood
are there the same, so too, the truth of the thing and of
the understanding are there the same, without any connotation of principle. But if the truth of the divine
understanding be taken as it is adequated to created
things, truth will remain the same to the extent that
God understands himself and others through the same
thing, but still in the understanding of the truth there
is added the relation of principle to creatures to which
the divine understanding is compared as measure and
cause. But every name, which does not import in divine things the relation of principle or what is from
a principle, or else imports also the relation of principle
to creatures, is spoken of essentially. Wherefore, if
in divine things truth be taken properly, it is spoken of
essentially; nevertheless truth is appropriated to the
person of the Son, just as art and the rest which pertain
to the understanding. Truth, however, is taken metaphorically or by likeness in divine things, when we take
it there according to that relation in which it is found in

created things, in which truth is spoken of in that the
created thing imitates its principle, namely, the [divine]
understanding. Wherefore, similarly, truth is predicated
in divine things in this way as the supreme imitation
of the principle which is proper to the Son, and according to this acceptance of truth, truth is properly
referred to the Son and referred to him personally, and
Augustine speaks thus in the book *on True Religion*, as
quoted above.

And thus the reply to the first is evident.

To the second it must be said that equality in divine
things sometimes imports the relation which designates
a personal distinction, as when we say that the Father
and the Son are equal, and according to that a real distinction is understood in the word equality. Sometimes,
however, a real distinction is not understood in the
word equality but only a distinction of reason, as when
we say that the divine wisdom and goodness are equal.
Whence, it is not necessary that it import a personal
distinction; and such is the distinction imported by the
word truth, since it is an equality of understanding and
essence.

To the third it must be said that although truth is
conceived by the understanding, nevertheless, the principle of conception is not expressed by the name of
truth as it is by the name of the Word: therefore, they
are not similar.

ARTICLE VIII.

Whether all truth is from the first truth

In the eighth place it is inquired whether all truth
is from the first truth. And it seems that that is not

the case. For it is true that this person committed fornication, but that is not, nevertheless, from the first truth. Therefore, not all truth is from the first truth.

2. But it was said that the truth of sign or of understanding according to which this true is said to be true is from God, but not the truth of sign or of understanding according to which this is referred to the thing.—But to the contrary, besides the first truth there is not only the truth of sign or of understanding, but also the truth of thing. If, therefore, this true is not from God in so far as it is referred to the thing, this truth of the thing will not be from God, and thus the proposition is advanced that not every other truth is from God.

3. Moreover, in order that the descent be made from the truth of proposition to the truth of the saying which expresses the truth of the thing, it follows: this person committed fornication, therefore it is true that he committed fornication. Therefore, the truth aforesaid consists in the fact that that act is joined to this subject. But the truth of the saying would not be from the composition of such an act with that subject, if the composition of the act were not understood under the deformity of the existing thing. Therefore, the truth of the thing is not only to the measure of the very essence of the act but to the measure of the deformity. But the act considered under its deformity is in no way from God. Therefore, not all truth of the thing is from God.

4. Moreover, Anselm, in the book *on Truth*, chapter 8,[26] says that a thing is said to be true when it is as it should be; and among the manners in which it can be said that a thing should be, he posits one manner according to which it is said that a thing should be, because, God permitting, it takes place. But the permission of God is extended even to the deformity of actuality.

[26] See above, vol. I, pp. 164-165.

Therefore, the truth of the thing pertains to that deformity. But that deformity is in no manner from God. Therefore, not all truth is from God.

5. But it was said that just as deformity or any privation whatsoever is said to be a thing which is not absolutely but in some one respect [*secundum quid*], so too it is said that truth holds not absolutely but in some one respect, and such truth in some one respect is not from God.—But, to the contrary, the true adds, over the thing that is, an order to the understanding. But although privation or deformity in itself is not absolutely the thing that is, nevertheless it is apprehended absolutely by the understanding. Therefore, although it does not have entity absolutely, it nevertheless has truth absolutely.

6. Moreover, everything relative to something [*secundum quid*] is reduced to that which is absolutely, as this statement, *The ethiopian is white with respect to tooth*, is reduced to this statement, *The tooth of the ethiopian is white*. If, therefore, some truth relative to something is not from God, then all truth absolutely will not be from God; which is absurd.

7. Moreover, that which is not the cause of the cause is not the cause of the effect, as God is not the cause of the deformity of sin, because he is not the cause of the defect in the free will from which the deformity of sin arises. But, as being is the cause of the truth of affirmative propositions, so non-being is the cause of the truth of negative propositions. Since, therefore, God is not the cause of that which is non-being, as Augustine says in the book of *LXXXIII Questions*, question 21 toward the middle, it remains that God is not the cause of negative propositions, and so not all truth is from God.

8. Moreover, Augustine says in the book of *Solilo-*

quies, part II, chapter 5, that the true is that which is constituted as it seems. But some evil is constituted as it seems. Therefore some evil is true. But no evil is from God. Therefore, not all that is true is from God.

9. But it was said that evil is not seen through the species of evil but through the species of good. But on the contrary, the species of good never makes apparent anything but the good. Therefore, if evil is not seen save through the species of good, then evil never appears save as good; which is false.

BUT TO THE CONTRARY concerning the statement in *I Corinthians* 12[27] on this question, *No man can say that Jesus is the Lord, but by the Holy Spirit,* Ambrose says, *Every truth by whomsoever pronounced is from the Holy Spirit.*

Moreover, all created goodness is from the uncreated goodness, which is God. Therefore, for the same reason, all truth is from the first truth, which is God.

Moreover, the reason of truth is completed in the understanding. But all understanding is from God. Therefore, all truth is from God.

Moreover, Augustine in the book of *Soliloquies* part II, chapter 5, says that the true is that which is. But all being is from God. Therefore, all truth.

Moreover, as *one* is converted with *that which is,* so too is *true.* But all unity is from the first unity. Therefore, all truth too is from the first truth.

I REPLY that it must be said that in created things truth is found in things and in understanding, as is evident from what has been said: in the understanding as it is adequated to the things of which it has knowledge; but in things as they imitate the divine understanding which is their measure, as art is the measure

[27] Vers. 3.

of all things made by art; and in another way as they are formed to make a true apprehension of themselves in the human understanding, which is measured by things, as is pointed out in book X of the *Metaphysics*. The thing, however, existing without the soul, imitates by its form the art of the divine understanding, and it is formed to make a true apprehension of itself in the human understanding by that same form by which, likewise, each thing has its being; wherefore, the truth of existing things includes in its principle [*ratio*] their entity and superadds the relation [*habitudo*] of adequation to the human or divine understanding. But negations or privations existing outside the soul do not have any form by which they might either imitate the exemplar of the divine art or bring forth a notion of themselves in the human understanding; but that they are adequated to the understanding is from the part of the understanding which apprehends their reasons. Thus, therefore, it is evident that when one speaks of a true stone and true blindness, truth is not related to the two in the same manner. For truth predicated of the stone includes in its principle the entity of the stone and superadds the relation to the understanding which is caused, likewise, from the part of the thing itself, since it has something according to which it can be referred; but the truth predicated of blindness does not include in itself the privation which is blindness, but only the relation of blindness to the understanding, which does not have something likewise from the part of blindness itself in which it is sustained, since blindness is not adequated to the understanding from the part of anything which it has in itself.

It is evident, therefore, that the truth found in created things can comprehend nothing other than the entity of the thing and the adequation to the understanding, or

the adequation of the understanding to things or the
privations of things; each of which is from God, because
both the form itself of the thing by which it is adequated
is from God and the true thing itself as well as the good
of the understanding, as is pointed out in the VIth book
of the *Ethics*, chapter 6, and book X, chapter 4 about
the middle, that the good of each thing consists in its
own perfect operation. The perfect operation of the
understanding, however, is only as it knows the true;
wherefore, its good consists in this, in so far as it knows
in this manner. Wherefore, since all good is from God
and all form, it is also absolutely necessary to say that
all truth is from God.

To the first, therefore, it must be said, that when it is
argued thus: Every true thing is from God; it is true
that this person has fornicated; the fallacy of accident
occurs, as can be seen from what has already been said
in the body of the article. For when we say that to
fornicate is true, we do not say it as if the defect implicated in the act of fornication were included in the
reason of truth; but true predicates only the adequation
of it to the understanding. Wherefore, it must not be
concluded: That this person commits fornication is from
God; but that the truth of it is from God.

To the second it must be said that deformities and
other defects do not have truth as other things do, as is
evident from what has been said, and therefore, although the truth of defects is from God, it can not be
concluded from that that the defects are from God.

To the third it must be said that according to the
Philosopher in the VIth book of the *Metaphysics*, truth
does not consist in the composition which is in things
but in the composition which the soul makes; and therefore truth does not consist in the fact that this act with

its deformity inheres in the subject; for that pertains to the principle [*ratio*] of good and evil; but in the fact that the act adhering thus in the subject is adequated to the apprehension of the soul.

To the fourth it must be said that good, due, right, and all notions of this sort are in one way related to the divine permission and in another way to other signs of the divine will. For in the other signs of the divine will good is referred both to that which falls under the act of the will and to the very act of the will, as when God enjoins honor of parents, and that very honor of parents is itself something good. But in permission it is referred only to the act of the one permitting and not to that which falls under the permission: therefore, it is good that God permit a deformity to occur, but it does not follow from that, that the deformity itself has any other rightness.

And the solution to the fifth is apparent from this.

To the sixth it must be said that truth which corresponds to negations and defects is reduced to truth absolutely, which is in the understanding, which is from God; and therefore the truth of defects is from God, although the defects themselves are not from God.

To the seventh it must be said that non-being is not the cause of the truth of negative propositions, in the sense of making them in the understanding; but the soul itself does this, conforming itself to non-being which is outside the soul: therefore, non-being existing outside the soul is not the efficient cause of truth, but, as it were, the exemplary cause. The objection, however, proceeded from the efficient cause.

To the eighth it must be said that although evil is not from God, nevertheless, the fact that evil is judged as it is, is from God: wherefore, the truth by which it is true that evil is, is from God.

To the ninth it must be said that although evil does not act upon the soul except by the species of the good; nevertheless, because it lacks good, the soul seizes in it upon the principle of the defect, and in that it conceives the principle of evil; and thus evil seems evil.

ARTICLE IX.

Whether truth is in sense[28]

In the ninth place it is inquired whether truth is in sense, and it seems that it is not. For Anselm says in the book *on Truth*, chapter 11,[29] that *truth is rightness perceptible to the mind alone.* But sense is not of the nature of the mind. Therefore, truth is not in the sense.

2. Moreover, Augustine in the book of *LXXXIII Questions*, question 5, proves that the truth of the body is not known by the senses; and the reasons for it are stated above. Therefore, truth is not in sense.

To THE CONTRARY, Augustine, *on True Religion*, chapter 36, says that truth is that by which that which is, is shown. But that which is, is shown not only to the understanding but also to the sense. Therefore, truth is not only in the understanding, but also in sense.

I REPLY that it must be said that truth is in understanding and in sense, although not in the same way. For in the understanding, it is as consequent to the act of the understanding and as known by the understanding; for it is consequent to the operation of the understanding, as the judgment of the understanding is of the thing according to which it is; but it is known by the understanding as the understanding reflects upon its

---

[28] Cp. *Summa Theologica* II, q. 16, a. 2.
[29] See above, vol. I, p. 172.

act, not only as it knows its act, but as it knows the relation of it to the thing. This it can not know except by knowing the nature of the act itself, which cannot be known unless the nature of the active principle, which is the understanding itself, in whose nature it is to be conformed to things, is known; wherefore, the understanding knows truth according to this, that it reflects upon itself. But truth is in sense as a consequent to its act; namely, when the judgment of sense is concerning the thing as it is; but nevertheless it is not in sense as known by sense: for if the sense judges truly concerning things, it still does not know the truth by which it judges truly; for although sense knows that it perceives, it still does not know its nature and, consequently, does not know the nature of its act nor the relation of it to the thing and, therefore, does not know its truth. The reason for this is that those things which are most perfect in the things which are, such as intellectual substances, return to their essence with a complete return: for in the fact that they know something placed outside themselves, they proceed in a certain fashion outside themselves, but as they know that they know, they begin, then, to return to themselves, because the act of cognition is medium between the knower and the known. But this return is completed as they know their own essences; wherefore, it is said in the book *on Causes*, proposition XV, that each thing knowing its essence returns to its essence with a complete return. But sense, which of all other things is the nearest to intellectual substance, begins to return to its essence not only because it knows the sensible but also because it knows itself perceiving. However, its return is not completed, because the sense does not know its own essence. Avicenna assigns this reason for it, that sense knows nothing except by a corporeal organ. But it is not possible that an organ fall medium between a sensitive power and itself. But the natural insensible powers in no way return upon themselves because they do not know themselves, as fire does not know itself heating.

From these things, therefore, the solution to the objections is evident.

ARTICLE X.

Whether any thing is false[30]

In the tenth place it is inquired whether any thing is false, and it seems that no thing is. Because according to Augustine in the book of *Soliloquies*, part II, chapter 5, the true is that which is. Therefore, the false is that which is not. But that which is not, is not any thing. Therefore, no thing is false.

2. But it was said that the true is the differentia of the thing which is, and therefore, as the true is that which is, so also is the false.—But, on the contrary, no differentia which is divisive is converted with that of which it is the differentia. But the true is converted with that which is, as has been said. Therefore, the true is not a differentia divisive of the thing which is, so that some false thing can be spoken of.

3. Moreover, truth is the adequation of thing and understanding. But every thing is adequated to the divine understanding, because nothing can be in itself otherwise than the divine understanding knows it. Therefore, every thing is true: therefore, no thing is false.

4. Moreover, every thing has truth from its form; for a man is called true by the fact that he has the true form of man. But no thing is, which does not have

[30] Cp. *Summa Theologica* I, q. 17, a. 1.

some form, because all being is by form. Therefore, every thing whatsoever is true: therefore, no thing is false.

5. Moreover, as good and evil are constituted, so too are true and false. But because evil is found in things, evil is not substantified except in good, as Dionysius[31] and Augustine say. Therefore, if falsity is found in things, falsity is not substantified except in the true; this does not seem to be possible since in that case true and false would be the same, which is impossible, just as man and white are the same, because whiteness is substantified in man.

6. Moreover, Augustine in the book of *Soliloquies*, book II, chapter 1, raises the following objection: If some thing is called false, it is either by that which is like or by that which is unlike. If by that which is unlike, there is nothing which can not be called false, for there is nothing which is not unlike something. If by that which is like, all things protest that they are true by that to which they are like. Therefore, in no manner can falsity be found in things.

1. BUT TO THE CONTRARY, Augustine, in the *Soliloquies*, book II, chapter 15, toward the middle, defines the false thus: the false is *that which is accommodated to the likeness of any thing and does not pertain to that whose likeness it bears.* But every creature bears the likeness of God. Since, therefore, no creature pertains to God himself by the mode of identity, it seems that every creature is false.

2. Moreover, Augustine says *on True Religion*, chapter 34, a little after the beginning: *Every body is true body and false unity.* But this is said so far as it imitates unity and is, nevertheless, not unity. Since, therefore, every creature whatsoever, by each of his perfections,

[31].*On Divine Names*, chapter 6.

imitates the divine perfection and is none the less infinitely removed from it, it seems that every creature is false.

3. Moreover, just as true is converted with that which is, so too is good. But from the fact that good is converted with that which is, there is nothing to prevent some thing being found evil. Therefore, from the fact that true is converted with that which is there is nothing to prevent some thing being found false.

4. Again, Anselm, *on Truth*, chapter 2,[32] says that the truth of a proposition is of two sorts: one, when it signifies what it has undertaken to signify, as this proposition, Socrates sits, signifies that Socrates sits whether Socrates sits or does not sit; the other, when it signifies that for which it was made, for it was made in order to signify a thing is, when it is; and according to this, a statement is properly called true. Therefore, for the same reason, any thing will be called true when it fulfills that for which it is, and false when it does not fulfill it. But each thing which falls short of its end, does not fulfill that because of which it is. Since, therefore, there are many such things, it seems that many things are false.

I REPLY it must be said that, as truth consists in the adequation of thing and understanding, so falsity consists in their inequality. The thing, however, is compared to the divine and to the human understanding, as was said above in articles 5 and 8 of this question; but it is compared to the divine understanding as a thing measured to its measure, in respect to those things which are spoken of or found in things positively, because all things of this sort arise from the art of the divine understanding; in another way, as the known to the knower,

[32] See above, vol. I, pp. 153-156.

and so negations and defects are adequated to the divine
understanding, because God knows all things of this sort
although he does not cause them. It is evident, therefore, that the thing existing by either privation or defect,
so far as it is constituted under any form whatever, is
adequated to the divine understanding. And so, it is
evident that any thing whatever, in comparison to the
divine understanding, is true, as Anselm says in the book
on Truth, chapter 7:[33] *Therefore, truth is in all things*
which are beings, because they are in that respect, what
they are in the supreme truth. Wherefore, by comparison to the divine understanding, no thing can be false
but, by comparison to the human understanding, an inequality of the thing to the understanding is now and
then found which is caused in a measure by the thing
itself; for the thing causes a notion of itself in the soul
by those things which appear concerning it outside the
soul, because our knowledge takes its beginning from
sense, of which the sensible qualities are themselves the
object, wherefore, too, in the Ist book *on the Soul* it is
said that accidents contribute a large part to learning
essence [*quod quid est*], and therefore, when sensible
qualities appear in any thing, indicating a nature which
does not underlie them, that thing is said to be false;
wherefore, the philosopher says in the VIth book of the
Metaphysics that those things are said to be false which
are formed to seem either such as they are not or what
they are not, as false gold, in which the color of gold
appears on the outside and other accidents of that sort,
when nevertheless the nature of gold does not underlie
the accidents within. However, a thing is not in such
wise the cause of falsity in the soul that it causes falsity
necessarily, because truth and falsity clearly exist in the
judgment of the soul, but the soul, in so far as it judges

[33] Cp. above, vol. I, p. 164.

of things, does not suffer from things, but in a certain
wise acts. Wherefore, a thing is not said to be false
because it always causes a false apprehension of itself,
but because it was formed to cause the apprehension
through those things which appear concerning it. But
since, as has been said in this article and in articles 5
and 8, the comparison of the thing to the divine understanding is essential, it is said to be true in itself
according to that; but the comparison to the human understanding is accidental, and according to it, it is not
called true absolutely: therefore, speaking absolutely,
every thing is true and no thing is false; but in some
one respect [*secundum quid*], namely, in their order to
our understanding, some things are called false; and
therefore, it is necessary to reply according to the
principles of both parts.

To the first, therefore, it must be said that the following definition, *the true is that which is*, does not express
the principle [*ratio*] of truth perfectly, but only, as it
were, materially, except as it signifies that the affirmation of the proposition is; namely, that it be said that
that is true which is said or understood to be as it is
in the thing; and so likewise, that is said to be false
which is not, namely, that which is not as it is said or
understood to be; and this can be found in things.

To the second it must be said that the true, properly
speaking, can not be the differentia of that which is; for
that which is does not have any differentia, as is proved
in the IIIrd book of the *Metaphysics*; but anything true
is related to that which is by the mode of differentia, as
is also any good, in so far, that is, as it expresses something concerning that which is, which is not expressed
by the name of that which is; and, according to this,
the intention of that which is is undetermined with

respect to the intention of the true; and so, the intention of the true is related to the intention of that which is, in a certain way, as differentia to genus.

To the third it must be said that that reasoning must be conceded, for it proceeds from the thing in its order to the divine understanding.

To the fourth it must be said that although any thing whatsoever has some form, nevertheless, not every thing has that form the judgments of which are shown externally by sensible qualities; and it is called false for that reason, in so far as it is found apt to cause a false estimation of itself.

To the fifth it must be said that something existing outside the soul is to that extent called false, as is evident from what was said in the body of the article, because it is formed to cause a false estimation of itself, when it moves the cognitive power; wherefore it is necessary that that which is said to be false, be something that is. Wherefore, since each thing which is is true, in so far as it is a thing which is, it is necessary that falsity existing in things be founded on truth; for this reason Augustine says in the book of *Soliloquies*, chapter 10 a little from the beginning, that the tragedian who represents true persons in the theatre would not be false if he were not a true tragedian; in the same way, a painted horse would not be a false horse, if it were not pure picture. It does not follow, however, that the contradictory is true, because the affirmation and negation, in the respect in which they assert the true and the false, are not referred to the same thing.

To the sixth it must be said that a thing is said to be false according as it is formed to deceive; when I say *deceive*, however, I mean a certain action inducing defect. Nothing, however, is formed to act except as it is

being; but all defect is non-being. Yet each thing so far
as it is that which is, has a likeness to the true; so far
as it is not, however, it recedes from likeness to it. And
accordingly, that which I say *deceives*, in the respect
that it derives from action, has its origin from likeness;
but with respect to the fact that it imports a defect (in
which the principle of falsity consists formally) it
arises from unlikeness; and, therefore, Augustine says
in the book *on True Religion* and book II of the *Soliloquies*, chapter 15 toward the middle, that falsity arises
from unlikeness.

To the first, therefore, of the objections which are
raised to the contrary, it must be said that the mind is
not formed to be deceived by any likeness whatsoever,
but by a great likeness in which an unlikeness can not
easily be found; and therefore, the mind is deceived by
a greater or a lesser likeness as it has greater or lesser
perspicacity for finding the principle of likeness and unlikeness. Nevertheless, it should not be stated absolutely
that some thing is false by the fact that it leads into
error, howsoever great the error may be, but by the fact
that it is formed to deceive many men or wise men. But
although creatures bear in themselves some likeness to
God, nevertheless, an extremely great unlikeness underlies that, so that it happens only from great stupidity
that the mind is deceived by such likeness. Wherefore, from the aforesaid likeness and unlikeness of creatures to God, it does not follow that all creatures should
be said to be false.

To the second it must be said that certain persons
have judged God to be body; and since God is the unity
by which all things are one, they have, consequently,
reckoned body to be that very unity because of that
likeness of unity. Body is called a false unity, then,

in so far as it has led or could lead some into the error that it be thought unity.

To the third it must be said that perfection is of two sorts, namely, first and second. First perfection is the form of each thing through which it has being; therefore, no thing is without that perfection while it still endures; the second perfection is the operation which is the end of the thing or that because of which it arrives at the end; and now and again, a thing may lack this perfection. The principle of the true in things results from the first perfection; for from the fact that a thing has form, it imitates the art of the divine understanding and it produces a notion of itself in the soul. But there results from the second, in the thing itself, the principle of goodness, which arises from the end; and therefore, evil absolutely is found in things, but false is not.

To the fourth it must be said that according to the Philosopher in the IIIrd book of the *Ethics* and the VIth book of the *Metaphysics*, the first truth is the good of the understanding; for the operation of the understanding is perfect in so far as its conception is true; and since discourse is the sign of the understanding, therefore, truth is its end. However, it is not thus in other things, and because of this it is not similar.

Article XI.

Whether falsity is in sense[34]

In the eleventh place it is inquired whether falsity is in sense, and it seems that it is not. For the understanding is always right, as is pointed out in the IIIrd book *on the Soul*. But the understanding is the superior part in man. Therefore, other parts of man too fol-

[34] Cp. *Summa Theologica* I. q. 17. a. 2.

low rightness, as in the larger world too the inferior motions are disposed according to the superior motion. Therefore, sense too which is the inferior part of the soul, will always be right: therefore, falsity will not be in it.

2. Moreover, Augustine says in the book *on True Religion*, chapter 36 in a digression toward the end, and chapter 33 about the middle: *The eyes themselves do not deceive us, for they are able to report to us absolutely nothing except their own affection. But if the senses of the body report all things as they have been affected, I do not know what more we should require of them.* Therefore, falsity is not in the senses.

3. Moreover, Anselm, in the book *on Truth*, chapter 6,[35] says: *It seems to me that truth or falsity is not in sense but in opinion*; and so you have what was stated.

BUT TO THE CONTRARY, there is what Anselm says in the book *on Truth*, chapter 6:[36] *Truth is in our senses, but not absolutely, for things sometimes deceive.*

Moreover, according to Augustine in the book of *Soliloquies*, chapter 15 in the middle, that is ordinarily called false which is removed far from verisimilitude, but has still some imitation of the truth. But the senses have a certain likeness of some things which are not thus in the nature of things, as sometimes one seems two, as when the eye is pressed. Therefore, falsity is in sense.

But it was said that sense is not deceived in proper sensibles but only concerning common sensibles.—But to the contrary, whenever something is apprehended of a thing otherwise than it is, the apprehension is false. But when a white body is seen through the medium of a green glass, the sense apprehends it otherwise than it

[35] See above, vol. I, p. 161.
[36] See above, vol. I, p. 160.

is, because it apprehends it as green and judges it so,
unless a prior judgment be present by which the falsity
is revealed. Therefore, sense is deceived even in proper
sensibles.

I REPLY that it must be said that our knowledge, which
takes its beginning from things, proceeds in the following order, first it begins in sense, second it is perfected
in understanding; so that sense is found in a certain
manner medium between understanding and thing; for
it is compared to things, as the understanding is, and
it is compared to the understanding, as some things are;
and therefore, truth or falsity may be said to be in sense
in two ways. In one way according to the order of
sense to the understanding, and in that way sense is
said to be false or true as things are, in so far, namely,
as they make a true or false estimation in the understanding. In another manner, according to the order of
sense to the thing, and so truth or falsity is said to be
in sense, as in the understanding, in so far, namely, as it
judges that that which is, is, or that that which is not,
is not. If, therefore, we speak of sense according to
the first way, then, in a certain manner, falsity is in
sense and in a certain manner falsity is not in it: for
sense is both a certain thing in itself and it is also indicative of some other thing. If, therefore, it is compared
to understanding as any thing is, then falsity is in no
wise in sense compared to the understanding, because as
sense is disposed, so it shows its disposition to the understanding; wherefore Augustine says, in the authority
quoted in argument 2 of this question, that it is able to
report absolutely nothing except its own affection. If,
however, it is compared to the understanding as it is
representative of another thing; since it sometimes represents the thing to the understanding otherwise than it is,

sense is called false in so far as it is formed to make
a false judgment in the understanding, although it does
not do it necessarily, as has been said also of things;
because as the understanding judges of things, so too it
judges of these presentations which are offered by the
senses. So, therefore, sense compared to understanding
always makes a true estimation of its own disposition in
the understanding, but not of the disposition of things.
If, however, sense be considered as it is compared to
things, then there are truth and falsity in sense in the
manner in which they are in the understanding. However, truth and falsity are found in the understanding
first and principally in the judgment of one who compounds and divides; but it is found in the formation of
the quiddities only by their order to the judgment which
follows from the above mentioned formation. Wherefore,
truth and falsity are spoken of properly in sense in the
respect that it judges of sensible things; but there is
no truth or falsity properly there in the respect that it
apprehends the sensible, but only according to the order
to the judgment which follows from the aforementioned
formation, as, namely, such a judgment is formed to
follow from such an apprehension. The judgment of
the sense, however, concerning certain things is natural,
as, concerning proper sensibles; concerning other things,
however, it is, as it were, by a kind of comparison
which the cogitative faculty in man (which is a power
of the sensitive part) makes, in the place of which
there is in other animals a natural estimation, and
so the sensitive faculty judges of common sensibles
and of accidental sensibles. The natural act of any
thing, however, is always in one mode, unless it is
impeded by accident, whether because of an intrinsic
defect or because of an extrinsic impediment; wherefore

the judgment of sense concerning proper sensibles is
always true, unless there be an impediment in the organ
or in the medium; but in common sensibles and accidental sensibles the judgment of the sense is now and
again deceived. And thus it is evident how there can
be falsity in the judgment of sense.

But concerning the apprehension of sense it must be
known that there is a certain apprehensive faculty which
apprehends the sensible species when the sensible thing
is present, as sense proper; and there is a certain faculty
which apprehends it when the thing is absent, as the
imagination; and therefore, sense always apprehends
the thing as it is, unless there is an impediment in the
organ or in the medium; but imagination apprehends the
thing mostly as it is not, because it apprehends it as
present when it is absent; and therefore the Philosopher
says in the IVth book of the *Metaphysics* that sense is
not the master of falsity, but fantasy is.

To the first, therefore, it must be said that in the
larger world superior motions take nothing from inferior but contrariwise. But in man understanding
which is superior receives something from sense, and
therefore it is not similar.

To the others the solution appears easily from what
has been said in the body of the article.

Article XII.

Whether falsity is in the understanding[37]

In the twelfth place it is inquired whether falsity is
in the understanding; and it seems that it is not. Be-

[37] Cp. *Summa Theologica* I, q. 17, a. 3.

cause the understanding has two operations: namely, one by which it forms quiddities in which there is no false, as the Philosopher says in the IIIrd book *on the Soul*; another by which it compounds and divides, and in that there is likewise no false, as is shown by Augustine in the book *on True Religion,* chapter 36 not far from the end, who says this: *Nor does any one understand false things.* Therefore, falsity is not in the understanding.

2. Moreover, Augustine says in the book of *LXXXIII Questions,* in question 31 and question 22 in the beginning: *Every one who is mistaken does not understand that in which he is mistaken.* Therefore, the understanding is always true: therefore, falsity can not be in the understanding.

3. Again Algazeli says: *Either we understand something as it is or we do not understand.* But whoever understands a thing as it is, understands truly. Therefore, the understanding is always true: therefore, falsity is not in it.

But there is, TO THE CONTRARY, what the Philosopher says in the IIIrd book *on the Soul* that where there is composition of understandings there too are the true and the false. Therefore, falsity is found in the understanding.

I REPLY that it must be said that the word understanding is taken for that which knows the inmost depths of the thing; for *to understand* is, as it were, *to read within,*[38] for sense and imagination know only the exterior accidents; but understanding alone pertains to the essence of the thing. But, further, the understand-

[38] That is, it is suggested that the etymology of *intelligere* is *intus legere.*

ing engages in diverse manners in reasoning and inquiring from the comprehended essences of things.
Therefore, the word understanding can be taken in two
ways. In one way, as it is related only to that for
which the name was first imposed, and thus we are said
properly to understand when we apprehend the quiddity
of things or when we understand those things which are
known to the understanding as soon as the quiddities of
things are known, such as the first principles which we
know when we understand the terms; wherefore, the
understanding is called the state or having [*habitus*] of
principles. The quiddity of the thing, however, is
properly the object of the understanding; wherefore,
just as sense is always true concerning proper sensibles,
so too understanding is always true in learning essence
[*quod quid est*], as is said in the IIIrd book *on the
Soul*. But nevertheless, by accident falsity can arise
there, in so far, namely, as the understanding compounds and divides falsely, which happens in two ways;
either in so far as it attributes the definition of one thing
to another, as if it should conceive rational mortal
animal as the definition of an ass; or in so far as it
joins parts of the definition together which can not be
joined, as if it should conceive the definition of ass to
be irrational immortal animal; for the following proposition is false: Some irrational animal is immortal. And
thus, it is evident that a definition can not be false except
in so far as it implicates a false affirmation. This double
mode, however, is touched on in the Vth book of the
Metaphysics. Similarly, the understanding is not de
ceived in any way in first principles. Wherefore, it is
evident that if the understanding be taken according to
the action by which the name understanding is imposed,
falsity is not in the understanding. Understanding can
be taken commonly in another manner, as it is extended

to all operations; and thus it comprehends opinion and reasoning, and in that sense, falsity is in the understanding, but never if the resolution into first principles is made correctly.

And by this the reply to the objection is evident.

MATTHEW OF AQUASPARTA (1234/40–1302)

The work of Matthew of Aquasparta is indication of the status of the discussion of the problem of knowledge after the debates and condemnations of the 13th century and after the aristotelian labors of Albert the Great and Thomas Aquinas. Pupil and follower of Bonaventura, Matthew worked out a profound interpretation of Augustine, but he had at his command, too, the corpus of aristotelian learning. If, therefore, Thomas had departed from the ways of augustinism to make a place for the logic and science of Aristotle, Matthew turns the emphasis again from data, origins, and arguments to the eternal reasons behind arguments. Often his philosophy is explicit defense of the position of Bonaventura against the thomist aristotelianism, particularly at the points at which Thomas had found only *a posteriori* or only accidental knowledge possible. To safeguard the eternal reasons which were the mark of the presence of God and the end therefore of Matthew's philosophical inquiry, his attack is constantly against skepticism, and his argument is dotted illustratively with truths that are indubitably certain. His doctrines are transitional between the opposition of Bonaventura (who defended the ontological proof as an *a priori* argument) to Thomas (who refuted it and substituted in its place *a posteriori* demonstrations) and the doctrine of Duns Scotus (who defends the ontological argument but colors it to make it *a posteriori*), for Matthew defends the argument without the coloring which Duns Scotus was to give it.

With Duns he shares a philosophical distaste for skepticism and a corresponding flare for certainties; unlike
Duns he makes his certainties the mark of divine illumination, with reservations to be sure, for the divine light
is not the whole and only reason of knowing, but the
emphasis is still on that highest part of the soul, by
which Augustine taught that sure truths are known, and
on the eternal reasons, by which they can be known.

The adversaries, inherited from Augustine and transmitted to Duns Scotus, against whom Matthew proceeds from time to time with full array of logic, are the
academics; against them he shows the mounting absurd-
ity of the position which holds that the human mind can
attain to no truth. He uses in refutation a device, frequent in his works though somewhat strange in the
middle ages, of prefacing his attack on opponents with
an account of the historical development of their doctrine; in the first of the disputed questions *on Faith*, he
traces (with materials borrowed from Augustine) the
departure of the new Academics from the doctrine of
the old Academics, of Plato and his followers. With
Bonaventura he finds the solution of skepticism and of
the problems of knowledge in a combination of Plato
and Aristotle: Plato had supposed the entire explanation of knowledge was in the archetypal intelligible
world of ideal reasons, that the world of sensible things
could yield only opinion; Aristotle had supposed that
knowledge could be explained by its origin in sense,
memory, and experience, and by the activity of the active
intellect abstracting species from phantasms. Plato
could therefore account for wisdom, but his doctrines
had no place for knowledge; whereas Aristotle dealt
entirely in knowledge, for his philosophy had nothing
to say of the eternal light of wisdom. Augustine held
to the middle way, and considered our knowledge of

higher and of lower things, of things exterior and of ideal reasons.

The philosophizers who followed Aristotle, therefore, whom Matthew criticizes and among whose number must doubtless be included Thomas Aquinas, fall into an error less only in degree than that of the academics. They hold that the active intellect of man, working on the data of sensation, is sufficient to explain understanding, and though they acknowledge the presence of the divine light, it is not as a special cause of knowledge, but only as a general cause, and therefore not necessary for the explanation of knowledge in particular. It is this doctrine which commits them to the error of supposing that there is no knowledge which proceeds from the eternal causes to things, that demonstration *a priori* is impossible, that only demonstration based on experience is cogent to man, in that he knows no eternal essence. Many precious selfevident truths, besides the ontological argument, are rendered invalid if this is so. For Thomas, the basis of philosophic certainty had to be the complete and perfect return of the soul on itself. In the circle of that return the mind knew things, not as they are in themselves, but by a certain reflection; it knew itself, not intuit ely, but by its acts. For Matthew the mind had only to understand the signification of the name of God, that he is that than which a greater can not be conceived, to realize that he can not be conceived not to be; the mind knows individual things through themselves and properly, not accidentally, but by singular species; it knows itself and its conditions, too, not only by arranging universals in arguments, but intuitively by perceiving the essence itself and its habits objectively. The mind's basic certainties of things, of its self-perception, of God and eternal reasons are the rediscovered and reiterated principles and the chief body of Matthew's philosophy.

None the less the eternal reasons are not the only reasons of knowledge, but knowledge is begotten in us, as Aristotle held, by sense, memory, and experience, from which are derived the universals which are the principles of the arts and the sciences. The mind attains to the eternal divine reasons, not as the object at which its inquiry terminates; rather they are the object which moves the understanding and they move it to other things which it knows properly; they are the motive object and the reason of seeing, not the object seen. They are necessary to explain the nature of the mind, the things which the mind knows, the medium of knowledge (in virtue of which, for example, I can know *all equals* by the same principle of equality, and in virtue of which likewise *all who know equals* know them by the same principle), and finally the nature of judgment (by which things are pronounced good and true and beautiful).

For all the differences which might be found, some-times with the considerable labor of Matthew and pointed by his pertinacious criticisms, between the aristotelianism of Thomas and the augustinism of Matthew, truth is defined in the disputed questions *on Knowledge* by distinctions which strongly recall Thomas. There are three kinds of truth: first, the truth which is the very form or nature of the thing; second, the truth which is the comparison of the thing to the created understanding; third, the truth which is the comparison of the thing to the divine light. But the foundation which Thomas gave to truths did not seem to Matthew to establish them firmly enough in the eternal truths on which thinking and things depend. Matthew would revise the more cautious statement of Thomas to recognize not only that truth, whatever its origin, involves certitude, but that human certitude further involves the perception of necessary, immutable, eternal truths, in such wise that whatever is known certainly by intellectual knowledge is known in the eternal reasons and in the light of the first truth. This has been the conviction throughout the history of philosophy of those who remark that even the denial of truth involves the assertion of truth, that doubt about one's thinking or one's existence involves the recognition at least of the doubting mind, that, finally, any inquiry concerning beings so recognized must lead with little difficulty to the nature of a necessary being at the basis of all being. Opposition to them has recruited the party of philosophers who have hesitated, in varying ways, to make the truths which the mind discovers the literal and essential characterization of the things known in such truths. Within the ranks of those who oppose skepticism there is the opposition between those who with Matthew are impressed with the circumstance that necessary propositions can be found to encompass all the variety of things, and those who with Thomas would weaken the generality of that argument by further speculation, since the truths known thus certainly, are the truths of no individual essence.

MATTHEW OF AQUASPARTA

TEN DISPUTED QUESTIONS ON KNOWLEDGE [1]

QUESTION I.

The question is, whether for the knowledge of a thing the existence of the thing itself is required, or whether that which is not can be the object of the understanding.

But that the existence of the thing is required for knowledge, and that that which is not can not be understood, is shown thus:

1. Anselm in his book *on Truth* [2] says that there is one truth which is only efficient, another truth which is only effected, and another which is efficient and effected. The truth which is only efficient is the first truth; the effected truth is truth in understanding or in proposition; the efficient and effected is the truth of the thing, which is effected by the first truth and effects truth in understanding or in proposition. The truth of knowledge or the truth of proposition however is cause of no truth. But if the first truth were not, there would be no truth in the thing, for it is the cause of the latter: therefore, if there were no truth in the thing, there

[1] FR. MATTHAEI AB AQUASPARTA O. F. M., S. R. E. CARDINALIS, *Quaestiones Disputatae Selectae, Tom. I. Quaestiones de Fide et de Cognitione.* Quaracchi: Typographia Collegii S. Bonaventurae, 1903, pp. 219-269.

[2] Ch. X: see above, vol. I, pp. 170-171.

would be no truth in the understanding, since the truth of the thing is the cause of that.

2. Again, it was said that truth is not in the thing, but in the understanding, as the Philosopher says in book VI of the *Metaphysics*,[3] that *good and evil are in things, but true and false are in the understanding*; and this is so for the following reason, that truth states an adequation which is formally in the understanding, for that which adequates is. Against this it was objected, that an adequation is a certain relation; for nothing is said to be adequated to itself, but it is necessary that it be adequated to something else. If, therefore, truth is an adequation of thing to understanding and conversely, then necessarily it requires the existence of the thing. And if it is thus, since nothing is understood except the true; and the true is not in the understanding, except because it is in the thing, then the existence of the thing is required necessarily for knowledge.

3. Again, Avicenna in book I of the *Metaphysics*[4] says that that which is, is the first impression of the understanding; for the first thing that is impressed in the understanding is that which is: therefore, the understanding understands only that which is: therefore, that which is not can not be understood.

4. Again, the Philosopher, in the *Metaphysics* book II,[5] says, *As each thing is related to being, so it is related to the true*; but the true is the object of the understanding: therefore, as it is related to being, so it is related to knowledge: therefore, that which is not is not knowable.

5. Again, Augustine in book XII of the *Literal Commentary on Genesis*[6] says, *The understanding either understands and is true; or if it is not true, it does not*

[3] That is, book VI, ch. 4, 1027[b] 26-28.
[4] Ch. 6.   [5] Ch. I.   [6] Ch. 25, n. 52.

understand. But that which is not is not true: therefore, that which is not is not understood. The proof of the minor premiss: Augustine in book II of the *Soliloquies* after the beginning[7] says, *The true is that which is*.

6. Again, three things are required necessarily for knowledge, namely a *cognoscitive* power, which is the understanding, a *medium* or reason [*ratio*] of knowing, which is the species of the thing, and the *object* itself. In the case of a non-existent thing, therefore, there can be the cognoscitive power, there can be the reason of knowing; but, I ask, what is the object? If it is a thing existing outside, I have the proposition, that that which is not is not known. If it is the species or reason of knowing, to the contrary: the medium or reason of knowing can in no way be the object in so far as it is the medium, since it is not that which is known, but the reason of knowing; it is not understood, but the reason of understanding: therefore, it is necessary to posit some being which is the object of the understanding.

7. It was said that the understanding of a quiddity abstracts from being, for in every created thing quiddity and being differ, and therefore, it is not necessary that there be an actually existent thing, but that it be apprehended by the understanding and that it be represented to the understanding. Against this it may be objected that, when the thing does not exist, nothing remains except in the understanding; but whatever is in the understanding, is constituted in the reason of medium in the reason of species, and it is not that which is understood itself or the object, but it is the reason of understanding representing the object. Therefore, it is necessary to hold that the thing is which is the object of the understanding: therefore, that which is not is not understood.

[7] Ch. 5, n. 8.

8. Again, it was said that, although the thing known is not in itself or in actuality, it is nevertheless in cause or in potentiality. It was objected: if every created cause has been circumscribed, the understanding still understands the quiddity of man: therefore, if the quiddity of man is the object of the understanding, not as it is in the thing, for we suppose this, nor as it is in the created cause, then as it is in the first and uncreated cause. But that can not be the object, except the beatific object, which can not be in this life: or it would follow that the understanding by its natural forces could attain to knowledge of the first cause of being, which is erroneous and one of the articles reproved and excommunicated: therefore, there must be present also some object outside in fact: therefore etc.

9. Again, if it knows that which is not, it does not know it except by that species which the understanding has in itself. Then I inquire: either it knows the thing according to the being which it has in its proper genus or not. If not: then it does not know according to its true being, since it has its true being in its proper genus, not in the understanding; and it follows then, that it does not know truly. If according to the being which it has in its proper genus, then it does not know or understand that which is not, but some actual thing.

10. Again, according to the Philosopher [in the *Metaphysics* book VI],[8] there is no knowledge, neither speculative nor practical, of that which is accidentally. And the cause or reason of this is because of a defect of being or because of a defect of entity; but it is certain that that which is not recedes further from the reason of that which is than does that which is accidentally: therefore, there can much the less be speculative or practical knowledge of that which is not.

[8] That is book VI, ch. 2, 1026^b 2-3.

11. Again, each thing is more in its cause than in its effect; but the truth of knowledge is caused by the truth of things in their proper genus: therefore, truth is more in things than in the understanding or knowledge: therefore, without the truth of things there remains no truth in knowledge.

12. Again, Augustine in book XI *on the City of God*[9] says, *To some it seems wonderful, but nevertheless true, that this world could not be known to us, if it were not; but unless it were known to God, it could not be.* From which it is gathered that the knowledge of God is the cause of things and does not depend on things; but our knowledge is caused by things, and therefore depends on things. But because things depend on divine knowledge as a cause, it is impossible that things be without divine knowledge. Therefore, in the same manner because our knowledge depends on things as a cause, our knowledge can not be unless things exist.

13. Again, *as sense is related to the sensible, so is understanding to the intelligible*,[10] but sense can in no way perceive the thing, unless a sensible thing exist: therefore, the understanding in the same way can not understand unless the intelligible thing has being actually.

14. Again, I make two suppositions: one is that knowledge or science is not without assimilation, and Augustine says this in book IX *on the Trinity*:[11] *All knowledge according to species is like the thing which it knows.* The second is that the like is not like itself, but like the like. It is necessary however to assert in any assimilation, four things: two like extremes and two reasons of assimilation. On the part of the understanding, there-

---

[9] Ch. 10, n. 3.
[10] ARISTOTLE, *on the Soul*, book III, ch. 4, 429[a] 16-18.
[11] Ch. 10, n. 16.

fore, there are the understanding itself and the species by which it is assimilated; on the part of the thing known, the quiddity is the reason of assimilation; but the term or the extreme can not be unless there be a like thing: therefore, science or knowledge of a thing can not be without the existence of the thing.

15. Again, the argument was confirmed since the accident can not be without subject:[12] therefore, the accident needs and requires that the thing be; but that likeness is an accident: therefore, not without subject. If, therefore, there is true assimilation or true likeness of the understanding to the thing and of the thing to the understanding, then it is necessary to posit a thing assimilated, in which the assimilation is as in a subject.

16. Again, the agreement is greater and the distance less of an existing thing to a superexistent than of a non-existent thing to an existent; but since God is absolutely superexistent, he is not knowable or intelligible, according to Dionysius *on Divine Names*:[13] therefore, much less will the non-existent or that which is not, be knowable.

17. Again, God knows non-existent things, because he has their reasons; but the human understanding does not have the reasons of non-existent things: therefore, in no manner can it know or understand non-existents.

18. Again, knowledge and knowable are spoken of relatively, so that, notwithstanding, there is a real relation on the part of knowledge, which depends on the knowable; but a real relation can not be unless to a thing really existent: therefore, there can be no knowledge, unless there be a knowable or thing known, real and in actuality. The proof of the minor premiss is

[12] Aristotle, *Metaphysics*, book VII, ch. 1, 1028^a 20-25.
[13] Ch. I, paragraph 1.

apparent by the Philosopher in the *Categories*,[14] where
he says that the being of relatives is thus to be constituted with reference to something else that the relation
depends not less, but rather much the more, so far as it
is relation, on the object than on the subject: therefore etc.

19. Again, according to the Philosopher in book III
on the Soul[15] to understand is to suffer something, and
it is certain that what the soul suffers is only from the
thing understood. I ask therefore: either from the likeness or from the thing. If from the likeness, then it is
not knowledge except of concepts; if from the thing or
object, it is necessary that the object be really, since
as the Philosopher says,[16] it is impossible that a real
property be, unless it be in that which really is: therefore etc.

20. Again, according to the Philosopher[17] words are
signs of these passions, that is, of conceptions, which
are in the soul: the understandings or the conceptions,
however, are the signs of the things. It is certain, however, that the concepts depend on things more than the
words [*vox*], for they are related to them more immediately. But there are no true propositions if things do
not exist: therefore, by much the more there will be no
true understandings or concepts if things do not exist.
The proof of the minor premiss is by Boethius in book
V of the *Consolation of Philosophy*,[18] by the Philosopher
on the Categories, by Anselm *on Truth*,[19] who say that
from the fact that a thing is or is not, a statement is said
to be true or false.

[14] Ch. 7, *on Relations*, 6ᵃ 36-6ᵇ 7.
[15] Ch. 4, 429ᵇ 24-25.
[16] Cp. *Metaphysics*, book VII, ch. 1, 1028ᵃ 20-25.
[17] *On Interpretation*, ch. 1, 16ᵃ 4.
[18] Prose passage 3.
[19] See above, vol. I, p. 153.

21. Again, Augustine in book XV *on the Trinity*[20] says: Two things are required for verbal truth, that is, that it be thus in fact as it is in knowledge, otherwise, if one or the other is deficient, the word is not true. But in all knowledge the word is required necessarily: therefore, the existence of the thing is required necessarily.

22. Again, the knowable is the measure of knowledge:[21] therefore, things are the measure of our understanding. It is certain, however, that the measure is more perfect than the thing measured; but the thing does not measure except by adequation: therefore, the reason of adequation or adequation itself is more perfect in the thing than in the understanding: therefore, also truth, since truth is adequation. If, therefore, the measured thing is not without the measure: then there is no truth in the understanding without the truth of the thing: therefore, it is not understood without the existence of the thing.

TO THE CONTRARY: 1. Avicenna says in the first book of the *Metaphysics*[22] that it is manifest that that which is stated concerning something, must have being in some fashion in the soul. For propositions are not concerning a true thing, except by that which has being in the soul, and they are accidentally by that which is in exterior things: therefore, in like manner, conceptions, on which propositions are founded, are accidentally through those things which are in exterior things. But those things which are by accident, are not necessary to the being of anything: therefore, there are true conceptions and true propositions, when things do not exist.

2. Again, the Commentator says on book VI of the

[20] Ch. 13, n. 24.
[21] Cp. ARISTOTLE, *Metaphysics*, book X, ch. 15, 1057^a 11-12.
[22] Ch. 6.

Ethics:[23] *As an inferior art is related to a superior, as for example the art of hewing to the art of building, so sense is related to understanding.* But the inferior art is so related to the superior art that after it has prepared the material, the superior art, although the inferior be lacking, proceeds and completes the work in the prepared material: therefore, in the same manner, although sense and the sensible species are lacking, once the intelligible species have been prepared, the understanding will be able to operate concerning these latter and to understand by them.

3. Again, Anselm says in the *Monologium*:[24] *The work which is done in connection with any art, not only when it is done, but likewise before it is done and after it will be destroyed, is always no other in that art than the art itself,* but it is known that the artificer foresees and foreknows the work to be done according to that art, which nevertheless is not yet: therefore, he knows that which is not: therefore etc.

4. Again, the intellective power is more efficacious than the imaginative; but the imaginative power can truly imagine, by means of the image of the thing left in it, that which is not: therefore, by much the more the understanding can understand a non-existent thing through the species which it has in itself. The proof of the minor premiss is clear experimentally, since by the image which I have in me of men who are not, I imagine them truly and I remember them.

5. Again, in our understanding there are impressed the eternal and immutable reasons of things, as, *every whole is greater than its part* and *of anything whatever either an affirmation or a negation*; but these reasons do not depend on things: therefore, by these reasons

[23] Ch. 7, *on Wisdom.*
[24] Ch. 34

the understanding can understand, when the things do not exist.

6. Again, every proposition is necessary which is necessarily asserted in being denied; and in this way Augustine proves that truth is necessarily because the denial of truth asserts truth, thus in book II of the *Soliloquies*,[25] *If truth is not, it is true that truth is not; and every truth is true by truth:* therefore, if truth is not, truth is, and therefore it is necessary that truth be. Thus I argue in what was stated: if that which is not is not intelligible, it is intelligible that that which is not is not intelligible; for that is true, and all truth is intelligible: therefore, the proposition is necessary that that which is not is intelligible.

7. Again, according to the Philosopher[26] the true is extended to that which is and to that which is not. For just as it is true that that which is is, so also it is true that that which is not is not; but everything which is true is intelligible and can be the object of the understanding: therefore etc.

8. Again, the existence or non-existence of a thing is not necessary nor required for knowledge, except because by the existence of a thing the understanding is in one or another disposition; but the understanding is not changed from one disposition to another and is not in different dispositions because of the existence or the non-existence of a thing: therefore, existence or non-existence is not required for the knowledge of a thing.

9. Again, the object of the understanding is essence [*quod quid est*], according to the Philosopher;[27] but error occurs in no manner concerning essence—for it is

[25] Ch. 2, n. 2.

[26] *Categories, On substance*, ch. 5, 4ᵃ 25 ff; *Met.* IV, 7, 1011ᵇ 26-29.

[27] *On the Soul*, book III, chs. 4 and 6, 429ᵇ 16-18, 430ᵇ 27-31.

abstracted from space and time, being and non-being—
therefore the understanding, whether the thing exists or
not, can understand essence without error: therefore,
the existence of the thing is not required for the knowledge of the thing, but that which is not can be the
object of the understanding.

I REPLY, the present question is not of the signification
of names or words; for whether words signify the same,
when the things are existent or non-existent, and whether
names are imposed on things or concepts, that is a logical
question and does not in the least pertain to us. For
that same question, that same difficulty of the question
remains for every word, for every name, for every circumscribed proposition.

Therefore it seems to me that in the proposed question distinctions must be made with respect to *that
which is not or that which is* and with respect to the
understanding which knows.

With respect to that which is not I make the distinction that that which is not can be taken in two ways,
namely, that which is not absolutely, that is, that which
is in no way, neither in itself nor in cause, neither in
potentiality nor in actuality, which neither was nor
will be, neither is nor is it possible for it to be; and then
I say absolutely that *that which is not can in no way
be the object of the understanding.* For as Avicenna
says,[28] the first thing which occurs to the understanding,
and the first which is apprehensible by the understanding, is that which is: therefore, as nothing is not intelligible, so that which is not is not intelligible.

In another manner that which is not can be understood, not as that which is not absolutely, but that which
is not in some manner, as that which is not in actuality,

[28] *Metaphysics* book I, ch. 6.

but is in potentiality; as that which is not in itself, but is
in its efficient cause or exemplar. And I say in this
sense that that which is not can be the object of the
understanding and is intelligible.

This, moreover, is clear in the *first* place from
prophetic illumination and prevision of future things.
For if there is no certain knowledge of that which is
not, since the future thing is a thing which is not, then
no future thing can be known or foreknown, which is
contrary to the sacred Scripture and the catholic faith.

It is clear in the *second* place from the *disposition
of things that are to be done.* For if there were no
certain knowledge of things which are not, then, since
no one does a thing willingly unless also knowingly,
no one would be disposed to do anything, and then all
disposition would perish and all artificial operation.
Augustine shows this best in book IX *on the Trinity*:[29]
*We do nothing by the members of the body in our say-
ings and actions, which the morals of men either approve
of or condemn, which we have not come upon previously
within ourselves by a word uttered interiorly. For no
one wishing something does what he has not previously
said in his heart*; and in book XV *on the Trinity*[30] he
says:

> As it has been said of the Word of God: *All
> things are done through it,* in which God is said
> to have made the universe through his one be-
> gotten Word; so there are no works of man
> which are not first spoken in the heart. And in
> this is the likeness of our word to the Word of
> God, that our word can be, even if it is not
> followed by operation; but operation can not
> be, unless the word precedes it: just as the
> Word of God could be, if no creature existed,

[29] Ch. 7, n. 12.   [30] Ch. 11. n. 20.

> but no creature could be, except through him,
> by whom all were made.

If therefore nothing which is not, or is not actually existing, can be known, there would be no disposition of things to be done, and all things would be done by chance by man; which is absolutely absurd. Therefore it is necessary that something which is not, be understood; nor is the existence of the thing required for its knowledge, but knowledge necessarily precedes in some things.

In the *third* place it is clear from *the recollection of past things*. For it is certain that things which have passed are not. Therefore, if that which is not is in no manner known nor understood, then there is no memory of past things nor recollection of past things, which is absolutely false; for we recall yesterday and what transpired in it.—Again, if there were no recollection, there would be no continuation either in words or in deeds, nor any order or connection. For he who does not recollect past things can not know where a thing ceased and where it must begin, as Augustine shows in book X of the *Confessions*,[31] book XII of the *Literal Commentary on Genesis*,[32] and in book II *on Christian Doctrine*.[33]

In the *fourth* place it is clear from *the power and operation of the understanding*. For the understanding by its active power can abstract by the light of the active intellect universals from particulars, intelligible species from sensible species, quiddities from things actually existing. It is certain, however, that the universals as well as the intelligible species, as well as the quiddities of things concern no thing actually existent, but are related indifferently to existent and non-existent

---

[31] Ch. 8 ff.   [32] Ch. 16, n. 33.   [33] Ch. 9, n. 14.

things, and do not concern space or time, and therefore the existence or non-existence of the thing has nothing to do with understanding of this sort; and therefore, as the intellect can understand the quiddity of a thing by the intelligible species, when the thing is existent, so it can also when the thing is non-existent.

Secondly, distinctions must be made with respect to the understanding which knows.

For the understanding is spoken of in two ways, just as there is a double operation of the understanding. For there is a certain *simple* and *absolute* understanding, which apprehends and conceives the simple quiddities of things; another is the *concretive* and *compositive* understanding, which understands and apprehends that the thing is present in and under the determined circumstances of time.

If, therefore, it is asked whether the existence of the thing is required necessarily for the knowledge of the thing, I reply that if we speak of that operation, or of that manner of understanding, by which the thing is understood to be under the determined circumstances of time, the existence of the thing according to the requirements of time is required necessarily, that it be understood that it is when it is, and that it be understood that it will be when it will be, and that it has been when it has been; otherwise the understanding would be false, and by that fact would not be understanding. *For either it understands and it is true, or if it is not true it does not understand,* as Augustine says in book XII of the *Literal Commentary on Genesis*[34] and as has been touched on in the opposition to the argument. But truth of the *future* is founded on the cause, as Augustine says in book XI of the *Confessions*,[35] where he says that nothing is seen except as present.

[34] Ch. 25, n. 52. [35] Ch. 18, n. 24.

> Although, therefore, future things are said to
> be seen, the things themselves which are not
> yet, that is, which are future, are not seen,
> but their causes or signs perhaps, which are
> now; therefore, not future but present things
> are now perceptible to those seeing, from which
> things future are predicted as conceived by the
> mind; for example, I see the dawn, I foretell
> the sun will rise; what I see is present, what
> I foretell future.

The truth of the present thing, however, is founded on
a thing actually existent; the truth of a past thing on
the image or species of the thing, which remains in the
understanding, together with the comparison to the
thing which was but is not now, just as Augustine says
in the same book:[36] *My boyhood, which is not now, is
in past time which is not now, but when I recall it and
tell of it, I perceive the image of it, which is still in
my memory in the present time.* But whether images
of future things are presented likewise, as causes now
existing, he says he does not know.

If, however, we speak of the understanding with
respect to that simple, absolute, and pure operation by
which it apprehends and conceives the absolute quiddities of things, I say this: that the existence of the thing
is not needed for knowledge of this sort, nay, the existence or non-existence of the thing has nothing to do
with it. The reason for this has been touched upon
in part, as well with respect to the *quiddity* itself, as
with respect to the *understanding*, and with respect to
the *intelligible species*.

With respect to the *quiddity*, since as Avicenna says
in book V of the *Metaphysics*[37] and in many places: In

_____

[36] *Confessions,* Book IX, ch. 18, n. 23.   [37] Ch. 2.

says *on the Immortality of the Soul*,[39] nothing is so
eternal as the reason of a circle; and in book II *on the
Free Will*:[40] *That seven and three are ten never was
not, never will not be, but always was, always will be.*
And the Philosopher in book VI of the *Ethics*[41] says,
that *knowledge is only of things which are of necessity,
and not contingent to be constituted otherwise than they
are, and eternal.* Knowledge must be established therefore in something: *not in things*, since if all things pass
away, these truths remain, and if no thing exists, these
truths are—for when no man exists, it is true that man
is a rational, mortal animal—*nor in the created understanding*, for every understanding is mutable, and when
no created understanding exists, these true things still
are: therefore only *in the eternal exemplar*, where *the
origins of mutable things remain immutable and the
reasons of transient things do not pass away*, as
Augustine says in book I of the *Confession*.[42]

Further, the created truth is not other than a certain expression of the uncreated truth; and each created
truth is true in so far as it imitates that exemplar.
If therefore these immutable truths can not be understood, except where they are, and they are not immutable
except in art: then it is necessary that they be understood in art.

Moreover, if the truth of the thing is only a certain
expression and imitation of the eternal art, and if the
likeness of that truth expressing the first exemplar is in
our understanding, it is impossible that I understand
truly and with certitude any thing, except by application
in a certain manner and by relation to the external exemplar. Since therefore we understand the quiddity of

[39] Ch. I.
[40] Cp. above book II, ch. 8, n. 21, vol. I, p. 36.
[41] Ch. 3.   [42] Ch. 6, n. 9.

something and its definitive reason, the object of the understanding is not *only the concept* itself of the mind, nor *only the quiddity itself*, which is not in the nature of things; nor is the *eternal exemplar* the *reposing* and *terminating* object because it is the sole and blessing object of the blessed understanding; but it is the *quiddity itself conceived by our understanding, yet related to the art* or the eternal exemplar in so far as, touching our mind, it is constituted in the reason of the thing which moves our mind; and thence we conceive a true notion of things, and once the materials have been furnished from below by the senses, the principles of all the arts flow thence.   Wherefore Augustine in book I of the *Retractations*[43] contends against Plato who said that the arts are brought forth within souls, because the ignorant and unlearned return true answers concerning them, that, *It is more credible that they return true answers, when they are questioned well concerning certain disciplines although unlearned in them, because there is present to them, when they can seize it, the light of eternal reason, in which they see these immutable truths.*   And in chapter 8 of the same book touching on the same error and the error that to learn is to remember, because any one makes true replies when questioned in good order, he says: *It can happen that one may be able to do this, because there is an intelligible nature and it is connected not only with intelligible but also with immutable things, and it is done in such order that when one moves oneself to these things, to which one is connected, or to oneself in so far as one sees them, to that extent one replies truly concerning them.*   And in book X of the *Confessions*:[44] *The beautiful things caused through souls in artist hands, come from that beauty which is above souls.*

[43] Ch. 4, n. 4.   [44] Ch. 34, n. 53.

I have touched on these few things examining them in advance, because the way in which the mind sees all things in art or in the eternal reasons will be seen more clearly in the following questions.

To the first argument to the contrary of the position stated it must be said that truth *first and principally,* both in things and in understandings, is from the first truth. None the less it is *originally* from things and in things in respect of the understanding in natural knowledge; but *formally* it is in the understanding itself, according as it conceives the thing as it is, for then there is an adequation of thing and understanding. However, although truth is caused in the understanding by things with respect to *origin,* still it is not so caused with respect to *conservation* and *continuation*; nay, when things perish, truth remains in understandings, but with the irradiations of the uncreated light. Nor does the objection hold which contends that if the first truth were to cease to be (to suppose the impossible) truth would not remain in things, therefore etc.; since the first cause is the *effective* and *conservative* cause, so that, if its influence were removed, nothing would remain; but things outside, although they are the effective cause of truth in understandings, are not nevertheless the conservative cause. For when the influence of second causes is removed, there still remains the influence of the first cause. In what way, however, truth is caused in the understanding by things outside, will be seen elsewhere.

To the second it must be said that adequation is a *relation* and involves another thing. But since between knowledge and the knowable the relation is according to *being* on the part of *knowledge,* because it depends on the knowable; but in the *knowable* the relation is only according to *reason,* because the knowable does not depend on knowledge nor does it posit any thing: therefore, it need not be according to *fact* but only according to *reason,* as understood or apprehended by the understanding, with nevertheless a relation to the first exemplar, in which there is the reason of immutable quiddity.—I say, moreover, that it is adequation, because the understanding apprehends or understands the quiddity in the manner in which it is; because it does not understand it by perceiving being or non-being, space or time, as likewise it is not concerned with its own reason: therefore, the understanding is adequated to itself.

To the third it must be said that as Avicenna says, that which is, is the first thing that occurs to the understanding concerning the true thing, and therefore that which absolutely is not, as has been said, is not understood. But that thing which is, is not something determined, neither in actuality nor potentiality, neither present nor future, not man nor horse nor any thing of this sort, but that which is, which is superior to all these; and I say that that quiddity is the thing which is in the understanding and in the eternal exemplar, although it is not that which is actually in things, for that is not part of its meaning.

To the fourth the reply is clear, since the Philosopher means to say nothing more than that in the manner in which the thing is, in that manner it is knowable. If it is in actuality, it is known in actuality; if it is in potentiality, it is known in potentiality; if it is abstracted from actuality and potentiality and from all difference of being, it is knowable in that manner; and universally, as many times as that which is is spoken of, so many times the true is spoken of, and as often or in as many ways as it can be called true, in so many ways is it knowable, as has been seen.

To the fifth the reply is clear in the same way, for the intellect, in understanding the quiddity of the thing, which is its proper object, understands the true. But the true is not nothing, but is that which is something [*quod quid est = essence*] or it is that which the thing is; and therefore it is properly the true, and the reason of Augustine is properly suited to it. For since I understand what man is, I understand rational man, and this is that which man is immutably. Nor does Augustine mean that which is *actual being*, since that *being* is corrupted; but truth in itself is not corrupted when things are corrupted; for the reason of the thing remains always.

To the sixth the reply is clear through the things which have been said in the principal solution. For I say that something is the object there; it is not necessary that it be something actually existing, nor is that part of the reason of the object of the understanding; but it suffices that it be represented to the understanding and apprehended by the understanding.—Or, as has been said, the object is the quiddity itself, conceived by the understanding, but according as it is related to the eternal exemplar, which is related to the understanding in the reason of the thing which moves it.

To the seventh argument that, if every thing is circumscribed, nothing remains except in the understanding, I say that it is false, but that *the immutable reason* remains. For it is immutably true that man is animal etc.; but it is in the eternal exemplar which is constituted in the reason of the thing moving our understanding. Whence the *quiddity conceived* and *related to that exemplar* is the object of the understanding.—But that which the argument adds, that whatever is in the understanding, is constituted in the reason of medium and in the reason of the knower, could be said to be false. For the understanding forms a certain concept for itself from the species representing something to it, whether it be or not be in fact,—which thing it presents to itself; but that thing does not conduct to understanding, but leads to something else; and it is not necessary that that be in fact, nor is it in the reason of object, but it suffices that it can be in the concept of the mind.

To the eighth it must be said that, if every created cause is removed, there remains still the immutable *reason* of the quiddity of the thing, and likewise there remains the *species* in the understanding, by which it can form for itself the concept of the thing. Although therefore the quiddity itself can not through itself be the object of the understanding, nor can the concept itself alone, for then the understanding would be vain, nor would it understand the thing, but its concept; nevertheless I do not say that the exemplar itself is the terminating or reposing object of the understanding; for the argument would proceed in that way; but all these concur in the making of one perfect reason of the object, as has been explained, and that is the quiddity itself conceived or apprehended by the understanding, but according as it is referred to the eternal exemplar, which is related to the understanding in the reason of that which moves.

To the ninth it must be said that it knows [that which is not] through species, not according to the being which it has in its proper genus, for [the thing] is not in its proper genus and still [the understanding] knows the thing truly; for it knows the quiddity which differs from being, nor is the being [of the thing] from the understanding of it, but the understanding abstracts absolutely from being, as has been said frequently. Yet it knows by referring to the first cause and exemplar, which moves it in this knowledge.

To the tenth it must be said that it is not because of a defect of entity that there is no knowledge of that which is accidentally, but rather because of a defect of determination, in that they neither have a determined cause nor any one mode of being, but it is possible that they occur as if by infinite causes and in infinite modes; and therefore they can not be known by natural knowledge either in themselves nor in their causes. However, the quiddities of things, although they do not have actual being, because that is not in their reason, have still immutable truth according to Augustine and the Philosopher.[45]

To the eleventh it must be said that truth is not in *things* and in the *understanding* in the same manner. In things it is originally and causally in respect to the understanding, but in the understanding it is formally, as has been said above.[46] And because it is not in the same manner, therefore, there is no uniform comparison; for causally it is more in things, formally it is more in the understanding.

To the twelfth it must be said that God is cause of things, and things the cause of our knowledge in different manners. For God is the *whole* cause of things and cause of the *whole* of things: therefore, things depend on his providence. But things are not the *necessary* cause of our knowledge; for God could imprint on our understanding species of things through which we should know, as he imparts them to angels. Moreover, things are not the whole and only cause, but together with the light of our active intellect and the divine light; and therefore, if they are in some manner the *original* cause, still they are not the *conservative* cause, nor with re-

[45] Aristotle, *Metaphysics*, book XI, ch. 8, 1065[b] 1-4.
[46] To the first; see above p. 259.

spect to its conservation does our knowledge depend on things.

To the thirteenth it must be said that there is no similarity there, since sense does not have a power for the conservation of sensible species, as the understanding has of intelligible species; and therefore sense does not perceive unless the sensible thing is present, but the understanding understands even when the thing is destroyed. And because we have intelligible species in the understanding, but no sensible species in sense, therefore the Philosopher says in book II *on the Soul* that we understand when we wish, but we do not perceive.

To the fourteenth it must be said that, as has been said above,[47] there is no relation of the knowable to knowledge except according to reason: therefore, assimilation also is only according to reason; and because of this it is necessary to grant that something according to fact exists on the part of the intelligible, but only in apprehension; nor is it inconsistent that something be referred according to reason to that which is not. For I see that between some things there is a relation according to being with respect to either extreme, namely, when the extremes depend on each other, and the relation posits something in either extreme, as between father and son.—Between other things there is a relation with respect to one of the extremes according to being, but with respect to the other according to reason; and therefore with respect to the latter extreme [the relation] posits nothing; of this sort is the relation between knowledge and the knowable.—Between still other things there is a relation with respect to both extremes according to reason, as between God and creatures from eternity. For there were in God from eternity ideas of things that were to be made, which they call a relation to

[47] To the second; see above pp. 259-260.

things according to reason, for the relation posits nothing on the part of the divine essence nor on the part of things which were not. Therefore, where there is a relation or an assimilation according to reason, it is not necessary to posit extremes except according to reason.

To the fifteenth the reply is clear. For it has been said that that likeness posits nothing on the part of the knowable according to fact, but only according to reason; and therefore it is not necessary because of this to posit the thing. *Likewise*, that likeness is a true accident with respect to one thing [the knower], and therefore it is necessary to posit the subject according to the truth of the thing; but since in another respect [i.e., to the known] it is only an accident according to reason, therefore it is not necessary to posit a subject except according to reason.—If the question be urged, as it was urged in connection with quiddity above, whether it is something or nothing: if it is something, it is either accident, or substance, or creator, or creature: I say that it is not nothing but something. But because it is not something actually, it is not substance, nor accident, nor this, nor that, for that is the division of things actually existent. *Finally*, the understanding of the quiddity abstracts from all being.

To the sixteenth it must be said that the superexistent is knowable and intelligible. However, that which Dionysius says, that God is not knowable or intelligible, must be understood: *fully*, as he is knowable and by a *comprehensive* knowledge, for he is comprehensible to himself alone; nevertheless, he is knowable by an apprehensive knowledge both that he is and what he is, although not fully and perfectly.

To the seventeenth it must be said that God knows the things about to be made, for he has their practical and exemplar reasons; but the human understanding can not know future things, which do not have causes in nature except by revelation of God in whom are the reasons of things about to be made. Nevertheless, because when things exist, the understanding acquires for itself the species of things, therefore when things cease to exist, it knows things through those species, for although it does not have reasons which make, still it has reasons that have been made.

To the eighteenth the reply can be made from those given above. For there is relation according to *saying* or according to *reason* on the part of the knowable, according to *being* on the part of knowledge: therefore, it is not necessary to posit the knowable in being, but in reason.—But with respect to what the argument says, that a real relation is only in reference to the thing, and that it depends more on the object than on the subject, because the being of relatives consists in constituting themselves in relation to something else, I say that, according as a relation states an accident, it depends more upon the subject in which it is; according as it is a relation to something or a condition [*habitudo*], it depends more on the object, because it is in relation to it; and I add that a real relation is in reference to the thing; to the thing as it is, but to the thing according to the mode and requirement of the thing. And because it does not belong to the reason of it that it be actually nor that it have being, but that it be only apprehensible and conceived by the understanding and related to the first exemplar: therefore, to such a thing the real relation is such.

To the nineteenth I say that to understand, so far as the *beginning* of understanding is concerned, is to *suffer* something, but so far as its *complement* is concerned, understanding is in *action*. For to receive is to suffer, but to judge and distinguish are actions. First therefore it suffers—in the manner in which to receive is to suffer—from things, from which it receives, or from phantasms, but later it acts; and therefore it is not necessary that it be active always, unless perchance we wanted to say, as has been said, that it suffers in that it is moved by the eternal reasons.

To the twentieth it must be said that the cases are not at all alike as regards *knowledge* or conception and *statement*, for statement always states that something is or is not; and therefore, it is not true except when it states that that which is is, or that that which is not is not. And in like manner, our understanding, according to an operation related to the existence of things under determined circumstances of time, is not true except when it conceives or apprehends that that which is is or that that which is not is not. Nevertheless, as has been said, the understanding has another absolute and simple operation which abstracts completely from these: therefore, it does not depend on the being or non-being of things.

To the twenty-first it must be said that it is true of the operation of the understanding which is concerned with the existences of things; but it is not true of that operation which abstracts from these.—Or it can be said that when the understanding apprehends the simple quiddity of the thing, it conceives the true word, for it is in the thing as it is in knowledge. For the quiddity names a certain thing, of which the reason or intention is concerned neither with being nor non-being, and thus the understanding understands it: therefore, it understands as the thing is, and for this reason the word is true.

To the twenty-second it must be said that the knowable is the measure of knowledge, and things are the measure of our understanding: this is according to the saying that science and knowledge are then true when they are adequated to the thing; and this is when knowledge knows the thing as it is and according to its mode. And therefore the reason of adequation or the truth *originally* is from things, but *formally* it is in the understanding, and *exemplarily* it is in God. And because there are different modes of being, there is no uniform comparison, but there is always the fallacy of proceeding from the statement in some certain respect to the statement absolutely; still it is certain that in God *absolutely* it is more perfectly.—As regards what is objected, that the measured depends on the measure, it can be said that the knowable thing is; *is*, I say, not in actuality, but in the conception of the mind and in the eternal exemplar, and this suffices for the reason of the measure.

QUESTION II.

In the second place it is inquired whether whatever is known certainly in intellectual knowledge, is known in the eternal reasons or in the light of the first truth.

That the natural light suffices, however, for sure knowledge without the influence of those eternal reasons, is shown thus.

1. The Philosopher in book III *on the Soul*[48] says: *As there is in every nature something by which it is to be made all things and something by which it is to make all things, so it is in the understanding or in the soul;* for there is in the understanding that by which it is to make all things, and that is the active intellect; and that by which it is to be made all things and that is the possible intellect. But wherever there is a sufficient

[48] Ch. 5, 430ª 10-14.

active principle and a sufficient passive principle for all things, no further agent is required. Therefore, the soul by its active and its passive principles suffices for sure knowledge without special irradiation or the influence of the eternal reasons.

2. Again, Anselm *on the Virginal Conception*[49] distinguishes a triple course of things, namely *natural, voluntary,* and *wonderful.* According to the natural course, natural things are made; according to the voluntary course, voluntary things, which depend on the created will; according to the wonderful course, those things which are made above nature by the divine power. But it is certain that the act of knowledge pertains to the natural course, not to the wonderful, for knowledge is not miraculous: therefore, it is able to be by the natural intellective power without a supernatural agent or influence from it.

3. Again, Hugo in book I *on the Sacraments*[50] says toward the end, that *some things are above reason, some below reason, some beyond reason, some according to reason.* But to all those things which lie under the power of some agent, the power of that agent suffices without any other higher aid: therefore, to the natural knowledge of those things which lie under reason and do not exceed its faculty, the natural light suffices, if the common influence which conserves every creature is supposed.

4. Again, as the divine power is related to the operable, so the divine wisdom is related to the knowable or intelligible. But as regards those operables which do not exceed the faculty of a nature, the power of the nature, together with the common influence, suffices: therefore, to the knowables which do not exceed the faculty of that nature, the natural light suffices together

[49] Ch. 11.   [50] Part III, ch. 30.

with the general influence which is not withdrawn from
any creature.

5. Again, I posit a species abstracted from phantasms,
I posit an intellective power disposed, I posit a conversion of the force of the understanding upon it, and I
posit the common influence; but more things do not
seem to be required for knowledge: therefore, the soul
can know with certainty without any special influence
from above, since all these are in the power of the
nature.

6. Again, whenever any one sees some thing in light
or in some art, he must necessarily see that light or art
or rule in which he sees it. But it is certain that the
understanding of the wayfarer does not see that eternal
art, light, and rule, for that sight makes the blessed:
therefore, neither does he see in it.

7. Again, if all things are seen in that light and by
special influence of that light, then they who are nearer
to that light see more than those who are turned away
from that light. But it is certain that many who are
turned more from that light see more and know more
than those turned to it: therefore, that light is not the
reason of seeing, nor does one see in that light whatever
is seen.

8. Again, the Philosopher in book II of the *Metaphysics*[51] says: *As things are in respect of being, so they
are in respect of knowledge*; but the created form, together with the general influence of the Creator, suffices
for being: therefore, similarly for knowledge: therefore,
some special influence of an eternal light is not
necessary.

9. Again, Augustine in book IX *on the Trinity*[52] says:
*Just as the mind gathers knowledge of corporeal things
through the senses of the body, so it gathers knowledge*

[51] Ch. I, 993ᵇ 30-31.   [52] Ch. 3, n. 3.

of incorporeal things through itself, since it is incorporeal; but if it should need another and superior aid, it would not know through itself: therefore, it does not need a higher aid.

10. Again, Augustine in book XII *on the Trinity*[53] says that the soul sees these immutable truths or signs of the sciences *in a certain incorporeal light of its own kind, just as the eye of the flesh sees things which lie in the corporeal light*; but it is certain that no light is of the same kind [*genus*] as our soul except the created light, for the uncreated light is not in any genus: therefore, it does not know in the uncreated light, but in the created.

11. Again, according to the Philosopher,[54] *Nature does nothing in vain nor is it lacking in necessary things*; but it is certain that the rational creature was created by God because of some operation, and this is the intellectual operation: therefore, nature is not lacking to it: therefore, the soul has from its nature and in its nature these things which are needed for intellectual operation, without any influence from above, supposing always the general influence.

12. Again, the Philosopher in book III *on the Soul*[55] compares the possible intellect to the eye, color to the phantasm, the active intellect to light; for it is a certain condition [*habitus*] like light; but the presence of the visible object suffices for sensual vision, when the power of sight of the one seeing and when the light of the sun are disposed: therefore, in the same way the presence of the phantasm and the receptive power of the possible intellect and the light of the active intellect making

[53] Ch. 15, n. 24.
[54] *On the Soul*, III, c. 9, 432[b] 21-24.
[55] Ch. 5, 430[a] 14-17.

species, which are understood potentially, to be understood actually, suffice for intellectual vision.

13. Again, it is certain that the act of knowledge is a
certain natural act; but something supernatural is not
required for natural operations: therefore, either the
operation of the understanding in those things which do
not exceed the faculty of the nature, is not natural, or
if it is natural, nothing supernatural is required. But
that influence, whatever it is, is supernatural: therefore
etc.

14. Again, if we see in that light whatever we see, it
is only in two modes: either as in a *mirror*, and this is
impossible, for whoever sees something in a mirror, sees
the mirror itself; or as in a *medium* or reason of knowing, and then either the divine light itself is *by essence*
the reason of knowing (but that can not be, for whatever
it is, it is something of the soul or inhering in the understanding, but the divine essence can inhere in nothing)
or else it is *something which flows from the divine light*
into the mind knowing. But whatever it is, it is creature; but every creature is mutable: therefore, it does
not suffice for sure knowledge; or else it is necessary to
go on *in infinitum*, which is inconsistent.

15. Again, it is certain that the divine light is concerning the invisible things of God, for the divine light
is only God himself; but as the Apostle says[56] the *invisible things of God are clearly perceived from the
creation of the world, being perceived through the things
that are made:* therefore, if the divine light is the reason
of knowing the creature, and the creature is the medium
and reason of knowing the divine light, then knowledge
is circular, which seems to be inconsistent.

16. Again, since it was said that knowledge is by a
certain divine influence; *to the contrary:* where the thing

[56] *Rom.* 1:20.

itself is, the species of that thing is not necessary; but God or the divine light is most present to our understanding: therefore, there is no need of any influence.

17. Again, that influence either is creator or it is creature. Not creator, because it flows and is poured forth from God: therefore, it is not God. Not creature, since it is like a certain light flowing from the sun; but the light is not from nothing nor is it from anything materially: therefore, neither is that influence: therefore, it is not a creature: therefore, it is nothing, since it is neither creator nor creature.

18. Again, every agent of infinite power has power over its own operation through itself without the aid of another; but our understanding is of infinite power: therefore, it has power in its own intellectual operation without the aid of another. The major premiss is clear: the minor is proved by the Commentator on book XII of the *Metaphysics*[57] in which he says, that the movers of the celestial orbs are of infinite power and can perpetuate motion, because they are a power which is not in matter; but our understanding is a power not in matter: therefore etc.

19. Again, since it had been said that that light is seen in a certain manner in every thing seen and is known in every thing known, it was argued that what we see, we do not know by faith; but of that eternal good we have no knowledge except by faith: therefore, we do not see it. The minor premiss is proved by Augustine in book VIII *on the Trinity*,[58] who says: So long as *we walk by faith, not by the species* [*i.e. by sight*],[59] we assuredly do not yet see God.

20. Again, according to the Philosopher in book I? *on the Heavens and the World*,[60] the superior a nature is,

[57] Ch. 7.

[58] Ch. 4, n. 6.

[59] II *Corinth.* 5:7.

[60] Ch. 12.

the fewer things it needs for its perfection; but the rational creature is a very perfect creature in the order of the universe: therefore, it needs fewer things for its perfection. But inferior creatures do not need some special divine influence to accomplish their perfections: therefore, much less the rational creature.

21. Again, if the influence of the divine light or if the divine light itself is necessary to knowledge, it is not necessary only as the medium which elevates, but as the reason of assimilation. But since the understanding is formed by nature to know all things, it is necessary that through that influence it be assimilated to that light with respect to all knowable things. But no influence suffices for representing all knowable things, nor does any attribute that is known assimilate or represent except according to that reason, as goodness the good: therefore, it is necessary that either God himself by his essence is the reason of assimilation, which is false; or nothing else suffices: therefore, one does not know in God or in any special influence.

22. Again, certitude of knowledge is from the part of the medium; but that medium is related equally to all: therefore, all would know equally. But this is false: therefore, they do not know in that light.

23. Again, according to Augustine in book X *on the Trinity*,[61] the act of will necessarily supposes the act of knowledge; but there is not required any superior influence for the act of will, for the natural act I say, since it is inclined naturally to choosing the good: therefore, neither is it required for the act of knowledge.

24. Again, the argument is confirmed thus: that every thing which moves or tends to something, necessarily has something of that to which it is moved: but the will is moved naturally to God: therefore, it has by nature

[61] Chs. 1 and 2.

something of God: therefore, further influence is not required.

25. Again, the reason of knowing must be proportional to the knower and the object; but any light is more proportional than the divine light, nor is that divine light proportional: therefore, it is not the reason of knowing. Moreover, that another light is more proportional is seen, for there is the light of the blessed angel which is as it were of the same parentage as our understanding. That that divine light is not proportional is clear, since it exceeds infinitely both our understanding and the knowable object; and besides, if it were proportional, the understanding could see it.

26. Again, every power[62] which is reflexive on itself judges of itself and of all things which are in it; but [our mind] does not judge of the divine light nor of any influence of light, since by it and according to it, it judges of all things: therefore, there is no such light or influence in our mind.

27. Again, if that light is the reason of knowing in all knowledge, since that light represents all things equally, all things would be known equally, present things and future, hidden and manifest, necessary and contingent; but this is false: therefore etc.

28. Again, I ask: when I see some immutable truth, as, *every whole is greater than its part*, and *seven and three are ten*, what do I see? Either something created, or something uncreated; not something created, since nothing created is immutable or eternal; not something uncreated, because I see this perspicuously; but to see God perspicuously is to be blessed; but we are not blessed here on earth, nor is anyone who sees some immutable truth blessed: therefore etc.

[62] Cp. BONAVENTURA, *Sentences*, book I, d. 3, p. 1, q. 1, to the fourth; see above, p. 128.

29. Again, if God or the divine light necessarily pours forth something in any certain knowledge, since to know, according to the Philosopher, is in our power,[63] then that light or the influence of that light would be in our power; but this is false: therefore, neither the divine light nor any special influence of it is required necessarily for certain knowledge.

ON THE CONTRARY: 1. Augustine in book XI *on the City of God*[64] says: *Although in certain animals the sense of the eyes is much more keen for looking into the light than it is in us, yet they can not grasp the incorporeal light, by which our mind is in a certain manner irradiated, that we may be able to judge concerning all these things. For in so far as we grasp it, to that extent we have it in our power.* Therefore by the illumination of that light and by attaining it, we know whatever we know certainly.

2. Again, Augustine in book XII *on the Literal Commentary on Genesis*[65] says:

> The light by which the soul is illumined that it may see clearly all things understood truly either in itself or in that light, is God himself. But when the soul attempts to perceive that light, it palpitates and has no more power; nevertheless whatever it understands is thence; as it is able to, it sees what is above it, and aided by that light it sees likewise whatever it sees in itself by understanding.

Therefore etc.

3. Again, in book XII of the *Confessions*:[66] *If we both see that what you say is true, and if we both see that what I say is true, I do not see in you nor you in*

---

[63] *On the Soul*, II, ch. 5, 417ᵃ 23-24.

[64] Ch. 27, n. 2.   [65] Ch. 31, n. 59.   [66] Ch. 25, n. 35.

*me, but both in that which is above our minds in im-
mutable truth.*

4. Again, in book VIII *on the Trinity*[67] *Augustine*
says: *When the mind so pleases us, when we understand
well, that we prefer it to every corporeal light, it does
not please us in itself, but in that art by which it is
made. For something which is made is approved when
it is seen that it should have been made; this is truth
and the simple good.*

5. Again, Augustine says in book IX *on the Trinity:*[68]
*For we do not gather a general or special notion of the
human mind through likeness by seeing many minds by
the corporeal senses, but we perceive the immobile truth,
from which we define [perfectly], so far as we are able,
not of what sort is the mind of man, but how it must be
in the sempiternal reasons.* And in the same chapter[69]
he says: *And accordingly we judge of these senses according to this* [form of eternal truth], *and we perceive
it by the perception of the rational mind.* And in the
beginning of chapter 7[70] he says: *In that eternal truth
through which all things are made, we perceive with a
glance of the mind the form according to which we are,
and according to which either in ourselves or in bodies
we are occupied with any thing according to true and
right reason.* Therefore not only do we see and know
in it, but we see it.

6. Again in book I *on the Christian Doctrine:*[71]

The wise man, having acquired wisdom, is
wise; before he acquired it, he was not wise;
but still the wisdom itself neither was ever
unwise nor could ever be. If they did not see
it, in no manner would the wise set an im-

[67] Ch. 3, n. 5.   [69] N. 11.   [71] Ch. 8, n. 8 and 9.
[68] Ch. 6, n. 9.   [70] N. 12.

mutably wise life before a mutable life with
full faith. For they see the [immutable] rule
itself of truth by which they declare the former
to be better, nor do they see it anywhere except
above their own nature, since they see themselves as mutable. Whence it is common to all
for contemplating commonly and immutably.
And he who does not see this, is as one blind in
the sun, to whom the refulgence of the so clear
and present light, poured into the very places of
[his] eyes, is of no profit.

Therefore the same as before.

7. Again, Dionysius in the book *on the Angelic Hierarchy*[72] says: *Supermundane things are divided into
three kinds by the reason of the divine understanding:
into substance, power, and operation*; but the rational
soul is produced only by some special influence of
God: therefore, it operates only by some special influence.
But the proper operation of it is intellectual knowledge:
therefore etc.

8. Again, everything which has been made, has been
made according to some reason. However, that which
has been made rationally, must be known through some
reason: either, therefore, through that by which it was
made or through some other. If through another: it is
not known truly; if through the same: but all things
are made by eternal reasons: therefore, they are known
only by eternal reasons.

9. Again, such is the order in the powers of the soul,
that the lower power always consults the higher.
Whence the particular sense consults the common sense,
the common sense imagination, imagination inferior
reason, the inferior portion of reason the superior, ac-

[72] Ch. 11.

cording to Augustine in book XII of the *Literal Commentary on Genesis*,[73] since all visions are referred to judgment by intellectual vision. Therefore, the superior portion either judges according to itself or through something which is above it. If through something which is above it, there is nothing above the soul except the immutable truth: therefore etc. If according to itself: then nothing is superior to it, as Augustine says *on True Religion*.[74] If therefore something is above the mind: then it judges according to that and through that; but that, as has been said, is the immutable truth; therefore etc.

I REPLY: since the rational soul is constituted as in a medium between creator and creatures, and is ordered to the creator according to its superior part, but to creatures according to its inferior part, as Augustine says in many places, therefore there have been from antiquity many opinions concerning knowledge and the reason of knowing.

For Plato together with his followers considered that the whole reason of knowing comes from an archetypal or intelligible world and from ideal reasons, and considered that that eternal light concurs to sure [*certitudinalis*] knowledge in its evidence and as the *whole* and *only* reason of knowing, as Augustine states in many places, and particularly in book VIII *on the City of God*:[75] *God himself, who made all things, is the light of minds for knowing all things.*

But this position is utterly erroneous. For although it seems to establish the way of wisdom [*sapientia*] none the less it destroys the way of knowledge [*scientia*].— Moreover, if that light were the *whole* and *only* reason of knowing, the knowledge of things in the Word would

[73] Ch. 11, n. 24.   [74] Chs. 30 and 31.   [75] Ch. 7.

not differ from the knowledge of things in their own
genus, nor would the knowledge of reason differ from
the knowledge of revelation, nor philosophic knowledge
from prophetic, nor knowledge by nature from knowledge by grace.

Another position was that of Aristotle, as it seems,
who said that the whole reason of knowing is caused and
comes from the inferior way of sense, memory, and experience, together with the natural light of our active
intellect abstracting species from phantasms and making
them to be understood in actuality.   And thence he
considered that the eternal light is not necessary to sure
knowledge, nor did he ever speak of it.   And this
opinion of his is clear in book II of the *Posterior
Analytics*.[76]

Certain philosophizers follow this position, although
not completely, none the less asserting that that light is
the general cause of sure knowledge, but in no wise do
we attain to it, nor is any special influence of it necessary in natural knowledge: but that the light of the
active intellect, together with the species and likenesses
of things received and abstracted from things, suffices;
otherwise the operation of the nature would be voided,
and our understanding would understand only accidentally, and our knowledge would not be natural but
supernatural.   That which Augustine says, that all things
are seen through that light and in it, is not to be understood that the understanding attains to that light in some
way, nor that that light is something poured in specially,
but that eternal God imparts naturally the intellectual
light to us, in which we know and see naturally all knowables, which lie under reason.

But this position seems likewise to be defective in a
number of respects.   For although it furnishes the way

[76] Ch. 19, 99[b]19—100[a]18.

of knowledge, it wholly destroys the way of wisdom. It seems to diminish a great deal the reason and nature of the image. For the rational creature by the very fact that he is *in the image of God*,[77] inheres according to the highest part of him in the eternal rules, as Augustine says in book XII *on the Trinity*.[78] It seems none the less to overturn and subvert all the foundations of St. Augustine, whose authorities can in no manner be expounded otherwise. But this seems improper, since he is the doctor extraordinary, and the one whom catholic doctors and especially theologians ought to follow.

And therefore I think that a medium way is to be held to without prejudice, by saying that our knowledge is caused both by lower and by higher things, by exterior things and by ideal reasons.

For the understanding of this it must be noted that nothing is known or understood except the true. Truth, however, is triple or is triply, according as each thing has being triply, namely, in its own genus, in the created understanding, and in the eternal exemplar, as Augustine says in book V of the *Literal Commentary on the Genesis*[79] and Anselm in the book *on Truth* in chapter X.[80] Therefore we can speak of truth in three ways: by comparison to the matter which it informs, since (in that every created nature represents according to its grade the art by which it was made) the form itself or nature or essence, through which it imitates the very art or exemplar, is its truth; and it is true only in so far as it expresses that exemplar. In the *second* place we can consider truth by comparison to the understanding which it excites; and this is the created understanding and most of all the human understanding, since

[77] *Gen.* 1:27.

[78] Chs. 1 ff.

[79] Ch. 12, n. 28.

[80] See above, vol. I, p. 170.

we are speaking of that mode. For there is no nature which does not manifest and declare itself to the understanding as it is able. In the *third* place we can consider truth by comparison to the exemplar from which it emanates; this is the divine light and art, by which all things have been made.

Truth, however, according to its own reason is the reason of knowing and manifesting, as Hilary says that truth is declarative being. This reason, as it is the impressed reason of the creature, that is, the form itself or quiddity, is not sufficient itself to manifest or declare or move the understanding. Therefore God provided a certain intellectual light for our mind, by which it abstracts from sensibles the species of things exposed to it, purifying them and receiving their quiddities, which are in themselves the object of the understanding. Nevertheless, he imparted a natural faculty of judgment, by which our mind discerns the goods from the evil and the trues from the false. But this light is not sufficient, for it is defective and mixed with opacity, unless it is brought under and connected with that eternal light, which is the perfect and sufficient reason of knowing, and the understanding according to its highest part attains to and in a certain manner takes hold of that.

It attains, however, to that light or those eternal reasons as the reason of knowing, but *not* the *only* reason, for then knowledge in the Word would not differ, as has been said, from knowledge in the proper genus of the thing, nor knowledge of wisdom, from knowledge of science; nor does it attain to that light as the *whole* reason, for then we would not need the species and likenesses of things; which is false, since the Philosopher says,[81] and experience teaches, that they who lose one

[81] *Posterior Analytics* I, ch. 18, 81ᵃ 37-40.

sense necessarily lose the scientific knowledge which is derived according to that sense; therefore, although according to Augustine the mind according to its highest part attains to those rules, nevertheless that is undoubtedly true which the Philosopher says, that knowledge is begotten in us by way of sense, memory, and experience, from which the universal is gathered, which is the principle of art and science; nor does it attain to that light as *naked*, for then knowledge of the source would not differ from knowledge of the way; nor as *proper*, but in a certain way general. And therefore together with these it needs necessarily the likenesses of things abstracted from things as the proper, determined, and distinct reasons of knowing. And this Augustine shows in book IX *on the Trinity*,[82] saying that the illumination [*lumen*], truth, is from the higher, that is, from light [*lux*]; but shadows are from the lower, that is from phantasms. He says,

> The judgment of truth is strong and bright from above, and is firm in the most uncorrupted rules of its right; and if it is joined as it were to a kind of cloud of corporeal images, it still is not involved nor confounded. But there is this difference between the two: either I am to be led away as if from a clear sky by any cloud or by no cloud, or else I am accustomed to ascend as to the highest mountains, enjoying the free air in varying ways and I look upon the very serene light above and the very dense shadows beneath.

The mind or the understanding, however, knowing that light and the ideal reasons attains to and in a certain manner perceives them, not as an *object setting*

[82] Ch. 6, n. 10 and 11.

at rest, terminating, and leading to itself, but as an object *moving and leading to something else;* not as an *object of vision,* in which the glance of reasoning is fixed, but as a *motive object* and *reason of seeing;* not *fully, but in part;* not in its *clarity,* but in a certain *obscurity,* because it is not yet fully deiform. And therefore we see so *through it that we do not see it;* we see so that *we do not perceive ourselves* seeing, except when we have turned about, by ascending step by step from the senses of the body, until we come to the nature of the rational mind, and at length by transcending the mind itself we come to the immutable rules, as Augustine teaches in book VII of the *Confessions.* Whence he says in book XV *on the Trinity*:[83] We see so through it that we do not see it except through a mirror and in an enigma. And Anselm in the *Proslogium,* chapter 14:

> Why, O Lord, does my soul not perceive you, if it finds you? Or does it not find you when it finds the light and the truth? Or could it understand anything of you except by your light and truth? If, therefore, it has seen the light and truth, it has seen you; if it has not seen you, it has not seen the light and truth, or it is the light and the truth which it has seen and none the less has not yet seen you, because it has seen you only in some respect, but it has not seen you as you are.

That illumination, therefore, by moving our understanding insinuates a certain illumination in our mind, so that it sees as it were *objectively* and effectively by *the divine light,* but it sees *formally* by and in *that illumination,* which is continued and preserved in our minds by

[83] Ch. 6, n. 10; or ch. 9, n. 16.

the divine presence. Nor is it withdrawn from any knower, but aids all the good and evil indifferently according to the ordination and immutable disposition of its wisdom by which it cooperates in the intellectual operation.

Many reasons moreover can be adduced to the confirmation of this.

And the *first reason* can be taken from the part of the nature of the *knowing mind*, that is, the intellectual mind. For since our mind, according to Augustine through the whole length of book XII *on the Trinity*, has a double portion, one *lower*, deputed to administrating temporal things, another *superior*, assigned to contemplating eternal things; as the lower portion does not suffice without the higher for full judgment in the administration of these things, so neither does the higher portion suffice without eternal light. This portion, however, is that in which the image of God is; and this portion inheres in eternal rules, through which it defines and judges whatever it knows with certitude. Moreover, since there is found in the creature a triple mode or grade of conformity to God, namely as *trace*, as *image*, as *likeness*; trace means the comparison to God as to a causative principle, likeness means the comparison to God as to an infused gift: therefore, image, which is medium between them, means the comparison to God as to a motive object. Therefore, in the operations of the creature, which are his in so far as the creature is a trace, God cooperates as principle and cause; of this sort are natural operations. In those operations, further, which are his, in so far as the creature is a likeness, God cooperates as infused gift; of this sort are meritorious operations and those pleasing to God. In those operations, finally, which are his as image, he cooperates as motive object and reason; of

this sort are intellectual operations, in which the understanding perceives immutable truth. Whence Augustine
in book VIII *on the City of God* says, that *God is the
cause of subsisting, and the order of living, and the
reason of understanding*;[84] *the effector of natures, and
the good of actions, and the light of things known*;[85]
our principle, our good, our light;[86] *cause of the constituted universe, fountain for the drinking of felicity, and
light for the perceiving of truth.*[87]

The *second reason* is taken from the part of the
knowable thing. For everything which is known certainly, is necessarily immutable; and this is true not only
as regards the act of the understanding, which is in the
perception of terms, but also of first propositions and
inferences.—For our understanding seizes the significances of *terms* when it apprehends each of them by
definition. Definition, however, has to be made by superiors, and those superiors by other superiors, until
one arrives at the most general, which being ignored,
the inferiors could not be known definitively. For unless it is known what *that which is through itself* [*ens
per se*] is, the definition of substance can not be known;
nor can that which is through itself be known, unless
it is known with its conditions, which are the one, the
true, and the good. Since, however, that which is [*ens*]
could be thought of as diminished, as completed, as in
potentiality, as in actuality, as that which is in some
one respect only, as that which is absolutely, and thus
with the other conditions which are of that which is as
that which is—*privations, however, can not be known
except by affirmations* according to Augustine and the
Philosopher[88]—the understanding could not come, as

84 Ch. 4.   86 Ibid., ch. 10, n. 1.
85 Ibid., ch. 9.   87 Ibid., ch. 10, n. 2.
88 *On the Soul* III, ch. 6, 430ᵇ 22-23.

resolving fully, into the understanding of anything of created things that are, unless it is aided by the understanding of the purest, most actual, and most complete thing that is. Therefore, it can not know an imperfect, defective and incomplete thing which is, *nor can it know that such a thing differs very greatly from another, unless that which is absolutely perfect, be seen by the mind*, as Augustine says *on True Religion*.[89]

As regards the perception of *propositions*, it then comprehends and understands truly, when it knows such true propositions, and can not be deceived concerning them, as, *every whole is greater than its part*. For it knows that this can not be constituted otherwise; it knows, therefore, that this truth is immutable.—As regards the perception of inferences, it sees, comprehends, and understands, when it sees that the conclusion follows necessarily from the premises; and this not only in necessary terms, but in contingent terms, not only in things that are, but in things that are not. Therefore it does not see this necessity in a *matter*, no more in propositions than in inferences and relations, for every part and every whole can cease to be; nor in the *soul*, since *the soul is mutable and can suffer the mutability of error*, as Augustine says *on True Religion*[90] and in book XIV *on the Trinity*. Therefore it sees in the *exemplar of the eternal art* and in the ideal reason, in which things have an immutable relation according to the representation of that art. Therefore, all light of reasoning truly is kindled from that truth and in the attempt to reach it, as Augustine says *on True Religion*.[91]

Again, as was touched on in the preceding question,[92] truth is nothing other in the creature than a certain expression of the eternal art and exemplar, according

[89] Ch. 30, n. 55.
[90] Ch. 30, n. 56.
[91] Ch. 39, n. 72.
[92] See above, pp. 256-257.

to which it has been made; and every creature is so far true, as he imitates that exemplar according to his grade. Therefore, it is impossible that it be known truly, except by a certain application and relation to that rule and reason, by which it was made. Whence Augustine in book I of the *Soliloquies*[93] says:

> God is intelligible, likewise those signs of the disciplines are intelligible, yet they differ a great deal. For both earth and light are visible, but the earth can not be seen unless illumined by light. Therefore likewise those things which are treated of in the disciplines, which everyone concedes [to be] very true with no hesitation, it must nevertheless be believed, could not be understood, unless they were lighted by God as by their sun. Therefore, just as in that sun three observations may be made: that it *is*, that it *shines*, that it *illumines*, so in that most secret God there are a certain three [observations to be made]: that he *is*, that he *understands*, and that he *makes* others *to be understood*.

The *third reason* is taken from the part of the *medium of knowing*. The medium, however, in certain knowledge is necessarily certain. It would not however be certain, if it were not *common in all, immutable*, and *infallible*.

This is clear since I know *all* equals according to the same reason of equality, and according to the same [reason of truth] *every one* knows them truly and with certitude; according to the same reason of beauty all know all beautiful things; according to the same reason of unity, all single things. It must be *immutable* because

[93] Ch. 8, n. 15.

nothing can be known immutably except by an immutable reason. It must be *infallible*, otherwise it would
not be a sure reason of knowing, because it could not
give infallibility.

If therefore every creature and every created light
is contracted and limited and terminable and mutable,
but certain reason is uncontractible, immutable, interminable, then no created light or created reason can be
the medium in certain knowledge. Therefore, it is
necessary that all things which are known certainly
be known in the light of eternal truth and in immutable
rules. This is the argument of Augustine *on True Religion*[94] where he says that the reason of beauty is
neither protuberant in space nor unstable in time. For
it can not rightly be said that the round vessel is judged
according to it and the round denarius is not judged
according to it; or that equal years are judged according to it and equal months are not judged according
to it. None the less it is neither greater nor less in
space of time or place, for if it were greater we would
not judge the lesser according to it, nor if it were less,
would we judge the greater according to it. As it is
however we know all squares according to the same law
of quadrature, and we know all equals according to the
same law of equality: therefore, the interval of spaces
and of times is neither greater nor lesser, but its power
is above all.—The same Augustine in book II *on the
Free Will*[95] where he shows that the laws of justice and
the laws of numbers are common to all, concludes:

> But that beauty of truth and wisdom does not
> shut off those who come in a crowded multitude
> of hearers, nor does it move along in time, nor
> does it migrate in space, nor is it interrupted

[94] Ch. 30, n. 56.
[95] Ch. 14, n. 38; see above, vol. I, p. 55.

by night, nor is it blocked off by shadows, nor does it fall under the senses of the body; of all the world it is nearest to those turned toward it, it is present to all, eternal to all, it is absent from no place, it admonishes abroad, it teaches within,

it is present to all who contemplate.

The *fourth reason* is taken from the part of the judgment, since in all certain knowledge right judgment is necessary. The mind judges rightly however of all *sensibles*; it judges of all *beautiful things,* as reason of which we say, that this thing delights, and this thing makes an agreement, this makes an equality; it judges of all *natures,* what must be attributed to each by the law of nature; it judges of the *morals of men,* what must be praised, and what must be damned. Every judgment, however, must be right according to some rule and law which is absolutely beyond judgment. Therefore this law is either *below* the soul, or *in the soul itself,* or *the soul itself,* or *above it.* It is not below it, because the soul judges of all things which are below it; nor is it the soul itself nor in the soul itself, for the soul is mutable and every condition or habit which is in it is mutable, and likewise it judges of itself and of everything which is in it: therefore it is above the soul. No law, however, is above the soul except the law of immutable truth. Therefore, it judges whatever it judges rightly by the law of immutable truth. And this is what Augustine says *on True Religion* :[96] If the mind judges according to itself, there is no more eminent nature. Therefore, since it is itself mutable, another law which is more excellent must be sought.

[96] Ch. 30, n. 54 and 56.

But since this law of all arts is [absolutely] immutable, and since the human mind to which it is granted to see such law, can suffer the mutability of error, it is [sufficiently] clear that there is above our mind the law which is called truth. Nor must it be doubted, moreover, that the immutable nature which is above the soul is God; and the first life, the first essence, the first beauty and equality are there, where the first wisdom is. For this is that immutable truth which is rightly called the law of all arts and the law of the omnipotent artifex.

He says the same in book II *on the Free Will*,[97] and in book VI *on Music*,[98] but best of all in book XIV *on the Trinity*.[99]

Hence it is (*he says*) that the impious think on eternity, and condemn many things rightly and praise many rightly in the morals of men. Yet in what rules do they judge these things, unless in those in which they see how each one should live, even though they do not themselves live in that same manner? [Where do they see them?] For they do not see them *in their own nature*, since without doubt these things are seen by the mind, and it is known that their minds are mutable, and whoever sees this in these immutable rules sees the immutable rules. Nor in *the condition or habit* of their mind, since these rules are of justice, and their minds are known to be unjust. Where then are these rules [written], where does the unjust know what just is, where does he per-

---

[97] Ch. 12, n. 34; see above, vol. I, pp. 50 and 51.
[98] Ch. 12, n. 34.   [99] Ch. 15, n. 21.

ceive that that must be had which he himself does not have? Where are they written then except in the book of that light which is called *truth,* whence all just light is marked off and whence it is transferred into the mind of the man who does justice, not by passing into it, but by being imprinted on it, just as a figure passes into the wax and does not leave the seal? But he who does not do it, and yet sees what should be done, he is one who is turned from that light, by which he is nevertheless touched.

The authorities alleged in the preceding question hold for the present question too. I say this, therefore, that whatever is known certainly in intellectual knowledge, is known in eternal reasons and in the light of the first truth in the way in which it has been explained, by concluding it from the *knowing nature* and *the knowable thing* and *the certain medium* and also from *right judgment,* so that the *material* reason of knowing is from exterior things whence the species of the things to be known are furnished, but the *formal* reason is partly from within, that is, from the light of reason, partly from above, but *completively* and *consummatively* from eternal rules and reasons.

The arguments, which prove this, must be conceded. To the arguments to the contrary it must be said:

To the first that the philosophy of Aristotle did not attain to this point; nor is this surprising. For this reason I say that although there is in the soul an active intellect, whose property it is to make all things, and a possible intellect, whose property it is to be made all things, nevertheless that does not suffice. For to say *all* and to say the *whole* are different.[100]   It suffices for *all* things, but still not *totally*, for with it is required necessarily a further and higher light.

To the second it must be said that the intellectual operation concerning natural things is natural. God, however, works and cooperates in the operations of creatures according to the mode and requirement of their nature, as has been seen. And because the rational creature is the image of God or formed to his image, the very nature [*ratio*] of the image requires that he cooperate in its operations according to the mode of object moving, in that the mind is formed naturally to be moved and illumined by that light. Nor must the operation, because of this, be called supernatural or miraculous, because he cooperates with a nature operating naturally according to the grade and mode of its nature, which operation he takes away from none.

To the third it must be said that, in truth, as Hugo says, some things are above reason, and some below reason; and although they may lie under the power of a nature, still that nature has no power in them except by a higher light, because this follows from the reason and requirement of the nature and from its nobility, just as the eye has power in those things which fall under its visual power, but not without the light of the sun or some other extrinsic light, because such a power and such an operation require it.

To the fourth it must be said that in all action of the rational nature, as it is rational, God cooperates in a certain more special way and by a certain more special influence than in the actions of other creatures. If, however, the argument runs from a comparison with other natures, in which he does not cooperate in *power* by some special influence, that therefore he does not

[100] ARISTOTLE, *Metaphysics* V, c. 26, 1023^{b} 26-1024^{a} 11.

cooperate in *wisdom* in intellectual operations: it is clear that they are not alike, since by the very fact that it is the image of God, the rational nature is ordered to God as to its object, and therefore God cooperates in its operations as motive object.

To the fifth it must be said that the light of the active intellect does not suffice to abstract intelligible species, nor does the natural judgment suffice to judge nor does the intelligible species which is made, suffice to manifest the thing perfectly, even if a common and a general influence be supposed, unless the divine light itself aids, touching and moving our mind and illumining it to this end, that it may be able to know certainly and indubitably, for the reasons above mentioned.

To the sixth the reply is clear. For it has been said that the understanding necessarily attains that light, that it sees that light; but not as the object which sets it at rest, on which it fastens its glance, for such sight makes one blessed, but as the object moving, not leading to itself, but leading to something else; just as the eye seeing in the light of the sun sees the light of the sun, not as object, but as it is the reason and medium of seeing.

To the seventh the reply is clear, since if those reasons were the *whole* and *only* reason of knowing, it would be true that he who is nearer them would see more in them and would see more things in them; but since they are neither the whole nor only reason, but together with created reasons, therefore not he who is nearer, but he who acquires more reasons, sees more things in those reasons.—Or it must be said that they see more who are moved more to them. But if some are nearer to that light considered as it moves [*in ratione moventis*] the *affect*, but not considered as it moves the *understanding*, because they do not move themselves to those reasons as to a light, but rather as to a fire, and therefore they receive more heat, in such wise that none the less they do not receive more splendor; but others contrarily.

To the eighth it must be said that that statement must be understood to mean that the more anything has of being, the more it is knowable by its own reason. Otherwise they are not similar, since the *being* of the thing is something absolute; and therefore the principles proper to it, together with the general maintenance of the creator, suffice for it. But *knowing* means the comparison to the understanding, which the thing moves; therefore, more is required for knowledge than for being, as well from the part of the knowable thing as from the part of the knowing understanding.

To the ninth it must be said that Augustine does not mean to exclude the aid of the light or of those reasons, but the aid of the senses. Therefore he wishes to say no more than that he knows corporeal things with the senses mediating, but he knows incorporeal things without the aid of the senses; just as, if we were to say that the eye through itself sees color, the benefit of light would not be excluded because of that.

To the tenth it must be said that that statement [*auctoritas*] of Augustine is absolutely to the contrary, as is clear to one considering it diligently. For he means there, in the entire context, that to that eternal light something of our own is subjoined in the natural order, and in that one sees whatever one sees. Nor does Augustine speak of kind because of some community of nature, as it is common to speak of kind or genus, but he calls it kind because of a certain conformity, because that light is intelligible and our soul is intellectual; that light is spiritual and our soul spiritual, in the manner in which it said in *Acts* 17:[101] *we are the kind of God.*

[101] Ver. 28; *genus* is usually rendered *offspring*, instead of *kind*, in translation.

To the eleventh it must be said that, in truth, nature is not lacking in things necessary to the rational creature but it provides for it in a more sublime way than for other natures. And although without the influence of that light it could not go forth into the actuality of certain knowledge, nevertheless it is not said to be lacking or deficient, because that light always assists it and is always present to it. Nor does this derogate from its nobility, but rather it attests to its great dignity.

To the twelfth it must be said that, as the Philosopher holds, the active intellect is like light, the possible, like an eye, the phantasm, like color. But then the likeness does not hold, since, just as for corporeal vision color itself and the visual organ and the power, together with the natural and complanted light, do not suffice without the benefit of the superior light, so too for intellectual vision the phantasm does not suffice for moving, nor the possible intellect for receiving, nor the light for abstracting and making species to be understood actually, without the aid and benefit of the divine light. For the light of the active intellect is like the light connatural to the eye, but the divine light is like the light of the sun.

To the thirteenth it must be said that without doubt knowledge is a certain operation natural to the intellectual nature, and this influence or cooperation can in a certain manner be called *natural*. Because of this, the distinction must be made that *natural* can be used in two ways: either *what is caused* from the principles of nature, and in this way that influence is not natural but supernatural; or in another way, *what is never absent* from nature and accompanies nature inseparably, and in this way that influence can be called natural.

To the fourteenth it must be said that one does not see in that light as in a *mirror*, because then one would see that light openly, but as in a *reason*, so that the divine light is by its essence an *effective* and *motive* reason, but that influence which we assert is a formal reason. And as regards the objection that is made, that that creature is mutable, I say that although the creature is and is mutable of itself, still it is not inconsistent that sure knowledge be from it *formally*, since it is from God *effectively*. Just as what we say of grace, that it elevates the soul above itself and moves it, is not to be understood effectively, but formally, for God does it through grace. It is thus in the question stated.

To the fifteenth it must be said that it is not inconsistent that by different modes the creator be the reason of knowing the creature and the creature the reason of knowing the creator. For the creator is the *motive* and *effective* reason of knowing, but the creature is the *manuductive* reason of knowing the creator and therefore knowledge is not circular, because it is not according to the same mode.

To the sixteenth it must be said that on the contrary where the thing itself is, its species is necessary, for even though God be most interior to the mind, still considered as [*in ratione*] that which *moves* his influence is necessary, or his species by which mediating he moves, for the mind could not be moved unless something were done in it. It is likewise necessary considered as that which *informs*, for God can not be the form of the understanding; but the reason of knowing is the form inhering to the understanding.

To the seventeenth it must be said that that influence is a creature and created from nothing. As to that which the argument says of the corporeal light, I say that the corporeal light is something made and a creature. For not only is something called a creature because it is made immediately from nothing, but because it is made from something or from something which has been made from nothing. Whence is it then? I say that it is from the luminous, not materially but originally, as the species of the thing is from the thing itself.

To the eighteenth it must be said that something can be called infinite in two ways, namely, by actuality or by duration. Therefore neither the movers of the orbs nor the understandings are infinite by an infinity of actuality; and if the Commentator said that, he erred; but they are infinite in duration, and therefore they can perpetuate motion. The argument, however, proceeded from the infinity of actuality, and therefore it does not hold.

To the nineteenth it must be said that not every sight removes a knowledge which is by faith, but the vision of that light as the object which brings to rest and terminates and in its clarity [does]; in which mode it is not seen along the way; it is seen as *object moving* and as *reason of seeing*, as has often been said.

To the twentieth it must be said that according to the Philosopher in the same place, some things are whole in goodness; and these acquire their perfection with no movement, such as God. Others are very close to integral goodness; and these acquire their perfection with very few movements, There are others which are ordered to great goodness, but are none the less removed from that perfection; therefore, they acquire their perfection with many movements. There are some, which are ordered to slight perfection; and those of this sort arrive at it with few movements. Some to no perfection; and they are immobile, because motion is for the acquiring of some perfection. The first is God; the second is the order of Angels; the third is the order of rational creatures, such as men; the fourth is the order of brute animals; the fifth is the order of higher elements; in the last and lowest place is earth. Nor is there a likeness of man and lower creatures, because he is ordered to some noble operation, that the divine light may be to him as an object moving and a reason of operating; and this is the mark of great nobility, just as it is a mark of nobility in sight (which although it is more excellent than the other senses, still needs the aid of light, which is the reason of seeing for it) that light is not necessary in the operations of other senses.

To the twenty-first it must be said that God himself through his essence is the *effective* reason of assimilating; but that influence is the *formal* reason of assimilating. In God, however, all things shine forth; but he does not lead to knowing by natural knowledge except only those things the species of which are received from things, whether corporeal or spiritual. And I think that there are different influences and different species according to the diversity of knowers, according to the plurality of reasons of different things.

To the twenty-second the reply is clear thus: that that light is not the whole or only reason of seeing, but together with reasons and species received from things. And therefore all do not see equally, because all do not receive species from things equally.—Moreover, although it is constituted equally, so far as it is from its own part, all do not move themselves or turn to it equally, and because of this they do not see equally.

To the twenty-third it must be said the minor premiss of the argument is false, since, just as the *understanding* would never know anything certainly without the illumination of that truth, so the *affect* would never love anything in good order without the affection of that goodness; but clearly Augustine means that in sins only blessedness is desired. And although it be moved naturally, still this is from its nature, and just as truth illuminating aids the understanding, so goodness affecting in a certain manner aids the affect.

To the twenty-fourth I say that it has something; and this is that influence affecting our affect, which it does not have naturally from its principles, nor from itself, but because this is never absent from it. It has likewise a conformity according to image.—If it be asked, whether the nature left to itself could be moved, I say no. And is it not the image of God? It is by all means. But still it is the property of the reason of the image, that it be borne in it as in the motive object, because of which they can not be separated.

To the twenty-fifth it must be said that the divine light is proportional both to the cognoscitive power and the cognoscible object, not by a proportion of commensuration, but of a certain order, because the *rational nature*, by the very fact that it is an image, is ordered to that object; likewise the cognoscible is formed naturally to be illuminated by that light as by a certain sun of its own, according to Augustine. The illumination of the angelic understanding, on the other hand, in so far as blessed, is not proportional to it by a proportion of order, although it is by a proportion of comparison and commensuration. Nor is it superior in this to the rational soul. For as Augustine says *on True Religion*[102] and in the *LXXXIII Questions*:[103] *In that it is the image of God, it is formed immediately by truth itself, with no creature interposed*; and in book X *of the City of God*:[104] *The angelic and the rational spirit are illumined by the same light.* It is, however, a natural

[102] Ch. 44, n. 82.   [104] Ch. 2.
[103] Quest. 51, n. 2 and 4.

any restatement of his doctrine: no modern language
constructed to carry the force of his distinctions, and
restatement therefore either distinctions must be
printed by approximate translation, or new expressions
must be invented as strange and as difficult as the latin
rms of Duns.

The intellectual heritage of Duns Scotus has been
subject of frequent discussion, but the polemical character of the discussions has not infrequently disguised
rather than disclosed his philosophical ancestors. The
selection which follows is not an unfair sampling of the
apologetic force he finds in the aristotelian system for
the defense of the doctrines of Augustine. Coming after
the departure of Thomas from pure augustinism, the
defense can be considered a restatement of the older
philosophy; but like the philosophy of Thomas it is a
restatement with a modification. Thomas had considered
the one Truth which Augustine discussed limited to the
truth which is involved in the adequation of things to
the divine understanding, but he had imported besides
the discussions of Aristotle for the statement of the
rich and shifting variety of truths which are adequations
of things to the human understanding; the one truth of
God is basic, but the statement of its being alone is
inadequate to characterize the truths of things and of
intellect. Duns Scotus reversed the thomist procedure:
he seeks the formal ground of certainty in the many
truths in which the mind is engaged; he finds infallible
truths and formalities which lead him back to the discovery, with Augustine, of eternal truths above the mind
to which the mind is directed. Broadly it may be said
that, whereas Thomas was led, impressed with the fact
that individuals of the same species differ only in
number and not in kind, to state a metaphysics built
upon substances unknown in their individuality, so em-

proportion, as it is borne by the nature into itself as into
an object moving, but not bringing to rest.

To the twenty-sixth it must be said that judgment of
the thing is double. For there is judgment of *discernment*, whether the thing is, and that this is not that; and
judgment of *authority* and as it were of definition, as
what a thing should be. The mind judges of the divine
light in the first manner, otherwise it would not know
it; it does not judge of it in the second way. The
argument proceeded in this second way, therefore it does
not hold.

To the twenty-seventh it must be said that when those
reasons are observed and seen in their clarity and as
the whole and only reason of knowing, future things
will be seen equally with present, contingent things with
necessary. But since they are not seen thus here on
earth, therefore neither are they all seen equally. Yet
it must be understood that, although God is absolutely
simple and uniform, still that eternal light, as it is an
exemplar, represents certain things as if outwardly and
openly, certain as if profoundly and in hiding. The
first are those which are made according to the necessary
ordination of the divine art, and the second those which
are made according to the dispensation of the concealed
will; and therefore natural things are known in that
natural light by the judgment of reason, but supernatural things and future things only by the gift of
heavenly revelation.

To the twenty-eighth it must be said that when I see
these immutable truths as the object *terminating*, I see
something *created*; when I see them as the object moving, I see something *uncreated*. This created thing,
however, is not immutable absolutely, but by supposition [i.e. by something which may stand for it immu-
tably]: therefore, certitude does not come from these

truths *absolutely* but *only in some one respect*. I see therefore a certain true concept in my soul objectively from the presence of knowable species, yet related to immutable reasons.

To the twenty-ninth it must be said that the influence of the light is not in our power, in the sense that we either make or produce it, or we should constrain God to pour it forth; but the influence is always present in accordance with the immutable ordination of divine liberality, nor is it ever withdrawn from any knower, but always aids him; and to that extent it could be said to be in our power.

JOHN DUNS SCOTUS (1266/1274–

Notwithstanding a growing interest in Dun and notwithstanding an increasing number of s his philosophy, the statement of his thought estimation of its importance are hazardous undert A variety of reasons explain why this should There is no critical edition of his works; examinati the authenticity of writings attributed to him has off one by one half a dozen important philosoph works which went under his name a century ago; t highly technical terminology which he evolved for th statement of his subtle philosophy can be worked with apparent cogency into a variety of interpretations; the content of Duns's philosophy, finally, is dependent on the emphasis the interpreter wishes to make, and dependent also on which of the works of doubtful authenticity he chooses to admit into the canon of Duns's writings. It would seem now that only five major works continue of undoubted authenticity—the treatise entitled *on the First Principle* (but not the treatise entitled *on the First Principle of All Things*), the *Questions on the Metaphysics* (but not the *Exposition on the XII Books of the Metaphysics*), the two Commentaries on the Sentences of Lombard, entitled the *Oxford Work* and the *Parisian Reportata*, and some *Quodlibetal Questions*. One effect of this limitation of authentic works has been the happy elimination of the contradictions, which it had been customary to find in the doctrines of Duns Scotus. But the subtlety and the technical detail of his philosophical analyses leave contradictions enough phasizing the fundamental unintelligibility of the thing which is, as it is, unadequated to the understanding; Duns Scotus, in his persistent search for the bases of certitude, recognized that the individual is handled in knowledge by distinctions (there is a real distinction, a distinction of reason only, and a formal distinction from the part of the thing), and expressed a theory of knowledge which emphasizes the status of the distinctions which the intellect discovers. The much agitated question of whether Duns refuted Thomas to state a greater synthesis of medieval thought, or whether he refined Thomas of questionable doctrines and reconciled him with Augustine, resolves itself into the question, simpler historically but more difficult of philosophical determination, of how a metaphysical inquiry with an aristotelian augustinian background will differ from an inquiry into formally verifiable certainties conducted on much the same background.

Here, as elsewhere, therefore, the inquiry into intentions and backgrounds may be abandoned for the examination of philosophical differences that appear in the doctrines themselves. If the difference is as it has been stated to be, it should appear particularly clearly in the status of the individual in each system. For Thomas, matter is the principle of individuation; that individuals of the same species differ, not in kind, but only in number, is the consequence of that principle. For Scotus, the principle of individuation is in the form, not merely in the matter; the essence of each individual contains the principle of contraction and limitation which restrains the universality of the species: the ultimate reality of the thing which is (*ens*) contracts the specific form. This is the doctrine of *hecceity*, according to which the characteristics of individuation are not to be found in quantity or in any other attribute of body, as Thomas's doctrine seems to state, but in a formal distinction derived from the thing. This is the significance of the much misinterpreted doctrine that being (*esse*) is no different from essence (*essentia*): the characteristics of individual things are intelligibly different; it is the possibility of formal differentiation and description which the hecceity preserves for the individual. Where Thomas was concerned to emphasize the specific and generic identity of different individuals, Duns was concerned with the notion, not necessarily contradictory, that each thing that is (*ens*) has some being (*esse*) of its own. Thomas followed Avicenna in holding that the mind conceived that which is (*ens*) in conceiving anything: whatever else is conceived must be as superadded to that first conception; Duns Scotus, on the other hand, considered that which is as particular, and as known in each case by the hecceity peculiar to the particular thing. Whereas Thomas, therefore, can express the relation of the true and the good by saying that they are convertible with that which is, for the one superadds to that which is an order to the understanding, the other an order to the appetite; Duns Scotus explains the relation by pointing out that the good and the true are different formally but identical in the thing.

The alterations that occur in the demonstrations of the existence of God are similar symptoms of the alteration of outlook toward a problem, analyzed in very similar fashion but with emphases diametrically opposed. Thomas is again concerned with the reality of first substances, individual things (of which properties, differences, genera, species can be predicated and in which accidents are present, but which can not, in turn, be predicated of anything). His refutation of the *a priori* demonstrations of God, his substitution of five *a posteriori* demonstrations for them are recognition of the fact that nothing is known save knowledge derived from experience of individual things, but that on the other hand the changes of individual things and the instabilities of sensible knowledge can not be explained save by a first mover, a first cause, a source of goodness; but that first cause is not itself known. Duns Scotus, too, holds that an *a priori* proof of the existence of God is impossible, but unlike Thomas he does not refute the ontological argument of Anselm, but "colors" it so that it is *a posteriori* rather than *a priori*. If the notion of God can be shown to be possible, it can be shown by that to be necessary; if a first efficient cause, if a final end, if a supreme perfection are possible, analysis of that possibility will show that they are necessary. Duns's proofs of the existence of God, therefore, begin like those of St. Thomas from knowledge occasioned by experience, but where Thomas seeks in experience some contingent thing which requires for its existence the existence of God, Duns Scotus consistently seeks out necessary truths and relations of thought implicated in the propositions which are necessarily true, independent of the experience that occasioned them. For this reason too the infinity of God plays a very important role in the analysis; an infinite first efficient cause, an infinite supreme intelligence, an infinite supreme good are concepts which can be analyzed as necessary formal background to the effects, the knowledge, the desires of this world.

The origin of all sciences in experience, the abstraction of universals, the activity of the mind compounding and dividing are familiar aristotelian steps in the analysis Scotus makes of knowledge. But that the concepts of genera and species are univocal realities; that necessary and infallible truths are involved in the statement of the conjuncture of terms, concerns him more than the peculiar properties and accidents of that which is. His polemic is directed most frequently against the skeptics who would deny that man can know naturally, without divine illumination, any sure truths. His search, therefore, is often for infallible and certain truths, and he finds three orders of them, the truths of first principles and conclusions derived logically from them, the truths of experience, and the truths of selfconsciousness. Following Aristotle and Augustine he holds that the principles of the sciences are very certain, that even the possibility of truth in science is indication of the infallible truth of scientific principles, notwithstanding that all the truths of science may be themselves subjected to doubt; the doors are concealed from no one though the contents of the house may be unknown. For the truth of the principles no appeal need be made beyond understanding and the terms of the principle understood; knowing the terms, the understanding knows one term as including the other. The truth of a first principle is in the conformity of the composition of the terms to the terms so compounded; the understanding apprehending terms has in itself the necessary cause of the conformity of the act of composition to the terms it compounds. There is a subtle and very modern turn to this analysis: the truth of a first principle is not made to consist in some character of the terms or categories in isolation but rather in the relation perceived between them in the apprehension by the mind of the proposition which relates them. So, too, whiteness and whiteness stand related not by some disparate peculiarity of the two terms but in the formal relation *likeness*. The whole is greater than its parts, because the perception of the composition of the terms stated in the proposition and the perception of the terms themselves is impossible without the perception of the conformity proportion, as it is borne by the nature into itself as into an object moving, but not bringing to rest.

To the twenty-sixth it must be said that judgment of the thing is double. For there is judgment of *discernment*, whether the thing is, and that this is not that; and judgment of *authority* and as it were of definition, as what a thing should be. The mind judges of the divine light in the first manner, otherwise it would not know it; it does not judge of it in the second way. The argument proceeded in this second way, therefore it does not hold.

To the twenty-seventh it must be said that when those reasons are observed and seen in their clarity and as the whole and only reason of knowing, future things will be seen equally with present, contingent things with necessary. But since they are not seen thus here on earth, therefore neither are they all seen equally. Yet it must be understood that, although God is absolutely simple and uniform, still that eternal light, as it is an exemplar, represents certain things as if outwardly and openly, certain as if profoundly and in hiding. The first are those which are made according to the necessary ordination of the divine art, and the second those which are made according to the dispensation of the concealed will; and therefore natural things are known in that natural light by the judgment of reason, but supernatural things and future things only by the gift of heavenly revelation.

To the twenty-eighth it must be said that when I see these immutable truths as the object *terminating*, I see something *created*; when I see them as the object moving, I see something *uncreated*. This created thing, however, is not immutable absolutely, but by supposition [i.e. by something which may stand for it immutably]: therefore, certitude does not come from these truths *absolutely* but *only in some one respect.* I see therefore a certain true concept in my soul objectively from the presence of knowable species, yet related to immutable reasons.

To the twenty-ninth it must be said that the influence of the light is not in our power, in the sense that we either make or produce it, or we should constrain God to pour it forth; but the influence is always present in accordance with the immutable ordination of divine liberality, nor is it ever withdrawn from any knower, but always aids him; and to that extent it could be said to be in our power.

JOHN DUNS SCOTUS (1266/1274–1308)

Notwithstanding a growing interest in Duns Scotus, and notwithstanding an increasing number of studies of his philosophy, the statement of his thought and the estimation of its importance are hazardous undertakings. A variety of reasons explain why this should be so. There is no critical edition of his works; examination of the authenticity of writings attributed to him has cut off one by one half a dozen important philosophical works which went under his name a century ago; the highly technical terminology which he evolved for the statement of his subtle philosophy can be worked with apparent cogency into a variety of interpretations; the content of Duns's philosophy, finally, is dependent on the emphasis the interpreter wishes to make, and dependent also on which of the works of doubtful authenticity he chooses to admit into the canon of Duns's writings. It would seem now that only five major works continue of undoubted authenticity—the treatise entitled *on the First Principle* (but not the treatise entitled *on the First Principle of All Things*), the *Questions on the Metaphysics* (but not the *Exposition on the XII Books of the Metaphysics*), the two Commentaries on the Sentences of Lombard, entitled the *Oxford Work* and the *Parisian Reportata*, and some *Quodlibetal Questions*. One effect of this limitation of authentic works has been the happy elimination of the contradictions, which it had been customary to find in the doctrines of Duns Scotus. But the subtlety and the technical detail of his philosophical analyses leave contradictions enough in any restatement of his doctrine: no modern language is constructed to carry the force of his distinctions, and in restatement therefore either distinctions must be blunted by approximate translation, or new expressions must be invented as strange and as difficult as the latin terms of Duns.

The intellectual heritage of Duns Scotus has been subject of frequent discussion, but the polemical char- acter of the discussions has not infrequently disguised rather than disclosed his philosophical ancestors. The selection which follows is not an unfair sampling of the apologetic force he finds in the aristotelian system for the defense of the doctrines of Augustine. Coming after the departure of Thomas from pure augustinism, the defense can be considered a restatement of the older philosophy; but like the philosophy of Thomas it is a restatement with a modification. Thomas had considered the one Truth which Augustine discussed limited to the truth which is involved in the adequation of things to the divine understanding, but he had imported besides the discussions of Aristotle for the statement of the rich and shifting variety of truths which are adequations of things to the human understanding; the one truth of God is basic, but the statement of its being alone is inadequate to characterize the truths of things and of intellect. Duns Scotus reversed the thomist procedure: he seeks the formal ground of certainty in the many truths in which the mind is engaged; he finds infallible truths and formalities which lead him back to the dis- covery, with Augustine, of eternal truths above the mind to which the mind is directed. Broadly it may be said that, whereas Thomas was led, impressed with the fact that individuals of the same species differ only in number and not in kind, to state a metaphysics built upon substances unknown in their individuality, so emphasizing the fundamental unintelligibility of the thing which is, as it is, unadequated to the understanding; Duns Scotus, in his persistent search for the bases of certitude, recognized that the individual is handled in knowledge by distinctions (there is a real distinction, a distinction of reason only, and a formal distinction from the part of the thing), and expressed a theory of knowledge which emphasizes the status of the distinctions which the intellect discovers. The much agitated question of whether Duns refuted Thomas to state a greater synthesis of medieval thought, or whether he refined Thomas of questionable doctrines and reconciled him with Augustine, resolves itself into the question, simpler historically but more difficult of philosophical determination, of how a metaphysical inquiry with an aristotelian augustinian background will differ from an inquiry into formally verifiable certainties conducted on much the same background.

Here, as elsewhere, therefore, the inquiry into intentions and backgrounds may be abandoned for the examination of philosophical differences that appear in the doctrines themselves. If the difference is as it has been stated to be, it should appear particularly clearly in the status of the individual in each system. For Thomas, matter is the principle of individuation; that individuals of the same species differ, not in kind, but only in number, is the consequence of that principle. For Scotus, the principle of individuation is in the form, not merely in the matter; the essence of each individual contains the principle of contraction and limitation which restrains the universality of the species: the ultimate reality of the thing which is (*ens*) contracts the specific form. This is the doctrine of *hecceity*, according to which the characteristics of individuation are not to be found in quantity or in any other attribute of body, as Thomas's doctrine seems to state, but in a formal distinction derived from the thing. This is the significance of the much misinterpreted doctrine that being (*esse*) is no different from essence (*essentia*): the characteristics of individual things are intelligibly different; it is the possibility of formal differentiation and description which the hecceity preserves for the individual. Where Thomas was concerned to emphasize the specific and generic identity of different individuals, Duns was concerned with the notion, not necessarily contradictory, that each thing that is (*ens*) has some being (*esse*) of its own. Thomas followed Avicenna in holding that the mind conceived that which is (*ens*) in conceiving anything: whatever else is conceived must be as superadded to that first conception; Duns Scotus, on the other hand, considered that which is as particular, and as known in each case by the hecceity peculiar to the particular thing. Whereas Thomas, therefore, can express the relation of the true and the good by saying that they are convertible with that which is, for the one superadds to that which is an order to the understanding, the other an order to the appetite; Duns Scotus explains the relation by pointing out that the good and the true are different formally but identical in the thing.

The alterations that occur in the demonstrations of the existence of God are similar symptoms of the alteration of outlook toward a problem, analyzed in very similar fashion but with emphases diametrically opposed. Thomas is again concerned with the reality of first substances, individual things (of which properties, differences, genera, species can be predicated and in which accidents are present, but which can not, in turn, be predicated of anything). His refutation of the *a priori* demonstrations of God, his substitution of five *a posteriori* demonstrations for them are recognition of the fact that nothing is known save knowledge derived from experience of individual things, but that on the other hand the changes of individual things and the instabilities of sensible knowledge can not be explained save by a first mover, a first cause, a source of goodness; but that first cause is not itself known. Duns Scotus, too, holds that an *a priori* proof of the existence of God is impossible, but unlike Thomas he does not refute the ontological argument of Anselm, but "colors" it so that it is *a posteriori* rather than *a priori*. If the notion of God can be shown to be possible, it can be shown by that to be necessary; if a first efficient cause, if a final end, if a supreme perfection are possible, analysis of that possibility will show that they are necessary. Duns's proofs of the existence of God, therefore, begin like those of St. Thomas from knowledge occasioned by experience, but where Thomas seeks in experience some contingent thing which requires for its existence the existence of God, Duns Scotus consistently seeks out necessary truths and relations of thought implicated in the propositions which are necessarily true, independent of the experience that occasioned them. For this reason too the infinity of God plays a very important role in the analysis; an infinite first efficient cause, an infinite supreme intelligence, an infinite supreme good are concepts which can be analyzed as necessary formal background to the effects, the knowledge, the desires of this world.

The origin of all sciences in experience, the abstraction of universals, the activity of the mind compounding and dividing are familiar aristotelian steps in the analysis Scotus makes of knowledge. But that the concepts of genera and species are univocal realities; that necessary and infallible truths are involved in the statement of the conjuncture of terms, concerns him more than the peculiar properties and accidents of that which is. His polemic is directed most frequently against the skeptics who would deny that man can know naturally, without divine illumination, any sure truths. His search, therefore, is often for infallible and certain truths, and he finds three orders of them, the truths of first principles and conclusions derived logically from them, the truths of experience, and the truths of selfconsciousness. Following Aristotle and Augustine he holds that the principles of the sciences are very certain, that even the possibility of truth in science is indication of the infallible truth of scientific principles, notwithstanding that all the truths of science may be themselves subjected to doubt; the doors are concealed from no one though the contents of the house may be unknown. For the truth of the principles no appeal need be made beyond understanding and the terms of the principle understood; knowing the terms, the understanding knows one term as including the other. The truth of a first principle is in the conformity of the composition of the terms to the terms so compounded; the understanding apprehending terms has in itself the necessary cause of the conformity of the act of composition to the terms it compounds. There is a subtle and very modern turn to this analysis: the truth of a first principle is not made to consist in some character of the terms or categories in isolation but rather in the relation perceived between them in the apprehension by the mind of the proposition which relates them. So, too, whiteness and whiteness stand related not by some disparate peculiarity of the two terms but in the formal relation *likeness*. The whole is greater than its parts, because the perception of the composition of the terms stated in the proposition and the perception of the terms themselves is impossible without the perception of the conformity of the composition to the terms; the perception of that conformity is the perception of the truth of first principles. The truth of conclusions depends on the truths so perceived of principles and on the further truths of syllogistic deduction similarly established and similarly perceived.

It does not escape Duns Scotus that the objection may be raised, that if all knowledge is derived from experience, and if experience yields no certain data, the understanding must have its infallible truth of principles and conclusions concerning terms in which the senses are consistently deceived. He points out, however, that the truth of such principles does not depend on the data of the senses, but only on the understanding and the terms; the senses are not the causes but the occasion of such knowledge; and even if all the senses were deceived, or (which would be worse) if some of the senses were sometimes accurate and some sometimes illusory, the formal relation of the terms would still be known: it is true that black is not white, however unreliable the perception of white and black might be. Duns Scotus does not, however, concede that knowledge by experience is necessarily fallible. He engages, on the contrary, in an inquiry for necessary truths among the things of experience. The truth discovered reduces to a formal statement of a principle of natural causation: whatever the difficulties in discovering causes, it is none the less known infallibly that an effect occurring in many things from a cause which is not free is the natural effect of that cause. The discovery of causes must be through experience, by which the causal sequence must be traced in natures which remain the same under a diversity of accidents. When a particular causal connection is discovered it can sometimes be reduced to a principle which is known in itself, as the

frequent eclipse of the moon can be reduced to the
principle of interference by opaque bodies in the propagation of light; sometimes the causal connection perceived can not be reduced to a principle better known
than the terms themselves of the perceived connection.
In the last case the effect which is undergone by the
subject is known as the natural effect of the cause only
by repeated examination of the phenomena and not by
any other principle; this is the lowest grade of scientific
knowledge, and Duns recognizes the possibility that no
necessary knowledge is possible there of the actual
union of the extremes—as in the statement that a given
herb has such or such characteristics—but only a
knowledge that the union can occur; some effects, in
other words, are not connected essentially with the
subject.

Apart from the certainties of principles and conclusions, and of experience, there is a third class of
certainties which are concerned with our knowledge of
our own actions. These certainties are those familiar
perceptions found in Aristotle, Augustine, and Descartes,
that I know that I think, that I understand, that I hear,
however much I may be deceived in that which I think,
or understand, or hear. The illusions of the sense, Duns
recognized and treats in detail, but the certainty that
I am and perform the acts which I perceive in doubting
is untouched by such uncertainties. Moreover, the inquiry into the formal bases of certainties permits Duns
a very illuminating discussion of the illusions which
were to continue to distress philosophers centuries later:
the stick half-immersed in water which appears to be
bent and the perception of distant objects which appear
to be smaller than they are. When the senses concur
in their information concerning a thing, certitude is had
of the data of sensation by the principle of natural

causation. When the senses differ, recourse must be had to some other principle. Thus in the case of the stick which appears to be bent, sight reports it bent, touch reports it straight; the solution is not by balancing one sense against the other, for the senses are the occasion, not the cause of knowledge, but by the principle that a harder thing is not broken by contact with a softer thing which recedes from it. Similarly the sight of a distant object as smaller is known to be illusory, because of the principle that when a quantity is added to a quantity the original quantity is still identical with itself: the addition of distance does not alter the size of a thing perceived at a distance. In each case the illusion involved in perception is corrected not by positive knowledge acquired from perception, but from knowledge, occasioned to be sure by sensation, but in which the mind would not be deceived even if it were deceived in all its senses.

Contemporary logical and phenomenological inquiries are returning to a formulation of these problems in many ways similar to the statement of them made by Duns Scotus. It is unfortunate that the remarkable subtlety of his analysis of formally certifiable truths has been forgotten in large part; it is equally unfortunate that his contribution to the history of thought is stated most usually as refutation of the metaphysical doctrines of Thomas Aquinas, or else as reconciliation and intellectual permutation of the thomist doctrine with older doctrines. The philosophical perception of Duns Scotus is nicer than would be indicated by either such project. It is not safe to state the project of his philosophy in any single form, but it might be ventured that he was concerned to discover the necessary truths in the philosophical discussions he encountered in the writings and debates of his times. Possibly he may be said to be responsible for the turn of philosophic interest to the *evidence* of propositions and of truths. Certainly the word evidence and the search for it assumes for the first time in his works the dominant place which Ockham and the ockhamites continued to give it. Duns Scotus contributed, in any case, even if he did not initiate the inquiry, to making explicit what is required for the formal truth of propositions. It is not a little ironical, therefore, that his determined attack on skepticism and his statement of the bases of truth should have furnished the instruments and the terms by which later analyses, particularly by the ockhamites, discovered necessary truths, to be sure, but found them so inapplicable rigorously and so unfruitful of consequences that the body of human science had to be reduced to the status of probable knowledge. In Duns Scotus there is, however, the momentary pause in which the necessary truths involved in a subject matter of shifting terms and altering doctrines was revealed with great lucidity and technical elaboration.

JOHN DUNS SCOTUS

THE OXFORD COMMENTARY ON THE FOUR BOOKS OF THE MASTER OF THE SENTENCES

BOOK I. DISTINCTION III, QUESTION IV.[1]

THE QUESTION IS PROPOSED.—Finally, with reference to this matter of knowability, I ask:

Whether any sure and pure truth can be known naturally by the understanding of the wayfarer without the special illumination of the uncreated light?

PRINCIPAL ARGUMENTS.—And I argue that it can not. —Augustine says *on the Trinity*, book IX, chapter 6: *But we perceive the inviolable truth, from which we may determine perfectly, so far as we are able, not how the mind of each man is, but how it must be in the sempiternal reasons.* And again in chapter 6 of the same work: *When we approve or disprove something rightly, we are inwardly convinced in approving and disproving, all other criteria remaining unchangeably above our mind.* And again in the same work, chapter 6: *Grasping the ineffably beautiful art of such figures above the perception of the mind by simple intelligence.* And in chapter 7 of the same work: *Therefore in that eternal*

[1] B. IOANNIS DUNS SCOTI, *Commentaria Oxoniensia ad IV. Libros Magistri Sententiarum*, ed. P. Marianus Fernandez Garcia. Ad Aquas Claras (Quaracchi): Ex Typographia Collegii S. Bonaventurae, 1912, vol. I, pp. 357-383.

truth, from which all temporal things are made, we perceive by the vision of the mind the form according to which we are and according to which we perform anything with true or right reason, whether in ourselves or in bodies, and thence we have the true knowledge of things conceived as if a word within us. Again in book XII, chapter 2 of the same work: *But it is of more sublime reason to judge concerning these corporeal things according to incorporeal and eternal reasons.* Again in the same book chapter 14: *However not only do the intelligible and incorporeal reasons of sensible things located in places persist without local spaces, but also the reasons of motions extended in time exist simultaneously without temporal duration as intelligible and not sensible reasons.*

And that Augustine is speaking there of *eternal reasons* truly in God and not of *first principles*, is seen by the fact that he has said in the same place, that it is the privilege of few to attain to them; but if he were speaking of first principles, it would not be the privilege of few to attain to them but of many, because they are known to all. Again, in book XIV chapter 15, speaking of the unjust man who rightly praises and vituperates many things in the customs of men, he says: *By what rules do they judge these things except by those in which they see in some fashion how every one should live?* And at the end he adds: *Where then are they written unless in that book of that light which is called truth?* That book of light is the divine understanding. Therefore, he means that in that light the unjust man sees what actions are to be done justly. And this is to be seen by means of something which is stamped or impressed by it [the light], for he says in the same place: *Whence all just law is marked off, and it is transferred to the heart of man who does justice, not by migrating, but as if by being impressed, as the image passes from a ring to wax and yet does not leave the ring.* There-fore, we see in that light by which justice is imprinted in the heart of man; but that is the uncreated light. Again, in the XIIth book of the *Confessions,* chapter 25: *If both of us see the true, you do not see it in me, nor I in you, but both of us in that which is above the mind in immutable truth.*

There are moreover in many places many other au-thorities of Augustine to prove this conclusion.

To the contrary: *the Epistle to the Romans* 1:20: *The invisible things of God, understood by means of those things that have been made, are clearly compre-hended from the creation of the world;*[2] but these reasons are the invisible things of God: therefore, they are known from creatures: therefore, before the vision of them sure knowledge of creatures is had.

The opinion is expounded which holds that no sure and pure truth can be known by us naturally without special illumination of the uncreated light. In this question there is one opinion[3] that there is a natural order *per se* among *general intentions.*—We speak of the two intentions which are relevant to the question propounded, namely, of the intention of *that which is* [*ens*] and of *the true.*

a) The first intention is of *that which is.* This is proved by the statement of the book *on Causes* in the fourth proposition: *the first of created things is being,* and in the commentary on the first proposition: *being is of more vehement adherence.*

b) This is proved likewise by reason: because *entity*

---

[2] *A creatura mundi* is usually interpreted in english trans-lations, *since the creation of the world.*

[3] Attributed to Henry of Ghent.

is *absolute*: whereas truth indicates a reference to ar exemplar.—From this it follows that that which is can be known under the relation of *entity*, but not under the relation of *truth*.

c) This conclusion furthermore is proved from the part of the *intellect*: because *that which is* can be conceived by simple understanding, and hence *that which is true* is conceived; but the relation of *truth* is conceived only by the understanding *compounding* and *dividing*; simple understanding however precedes composition and division.

If therefore it is inquired, in the question proposed, concerning knowledge of *that which is,* or concerning *that which is true* of that which is, the reply is that the intellect can know *the true* thus by pure natural causes. —This is proved: because it is contradictory that a nature be untrained in its own operation, according to Damascenus, and that is more contradictory in a more perfect and superior nature according to the Philosopher in the second book *on the Heavens and the World,* where he speaks of stars, because it would be extremely contradictory for the stars to have a progressive power and not have the natural instruments for progression: therefore, since the proper operation of the intellect is to understand the true, it seems improper that nature should not concede to the intellect that which suffices for that operation.

d) But if we speak of the knowledge of *truth,* it is replied that as there is a *double exemplar,* created and uncreated, according to Plato in the first part of the *Timaeus,* that is, a made and an unmade or a created and an uncreated exemplar: the *created* exemplar is the *universal species* caused by the thing: the *uncreated* is the idea in the *divine mind*; thus there is a *double conformity* to the exemplar and a *double truth*: one is the

conformity to the *created* exemplar, and in this fashion
Aristotle stated that the truths of things are known by
their conformity to the intelligible species; and Augustine seems to say this in the IXth book *on the Trinity,*
chapter 7, where he holds that we have a special and a
general knowledge of things, each of which is collected
from sensibles, according to which we judge the truth
of anything that turns up, that the thing itself is such
or such.

But that we should have an absolutely *certain* and *infallible knowledge of the truth* of a thing through the
acquired exemplar in us, this is said to be utterly impossible.—And it is proved by a threefold reason, according to those holding this doctrine: the first reason
is taken from the part of the *thing* from which the exemplar is drawn: the second from the part of the *subject*
in which it is: the third from the part of the *exemplar*
in itself.

e) The *first* reason is this: that object from which the
exemplar is abstracted is *mutable*: therefore, it can not
be the cause of anything *immutable*; but sure knowledge
of any truth concerning anything is had of it under an
immutable relation: therefore, it is not had by such an
exemplar.

This is said to be the reason of Augustine in the
LXXXIII Questions, question 9, where he holds that
pure truth is not to be sought from sensible things, because sensible things change without intermission.

f) The *second* reason is this: the soul in itself is
mutable and passive to error: therefore, it can be rectified by nothing more mutable than itself that it err not;
but such an exemplar in it is more mutable than the soul
itself: therefore, that exemplar does not regulate the
soul perfectly that it err not.

This is said to be the reason of Augustine in the book

on True Religion: *Since the law of all arts is absolutely
immutable, and since the human mind, to which it has
been conceded to see such a law, can suffer the mutability
of error, it is sufficiently apparent that there is above
our mind a law which is called truth.*

g) The *third* reason is: no one has certain and infallible knowledge of truth, unless he has that by which
he can distinguish truth from verisimilitude; for if he
can not distinguish truth from *falsity* or *verisimilitude*,
he can doubt whether he is deceived: but truth can not
be distinguished by means of the aforesaid created
exemplar from verisimilitude, therefore etc.—*Proof of
the minor premiss*: such a species can represent itself
as itself, or in another fashion it can represent itself *as
object*, as is the case in dreams. If it represents itself
as object, it is falsity: if as itself, it is truth: therefore,
through such a species it is not known sufficiently distinctively when it represents itself as itself, and when it
represents itself as object; and thus it is not sufficiently
distinctive of truth from falsity.

h) From these considerations it is concluded that if it
happen that man knows a sure knowledge and infallible
truth, that does not happen to him by looking at an
exemplar derived from the thing by sensation, howsoever much it be purified and made universal, but it is
necessary that he look upon the *uncreated exemplar*.

And therefore this mode is stated: God, not as that
which is known, has the significance of an *exemplar*
looking to which pure truth is: for the known is in
general attribute, but he is the reason of knowing as
naked exemplar, and the proper reason of the created
essence. The fashion, however, in which he may be the
reason of knowing and not the *known* is shown in an
example: for just as the ray of the sun is sometimes projected from its source in an *oblique* line, sometimes in a

direct line: and although the sun is the reason of seeing of that which is seen in the ray projected in the first manner, nevertheless it is not seen as it is in itself; but the sun is the reason of knowing of that which is seen in the ray in the second manner, in such wise that it too is known; thus, therefore, the uncreated light illumines the angelic intellect as in direct view, and then as seen, it is the reason of seeing other things in itself; but it illumines our understanding, while we are on the way, as in an oblique view; and therefore it is the reason of seeing to our intellect and not the seen.

i) It is held, moreover, that the uncreated exemplar has a triple relation in respect to the act of seeing, namely, that of the *kindling light,* and that of the *changing species* and that of the *configuring character or exemplar.*

And from this it is concluded finally that a special influence is required, because just as that essence is not seen by us naturally in itself, so likewise, as that essence is the exemplar in respect to any creature, it is not seen naturally, according to Augustine when he writes on seeing God: *for it is in his power to be seen: if he wishes, he is seen, if he does not wish, he is not seen.*

j) Finally it is added that there is a perfect knowledge of truth when two exemplar species concur in the mind, one *inhering,* that is, caused, the other *having penetrated from without,* that is, not caused, in illuminating the mind. The mind conceives the *word of truth* perfectly when out of these two species of the thing it has compounded one reason or criterion for understanding the thing of which it is the criterion.

DIVISION OF THE QUESTION.—Against this opinion I show *first,* that these reasons are not the fundamental reasons of any true opinion, nor are they according to the intention of Augustine, but lead to the opinion of the academics.—In the *second* place, I show how that opinion of the academics, which seems to follow from these reasons, is false.—In the *third* place, I reply to those reasons, in so far as they do not hold.—In the *fourth* place I argue against the conclusion of this opinion.—In the *fifth* place, I resolve the question.—In the *sixth* place, I show how these reasons (in so far as they are Augustine's) lead to that intention of Augustine, but not that intention to which they were drawn here.

Article I.

IT IS SHOWN THAT THE PROPOSED REASONS ARE NOT THE FUNDAMENTAL REASONS OF ANY TRUE OPINION, NOR ARE THEY ACCORDING TO THE INTENTION OF AUGUSTINE, BUT LEAD TO THE OPINION OF THE ACADEMICS.

IT IS DEMONSTRATED THAT THE ABOVE MENTIONED REASONS LEAD TO ALL INCERTITUDE.—*In the first place, these reasons seem to lead to the impossibility of sure natural knowledge.*

a) In the first place this is so,[4] because if an object is changed continually, no certitude of it can be had under an immutable reason, nor indeed could certitude be had in any light, because there is no certitude when the object is known in another way than it is itself: therefore, there is no certitude in knowing a mutable thing as immutable.—It is evident likewise that the antecedent of this reason, namely, *that sensible things are changed continually*, is false; this is, indeed, the opinion attributed to Heraclitus in the IVth book of the *Metaphysics*.

b) In the same way, if there could not be certitude

[4] See above. e) p. 317.

because of the mutability of the exemplar which is in our soul,[5] since whatsoever is placed in the soul subjectively is mutable, so too the very act of understanding will be mutable, and therefore it follows that the soul is rectified by nothing in the soul that it err not.—It would follow likewise that the very act of understanding, since it is more mutable than the soul in which it is, will never be true, nor will it contain truth; which is false.

c) In the same way, according to this opinion, the caused *inhering* species concurs with that *penetrating* species; but when something which is incompatible with certitude concurs, no certitude can be had: for just as from a necessary and a contingent proposition only a contingent conclusion may be drawn, so from certainty and uncertainty concurring for some point of knowledge, no certain conclusion follows.

d) The same conclusion is likewise evident from the third reason,[6] because if that species abstracted from the thing concurs for all knowledge, and if it can not judge distinctly, because sometimes it represents itself as itself and sometimes it represents itself as object: therefore, whatever else concurs, no certitude can be had by which truth may be distinguished from verisimilitude.

e) Therefore these reasons are seen to lead to all incertitude and thus to the opinion of the academics.

It is proved that the aforestated conclusion is not according to the mind of Augustine.—I prove however that this conclusion is not according to the mind of Augustine:

a) Augustine in the IInd book of the *Soliloquies*: *Every one concedes without hesitation that the proofs of*

---

[5] See above, f) pp. 317-318.   [6] See above, g) p. 318.

the sciences are very true. And Boethius *De hebdomadibus*:[7] *A common conception of the mind is that which when heard anyone proves.* And the Philosopher in the IInd book of the *Metaphysics*: *First principles are known to all, like the door in a house,* because the door is concealed to no one, although things within the house may be concealed.—From these three authorities it is argued as follows: that which is proper to *all* members of any species follows from the *specific nature*: therefore, since everyone has infallible certitude of *first principles,* and further since the *form of the perfect syllogism* is naturally evident to every one, according to the Ist book of the *Prior Analytics,* but knowledge of the conclusion depends only on the evidence of the principles and on the evidence of the syllogistic inference; therefore any demonstrable conclusion can be known naturally to every one from premisses known through themselves.

b) In the second place, it is clear likewise that Augustine concedes the certitude of those things which are known through the *experience of the senses*; wherefore he says in the XVth book *on the Trinity,* chapter 12: *May we be spared from doubting that those things which we learn through the senses of the body are true, for through them we learn the heaven, the earth, and the things which are known to us in these, so far as he who made us and them wished us to know.* If therefore we do not doubt their truth and we are not deceived, as is clear, then we are certain of things known by way of sense, for *certitude* is had when doubt and deception are excluded.

c) In the third place it is evident that Augustine concedes in the same work book XV, the same chapter. certitude concerning our actions: *He lives whether he be*

[7] See above, p. 160, note 3.

asleep or awake, for it is part of living also to sleep and see in dreams.

d) But if you say: to live is not a second act but a first act; he continues in the same place: *If any one should say, I know that I know, he can not be mistaken,* even by reflecting as many times as you wish on the first known. And in the same work: *If any one should say, I wish to be happy, how would the reply be made not impudently, perhaps you are mistaken? And if he says I know that I wish this, and I know that I know this, then he can add a third to these two that he knows these two, and a fourth that he knows that he knows these two, and so he can proceed to an infinite number.* And in the same work: *If any one should say, I do not wish to err, will it not be true, whether he errs or does not err, that he nevertheless does not wish to err? And other arguments,* he says, *are found which hold against the academics who contend that nothing can be known by man.* And there follows in the same work, *There are then our three books*[8] *written in the first period of our conversion; the many arguments which have been found by the academics against the perception of truth will not in the least prevail on him who had been able to and has wished to read them and having read them has understood them.* Again in the same book XV, chapter 15: *Those things too which are known in such wise that they can not slip from the mind, since they are present and pertain to the nature of the mind itself, of which sort is the following, that we know we live; for this remains as long as the mind remains, and because the mind always remains, this also remains always.*

And thus the first article is evident, that the reasons of that opinion are not conclusive, and that this first opinion is false and against Augustine.

[8] *The Three Books against the Academics.*

Article II.

It is shown in what that opinion of the academics is false.

Division of the Article.—With respect to the second article, that the error of the academics has no place in any knowable things, it must be seen how infallible certitude can be had naturally of the three kinds of knowables mentioned above, namely, of *principles known through themselves* and of *conclusions*, secondly of *things known by experience*, thirdly, of *our actions*.

The certitude of first principles is shown.—With reference to certitude of *principles* I say this: that the terms of principles known through themselves have such an *identity*, that one term known *evidently* includes the other necessarily; and therefore the understanding compounding those terms, from the fact that it apprehends them, has in itself the *necessary* cause of the *conformity* of that act of compounding to the terms themselves of which the composition is and likewise the *evident* cause of that conformity; and therefore, that conformity is evident to it necessarily. The necessary and evident cause of that conformity it apprehends in the terms: therefore, the *apprehension* of terms and their *composition* can not be in the understanding, unless the *conformity* of that composition to the terms stands, just as whiteness and whiteness can not stand unless *likeness* stands. But this conformity of composition to terms is the *truth of composition*: therefore, the composition of such terms can not stand unless there is truth, and thus the perception of that composition and the perception of terms can not stand, unless the perception of conformity of composition to terms stands and thus the perception of truth, for the first percepts obviously include the perception of that truth.

The Philosopher confirms this reasoning by likeness in book IV of the *Metaphysics*, where he insists that the opposite of a first principle, such as, *it is impossible that the same thing be and not be*, can not come into the understanding of any one, because then there would be contrary opinions in the mind at the same time. This is undoubtedly true of contrary opinions, that is of opinions formally contradictory, for the opinion attributing being to something and the opinion attributing non-being to the same thing are formally contradictory.— Thus I may state in the question proposed that there is some contradiction to the intellections in the mind, although not a formal contradiction; for if there exists in the understanding a knowledge of the whole and the part and a composition of them, since they include as a necessary cause the conformity of the composition to the terms, and if there exists in the understanding this opinion, that this composition is false, contradictory ideas will be present: not formally, but the one notion will stand with the other, and nevertheless one will be the necessary cause of an idea opposed to the other; which is impossible. For just as it is impossible for white and black to be at the same time, because they are contrary formally, so it is impossible that white and that which is the precise cause of blackness stand, so it is necessary that it can not be without the other without contradiction.

THE CERTITUDE OF CONCLUSIONS IS SHOWN.—When the evidence or the certitude of first principles has been had, it is evident how certitude may be had of conclusions inferred from them, because of the evidence of the perfect form of the syllogism, since the certitude of the conclusion depends only on the certitude of the principles and on the evidence of the inference.

THE UNDERSTANDING DOES NOT ERR, ALTHOUGH THE SENSES ERR.—But will not the understanding err in this knowledge of principles and conclusions, if the senses are deceived concerning all the terms?—I reply, that with respect to this knowledge the understanding does not have the senses for cause, but only for occasion, for the understanding can not have knowledge of simples unless it has received that knowledge from the senses; still, having received it, it can compound simples with each other by its own power; and if from the relation of such simples there is a combination which is evidently true, the understanding will assent to that combination by its own power and by the power of the terms, not by power of the sense by which it receives the terms from without.—Example: if the reason of whole and the reason of greater are received from sense, and the understanding compounds the following: *every whole is greater than its part*, the understanding by its own power and that of these terms assents indubitably to this combination, and not only because it sees the terms conjoined in the thing, as it assents to the following, *Socrates is white*, because it saw that the terms are united in the thing.—Moreover, I say that if all the senses were false, from which such terms are received, or, what would lead even more to deception, if some senses were false, and some true, the understanding would not be mistaken concerning such principles, because it would always have in itself terms which were the cause of truth: just as, if the species of whiteness and blackness had been impressed miraculously in dreams on one blind from birth, and if they remained subsequently in waking, the understanding abstracting from them would compound the following proposition, *white is not black*; and the understanding would not be deceived concerning this, even though the terms be received from erring sense; for the formal relation of the terms, to which it has reached, is the necessary cause of this negative truth.

THE CERTITUDE CONCERNING THINGS KNOWN BY EXPERIENCE IS SHOWN.—Concerning the second type of knowables, namely concerning things known through experience, I say that although experience is not had of all singulars, but of a large number, and that although it is not always had, but in a great many cases, still one who knows by experience knows infallibly that it is thus, and that it is always thus, and that it is thus in all, and he knows this by the following proposition reposing in the soul, *whatever occurs as in a great many things from some cause which is not free, is the natural effect of that cause,* which proposition is known to the understanding, even though it had accepted the terms of it from erring senses; for *a cause which is not free* can not produce *as in a great many things* an effect to the opposite of which it is ordered, or to which it is not ordered by its form: but a casual cause is ordered to the producing of the opposite of the casual effect or to not producing it; therefore, nothing is the casual cause in respect to an effect produced frequently by it, and if it is not free, it is a natural cause.

That, however, this effect occurs by such a cause producing *as in a great many cases*, this must be learned through experience; for to discover such a nature at one time with such an accident, at another with such another accident, it must be discovered that, howsoever great might be the diversity of such accidents, such an effect always followed that nature; therefore, such an effect follows not through some accident accidentally of that nature, but through the very nature in itself.

But it must be noted further that sometimes experience is had of a conclusion, as for example, *that the moon is frequently eclipsed*; and then having supposed the conclusion because it is so, the cause of such a conclusion is inquired by the method of division, and sometimes one proceeds from the conclusion experienced to principles known from the terms, and then from such a principle known from the terms, the conclusion, previously known only by experience, can be known more certainly, namely, by the first kind of knowledge, for it can be known as deduced from a principle known in itself: just as the following is known through itself, that, namely, *an opaque object interposed between a luminous and a transparent object impedes the multiplication of light to such a transparent object*; and if it were found by division that the earth is such a body interposed between the sun and the moon, it will be known most certainly by demonstration based on the essence [*propter quid*] and through causes, and not only through experience as that conclusion was known before the discovery of the principle.

Sometimes, however, there is experience of the principle in such a manner that it is not possible to discover further by division the principle known through the terms, but one must stop at some truth which holds as in many cases, of which the extremes are frequently experienced united, as for example, that *a herb of such a species is hot*, nor is any other middle term discovered prior by means of which the passion is demonstrated of the subject because of its nature [i.e. *a priori*], but one must stop at this as at the first thing known by experience. Then although incertitude and fallibility may be removed by the following proposition, *the effect as in a great many cases of any cause which is not free is the natural effect of it*, nevertheless this is the last grade of scientific knowledge; and perhaps necessary knowledge is not had there of the actual union of extremes, but only of an aptitudinal union; for if the passion is another thing separated from the subject, it could without contradiction be separated from the subject, and the person who knows by experience would not have knowledge that it is so, but that it is formed apt to be so.

CERTITUDE CONCERNING OUR ACTIONS IS SHOWN.—Concerning the third type of knowable things, namely, concerning our actions, I say there is certitude concerning many of them just as of principles known through themselves, as is obvious from book IV of the *Metaphysics*, where the Philosopher says of the reasons of those who say that all appearances are true, that these reasons inquire whether we are now dreaming or awake: *All these doubts, however, amount to the same, for they all think that there is a reason for all things.* And he adds, *They seek the reason for things of which there is no reason, for there is no demonstration of a principle of demonstration.* Therefore, according to the same Philosopher in the same place, that we are awake is known through itself as is a principle of demonstration.

Nor does it matter that it is contingent, for as has been said elsewhere, there is an order in contingent things, because something is first and immediate; otherwise there would either be a regress *in infinitum* in contingent things, or else something contingent would follow from a necessary cause: both of which are impossible.

And as there is certitude concerning waking as concerning something known through itself, so likewise of many other actions which are in our power, as that I understand, that I hear, and thus of others which are perfect acts; for although there is no certitude that I

see white which is located without, either in such a
subject or at such a distance, because an illusion can
be caused in the medium or in the organ and in many
other ways, nevertheless there is certitude that I see,
even though an illusion be caused in the organ, which
illusion in the organ seems to be the greatest of illusions,
as for example, when an act is caused in the organ
itself, not by a present object, but such as is made naturally by a present object. And thus the faculty would
have its act, if such an illusion or passion were supposed,
and that would truly be what is called vision there,
whether it be action, or passion, or both. But if the
illusion were not caused in the organ itself, but in something proximate to it, which seems to be the organ, as,
if the illusion were not caused in the concourse of
nerves, but if the impression of the species such as is
naturally made by the object were caused in the eye
itself, still sight would see; because such a species, or
what is naturally seen in it, would be seen, for it would
have sufficient distance with respect to the organ of
sight, which is in the concourse of those nerves, as is
evident from Augustine in book VI *on the Trinity*,
chapter 2, because the remains of things seen, remaining
in the eye when the eyes are closed, are seen; and
according to the Philosopher *on Sense and the Sensed*,
because the fire which is generated by the violent elevation of the eye and which is multiplied as far as the
closed eyelid, is seen; these are true visions, although
they are not the most perfect visions, because there are
here sufficient distances of the species to the principal
organ of sight.

ON THE CERTITUDE OF THOSE THINGS WHICH ARE
UNDER THE ACTIONS OF THE SENSES.—But how is certitude had of those things which are under the actions of
the senses, as for example, that something outside is

white or hot as it appears to be?—I reply: either opposites appear to the diverse senses concerning something
known thus, or else not, but all the senses knowing it,
have the same judgment concerning it.—If in the second
manner, then certitude is had of the truth of such a
thing known by the senses, and by that proposition which
precedes, namely, *what occurs as in a great many cases
from something, is the natural effect of it, if it is not a
free cause*; therefore, since the same alteration [or im-
mutation] of sense occurs in a great many cases when
this thing is present, it follows that this sensitive alteration or the generated species [i.e. impression] is the
natural effect of such a cause, and thus such a thing
outside will be white or hot or such as is naturally
represented by the species generated by it as in a great
many cases.—If, however, the diverse senses have diverse judgments concerning something seen outside, as,
for example, sight says that the staff is broken of which
part is in water and part in air, and touch can discover
the contrary: as sight likewise always says that the sun
is of a quantity less than it is, and everything seen
from a distance is less than it is; in such judgments
there is certitude of what is true and of what sense
errs, by a proposition reposing in the soul more certain
than any judgment of sense and by the concurrent
actions of many senses, so that some proposition always
rectifies the understanding of actions of sense, as to
which is true and which is false, in which proposition
the understanding does not depend on the sense as on a
cause, but as on an *occasion*.—Example: the understanding has this proposition reposing in it, *nothing which is
harder is broken on the contact of something soft reced-
ing from it*; this is so known through itself from its
terms, that even if it were received from erring senses,
the understanding could not doubt that proposition, for

the opposite involves a contradiction: but that the staff is harder than water, and that the water withdraws from it, both senses testify this, as well sight as touch. It follows therefore that the staff is not broken as the sense of sight judges it broken; and thus the understanding judges, by something more certain than any act of sense, which sense errs and which does not with respect to the fracture of the staff.

In the same way from another part, that *the same quantity added to a quantity is absolutely equal to itself,* this is known to the understanding, howsoever much the knowledge of terms may be received from erring senses; but that the same quantity can be added to an object of sight nearby or distant, this the sense of sight as well as touch testifies: therefore, a quantity seen, whether nearby or at a distance, is equal: therefore, when sight testifies that it is less, it errs.—This conclusion is concluded from principles known through themselves and from the actions of two senses knowing it is thus in a great many cases; and thus wherever reason judges that the sense errs, it does this not by some knowledge acquired positively from the senses as from a cause, but through some knowledge occasioned from sense, in which it is not deceived even if all the senses are deceived, and through some other knowledge acquired from sense or from the senses as in a great many cases, which are known to be true by the often quoted proposition, namely, *that which occurs in a great many cases,* etc.

ARTICLE III.

A REPLY IS GIVEN TO THE REASONS IN SO FAR AS THEY DO NOT HOLD.

THE FIRST REASON OF THE CONTRARY OPINION IS SOLVED AND IT IS DEMONSTRATED THAT THE MUTABILITY

OF THE OBJECT IN ITSELF DOES NOT STAND IN THE WAY
OF CERTITUDE OF KNOWLEDGE.—With respect to the third
article, replies to the three reasons stated above must be
derived from these points.—To THE FIRST,[9] that is, to
the objection concerning the change of the object, the
antecedent is false; for sensible things are not in con-
tinual motion, but they remain the same in another
duration.   Nor is it the opinion of Augustine, but that
of Heraclitus and of his disciple, Trachilus, who did not
wish to speak but to move his finger, as is related in
the IVth book of the *Metaphysics*.[10a]—And likewise the
consequence does not hold, even if it were granted that
the antecedent was true, because then according to Aristotle, certain knowledge could still be had of this truth,
that all things are moved continually.—Again it does
not follow: if the object is mutable: therefore, what is
produced from it is not representative of anything under
the aspect [*ratio*] of immutability; because *mutability*
in the object is not the reason for producing; but the
nature of the object itself, which is mutable, is that
reason; that which is produced by it, therefore, represents the nature essentially, because the nature is essentially the reason for producing it; therefore, if there
is a nature, from which a nature has some immutable
relation to something else, that something else and that
nature, each through its own exemplar, are represented
as immutably united.   And thus, knowledge of the immutable union of them can be had through two exemplars
produced from two mutable things, not in so far as
they are mutable, but in so far as they are natures.

It is evident also that something can be represented
under the aspect of the immutable by a representative
which is mutable in itself; for the essence of God is

[9] See above, e) p. 317.

[10a] The reference is to Cratylus; see ARISTOTLE, *Met.* IV, 5,
1010a13.

represented to the understanding under the aspect of
the immutable by something entirely mutable, whether
it be a species or an act.—This is evident by a like case,
for something under the aspect of the infinite can be
represented by a finite.

THE SECOND REASON IS SOLVED.—To the second[10b] I
say that two kinds of mutability can be understood in
the soul: one from *affirmation* to *negation,* and conversely: as for example, from ignorance to knowledge,
or from not understanding to understanding. Another
is as from *contrary* to *contrary*: as for example, from
rectitude to deception, and conversely.—The soul, however, is mutable by the first mutability with reference
to any object, and such mutability is removed from it by
nothing existing formally in it; but it is not mutable
according to the second mutability, except concerning
those complexes which are not evident from their terms;
concerning those however which are evident from their
terms, it can not be changed according to the second
mutability, because the apprehended terms themselves
are the necessary cause of the conformity of the composition to those terms.—Therefore if the soul is mutable
from rectitude to error absolutely, it does not follow
that it can be rectified by nothing other than itself, for
it can at least be rectified by those objects concerning
which the understanding can not err, once it has apprehended the terms.

THE THIRD REASON IS SOLVED. To the third[11] I say:
if it had some cogency, it would hold rather against
that opinion which denies the intelligible species, for
that species which can represent itself as object in
dreams is a phantasm, not an intelligible species: therefore, if the understanding uses only a phantasm, through
which the object is present to it, and not any other

.10b See above, f) pp. 317-318.   11 See above, g) p. 318.

intelligible species, it does not seem that it can discern, through something in which the object lights up itself. truth from verisimilitude. But the reason does not hold when the intelligible species is posited in the understanding, for the understanding can not use that as the object in itself, for it is not possible to use the intelligible species in dreaming.

OBJECTIONS AND DOUBTS ARE SOLVED.[12]

a) If you object that the phantasm can represent itself or the object; that therefore the understanding can err because of that error of the faculty of phantasy or it can be bound so that it can not operate, as is evident in dreams and in frenzies, it can be said that if it be bound when there is such error in the faculty of phantasy, the understanding nevertheless does not err, because it does not then have any act.

b) But how will the understanding know or how will it be certain when the faculty of phantasy does not err, which however must not err in order that understanding may not err?—I reply: the following truth reposes in the understanding, that *a power* [i.e. a faculty] *does not err concerning the object proper and proportioned to it unless it is indisposed*; and it is known to the understanding that the faculty of phantasy is not indisposed in waking by such an indisposition which makes the phantasm represent itself as object, for it is known self-evidently [i.e. through itself] to the understanding, that when it understands it is awake, and thus it is that the faculty of phantasy is not bound in waking as it is in dreams.

c) But a further argument against the stated certitude concerning actions is the following: it seems to me that I see or I hear when I nevertheless do not see

[12] See above, *g*) *Proof of the minor premiss*, p. 318.

or hear: therefore, there is no certitude concerning this.
—I reply, that it is one thing to show, against some one
denying a given proposition, *that it is true*, and it is
another to show, to some one admitting it, *how it is
true*.—For example: in book IV of the *Metaphysics*,
when the Philosopher does not bring forward against
those denying the first principle the following incon-
sistency, that *contrary opinions would be in the soul at
the same time*, [since] they would concede this as a
premiss; but he shows them other inconsistencies manifest to them, although not manifest in themselves. But
to *those who accept the first principle* he shows *how* the
first principle is known, for it is known thus, that the
opposite of it can not occur in the mind; he proves this,
because otherwise contrary opinions could be present at
the same time: such a conclusion is more inconsistent
with itself than the hypothesis.

Thus at this point, if you contend against me that *no*
proposition is *known through itself*, I do not wish to
dispute with you: for it is shown that you are shameless,
because you are not persuaded, as is evident in your
actions, as the Philosopher argues in book IV of the
Metaphysics: for dreaming of obtaining something as if
hard by and later awaking, one does not pursue it, as
one would to attain it in waking if it were thus close by.
—But if you admit that *some* proposition is *known
through itself*, it is necessary that it can be known; and
concerning anything an indisposed power [i.e. faculty]
can err, as is evident in dreams: therefore, from the
fact that some things are known to be *known through
themselves*, it can necessarily be known when a power
is indisposed and when not; and consequently knowledge
can be had of our actions, because a power is disposed
so that those things are known through themselves which
appear to it to be known through themselves.

d) I say then to the form of that bit of sophistry, that just as it appears to one dreaming that he sees, so the opposite of any speculative principle known through itself may possibly appear to one; and still it does not follow that that principle is known through itself. Thus it does not follow that that which one hears is known through itself to one who hears it, for the indisposed power can err concerning either, but not the disposed power. And when it is disposed and when not, is *known through itself*; otherwise it could not be known that anything else is known through itself for it could not be known what was known through itself to the understanding, [that is,] whether it was that to which the understanding thus or thus disposed would assent.

ARTICLE IV.

IT IS ARGUED AGAINST THE CONCLUSION OF THE AFORE-STATED OPINION.

THE AFORESTATED CONCLUSION IS IMPUGNED BY FIVE REASONS.—With respect to the fourth article against the conclusion of the opinion, I argue thus:

a) I ask, what is understood by *sure* and *pure truth*?[13] Either the *infallible* truth, that is, truth without doubt or deception; and it has been proved above and it has been declared in the second and third articles that such truth can be had from pure natural things.— Or else the question is understood of the truth which is *a passion of that which is*; and then since that which is can be understood naturally, therefore also the true, since it is a passion of it. And if the true, then also *truth* by abstraction, because whatever form can be

[13] See above, h) p. 318-319.

understood as in the subject, can also be understood as in the abstract in itself and in the abstract from the subject.—Or in the third place, by truth is understood a *conformity to an exemplar*; and if it is to the created exemplar, the proposition is proved; but if to the uncreated exemplar, the conformity to that can not be understood except if that exemplar is known; for the relation is not knowable unless the extreme is known: therefore, what is assumed in the opinion is false, namely, that *the eternal exemplar is the reason of knowing, not the known.*

b) Moreover, in the second place thus: the simple understanding can know definitively that which it understands confusedly, by seeking by the method of division the definition of that which is known. This definitive knowledge seems the most perfect knowledge pertaining to the simple understanding. From such preliminary knowledge of terms the understanding can know the principle most perfectly, and from the principle, the conclusion: and in this, intellectual knowledge seems to be completed, so that necessary knowledge of truth does not seem to be had beyond the aforesaid truths.

c) Again in the third place: either the eternal light causes something prior naturally in actuality or not.— If it does, it does it either in the object or in the understanding.—Not in the object; for the object in so far as it has being in the understanding, does not have real being, but intentional being: therefore, it is not capable of any real accident.—If in the understanding, then the uncreated light does not change for the understanding of the pure truth, except through the mediation of its effect: and thus the common opinion seems to posit knowledge in the uncreated light as perfectly as this opinion for it posits that it is seen in the active intellect, which is the effect of the uncreated light, and more perfect than would be the accidental, caused light.

If, however, it causes nothing actual prior, either therefore the light alone causes the actuality, or the light together with the understanding and the object.—If the light alone, then the active intellect has no operation in the knowledge of the pure truth: which seems inconsistent because this operation is the most noble operation of our understanding: therefore, the active intellect which is the most noble faculty in the soul, concurs in some way in that action.

d) In the same way likewise according to the Philosopher, in book III *on the Soul,* the active intellect corresponds to the active reason, the possible intellect to the passive reason: therefore, the active intellect is related in some manner actively to whatever the possible intellect receives.

e) The following contradiction likewise which is brought forward at that point is derived from the aforesaid opinion by another method, for according to those holding this opinion, the agent using the instrument can not have an action exceeding the action of the instrument: therefore, since the power of the active intellect has no application in the knowledge of the pure truth, the eternal light using the active intellect will have no application in the knowledge or in the action of this knowledge of pure truth, so that the active intellect has there the relation of instrument.

f) If you say that the uncreated light together with the understanding and the object causes this pure truth, this is the common opinion, which considers that the eternal light, as the remote cause, causes all certain knowledge and truth.—Either therefore this opinion [which is being examined] will be contradictory, or it is not at variance with common opinion.

Article V.

THE QUESTION IS SOLVED.

THE FOURFOLD WAY IN WHICH NECESSARY TRUTHS CAN
BE SEEN IN ETERNAL RULES.—Therefore I say in answer
to the question, that it is necessary, because of the
statement of Augustine, to concede that *infallible truths
are seen* or understood or known *in eternal rules.*—Note
here in the first place that the *in* can be taken objectively, and this can be done in four ways: as in a *proximate object,* or as in *that which contains the proximate
object,* or as in that *by virtue of which the proximate
object moves,* or as in *the remote object.*

THE FIRST WAY OF SEEING NECESSARY TRUTHS IN
ETERNAL RULES IS EXPOUNDED.—For the understanding
of the first way I say that all actual intelligibles of the
divine understanding have intelligible being, and in them
all truths concerning them shine forth, so that the intellect, understanding them, and by virtue of them understanding the necessary truths concerning them, sees in
them, as in objects, those necessary truths.—The latter,
however, in so far as they are secondary objects of the
divine understanding, are truths (because they are in
conformity with their exemplar, namely, with the divine
understanding) and quiddities; they are light, because
they are manifestive, and they are immutable there and
necessary; but they are eternal in some one respect
[*secundum quid*], because eternity is a condition of an
existing thing, and they do not have existence except in
some one respect only.—Thus, therefore, we can in the
first place be said to see in the *eternal light,* that is, in
the *secondary* object of the divine understanding, which
is *truth* or the *eternal light* in the manner set forth.

THE SECOND WAY IS EXPOUNDED.—The second way is clear similarly, for the divine understanding contains these truths like a book, as that authority of Augustine states *on the Trinity*, book XIV, chapter 15,[14] that these rules are written in the book of eternal light, that is, in the divine understanding, in so far as it contains these truths. And although that book is not seen, still those quiddities or truths which are written in that book are seen. And to that extent our understanding can be said to see truths in the eternal light, that is, in that book, as in *that which contains the object*, and this is done according to the second way; or even in those truths which are *the eternal light in some one respect only*, just as we see in objects, and that is done according to the first way.—And either of these ways seems to be dependent on the understanding, for Augustine in book XII *on the Trinity*, chapter 14, says that *the relation or reason of the square body remains incorruptible and immutable*, etc.: but it does not remain thus except as it is the secondary object of the divine understanding.

A DOUBT CONCERNING THE FIRST WAY IS SOLVED AND THE THIRD IS EXPOUNDED.

a) There is, however, a doubt directed against the first way: for if we do not see these truths as they are in the divine understanding, because we do not see the divine understanding, how are we said to see in the uncreated light from the fact that we see in such light eternal in some one respect only, which has being in the uncreated light, as in the understanding which knows?

b) To this the third way affords answer, that those things, as they are a secondary object of the divine understanding, do not have being, except in some one respect only; however, a truly real operation does not

---

[14] See above, *Principal Arguments*, p. 314.

belong absolutely to any being in some one respect by virtue of itself; but if it belongs to it in some manner, it must be by virtue of something to which *being absolutely* [*esse simpliciter*] belongs.   Therefore, it is not the property of these secondary objects to move the understanding absolutely except by virtue of the divine understanding, which is being absolutely, and through which these objects have being in some one respect.   Thus, therefore, we see in the light which is eternal in some one respect as in a proximate object; but we see in the uncreated light according to a third manner, namely, as in a proximate cause, *by virtue of which the proximate object moves.*

c) In relation to this, likewise, it can be said that as regards the third way, we see in the uncreated light as in the proximate cause of the object in itself; for the divine understanding produces objects by its own actuality in intelligible being, and by its own actuality it gives to this object such being, and to that object such, and consequently it gives them such a reason of object, by which reason they first move the understanding to such certain knowledge.

And that it can properly be said that our understanding sees in an uncreated light, because the eternal light is the cause of the object, appears from a comparison, for we are said properly to understand in the light of the active intellect, although none the less that light is only the active cause, namely, either making the object in actuality, or by virtue of which the object moves, or both.

d) This double causality of the divine understanding, therefore, which is the true uncreated light, namely, that it produces secondary objects in intelligible being, and that it is that by virtue of which secondary objects already produced move the understanding actually, can, as it were, integrate a third member as the cause by which we are said truly to see in an eternal light.

THE OBJECTION IS SOLVED.—And if you object against these two modes integrating a third member as cause, because then it seems that we should be said to see in God willing, or in God as he is will, rather than in God as he is light, for the divine will is the immediate principle of any action directed outward; I reply: the divine understanding, in so far as it is prior in any manner in the act of the divine will, produces these objects in *intelligible* being; and thus in respect of them it seems to be a purely *natural* cause, for God is not a *free* cause in respect of anything except what presupposes before itself in some manner a willing according to the act of will; and just as the understanding as prior to the act of the will produces objects in intelligible being, so as prior cause it seems to cooperate with those intelligibles toward their natural effect, namely, that apprehended and compounded they may cause a *conformity of apprehension to themselves.* It seems therefore to involve a contradiction, that any understanding form such a composition, and the composition not be in conformity with the terms, although it is possible that it may not conceive those terms; for although God voluntarily constrains to the end that the understanding compound the terms or not, nevertheless, when it has compounded them, that that composition be in conformity with the terms seems to follow necessarily from the relation of the terms, which relation they have from the understanding of God causing those terms naturally in intelligible being.

COROLLARY.—It is apparent from this why special illumination is not necessary for seeing in eternal rules;

for Augustine does not hold that anything is seen in
them except truths which are necessary by the strength
of the terms, and there is the greatest necessity in such
things as well of remote cause as of proximate cause in
respect to the effect: for example, as well of the divine
understanding with reference to moving objects as of
those objects with reference to the truth of combination
of them. And although likewise there is not so great a
necessity to the perception of that truth, that the opposite involves a contradiction, nevertheless the necessity
is from the part of the proximate cause, with the remote
cause coassisting it, for the terms apprehended and
compounded are formed naturally to cause the evidence
of conformity of the composition to the terms, even
though it is held that God constrains terms to this effect
by a general influence, but not by a natural necessity.

But whether there is a general influence, or what is
more, a natural necessity of influencing the terms to this
effect, it is clear that no special illumination is needed.

THE DOCTRINE OF SAINT AUGUSTINE IS EXPOUNDED.—
That which has been assumed concerning the intention
of Augustine is evident from his own statement in book
IV *on the Trinity*, chapter 15, in which he speaks of
infidel philosophers: *Some of them were able to raise
the sight of their mind beyond any creature and to attain
to the light of immutable truth in howsoever small a degree, for not yet having attained which they deride many
christians who live meanwhile from faith alone.* Therefore, he holds that christians do not see the things they
believe in the eternal rules; but philosophers see many
necessary truths in them. In the same place, in book
IX *on the Trinity*, chapter 6: *Not as the mind of every
man is, but as it must be in sempiternal reasons,* as if to
say, contingent things are not seen there, but necessary

things.—And in the same work, book IV, chapter 16, he argues against those philosophers,

> Because they dispute most truly and because they persuade by most certain proofs that all temporal things are made by eternal reasons, have they therefore been able to perceive in those reasons themselves, or to gather from them, how many the genera of animals are, what the seeds of each are in the beginnings, what the mode is in increments, what the numbers are by conceptions, by births, by ages, by deaths, what motions in desiring those things which are according to nature and of avoiding the contraries? Have they not sought all these things, not by that immutable wisdom, but by the history of places and times, and have they not credited the things discovered and written by others?

Therefore he understands that those contingent things which are known only by the senses or are believed by stories, are not known by eternal rules; and yet special illumination is needed more in believing contingent things than in things known necessarily; indeed, special illumination is removed most especially in necessary truths and general illumination alone suffices.

THE OBJECTION AGAINST THE AFORESTATED EXPOSITION IS SOLVED.—To the contrary: why then does Augustine say in book XII *on the Trinity*, chapter 14, that *it is in the power of only few to attain by keenness of mind to the intelligible reasons*, and in the *LXXXIII Questions*, question 46, that only the pure of soul attain to them?— I reply: that purity must not be understood as a purity from vices, for in book XV *on the Trinity*, chapter 15,

he holds that the unjust see in the eternal rules what
is to be perceived in them,[15] and in book IV, in the
chapter quoted above, he holds that the philosophers saw
the truth in the eternal rules without faith; and in the
same question he holds that no one can be wise without
knowledge of ideas, in the manner in which Plato, for
example, would be conceded to be wise. But this *purity*
must be understood by elevating the understanding to
considering truths as they shine forth in themselves,
not only as they are revealed in the phantasm.

It must be considered here that the sensible thing outside causes a confused phantasm and single accidentally
in the faculty of phantasy, that is, representing the
thing according to quantity, figure, color, and other
sensible accidents; and as the phantasm represents only
confusedly and accidentally, so, many men perceive only
that which is by accident. Truths, however, are purely
and absolutely such from the *very nature of terms*, in
so far as those terms are abstracted from all things
conjoined by accident to them; for this proposition,
every whole is greater than its part, is true in the first
place, not as the whole is in a stone or in wood, but as
the whole is abstracted from all things with which it is
conjoined by accident; and therefore the understanding
which never understands totality except in the accidental
concept, as for example in the totality of the stone or
the wood, never understands the pure truth of this principle, for it never understands the absolute reason of
the term, by which truth is.

Therefore, it is in the power of few to attain to the
eternal reasons, because it is in the power of few to
have essential intellections, and of many to have such
accidental concepts.—But these few are not said to be

[15] See above, *Principal Arguments*, p. 314.

distinguished from others by a special illumination, but
by better natural powers, for they have an understanding which is more abstractive and more perspicacious, or
else because of a greater searching out, through which
one person succeeds in knowing those quiddities which
another, equally ingenious, but not inquiring, does not
know.

And in this manner is to be understood that saying
of Augustine concerning one looking out on a mountain
and having below the cloudy air and above pure light,
in book IX *on the Trinity*, chapter 6; for he who always
understands only the accidental concept, in the manner
in which phantasms represent such objects as accidental
entities, is like one placed in a valley surrounded with
cloudy air; but he who separates quiddities by understanding them absolutely by an essential concept, which
quiddities notwithstanding are apparent in phantasm
with many other accidents joined to them, has the lower
phantasm, like cloudy air, and he is in the mountain,
in so far as he knows that truth, and he sees the true
above, as that superior truth in the power of the uncreated understanding, which is the eternal light.

THE FOURTH WAY OF SEEING NECESSARY TRUTHS IN
ETERNAL RULES IS EXPOUNDED.—And in this last manner
it can be conceded that pure truths are known in the
eternal light as in a *remote known object*, for the uncreated light is the first principle of speculative things
and the final end of practical things; and therefore
speculative as well as practical things are derived from
principles themselves. And therefore the knowledge of
all, of speculative as well as practicable, by principles
derived from the eternal light as known, is more perfect
and purer than knowledge derived by principles in the
class itself, as has been said in the question on the sub-

ject of theology, and it is more eminent than any other kind whatsoever. And in this manner the knowledge of all things pertains to the theologian, for to know that a triangle has three sides, as it is a certain participation of God, and having such an order in the universe that it expresses as it were the perfection of God, this is to know that the triangle has three sides in a more noble way than by the reason of triangle: and thus to know that one must live temperately because the final beatitude is to follow, which consists in attaining to the essence of God in himself, is to know this practical knowable more perfectly than by any principle in the class of morals, as for example by this, that *one should live honorably*.

And in this manner Augustine speaks of the uncreated light as known, in book XV *on the Trinity*, chapter 27, where addressing himself, he says, *Certainly therefore you have seen many true things and you have drawn them from that light in which you saw them shining forth to you; turn your eyes up to the light itself and fasten them on it if you can; for thus you will see what distinguishes the nativity of the Word of God from the procession of the Gift of God.* And a little later, *This light has shown these and other things similarly certain, to your interior eyes. What cause is there therefore why you can not see with fixed glance that light itself, save only weakness?* etc.

THE PRINCIPAL ARGUMENTS ARE SOLVED.—From the things that have been said it is clear concerning all the authorities of Augustine to the contrary[16] and the authorities of Augustine which occur concerning this matter, can be expounded according to some of the mentioned modes of seeing.

[16] See above, pp. 313-315.

ARTICLE VI.

IT IS SHOWN HOW THE REASONS OF THE CONTRARY OPINION
PROVE THE INTENTION OF AUGUSTINE, BUT NOT THE IN-
TENTION FOR WHICH THEY ARE BROUGHT FORTH HERE.

With respect to the sixth article it must be seen how
those three reasons stated for the first opinion prove
something of truth in so far as they are taken from
Augustine, although they do not prove that false conclusion for which they were adduced.

ANOTHER SOLUTION OF THE REASONS OF HENRY.

a) It must be known here that from sensible things
as from a primary and essential cause, pure truth must
not be expected, for the knowledge of the sense is truly
something by accident, as has been said,[17] although
some acts of the senses are certain and true; but by virtue
of the active intellect, which is a participation of the
uncreated light, illumining the phantasms, the quiddity
of the thing is known, and from this, true purity [of
truth] is had.—And by this the first argument of
Henry[18] is solved; and it no longer holds according to
the intention of Augustine.

b) To the second reason of Henry[19] I say that the
soul is mutable from one disparate act to another, according to the diversity of objects, because of its own
unlimitedness and immateriality, for it is in respect to
any thing that is; in the same way from actuality to
non-actuality, for it is not always in actuality; but in
respect of first principles, the truth of which is known
from the terms and in respect of conclusions deduced

[17] See above, p. 346.   [19] See above, f) pp. 317-318.
[18] See above, e) p. 317.

evidently from the terms, it is not mutable from contrary to contrary, from true to false. For the rules rectify the thing understood in the light of the active intellect; and although the intelligible species itself of the terms is mutable in being, still in representing in the light of the active intellect, the intelligible species represents immutably, and the terms of the first principle are known by two intelligible species, and thus that union is true and certain evidently.

To the third[20] it must be said that the conclusion is against him, for he posits only sensible species or phantasms [i.e. sensible impressions or images];[21] there is no conclusion concerning intelligible species representing the quiddity.

It must be said, however, that if the sensitive powers are not impeded, the sensible species represents the thing truly; but in sleep the powers of the exterior senses are bound: therefore, the imaginative faculty, conserving the sensible species, in accordance with the diversity of flux of the humors of the head, apprehends them as the things of which they are the likenesses, for they have the force of things, according to the Philosopher, *on the Motions of Animals.*—The third reason proves no more than this.

[20] See above, g) p. 318.
[21] See above, pp. 334-335.

WILLIAM OF OCKHAM (c. 1300-1349)

William of Ockham presents the spectacle (which
has had not a few parallels) of a philosopher, generally
conceded to be of the first importance, whose reputation
would seem undiminished by the fact that none of his
logical, physical, or philosophical works have been published since the seventeenth century. The present selec-
tions were translated from what is probably the last
(the second) edition of the *Quodlibeta*, that of Strasbourg, 1491.[1] There are indications, too, that some of
the manuscripts still available contain works of his, if
they are proved to be genuinely his, which have never
been published. With his political writings he has fared
better, for the interest in his political theories and the
scholarly examinations of them have been more constant
and more exacting. Yet despite the paucity of editions in
recent centuries, the large number of manuscripts of
his philosophical works in the libraries of Europe indicates that at least the beginnings of his reputation were
built on a broader circulation of his doctrines.

His reputation for nominalism, which has achieved
widest currency, grows from the interpretation he made
of the aristotelian logic. In the processes of learning

[1] The text of that edition has been followed in all respects
except the paragraphing and the numbering and arranging of
the arguments, in which more recent conventions have been
introduced by the present editor. The other edition (GUILLERMI
HOKAN, *Quodlibeta,* ed. by Cornelius Oudendiick. Paris:
Petrus Rubeus, 1487) has, however, been consulted and in
some instances variant readings have been adapted, and omissions supplied, from it.

(or he would say, according to the primacy of generation) the individual thing is known first. No universals,
only individuals, exist outside the mind, and it is from
those extramental realities that knowledge has its first
beginnings. Even to ask whether the terms of a proposition or the ideas of the mind are anything outside the
mind is to raise a question irrelevant to science; science
is science, not dependent on whether concepts are only
in the mind or not, but dependent on whether or not
concepts stand for things outside the mind. To hold
that terms and concepts are not things, but stand for
things, is not, however, an isolated answer to the problem of the universal, and the statement of only that
aspect of Ockham's doctrine is insufficient to characterize
what is usually referred to as his nominalism, for it
misses the essential realism of the doctrine. If it is
true that the universal is nothing in things outside the
mind, no more is the individual thing which is outside
the mind suited to enter the mind. The theory of
knowledge which William of Ockham set up, was less
concerned with the construction of a metaphysics to
reduce thought to being than with the examination of
the means of which thought disposes to know the things
that are.

If, then, the origin of the arts and sciences is in
experience, knowledge none the less consists in ideas;
the first object according to the primacy of generation
is the individual thing, but the first object according to
the primacy of adequation is the universal. Since ideas
are not properly parts of the things outside the mind,
but rather signs for those things, the center of the
problem of knowledge is the problem of signification.
A sign, Ockham defines, as that which causes something
to come into knowledge and which is formed to stand for
that thing. Terms stand for (*supponens*); individual

things are stood for (*suppositum*). But two intentions are distinguishable in the mind: the first intention is the act of the understanding signifying things themselves which are not signs of something else; the second intention is the act of signifying first intentions. Signs, moreover, may be divided into three kinds, written terms, spoken terms, concepts. Since universals are concepts or terms, the place of universals in thought depends on the circumstance that they have only objective (that is mental) being, and no subjective being outside the mind, that they are predicable of many things, but are the essence of no thing, that in short, the being of universals is their being understood (*esse eorum est eorum cognosci*).

The mind has two powers, the intuitive power by which it contemplates individual things, and the abstractive power by which it separates things into their elements or forms general ideas applicable to many things. The origin of knowledge is in sensible intuitive perception, but apprehension by sensation is insufficient to account for knowledge, even if the judicative power of the understanding be added to it. The act of apprehending and the act of assenting are distinct, in both the processes of understanding and the processes of sensation. By sensation, that a thing is is perceived: desire is the assent to that perception; but though sensitive sight may suffice to cause an act of the sensitive appetite, it does not suffice to cause intellectual assent to the contingent proposition that such and such a thing is. For that there is required an intellectual intuition. The apprehension of such a proposition, moreover, and the judgment of it are distinct, for it may be shown that the act of doubting a proposition is possible simultaneously with the demonstration of the proposition. Finally, not only does sensation know things, and understanding

know terms, intuitively, but in the same way the understanding knows itself intuitively, for it knows its own
states, and it is possible for it to form a contingent
proposition concerning either understanding or will to
the effect, for example, that understanding is, or will is.
Intuitive knowledge, therefore, is not merely, as has
frequently been supposed in exposition of William of
Ockham, the perception of things which are, as they are
actually; it must be broadened by the notion of intellectual intuition to include whatever can be in effect or
was at some time in the nature of things.

The processes of logic presuppose an apprehensive act of some sort. Abstractive knowledge presupposes intuitive knowledge, and nothing can be known
in itself unless it is known intuitively. Intuitive knowledge is knowledge in virtue of which it can be known
whether or not a thing is. This dependence of logic
on intuition is not, however, made the basis of an empiricism, for once terms have been defined, they may be
known directly. The statement of the dependence is
only the recognition that before terms can be combined
properly according to the laws of logic, the terms themselves must be apprehended: sometimes that apprehension is of a term which indicates the existence of a thing
outside the mind; sometimes it indicates only another
term, sometimes an idea, or a passion, or an intention of
the mind itself; sometimes, and this is the case that is
of particular interest to the logician, it is the apprehension of a complex of terms. The judgments of logic
have to do with such complexes of terms in propositions.
This prelogical apprehension introduces into Ockham's
discussion of truth a word, somewhat strange to the
aristotelianism of his predecessors, which he probably
learned from Duns Scotus. His search is for *evident*
knowledge; to know a proposition *evidently*, recourse

can be had to no logical device, save that of tracing back to a proposition to which assent is given because its statement is as things are apprehended in fact to be. The evidence of that perception, sensitive or intellectual, is intuitive. Evidence is that quality of the proposition in virtue of which it is seen to be true. In the body of logic, on the other hand, assent to a proposition is referred to a whole complex of assenting and dissenting. Not to trace the concatenation further, assent to the proposition, *man is an animal* (for example) involves not only the assertion that that proposition, in itself and absolutely, is true, but assent also to the proposition, *this proposition man is an animal is a true proposition*, for the assent is to the complex of terms which constitutes the original proposition. Propositions known through themselves, however, are different from propositions in general. Propositions like, *the whole is greater than its parts, God is three and one, God is not the devil*, require for assent nothing more than the apprehension of their terms. The first principles of any science would be of this latter sort. In selfevident propositions the assent is not to the complex of terms as object; only the apprehension of individual things is presupposed, although the assent is not an assent to individual things.

It involves no contradiction, therefore, that the same conclusion can be known by experience and by demonstration; that, even more, the same conclusion can be proved *a priori*, *a posteriori*, and by authority. To hold this is not to forget that all intellective knowledge presupposes the sensitive imagination of the interior and exterior senses, nor that all evident knowledge is based on intuitive perception. Every discipline begins with individuals and derives from experience the universal which is the principle of the art or the science. But though all knowledge has its origin from the senses, and though every discipline is based on individuals, yet no discipline treats properly of individuals as such, and no science is properly of individuals; but both have to do with universals which stand for individuals.

The science of logic is concerned with the ways in which terms can be manipulated to stand adequately for things, and in this analysis of knowledge it is not surprising that Ockham's examination of the devices of logic should be one of his principal concerns and one of his chief claims to fame. He wrote two logical works: a commentary on the aristotelian logic called *A Golden and Extremely Useful Exposition of the Ancient Art* and another work called the *Sum of All Logic*. Both display in the sequence of the subjects treated the presence of the theory of knowledge they exemplify, for they take up in turn, terms, judgments (propositions), arguments (syllogisms). In this, as in the metaphysics and the physics, there is no departure from Aristotle, save in so far as this is an interpretation of Aristotle. For the *Categories* of Aristotle, Ockham conceived, dealt not with things but with words indicating intentions or ideas, and the remaining books of the *Organon* devised the ways of combining and separating words in propositions and relating propositions in syllogisms and consequences. The exposition of Ockham's contribution to the philosophy of knowledge is more difficult, therefore, than the exposition of the contributions of most of his predecessors. For whereas the examination of the nature of knowledge turned the augustinians for the most part to the contemplation of God or to the investigation of nature preliminary to the discovery of God; and whereas for Thomas Aquinas, knowledge suggested problems concerning judgment and thought and things (for, since such opuscula as *The Sum of All the Logic of Aris-*

totle are apocryphal, Aquinas prepared commentaries for only the *on Interpretation* and the *Posterior Analytics* out of all the books of the *Organon*); Ockham was turned from the same problems to the consideration of the principles and causes of physics and the mechanisms and rules of logic. Of God he found nothing that could be known evidently by demonstration. The three principles of natural generation and the four causes he could expound with the thomists, but the emphasis had changed, for his principle of economy, the famous razor, which would not permit him more elements in explanation when fewer would suffice, disposed of the metaphysical entities on which the thomists grounded their confidence that things were as they were thought to be: there ceased to be need of the thomist intentional species, their rational immaterial soul which is the form of the body, their God known *a posteriori* since he could not be known *a priori*. Faith saved much of the rational psychology and all the theology. But for the foundation of certainty Ockham went not to intentional species or to the return of the soul upon itself, but to the intuition of first principles, to the classification of terms, concrete and abstract, categorematic and syncategorematic, of first and second imposition, of first and second intention, to the classification of syllogisms, demonstrative and topical, categorical and hypothetical, to an illuminating, though largely forgotten treatment of definition, consequences, induction.

His was not, of course, the first instance in the middle ages of concern with such problems, but the turn which he gave to their resolution was a turn which the philosophers of more than a century were to continue to give to the problem of truth. The terms of the problem were to be apprehension and judgment; and in the ways of immediate perception and in the peculiarities of propositions, the solution lay. It was not long after—considerably before the beginning of the eighteenth century —that the certainties of Ockham were treated as the certainties of Augustine and those of Thomas had successively been treated: as the augustinian divine illumination yielded to the thomist doctrine of abstraction, which was perhaps, as its proponents usually insisted, not inconsistent with it, but which none the less made the subject of philosophy not God and his nature and acts, but the soul and things: as the ockhamite doctrine that universals are terms which stand for things, rather than as Thomas supposed, forms derived by the activity of the active intellect which abstracted them from a universe actual in being but potential in being understood, again shifted the emphasis (though the attitudes again might possibly be reconciled) from the nature of being and the soul to the examination of natural generation and propositions; so too the men who may be considered followers of Ockham in the fourteenth century, in physics deserted evident propositions to discuss contingent propositions about the acceleration of freely falling bodies, inertia, center of gravity, and in the problem of knowledge granted the certainty of first principles and of sense perceptions, but insisted on the contingency of all other propositions, since the certainties of principles could not be used to generate a system from the stated certainties of perception. The history of aristotelianism will have to be written more fully before the importance or the originality of Ockham's contribution can be estimated, and he will appear to better advantage in the statement of the logician than in broader exposition. Whether or not the men who succeeded him followed in his footsteps must remain even then an arduous question, for when it is a problem of whether or not an interpreter truly interpreted Ockham, each successive interpretation must be another step in an infinite regress such as abound in the history of philosophy. Philosophically it suffices that later developments no more superseded his thought than his thought had superseded that of Duns Scotus; or than Duns had superseded Thomas; or Thomas, Augustine. Doubtless the sequence of philosophers in this progress down through the fourteenth century suggests the stages of what has been called the secularisation of philosophy—such a description, however, intrudes the judgment of a moralizing present, tracing the evolving past, and also approving its outcome. The principles of the succeeding philosophies of the middle ages could, of course, be applied still to explain the mechanisms of becoming and the nature of being. One philosophy is deserted for another most usually because of a hope that the new philosophy will explain more readily an aspect which the old may seem to have left untouched, rarely because something in experience truly dictates the change; a well formed philosophy is demonstrably wrong only on other principles than those on which it was developed. In that fact doubtless is one justification of the study of the history of philosophy, that the principles which philosophers long dead had evolved are not infrequently fertile of philosophical statement and explanation to which the better remembered principles with which their successors thought to refute them are inadequate.

WILLIAM OF OCKHAM

THE SEVEN QUODLIBETA[1]

Quodlibet I.

Question XIII.

Whether that which is known by the understanding first according to a primacy of generation is the individual.

PRINCIPAL ARGUMENT. And it seems in the first place that it is not. For the universal is the first and proper object of the understanding. Therefore, in point of primacy of generation it is known first.

To THE CONTRARY, the object of sense and the object of understanding are absolutely the same. But the individual is the first object of sense by such a primacy: therefore etc.

CONCLUSION. The meaning of the question must be stated first here. In the second place the question is to be answered.

1. With respect to the first part it must be known that individual is taken here not as every thing which is one in number, for taken thus, each and every thing is individual. But it is taken to mean that thing which

---

[1] *Quodlibeta septem una cum tractatu de sacramento altaris Venerabilis inceptoris fratris Guilhelmi de Ockam anglici, sacre theologie magistri, de ordine fratrum minorum,* Strasbourg, 1491.

is one in number and is not a sign, whether natural or voluntary (or at good pleasure), common to many things, for the written word, the concept, and the spoken word, which are significative of many things, are not individuals, but only the thing which is not a common sign is individual.

In the second place [with respect to this first part] it must be known that this question is not understood to be about any knowledge whatsoever of the individual, for any universal knowledge taken thus is knowledge of the individual. For nothing is understood by such universal knowledge except an individual and individuals. However, such knowledge is common; but the question is understood to be about knowledge which is properly speaking simple and individual.

2. With respect to the second part, having supposed that the question is understood to be about knowledge properly individual, then I say first that, taking individual in the said manner to mean knowledge which is properly individual and simple, the individual is known first.

This is proved by the following reason, that the thing outside the soul which is not a sign is understood by such knowledge first. But every thing outside the soul is individual: therefore etc.

Moreover, the object precedes its own act and is first in the primacy of generation. But nothing precedes such an act except the individual: therefore etc.

In the second place [with respect to the second part] I say that knowledge which is simple and peculiarly individual and first by such a primacy is intuitive knowledge. That this knowledge, however, is first, is evident because of the fact that abstractive individual knowledge presupposes intuitive knowledge in respect to the same object, and not conversely. Moreover, that it is prop-

erly and peculiarly individual is evident from the fact
that it is caused immediately by the individual thing, or
it is its nature to be caused by it, nor is it its nature to
be caused by any other individual thing, even of the
same species.

3. In the third place, I say that the abstractive knowledge which is first by the primacy of generation and
simple (1) is not knowledge peculiarly individual, but
(2) on the contrary is sometimes, nay always, common
knowledge.

(1) The first is evident because one does not have
properly simple knowledge of any individual at the
moment when specific knowledge of the individual can
not be had; but now and then there is such knowledge
[i.e. abstractive knowledge which is not properly indi-
vidual], as is clear in the case of something coming from
a distance which causes a sensation by virtue of which
I am able only to judge that that which is seen is a
being. It is manifest that in that case the abstractive
knowledge which I have first according to the primacy of
generation is knowledge of being and of nothing lower.
And consequently it is not a concept having to do with
the species nor is it a proper concept of the individual.

(2) The second is clear because no abstractive simple
knowledge is more the likeness of one thing than another
in respect of like things, nor is it caused by a thing, nor
is it its nature to be caused by it: therefore, no such
knowledge is properly an individual knowledge; but all
such knowledge is universal.

DOUBTS. But perhaps there are some doubts at this
point. First because it seems that intuitive knowledge
is not proper knowledge, because whatever is given by
intuitive knowledge is assimilated equally to one individual and to another which is like it, and it represents

one individual equally with the rest. Therefore, it does not seem to be knowledge of one thing more than another.

The second doubt is that if first abstractive knowledge is occasionally a knowledge or concept of being, such as was given in the case of something coming from a distance, then in the same way first intuitive knowledge in the same situation will be knowledge of all being, because it is impossible that there be many simple proper concepts of the same thing. But I can have one perception of one thing coming from distant places, by which I only judge it to be being, another by which I judge it to be animal, a third by which I judge it to be man, a fourth by which I judge it to be Socrates. But these perceptions are not of different kinds [*ratio*]: therefore, all of them can not be proper notions of the same individual thing.

The third doubt is that it seems that first abstractive knowledge is most of all proper, since the object is approximated in the manner in which it should be, because we are able by the first abstractive knowledge to recall the same thing previously seen, which could not be done if abstractive proper knowledge were not had concerning the same thing previously seen.

The fourth doubt is that it seems from what has been said already, as if the concept of the genus could be abstracted from one individual, for example the concept of animal, as is evident in the case of one coming from distant places, since I have a perception such that I can judge by it that that is an animal.

RESOLUTION OF DOUBTS. I say, therefore, to the first of these doubts that intuitive knowledge is proper individual knowledge, not because of the greater assimilation to one thing than to another, but because it is caused naturally by the one and not by the other, nor can it be caused by the other. If you say that it can be caused by God alone, that is true, but it is the nature of such a perception to be caused by one created object and not by another. And if it is caused, it is always caused by one object and not by another. Whence it is no more called intuitive proper singular knowledge because of likeness, than it is called first abstractive knowledge, but only because of causality; nor can any other cause be assigned.

To the second doubt I say that sometimes those perceptions are of the same species and differ only as more and less perfect in the same species, as, if a concept were perceived from parts of the same reason or kind [ratio], in which there were no more accidents sensible to sight, then by the approximation of that visible, as for example white, perception is intensified and is made clearer. And in this way one and another individual can be caused, for such a perceived thing is being or body or color or whiteness. But you say that those things differ in species which can not cause an effect of the same species; but clear and obscure vision are of this sort, therefore etc.: I say that whenever causes which are augmented and intensified can not cause an effect of the same species, they differ in species then and not otherwise. Now, however, this perception, when it is augmented and intensified, can accomplish every effect that a clear sight can; and consequently they are of the same reason or of the same species. Yet clear perception and obscure perception are sometimes of different species, as for example when different objects are seen, as, if something were seen colored in different colors, according to a lesser and a greater approximation. But these perceptions are not of the same object but of different objects.

To the third doubt I say that by seeing something I

have some proper abstractive knowledge; but this is not simple but composed from simples. And this composite notion is the beginning of recollection, for by it I recall Socrates, because I saw him formed thus or figured thus, colored thus, of such a length, breadth, and in such a place; and by that composition I recall that I have seen Socrates. But if you circumscribe all simple concepts except one, I no more recall Socrates because of it, than I recall another man extremely like him. Whence I can recall that I have had sight of a man; but I do not know whether it is Plato or Socrates; and therefore a simple abstractive notion is not proper absolutely; but a composite notion can well be proper.

To the fourth doubt I say that the concept of genus is never abstracted from one individual. To the other argument [of this doubt] concerning something coming from distant places, I say that I judge it to be animal because I have previously the concept of animal, which concept is the genus; and therefore by the concept I am led to recollective knowledge. Whence if I did not previously have the concept of the genus of animal, I would judge only that this thing seen is something.

And if you ask what abstractive conception is first formed by the medium of intuitive knowledge, I say sometimes only the concept of that which is or being, sometimes the concept of genus, sometimes the concept of the most special species according to whether the object is less or more removed. The concept of that which is or being, however, is always impressed, because when the object is approximated in the required manner, the specific concept and the concept of being are caused at the same time by the individual thing without.

To the principal argument I say that the universal is the first object by the primacy of adequation, not by the primacy of generation.

Quodlibet I.

Question XV.

Whether our understanding by its nature [pro isto statu]
knows sensible things intuitively.

Principal argument. And it seems in the first place
that it does not, because sensitive sight suffices together
with abstractive knowledge for the knowledge of sensible
things: therefore, intuitive sight is superfluous.

To the contrary, whatsoever perception sense can
accomplish, understanding also can accomplish: but this
is proper to the perception of sense: therefore etc.

Conclusion. To this question I say that our understanding does know sensible things intuitively, because
our understanding knows evidently the first contingent
proposition concerning sensibles: therefore, it has an
incomplex conception sufficient to cause this complex conception evidently; but abstractive knowledge of sensibles
does not suffice: therefore etc.

To the arguments to the contrary,[2] I say that in
holding the sensitive soul to be the same form as the
intellective soul it is not necessary to say that the sensitive sight is received in the intellective soul; but it is
received in the body or in the soul which is distinct from
the intellective soul in the body. For if it were received
in the intellective soul, then a separated soul, at least by
the power of God, could have in itself all such sensation
and it could perceive; which does not seem to be true;
because if it were thus, the angel would lack some
natural perfection, for it seems that the angel also could

[2] The statement of the *arguments to the contrary*, to which
the following are replies, seems to be lacking.

have such forms naturally; for corporeal things would be only the efficient causes of these forms. But if they are diverse forms, as I believe that they are, then I say that the sensitive seeing does not suffice to cause assent to a contingent proposition however much it may suffice to cause an act in the sensitive appetite; for they are not similar in that the same form would then be subject of the sensation and of the act of desiring. If you say that the intellective and the sensitive are not distant from each other in location, that does not hold, for what sees and what assents must be the same in number [i.e. the same individual]. The question concerning the understanding of the head and of the foot has been answered above.

To another [argument to the contrary], I say that there is a difference between sensitive seeing and intellectual seeing, which is noticed by us partly through reason, partly through experience. By experience because the child sees by sensitive sight and not intellectual; for he does not understand by reason that the separated soul can have intellective sight, not sensitive.

To another [argument to the contrary], I say that the separated soul can have such sight, otherwise the separated soul could not have knowledge of sensibles. Similarly, the angel can have such knowledge: therefore, the separated soul likewise. To the proof of this I say that the separated soul can naturally see the complex and incomplex secrets of hearts in the mind of the angel.

To the Scripture I say that the statement is of a fact and natural power suspended from actuality.

To another [argument to the contrary], I say that it requires speech and illumination for two reasons. The first is that perhaps it is not permitted to understand naturally what it could understand [super]naturally.

The second, that many things are revealed to one angel which are not revealed to another nor to the separated soul, as was said in the question on the speech of angels.

To another [argument to the contrary], I say that one can not acquire the sight of God and beatitude naturally, because it can not be caused except by God alone. And further it does not follow: he can see the less visible, therefore, the more visible, just as it does not follow that my understanding can see whiteness which is less visible, therefore, it can see the angel which is more visible; and this is so because the sight of the angel can not be caused in me naturally, and thus it is in this question.

To another [argument to the contrary], I say that sensitive sight is the partial cause of intellectual sight, but it is not the partial cause of the act of assenting without the intellectual seeing, for complex knowledge presupposes incomplex knowledge in the same subject; just as the will can not proceed to action, unless knowledge precedes in the understanding, howeversomuch intuitive knowledge there be in sense.

To another [argument to the contrary], I concede that sensitive sight is subjectively in the sensitive appetite, for sense and appetite are the same: therefore, whatever is subjectively in one is also subjectively in the other.

To THE PRINCIPAL ARGUMENT, I say that sensitive seeing does not suffice, but requires intellectual seeing etc.

QUODLIBET V.

QUESTION V.

Whether intuitive and abstractive knowledge differ.

PRINCIPAL ARGUMENT. And it seems that they do not, because a plurality must not be asserted without necessity, but the same notion, according to substance, can be called intuitive when the thing is present, and abstractive when the thing is absent, in that intuitive knowledge connotes the thing present, and abstractive, the thing absent.

To THE CONTRARY, a contingent proposition can be known evidently by the understanding, as for example that this whiteness is, and not by abstractive knowledge, for that knowledge abstracts from existence; therefore by intuitive knowledge: therefore they differ really.

THE CONCLUSION of this question is certain and can be proved by the separateness of the acts of the two kinds of knowledge; but how they differ is doubtful. And I say for the present that they differ in two ways. In one way in that by intuitive knowledge assent is given to a contingent proposition,[3] and by abstractive knowledge it is not. In another way through the fact that by intuitive knowledge I not only judge that a thing is when it is, but also that it is not when it is not; by abstractive knowledge I judge in neither of these manners. The second is manifest. I prove the first because although it is contradictory that the same idea be the total cause of one judgment and of the contrary of the judgment in respect of the same experience of it, yet it is not contradictory that it be the partial cause of one judgment when the thing exists and that it be the partial cause of the contrary judgment when the thing does not exist, and thus it is in the question proposed. Furthermore, God sees by the same idea that the thing is when it is and that it is not when it is not: therefore, it can be thus without contradiction in the case proposed.

1. BUT TO THE CONTRARY, if this is granted, it follows that God could not cause in us a single act of knowing by which it appears to us that a thing is present

[3] The 1491 edition has *primo* instead of *propositioni*.

when it is absent; which is false, since this does not involve a contradiction. The assumption is proved, because that knowledge is not intuitive because of the thing, since by intuitive knowledge the thing appears to be when it is and not to be when it is not; nor abstractive knowledge, since by abstractive knowledge the thing does not appear to be present.

2. Moreover, that which agrees with an act according to the substance of the act, if the substance of it remains the same, whatsoever else is posited it can still agree with it. But the substance of seeing remains the same by the divine power when no thing exists: therefore, it is not contradictory for it to cause at least partially such an assent as previously, now that the thing does not exist; and consequently, that can be proper to it.

3. Moreover, if this is granted it follows that seeing could be, and yet by it the thing would appear neither to be nor not to be. The consequence is contrary to fact. The assumption is proved by the following common principle: where any one at all of certain given things is in accord with a given thing contingently, if there is no contradiction God can make that thing without all those certain things at once. For thus it is proved most cogently that matter can be without any form. But by virtue of seeing, some one can sometimes know that a thing is and sometimes know that it is not: therefore, there is no contradiction that neither being or non-being accords with it.

4. Moreover, if this is granted, God could not cause evident assent in respect of the following contingent proposition, *this whiteness is*, when whiteness is not existent, for the sight of whiteness causes the evident assent in respect of the proposition, *this whiteness is not*; and the understanding does not seem to assent to the opposite.

1. To the first of these I say that God can not cause in us knowledge such that by it a thing appears evidently to be present when it is absent, for that involves a contradiction, because such evident knowledge conveys that it is thus in fact as is denoted by the proposition to which assent is given. And consequently since evident knowledge of this proposition, *the thing is present*, conveys that the thing is present, it is necessary that it be present; otherwise it would not be evident knowledge. And you posit that it is absent. And thus from that hypothesis there follows a manifest contradiction with evident knowledge, namely, that the thing is present and that it is not present. And therefore God can not cause such evident knowledge. Nevertheless, God can cause a creditive act by which I believe that a thing which is absent is present. And I say that that creditive idea will be abstractive, not intuitive. By such an act of faith a thing can appear to be present when it is absent; yet not by an evident act.

2. To the other I answer by conceding that if the sight of the thing remain by the power of God when the thing is non-existent, it is not inconsistent for vision to cause partial assent, if all other causes requisite concur, but it is inconsistent that it cause such assent totally and partially without other causes; and thus since the existence of the thing is the partial cause of that evident assent, it is impossible that it be caused naturally without the existence of the thing.

3. To the other, I concede the principle and the conclusion and the whole deduction, for it is not a contradiction that seeing be and still by that seeing I neither judge the thing to be nor not to be, because God can make sight without any such assent; but this can not be done by nature.

4. To the last, I say that God can not make evident

assent of the following contingent proposition, *this whiteness is,* when the whiteness is not, because of the contradictions which follow, because evident assent conveys that it is thus in fact as is conveyed by the proposition to which assent is given; but by this proposition, *this whiteness is,* is conveyed that this whiteness is, and consequently if the assent is evident, this whiteness is, and it has been asserted that this whiteness is not; and thus that hypothesis involves manifestly a contradiction with evident knowledge, namely, that whiteness is and that it is not. And yet I concede that God can make assent which is of the same species with that evident assent in respect of that contingent proposition, *this whiteness is,* when it is not; but that assent is not evident, because it is not in fact as is conveyed by the proposition to which assent is given.

And if you say that God can bring about evident assent of this contingent by way of the existence of this thing as a mediating secondary cause: therefore, he can do it by himself alone; I reply that this is the fallacy of a figure of speech; as the following argument, God can bring about a meritorious act with a created will mediating: therefore, he can do it by himself alone. And this is because of the different connotation herein.

To THE PRINCIPAL ARGUMENT I say that there is a necessity of asserting a difference between these kinds of knowledge.

QUODLIBET VI.

QUESTION VI.

Whether there can be intuitive knowledge of a non-existent object.

PRINCIPAL ARGUMENT. And it is argued that there can not be, because it is a contradiction that sight be and nothing be seen: therefore, it is a contradiction for sight to be and for the object seen not to be.

To THE CONTRARY, sight is a quality absolutely distinct from the object: therefore, it can be without contradiction without the object.

CONCLUSION. 1. In this question I assert two conclusions. The first is that there can be by the power of God intuitive knowledge concerning a non-existent object; this I prove first by an article of faith: I believe in God, father almighty; which I understand thus, that everything which does not involve a manifest contradiction is to be attributed to the divine power; but for this to be done by God does not involve a contradiction: therefore etc. Moreover, in that article is based the following famous proposition of theologians: *whatsoever God produces with secondary causes mediating, he can produce and conserve immediately without them.* From this proposition I argue thus: every effect which God causes with a secondary cause mediating he can produce immediately through himself. But he has power in intuitive corporeal knowledge with the object mediating: therefore, he is effective in it immediately through himself. Moreover, every absolute thing distinct in place and subject from another thing can exist by the divine power if the other absolute thing has been destroyed. But the sight of the stars in the sky which I see is of this sort: therefore etc.

And if you say that according to this opinion it follows that God can be seen beatifically and intuitively, when his actual presence is not displayed, as [*in ratione*] an object actually present to the understanding itself: which is false and erroneous; I reply that there is a condition involved in arguing that because God can make such a vision without a created object on which it depends only as on a second cause, therefore God can be seen intuitively and beatifically, when his actual presence is not displayed, as [*in ratione*] an actuality present to the understanding itself, on which object that vision depends as on a first cause. For although, according to the doctors, God can produce effects proper to secondary causes without those secondary causes, still he can not produce any effect without a first cause. Whence just as it is not possible that color cause effectively the sight of color in the eye unless it is actually present, so it is not possible that God cause sight in the understanding unless he has displayed his actual presence.

2. The second conclusion is that intuitive knowledge can not be caused or conserved naturally when the object is not existent. The reason of this is that a real effect can not be produced from non-being to being nor conserved by that which is nothing, and consequently, naturally speaking, a producing cause is required for existing as much as a conserving cause. And if you say that if one sees the sun and later enters a dark place, it appears to one that one sees the sun in the same place and of the same magnitude: therefore, the sight of the sun remains when it is itself absent; and for the same reason it would remain if it were itself non-existent; I reply that the sight of the sun does not remain, but there remains some quality, namely, the light impressed on the eye, and that quality is seen; and if the understanding forms such a proposition as this, *the light is seen in the same place* etc. and assents to it, it is deceived because of that impressed quality which is seen.

To the principal argument I say that it is a contradiction for sight to be and for that which is seen not to be in effect and for it not to be able to be: therefore, it is a contradiction that a chimera be seen intuitively. But it is not a contradiction that that which is seen be nothing in actuality outside the soul, so long as it can be in effect or was at some time in the nature of things. It is thus in the question proposed. Whence God saw from eternity all makeable things and yet none were from eternity.

QUODLIBET V.

QUESTION II.

Whether the same conclusion in number can be known evidently by demonstration and experience.

PRINCIPAL ARGUMENT. 1. And it seems that it can not, because seeing the thing and later not seeing it, one forms simple absolute concepts of different kinds [*ratio*]: therefore, composite conclusions from them will be of different kinds [*ratio*], of which the nature of one is to be known by demonstration, that of another to be known by experience. The consequence is clear of itself. The antecedent is proved because otherwise the way-farer and the blessed would form equally evident propositions concerning God, because they would be composed from concepts of the same kind; which is false.

2. Moreover, the necessary is not contingent, but the conclusion of a demonstration is necessary; and the proposition known by experience immediately is contingent: wherefore etc.

TO THE CONTRARY, the following conclusion can be known by experience, *all fire is heat-giving*; and the same conclusion in number can be known by demonstration by heat as by a middle term: therefore etc.

CONCLUSION. To this question I say briefly that the same conclusion not only in species but in number can be known evidently by demonstration and by experience and by the same condition in number. This I prove because some condition verificative of the conclusion is acquired from experience and no other from knowledge. This is clear inductively, and knowledge of the same conclusion is acquired by demonstration: therefore etc.

Moreover, demonstration based on the nature of things [*propter quid*, i. e. *a priori* demonstration] and demonstration on the grounds of some one thing only [*quia*, i. e. *a posteriori* demonstration] can cause knowledge of the same species in respect of the same conclusion: therefore, in the same manner demonstration and experience can do it.

Moreover, a principle and a conclusion differ in this, that a principle can be known only from its terms or by experience without demonstration; but the same conclusion can be known evidently by experience and by demonstration.

Moreover, causes distinct in species can have effects of the same species; this is clear above: therefore, it is thus in the question proposed.

1. BUT TO THE CONTRARY, a single proposition is not more evident or less evident. But a proposition which is formed with sight mediating is compounded from conceptions more evident than the proposition which is formed with only demonstration mediating, because seeing a thing one assents more evidently than having a demonstration only without experience: therefore etc.

2. Moreover, if the condition of the conclusion caused by demonstration and [that caused by] experience are of the same species, then no way is apparent for proving a distinction of species between the acts of believing, of having an opinion, and of knowing, because the conclusion is the same in itself, and thence the premises can cause an act of the same species: therefore etc.

3. Moreover, knowing a conclusion by demonstration

or experience, howsoever much that assent may be intended, one would never assent so evidently as when
one has demonstration and experience. For otherwise
assent could be increased by frequent repetition of that
demonstration to equal evidence with that which experience caused; which is false: therefore, these kinds
of knowledge differ in species by the following principle,
*those things which have no power in effects of the same
kind* [ratio] *are not of the same kind.*

4. Moreover, if thus the same conclusion is in the
syllogism from true premises and from false premises,
the false premises would cause assent of the same
species with the true premises, and consequently the
sophistical, the falsigraphic, and the demonstrative syllogisms will cause knowledge of the same species.

5. Moreover, the same conclusion in number can be
proved from the thing philosophically from speculative
premises and can be demonstrated by practical premisses, such as the following, *the act is generative of the
habit or condition.* Therefore, if this assent will be the
same, then the same knowledge will be practical and
speculative; which seems absurd.

RESOLUTION OF OBJECTIONS. 1. To the first of these
I say that the same proposition can not be more evident
and less evident at one and the same time to one and the
same person; nevertheless the same proposition can at
one and the same time be more evident to one and less
evident to another. In the same way the same proposition can be less evident to one person at one time and
more evident to the same person at another time.

For proof of this, I say that if some one knows
a conclusion at one time by demonstration only and at
another time knows the same conclusion by demonstration and experience, then to such an one that conclusion
is first less evident and later more evident.

2. To the other I deny the consequence, because the act of having an opinion of and the act of knowing the same conclusion are formally contradictory, because one is evident and the other is unevident and entertained with fear. Two such, however, can not at the same time be in the same understanding, and consequently they are distinct in species; just as it is proved that the acts of loving and of hating the same man differ in species because they are contradictory formally.

For proof of this, I say that not all premisses can cause knowledge of a conclusion of the same species, but some can and some can not, because it is certain that the premisses of a sophistical syllogism and of a falsigraphic syllogism do not cause knowledge of the same species in respect of the same conclusion. In the same way premisses of creditive, opinionative, and demonstrative syllogisms in respect of the same conclusion do not cause assent of the same species, but rather opposed assents, as faith, opinion, knowledge are opposed. And therefore I say that some causes of different kinds [*ratio*] can sometimes cause effects of the same species, but not all causes of different kinds can do this. Nor is any other cause to be sought than that that is the nature of the thing.

But there remains a doubt with reference to this: how is a determination of species proved between these acts? The reply is proved by reason of the contradiction between the acts of knowing, having an opinion, and believing in respect of the same conclusion.

3. To the other I say that if that argument were conclusive, it would prove that heat which is caused by the sun and by fire, and heat which is caused by two fires are not of the same species, because howsoever much the power of the sun were increased it can not by itself cause such perfect heat as it can together with

fire. And likewise howsoever much the power of one
fire be augmented, it can not by itself cause so perfect
heat as with another fire. And consequently these heats
would be of different species by this argument; which is
false. Therefore I say that just as the power of the
sun can be increased so much that it can cause as perfect
heat as fire can cause by itself without the sun, and yet
with the sun it can cause a still more perfect heat than
this, so by demonstration assent can so be increased to
a very great degree, if possible *in infinitum,* that it is
equally evident and equally perfect as that assent which
experience would cause by itself without demonstration.
Nevertheless, it can never be increased by demonstration
so much that it causes assent equally perfect and equally
evident by itself without experience, as it can cause together with experience. And the principle quoted is to
be understood in this sense: *those things which have no
power in any effect of the same species are of different
kinds* [ratio] *or species, and otherwise they are not.*

4 and 5. To the last I say that the same conclusion
can be in the syllogism from true premisses and from
false, but besides that, the consequence does not hold:
that therefore, these premisses can cause knowledge of
the same species, because I have not said universally
that all premisses cause assent of the same species, but
I have said particularly that some premisses etc. And
therefore I say that false premisses are not formed
naturally to cause assent of the same species with true
premisses. For false premisses cause opinion; true
evident premisses cause evident assent. However, if
they are believed, they cause faith.

1. To the principal argument I say that, seeing a
thing and later not seeing it, one can form two propositions composed from abstractive conceptions, as Paul
after the rapture. And one is composed from concep-

tions causing evident assent and the other not, but [the latter] will be [un]evident, as that proposition which he had of God before the rapture which was only believed by faith; and he had another after, which was evident to him by demonstration before the rapture, and the same demonstration in species or in number was more evident after the rapture, with the vision of God mediating.

2. To the other I say that the necessary is not known through the contingent syllogistically as through premisses, but evident contingent knowledge can be the efficient cause partial to causing evident knowledge in respect of the necessary; and thus it is in the question proposed.

QUODLIBET V.

QUESTION VI.

Whether the act of apprehending and the act of judging[4] differ really.

PRINCIPAL ARGUMENT. And it seems that they do not, because it is a contradiction that there be a demonstration in the soul if the soul does not know the conclusion; but demonstration can be in the soul with only the composition of the propositions of the demonstration: therefore, knowledge is something of demonstration. Not the principle nor any term: therefore, the conclusion.

TO THE CONTRARY, they can be separated: therefore, they differ. The antecedent is clear, because some propositions are neutral, to which our understanding does not assent nor dissent at first, and later it assents because of some middle term.

[4] The 1487 edition has (erroneously) *act of seeing.*

CONCLUSION. I reply that I shall first assert two distinctions. Secondly I shall answer the question.

Concerning the first I say that *assent* is of two sorts. One by which the understanding assents that something is or that something is not, or that something is good or white; another by which the understanding assents to some complex.

The second distinction is that *apprehension* is of two sorts. One is composition or division, or the formation of a proposition; there is another, which is a knowledge of the complex itself already formed, as knowledge of whiteness is called apprehension.

In the third place I state two conclusions

1. The first is that the act of assenting taken in either mode is different from the [first] apprehension which is the formation of the proposition. This I prove first as follows. The same conclusion is proved *a priori* and *a posteriori* and by authority as has been shown before. If therefore the conclusion or the formation of the conclusion were knowledge, which is an act of assenting, it follows that then the same knowledge would be *a priori* and *a posteriori*. In the same way faith and opinion; and the same conclusion would at one and the same time be evident and not evident to the same person, because it is by hypothesis knowledge and faith. For the same conclusion in number can first be believed and later be known.

Moreover, the act of doubting is not contradictory to the conclusion of the demonstration, because it is not contradictory to the subject nor the predicate, nor the copula; but the act of doubting is incompossible with knowledge. Therefore, knowledge is not the conclusion nor the formation of the conclusion.

Moreover, the act of believing and the act of knowing are simple and brought forth of necessity immediately.

The conclusion itself however is composite, because the composition of the conclusion is the conclusion and not part of it.

2. The second conclusion is that assent, taken in either mode, differs from the second apprehension which is knowledge of the complex already formed. I prove this first as follows: believer and unbeliever contradict each other concerning this article of faith, *God is three and one*. Either, therefore, this article formed in the mind is apprehended and known by both, or not. If it is and the act of believing is not in both, then the act of believing differs not only from this article formed in the mind, but also from the apprehension of it. If not, it is apprehended in both.

To THE CONTRARY, it may be argued by asserting all things in these two to be equal, except the act of believing, and then it is manifest that one can apprehend that article. In the same way no one assents or dissents except concerning something known; but the unbeliever dissents from this article immediately and denies it: therefore, he knows this article.

Moreover, the apprehensive act causes the judicative act: therefore, they differ. The consequence is manifest. The antecedent is proved by experience, for however frequently one apprehends a complex and does not at first assent, if later because of some middle term one should assent to it only once, one is inclined later promptly to assent to it, and not from the habit of assenting, because as yet it is not had so perfectly that it could incline to that assent: therefore, that promptitude is effectively from the apprehensive habit. But no habit inclines to another act except with its own act mediating: therefore, the apprehensive act immediately causes the judicative act.

Moreover, some apprehend a neutral proposition to

which they neither assent nor dissent: therefore, apprehension, assent, and dissent differ.

Moreover, some first deny a proposition, and later concede it, and apprehend it always: therefore, this apprehension differs from the assent and dissent, for it is related successively to both when one denies and when one concedes.

To THE PRINCIPAL ARGUMENT it is said that it is no contradiction for a demonstration to be in the soul without the act of knowing, because the act of doubting is not contradictory formally to the conclusion nor to the demonstration: although perhaps it is contradictory to it virtually; and consequently by the power of God the act of doubting could be caused in the soul at the same time with the demonstration.

QUODLIBET IV

QUESTION XVII.[5]

Whether every act of assenting presupposes an act of apprehending with respect of the same object.

PRINCIPAL ARGUMENT. And it seems that it does, because the understanding assents only to what it considers true, nor does it dissent except to what it considers false. But the understanding considers nothing true or false except what is known and apprehended: therefore, all assent necessarily presupposes apprehension.

To THE CONTRARY, having formed the following immediate proposition, *every whole is greater than its part,* without any apprehension of the proposition, the understanding straightway assents necessarily: therefore, that assent does not presuppose apprehension.

[5] This question is numbered XVI in the 1487 edition.

CONCLUSION. Here I shall first make a distinction. Secondly I shall answer the question.

Concerning the first I say, as has been said elsewhere, in quodlibet III, question VI, that the act of assenting is of two sorts: one by which I assent that something is or is not, as I assent that *God is three and one*, and that *God is not the devil*; and yet I do not assent to God or to the devil, but I assent that God is not the devil. Whence by the power of word I assent by the latter act to no thing, yet by the same act I apprehend God and the devil, because every act of assenting is an act of apprehending and not conversely. Another kind is the act of assenting by which I assent to something so that the act of assenting is referred to something by assenting or dissenting to a complex, as by assenting to this proposition, *man is an animal*, because I consider that it is true, and I assent not only to this proposition, *this proposition man is an animal is a true proposition*, in which this proposition, *man is an animal*, is subject, but I assent to this proposition, *man is an animal*, in itself and absolutely; and this is so because I know that as it is in fact, so it is conveyed by this proposition.

Concerning the second I say in general that the first assent never presupposes necessarily the apprehension of a complex, because this assent is not in respect of a complex as object, but it presupposes the apprehension of individual things, although the understanding may not assent to the individual things. But the second assent, naturally speaking, presupposes necessarily the apprehension of a complex, and this indifferently,[6] whether that complex is compounded of conceptions of [individual] things or not. And the reason is that this assent has a complex for object. Now, however, none

---

[6] The 1491 edition has *et in hoc differunt* instead of *et hoc indifferenter*.

of us naturally assent or dissent except concerning that which is known and apprehended: therefore, it is impossible that I assent to some complex naturally unless I apprehend it.

1. But to the contrary, if the understanding form this proposition, *the whole is greater than its part,* having circumscribed all other apprehension of the complex except this composition, this evident assent is caused instantly. Otherwise it would not be a proposition known through itself. In the same way if this understanding form the proposition, *God is three and one,* without any other apprehension, it can, together with a command of the will, cause an act of belief of that article: therefore, such assent does not presuppose apprehension.

2. Moreover, apprehension of a complex is not a proposition, because the understanding can form a proposition although it does not know it or apprehend it, just as I can know a stone although I do not know that knowledge. Nor is the apprehension part of the proposition, because every part of the proposition can be knowledge of an external thing and no other knowledge is necessary to the act of assenting.

3. Moreover, assent with respect to a thing is one thing and assent with respect to a complex is another, just as apprehension of a thing is one thing and apprehension of a complex another. Therefore assent at least in respect of a thing does not presuppose apprehension of a complex.

1. To the first of these [arguments to the contrary] I say that the argument, as well with respect to the act of assenting in common as with respect to the act of believing the article, proceeds from the first assent and not from the second.

2. To the second I say that the apprehension of a complex is neither a part of the proposition compounded

from notions of external things, nor is it the proposition itself, although it could be part of another proposition; but it is another kind of knowledge distinct as well from proposition as from assent; and assent which has a complex for object presupposes this knowledge; and this is true not only when one assents to a complex which is compounded from conceptions of things, as in the following, *man is an animal, man is not an ass,* but also when one assents to some proposition whose subject and predicate are propositions; propositions concerning the sense of a composition are commonly of this sort, such as the following, *this proposition, man is an animal, is true, or necessary, or contingent;* or *this proposition, man is an ass, is impossible,* etc. because in order that I may assent to such complexes it is necessary that I first apprehend and know them.

3. To the third I say that there is no assent in respect of the thing because nothing is said when I assent to a stone or an ox.

To THE PRINCIPAL ARGUMENT the answer is clear from what has been said.

QUODLIBET IV.

QUESTION XIX.[7]

Whether first and second intentions are really distinct.

PRINCIPAL ARGUMENT. And it seems that they are not, for an essence of the reason is not distinct really; but intentions, as well first as second, are only entities of the reason: therefore etc.

To THE CONTRARY, first and second intentions are

[7] This question is numbered XXXV in the 1487 edition.

things, and are not the same things but distinct things: therefore, they are distinguished really.

CONCLUSION. In the first place, what first and second intentions are must be considered here. In the second place the question must be answered.

Concerning the first I say that both first and second intention can be taken in two ways, broadly and strictly. Broadly the first intention is said to be the intelligible sign existent in the soul which does not signify an intention or a concept in the soul or any other signs precisely, and I say this, whether sign be taken for that which can stand [for a thing] in a proposition and be part of a proposition, of which sort are categorematic terms, or whether sign be taken for that which can not stand [for a thing] nor be the extreme terms of a proposition when it is taken significatively, of which sort are syncategorematic terms. And in this manner not only mental categorematic terms which signify things which are not themselves significative, but also mental syncategorematic terms and verbs and conjunctions and others of this sort are called first intentions.

EXAMPLE. For in this manner not only the concept of *man* which signifies all men and can stand for them and be part of a proposition, and the concept of *whiteness*, and the concept of *heat*, and such concepts are properly called [first] intentions; but such syncategorematic concepts as the following, *if, nevertheless, not, while, is, and, runs, reads,* are called first intentions, and this is because although they do not stand, taken in themselves, for things, yet conjoined with others they make the others stand [for things in diverse manners, as *every* makes *man* stand for][8] and be distributed over all men, as in this proposition, *every man runs*; and

[8] Omitted in the 1491 edition.

yet this sign *every* signifies nothing through itself, because it signifies neither an external thing nor an intention of the soul.

But strictly the first intention should be a mental name formed precisely to be the extreme term of a proposition and to stand for a thing which is not a sign; as the concept of *man,* of *animal,* of *substance,* of *body.* And briefly all mental names which naturally signify individual things which are not signs.

In the same way, taken broadly, that concept of the soul is called a second intention, which signifies not only the intentions of the soul which are natural signs of things (of which sort are the first intentions taken strictly) but also as it were mental signs signifying at will syncategorematic mental signs. And we have perhaps in this way only a word corresponding to the second intention.

However, taken strictly, that concept is called a second intention which signifies precisely intentions naturally significative, of which sort are *genus, species, difference,* and others of this sort, for as the concept of man is predicated of all men, as in saying, *this man is a man, that man is a man,* and thus of the others, so too one common concept, which is the second intention, is predicated of first intentions which stand for things, as in saying, *man is a species, ass is a species, whiteness is a species, animal is a genus, body is a genus, quantity is a genus;* in the manner in which *name* is predicated of different names, as in saying, *whiteness is a name, man is a name;* and this second intention thus signifies first intentions naturally and can stand for them in a proposition, just as the first intention signifies external things naturally and can stand for them.

Concerning the second, some say that first and second

intentions are certain fictive entities which are only objectively in the mind and nowhere subjectively.

ON THE CONTRARY when a proposition is verified by things, if two things suffice for the truth of it, it is superfluous to assert another thing; but according to all such propositions as, *man is understood: man is subject: man is predicate: man is a species: animal is a genus,* and similar propositions in which such fictive being is asserted, the propositions are verified by things, and two things suffice for verifying all such propositions: therefore etc. The assumption is proved because having posited knowledge of man in the understanding, it is impossible that this proposition be false, *man is understood.* In the same way, having posited the intention of man in common and the intention of subject in common, and having formed this mental proposition, *man is subject,* in which one intention is predicated of the other, it is necessary that this proposition be true, *man is subject,* without anything fictive.

Moreover, such a fictive thing hinders the knowledge of the thing: therefore, it is not to be asserted because of knowledge. The assumption is proved because that fictive thing is neither the idea, nor is it the external whiteness known, nor is it both together; but a certain third thing, medium between knowledge and the thing: therefore, if that fictive thing is understood, then the thing outside is not understood, and then when I form the following mental proposition, *God is three and one,* I do not understand God in himself but that fictive thing; which seems absurd.

Moreover, for the same reason, in understanding other things God would understand such fictions; and so from eternity there was coordinated as many fictive beings as there could be different intelligible beings which were so necessarily that God could not destroy them; which seems false.

Moreover, such a fictive being does not have to be posited in order that a subject and predicate may be had in a universal proposition, because the act of understanding suffices for this: for that fictive being is as individual in being and in representing as the act. This is evident from the following, that one fiction can be destroyed while another remains as actual, for either that fiction depends essentially on [some] act [of reason] or not. If it does, then, when one act ceases, that fiction is destroyed, and yet the fiction remains in another act, and consequently there are two individual fictions as there are two acts. If it does not depend on this individual act, it does not consequently depend essentially on any act of the same reason, and thus that fiction will remain in objective being without any other act; which is impossible.

Moreover, it is no contradiction that God form such real knowledge without such a fiction [for knowledge does not depend on such a fiction] essentially; but the contradiction is that the intention be posited in the understanding lest something be understood: therefore, the intention must not be posited because of a common intention.

Therefore, I say that as well the first intention as the second intention is truly an act of understanding, for by the act can be saved whatever is saved by the fiction. For in that the act is the likeness of the subject, it can signify and stand for external things; it can be the subject and the predicate in a proposition; it can be genus, species etc. just as the fiction can. Wherefore it is clear that the first and second intention are really distinct, for the first intention is the act of understanding signifying things which are not signs. The second intention is the act signifying first intentions. Therefore they are distinguished.

As REGARDS THE PRINCIPAL ARGUMENT it is clear that both first and second intentions are truly real entities, and they are truly qualities subjectively existent in the soul: therefore etc.

QUODLIBET V.

QUESTION XXV.[9]

Whether the absolute, connotative, and relative concepts are really distinct.

PRINCIPAL ARGUMENT. And it seems that they are not, because plurality must not be asserted without necessity; but this is not necessary: therefore etc.

TO THE CONTRARY, words are distinct: therefore, concepts; the consequence holds because they are ordered signs.

CONCLUSION. I reply that the conclusion is certain according to the philosophers. For the concept of man is absolute; the concept of white is connotative; and the concept of father is relative; and they do not coincide except as inferior and superior, for every relative concept is connotative, and not conversely.

But it is doubtful how they differ. And therefore I say that they differ in this, that the absolute concept signifies all the things it signifies equally in the first and single mode of signifying, namely, in the direct mode, as is clear from this name *man* and similar words, for it signifies all men equally, and not first one and secondarily another. Nor does it signify one directly and another obliquely. And such a name is truly predi-

⁰ This question does not appear in the 1487 edition.

cated of something without the addition of any term in
an oblique case, as *Socrates is a man*, although he is not
a man of anything. And such a name, properly speaking, does not have a definition expressing the essence
of the name [*quid nominis*].

The connotative name, however, properly signifies one
thing first and another secondarily, and one thing directly and another obliquely. And such a name properly
has a definition expressing the essence of the name, nor
can it be predicated truly of anything unless an oblique
case can be added to it. An example of this is in the
concept *white* and in similar concepts. For first it signifies *white* and secondarily *whiteness*; it signifies the
subject directly, and whiteness obliquely. Nor can
Socrates be white unless this is true; Socrates is white
by whiteness; Socrates is so much by quantity; long
by length.

The concrete relative concept, however, has in the
highest degree the aforesaid conditions which this connotative concept has. But they differ in that whenever
the connotative concept is predicated truly of anything,
its abstract can properly be added to it only in an
oblique case, for nothing is white unless it is white by
whiteness, nor warm unless it is warm by warmth. But
when the relative concept is predicated truly of anything, an oblique case which is not the abstract of it can
always properly be added to it. An example is in the
case of *master, father*, and others, for Socrates is not
master unless he is master of some servant. Nor can he
be a father unless he is father of some son. Nor can he
be like except to some one having a like quality. Nor
equal except to some one having quantity; and thus it is
with all relative nouns.

To THE PRINCIPAL ARGUMENT the conclusion is clear
from what has been said.

QUODLIBET II.

QUESTION XII.

Whether the direct and reflex act are the same act.

PRINCIPAL ARGUMENT. And it seems in the first place that they are, because otherwise there would be a process *in infinitum* in reflex acts: therefore etc.

TO THE CONTRARY, in us the understanding and its object are not the same; but the direct act is the object of the reflex act: therefore etc.

CONCLUSION. In the first place I shall expound here the meaning of the question. In the second place I shall reply to the question.

Concerning the first I say that the direct and reflex acts are not taken here in their proper sense, for that is called reflex properly, which begins from a given thing and terminates in the same thing. And therefore no act is properly called reflex. But direct and reflex are taken improperly, for that act is called direct by which the understanding understands an object outside the soul, and that act reflex by which this direct act is understood.

Concerning the second I say that the direct act and the reflex act are not the same act. I prove this first as follows. Whatever is known by a power through some act of a kind [*ratio*] other than the object, can be known through a consimilar act by another power of the same kind. But one angel knows the act of another angel by an act distinct from the act known: therefore, the angel whose act is known by the other can know its own act by a knowledge consimilar to this knowledge which another angel knows. But that knowledge is distinct in species from the object: therefore, it is other. For this reason seems more cogent than all the others which are relative to this part.

Again, intuitive knowledge and abstractive knowledge are distinct; that is certain; but abstractive knowledge can be known intuitively as is clear in the first quodlibet: therefore etc.

Again, the direct and the reflex acts of will are not the same: therefore, the understandings of them are not the same. The antecedent is clear because the act of love and of hate are not the same; but some one sometimes loves hate: therefore etc.

1. To THE CONTRARY, if this is so, then infinite acts could be at the same time, because there is a process *in infinitum* in them; and the posterior always requires that the prior exist, just as intuitive knowledge requires naturally the existence of the object.

2. Moreover, there would then be some act which could not be apprehended intuitively by the understanding.

1. I REPLY, therefore, to the first of these by conceding a process *in infinitum* in abstractive but not in intuitive ideas. The first is clear because any intuitive and abstractive knowledge can be known abstractively when it is not itself existent. For this perception can cease and then it can be known abstractively; and that knowledge can cease and then be known in another abstractive idea; and thus *in infinitum*. But from this there does not follow any actual infinity nor any great magnitude, as for example that a thousand perceptions exist at the same time, which we do not experience: therefore, in this process there is given an ultimate perception which can not be seen. For of it we have experience through its status itself [i.e. through the fact that perception comes to rest in it]. But what the cause is I do not know.

And by this the conclusion to the other argument and to the principal argument is clear; obviously no multitude follows from this necessarily.

2. The second is clear likewise, because in intuitive ideas the posterior always requires that the prior exist; and therefore if there were a process *in infinitum*, one greatest multitude could be made; which is not true.

QUODLIBET I.

QUESTION XIV.

Whether our understanding by its nature [pro isto statu] *knows its own acts intuitively.*

PRINCIPAL ARGUMENT. And it seems in the first place that it does not, for nothing is known by the understanding except that which previously fell under sense; but acts of understanding were never under sense: therefore etc.

To THE CONTRARY, abstractive knowledge presupposes intuitive. But intellectual conceptions are known abstractively: therefore, intuitively.

CONCLUSION. Replying to this question I say that our understanding does know its own acts intuitively. And the reason is that a contingent proposition is formed concerning the knowledge of the understanding and concerning the will, which is known evidently by our understanding, namely, such a proposition as the following, *there is an understanding, there is a will*: therefore, either by means of intuitive or abstractive knowledge of the act of understanding. If in the first manner, the proposition is granted. The second can not be held because abstractive knowledge is abstracted from an actual existence.

Again, experimental knowledge is not without intuitive knowledge; but one who lacks all intuitive sensitive knowledge, experiences intellectual knowledge: therefore etc.

RESOLUTION OF OBJECTIONS. To the first argument to the contrary, I say that that does not follow because there would then be infinite perceptions in actuality. For proof of this I say, that if it is held that direct and reflex acts are not distinct, it can be said that the seeing of a stone is seen by itself when the stone is seen. And then it can be said that that proposition which is composed from the seeing of the stone and the concept of the stone can not remain when the seeing of the stone is not, although another proposition which is composed out of these conceptions can remain without the sight of the stone. But if it be held that the reflex act is distinct from the direct act, I say that the seeing of the stone will be by another seeing, but in the end one will come to a seeing which is not seen by a seeing naturally distinct from it, although it could be seen if there were no impediment, and I concede a regress *in infinitum* by the divine power; but speaking naturally there will be a seeing which can not be seen; and for the following reason, that our understanding is a limited power: therefore, it has power only for a certain number of sights and not for more. But in what seeing one must stop I do not know. Perhaps one should stop in the second seeing, because it perhaps can not be seen naturally.

To another [objection] I say that one can not experience the first and the second seeing equally and so *in infinitum*, because one is stopped at some sight which can not be seen because of the limitation of the understanding, which has power for so many sights and no more. I concede, none the less, that one can naturally have several perceptions at once, at least two or three of the same object.

To another [objection] I concede that I assent evidently to the following proposition, *I see*. And I say that the assent is caused by the seeing of that seeing; but from this it does not follow that there will be infinite perceptions at the same time; nor can there be a process *in infinitum* naturally; but a stop must be made at some seeing which is not naturally visible. Nor can one assent evidently to a complex formed as the following, *I see that sight at which the seeing has come to a stop.*

To another [objection] I concede that if there were in the soul a second sight, it could be seen if there were no impediment, and yet if it were in my soul I would not be able to see it, because the first act impedes the second so that it can not be seen with the first seeing. And I say it is not impossible, by the fact that it is in the understanding, that it could not be seen because if it were in the understanding it could be seen through itself; but because it is in the understanding at the same time as another act, it comes about that it can not be seen. And I say that I experience the vision of a stone, but I do not experience the vision of that vision. And by that reason the example of Augustine in book VI *on the Trinity*, chapter 8 near the end, is explained, in which he says that he often read and did not know what he read; clearly this happened because of destruction through the act of the other power, and still there is no contradiction between those acts, just as likewise a man intent on seeing does not perceive himself hear, when nevertheless he hears, and yet between sight and hearing there is no contradiction. So it is in the question proposed that although there is no contradiction between the last perceiving to which one comes naturally and the perceiving of that or of any of the preceding perceivings, yet one act can impede the other by the fact that it is.

To another I say that I am certain that I understand a stone in virtue of the sight of the stone, and in virtue of the perception of the first sight, and sometimes perhaps in virtue of these perceptions and in virtue of some proposition habitually known. For example, I am certain that I understand by experience because I see the seeing of the stone. But I am certain that I understand the stone by discourse from effect to cause as I know fire by smoke, when I see smoke alone, and this is so because I have on another occasion seen smoke caused by the presence of fire. And in the same manner because on another occasion I have perceived intellectually such a seeing caused in me by the presence of a stone.

Again I argue, such effects are of the same species, as has been expounded above in reference to the speech of angels. The proposition habitually known is this, *all such effects of the same species have causes of the same species.* I do not say in general all effects of the same species have a cause of the same species.

To THE PRINCIPAL ARGUMENT I say that Aristotle says that nothing of those things which are external is understood unless first it falls under sense, and they are sensibles only according to sense, and that authority is true concerning them, but concerning spirits it is not.

QUODLIBET II.

QUESTION X.

Whether the sensitive soul and the intellective soul are really distinct in man.

PRINCIPAL ARGUMENT. And it seems in the first place that they are not, for there is only a single being of a single composite thing: therefore, only a single form, for the form gives being.

To THE CONTRARY, any animal is prior in nature to man: therefore, man is by one form and animal by another.

CONCLUSION. I reply to this question that they are distinct; but it is difficult to prove this, because it can not be proved from propositions known through themselves. I prove, nevertheless, that they are distinct really.

1. In the first place thus. It is impossible that there be contraries at the same time in the same subject; but the act of desiring something and avoiding or rejecting the same thing are contrary in the same subject: therefore, if they are at the same time in the nature of things, they are in different subjects; but it is clear that they are at the same time in man, for this same thing which man desires by the appetite he rejects by the understanding.

And in the same way by Aristotle in book III *on the Soul*, where he says that there are in the same person contrary appetites, that is, they would be contrary if it was their nature to be received in the same subject. If you say that these appetites are called contrary because they are inclinative to contrary effects, and they are thus virtually contrary, because the one inclines to pursuing, the other to flight, which is incompossible with the first, and such contraries can well be in the same subject; but they are not formally contrary; on the other hand by that reason you would say just as easily that willing and denying are not contraries formally, but only virtually, for it is their nature to incline to contrary effects, and thus the way disappears for proving anything to be contrary.

Moreover, the same substantial form can not at one

and the same time have two acts of desiring in respect
to the same object. But in man there are frequently acts
at the same time of willing some good and of desiring
it by the sensitive appetite: therefore, these acts are
not in the same subject.

Moreover, the same form does not bring forth at one
and the same time an act of desiring something naturally
and something else freely; but man wishes something
freely, and the sensitive appetite desires it naturally:
therefore etc.

2. In the second place I argue thus principally.
Sensations are subjectively in the sensitive soul
mediately and immediately; and they are not subjectively in the intellective soul: therefore, they are
distinct. The major premiss is clear because nothing
else can be assigned as the subject of sensations except
the sensitive soul or power. And if the power is an accident of the soul, it will be subjectively in the sensitive
soul; this is proved because otherwise every apprehension of the sensitive soul would be an act of understanding, for it would be subjectively in the intellective
soul. Similarly, then, the separated soul could perceive,
for sensation is therefore subjectively in the intellective
soul, and God can conserve every accident in its subject or in any other; and consequently he could conserve
the sensitive soul in the separated soul; which is absurd.
If you say that the composite whole is the immediate
subject of sensation or of the sensitive power, and no
form; on the contrary, accident is not more simple than
its first subject, as will be shown clearly at another
time: therefore, sensation, since it is a simple accident,
can not be subjectively and immediately in the composite
and first [subject]. In the same way having granted
this, those powers would not be powers of the soul more

than of the body: wherefore, they are not subjectively more in one than in another.

3. In the third place I argue thus. The same form in number is not extended and unextended, material and immaterial; but the sensitive soul in man is extended and material, and the intellective soul is not, for it is all in all etc.

OBJECTIONS. But against these [arguments] there are arguments of many sorts.

1. In the first place thus, that Augustine in his book on Ecclesiastical Dogmas attacks two souls in man and says that it is the error of some.

2. In the second place, that either that sensitive soul remained three days with the body or with the soul; and whichever be granted it follows that Christ was not dead univocally with other men, or else he was corrupted and then Christ put off one soul which he had taken on; which is contrary to the holy doctors.

3. In the third place, that the Parisian article says the doctrine that, when the rational soul recedes from the body, the animal remains still alive, is an error. But if they are distinct the sensitive soul remains after the separation of the intellective, for nature proceeds in the same order in generating and in corrupting. But in generating, the sensitive is introduced prior to the intellective if they are distinct; and the Philosopher says this in his book on Animals.

4. Again, if the sensitive soul remains without the intellective, that composite would be neither man nor rational animal; and thus it would not be rational nor irrational.

RESOLUTION OF OBJECTIONS. 1. I reply and I say to the first of these, that Augustine attacked two intellective souls in man of which one is from God and the

other from the devil; and this is the mind of Augustine
if any one examines his book in that place.

2. To the second I say that the sensitive soul of Christ
in those three days remained where God pleased, but
thus that it was always united to deity. But whether
it remained with the body or with the intellective soul,
only God knows; yet both can well be said. And I
deny that he was not then dead univocally with other
men, because for the same reason it could be said that he
was not univocally dead, for the body of Christ is not
corruptible as the bodies of other men are corruptible:
therefore, it does not follow that he was not univocally
dead because of the separation of the intellective soul.

3. To the third I say that after the separation of the
intellective soul the sensitive soul does not remain, nor
was the sensitive soul introduced in the generation of
man prior in time to the intellective. To the Philosopher I say that the sensitive soul is prior in nature in
the body, but not prior in time, for they are introduced
and expelled at the same time.

4. To the last I say that if by the power of God the
sensitive soul remained in the body, that composite
would be alive, and still it would be neither rational
animal nor irrational, nor would it be animal truly contained under animal, which is the genus. And the reason
of this is that it would not be a being complete through
itself in the genus, but it would be its nature to be an
essential part of something existing through itself in the
genus; and no such thing would be through itself in the
genus of substance, or in any other genera essentially.
Nor would any genus be predicated of it essentially in
the first manner. Yet if all that which has this sensitive soul be called animal, then this is truly animal; but
then animal would be spoken of equally of that and of
other animals.

To the principal argument I say that there is only one total being of man, but many partial beings.

Quodlibet II.

Question XIII.

Whether the act of a more perfect object is more perfect.

Principal argument. And it seems in the first place that it is not, because if it were, then the act of an infinite object would be infinite and consequently every act in respect to God would be infinite.

To the contrary, if it is not, then there would be no way of proving that any act is more perfect than any other.

Conclusion. I shall first set down one distinction here. In the second place I shall reply to the question.

Concerning the first I say that for anything to be more perfect than another thing can be taken in two ways. In one way according to things distinct in species. In a second way in those things which are of the same species. In the first way the angel is more perfect than man and man is more perfect than the ass. In the second way one whiteness is more perfect than another, and any form in which there are more parts of the same quantity of mass or power than in another form of the same species, as one whiteness is more perfect than another, because it has more parts of whiteness of the same quantity, and in the same way one love is more perfect than another.

Concerning the second article I assert two conclusions.

1. The first is that it is not necessary that the act of the more perfect object always be more perfect; and this is so whether the object be complex or incomplex.

And I prove this first as follows. A principle is a more perfect object than the conclusion, and in respect of the same principle there can be acts of erring and of doubting, both of which are more imperfect according to species than the act of knowing: therefore, an act related to a more perfect object can be more imperfect than the act of a more imperfect object.

Moreover, let us take two incomplex objects, such as an angel and a man. Then I argue thus: the act of hating is more imperfect in respect of either than the act of loving; but I can hate the angel and love the man: therefore etc.

Moreover, a remiss act is more imperfect than an intense act, at least speaking of perfection of the second sort, although it may not be necessary that it be thus always in the first sort, but [it is] when some one loves a better and more perfect object less intensely; and this holds as well of objects of the same species as of objects of different species, as a man sometimes loves the greater love with less intensity than the lesser love, and loves the angel less than the man, which is clear because sometimes he thinks less intensely of the more perfect object than of the more imperfect object.

2. The second conclusion is this. The act of the more perfect object can always be more perfect than the act of the more imperfect, so that some act in respect of the more perfect object is more perfect than any act in respect of the more imperfect object, as well complex as incomplex.

Wherefore it must be known that in respect of the same object, as well complex as incomplex, there can be different acts, just as in respect of the same conclusion there can be different acts, such as erring and doubting. And similarly in respect of the same thing there can be the act of loving and of hating. And although the act of erring could be more perfect than some act in respect of the more perfect object, yet the most perfect act among these is the act more perfect in respect to the more perfect object than any act in respect to a more imperfect object. Just as the most perfect act in respect of one more perfect conclusion is more perfect than any other act in respect of a more imperfect conclusion. And in the same way I conclude of incomplex objects distinct in species. However, the most perfect act in respect of the more perfect object is more perfect than any other act in respect of a more imperfect object. Just as the most perfect act which is brought forth concerning an angel is more perfect than any other act which is brought forth concerning a man. I prove this as follows: because those two are of different species, and the most perfect act in respect of the more imperfect object is not more perfect than the most perfect act in respect of the more perfect object, as appears manifestly: therefore, since one act is necessarily more perfect than another, by the fact that they differ in species, it follows that the most perfect act in respect of the more perfect object is more perfect than the most perfect act in respect of the more imperfect object. But that these acts are distinct in species, is proved because contrary acts in respect of the same object differ in species, such as the act of erring and knowing: therefore, much the more the most perfect acts of objects distinct in species. If you say that the acts of complex objects are of different species, but not the acts of incomplex objects, there is not, on the contrary, greater reason for the latter than for the former. Moreover, then the act of hating would be of the same species as the act of loving, for both are in respect of incomplex objects. In the same way the vision of a creature according to this could be beatific, because if it is of the same species as the vision of God to whomsoever it should be intended, it would arrive at an equal grade with the beatific vision.

To THE FIRST PRINCIPAL ARGUMENT I say that such a mode of arguing does not hold, unless it happens to fill in proper order the process *in infinitum,* that is, when the act in respect of the infinite presupposes of necessity infinite acts of infinite objects having an order according to greater and less perfection. But it is not thus in the question proposed, as is manifestly clear, because God can be understood and loved after or before any created object, and the act by which he is loved is necessarily finite.

1. To THE CONTRARY, if the act in respect of the infinite is finite, and the act of anyone in respect to that which is a created subject is similarly finite, since the act in respect of the infinite exceeds the other act in respect of the other subject in a double proportion, as I suppose, God can therefore make some object doubly more perfect than A, and let that be B. Then the most perfect act in respect to B, according to what has been said, exceeds the most perfect act in respect to A doubly. And again let God make an object excelling B doubly, and let that be C. Then because the most perfect act in respect of C excels the most perfect act in respect of B doubly, and because consequently by chance the most perfect act in respect of B is made equal to an act which is in respect of the infinite, it follows necessarily that the most perfect act in respect of C exceeds the act in respect of the infinite doubly, and thus an act in respect of the infinite would exceed in perfection an act in respect of the infinite.

To this answer can be made in a number of ways. In one way by positing a status among species distinct in respect to perfection [i.e. a species than which there

could not be one more perfect], because then the chance
is not possible, and therefore if the act in respect of the
infinite exceeds in a double perfection the act in respect
to that which is an individual of the highest species, God
could not make another species in double perfection of
that, and thus according to this way the argument is
made void.

1. But against that there is that difficulty of the
process *in infinitum* of acts of understanding by reflex
acts, of which each posterior is more perfect than the
prior. Because of the more perfect object I say that
the more perfect act having whiteness for object is
more perfect than whiteness: therefore, the first reflex
act is more perfect than the direct act because of a more
perfect object. For the same reason the second reflex
act is more perfect than the first, and thus with all:
therefore, there can be a process *in infinitum* in objects
distinct in species according to greater and less perfection.

I say that it can be said in answer to this that in such
things there is a process *in infinitum*, and one would
never arrive none the less at any act of perfection equal
to A. And thus it can be said in the question proposed,
notwithstanding such a process *in infinitum*, one never
arrives none the less at any equally perfect act, such as
an act in respect of the infinite. And this is so because
they are of different kinds [*ratio*], nor is it the nature
of the one to be equalled to the other in perfection. If
you say that the act in respect of the infinite excels the
direct act in a certain proportion of quantity, let us say,
twenty times, and the first reflex act excels the first
direct act in as much perfection, and the second excels
the first as much or in as much, and the third excels
the second as much; but every finite amount is transcended by the addition of the same quantity: there-

fore, one must come to some reflex act which will be
more perfect than the act in respect of the infinite.

I say here that properly speaking it is not to be conceded with respect to proportion that the act in respect
of the infinite exceeds the direct act in equal proportion,
because this is true only when one happens to suppose
equal or unequal parts by the composition of which something more perfect is made, as is the case with two parts
of water and fire; and thus with similar things. But in
the question proposed there is an excess of one act over
another act according to itself whole and totally, so that
every part of one exceeds the whole of the other, not
only in species but also in perfection, just as every part
of whiteness is more perfect than any blackness.

So I say that that proposition which has been accepted, *every finite* etc., has truth in those things which
are of the same kind [*ratio*], in which one is added
truly to the other, just as a part of water is added to a
part of water, and a part of whiteness is added to the
preceding whiteness. It has truth likewise when it happens to assert an equal part and another part exceeding.
But it does not have truth in those things in which one
can proceed *in infinitum* according to perfection by the
addition of some things not of the same quantity, but of
some things of the same proportion, which according to
themselves as wholes are unequal, and yet one never
comes to any great perfection of quantity, for one does
not come in the least to the perfection of substance, and
thus it is in the question proposed concerning reflex
actions.

1. But still the position advanced is proved because
when something is added to something else according to
your gloss, that if someone grieves concerning something sad, he will grieve so much more concerning something greater, as a man grieves more because he is

punished for two days than for one day, and so forth for the rest. And consequently through an infinite time he will grieve infinitely, and here a part of grief is added to part.

2. Moreover, a remiss habit sets up a difficulty for the will, and the more intense the habit the greater the difficulty: therefore also, some habit sets up an impossibility for conquering the sensitive appetite.

1. Replying to the first of these I say that it is possible that one man be saddened as much and not more concerning an infinite intensive pain than another man may be, or the same man at another time, concerning a finite pain. And if you argue in the same manner as above concerning that man who according to right reason sorrows so much, that he sorrows more concerning a greater thing, etc., I say that it is possible that he sorrow according to right reason, as much by fear of a finite pain as another man, or the same man at another time, concerning an infinite pain. The reason of this is that every creature is limited, and therefore has power for so great an effect and not a greater. And therefore when he comes to the ultimate to which he is able to go, then he can do no more.

To the contrary, right reason declares repeatedly to you that you grieve more concerning an infinite pain than concerning a finite pain. I say that that is not so, but it would be necessary that one grieve more, if one could. And in the same way it can be said that such a man who is in the ultimate act can desire the vision of God as intensively through one time as through infinite time, because of the defect of his power.

If you say: I assert that God may cause grief concerning infinite pain and desire of beatific vision to endure *in infinitum*; since he is not himself limited, he can communicate infinite grief concerning infinite pain; this can be said in two ways. First from any such quality caused by God, God can make a more intense quality *in infini-tum*; but one will never arrive at the infinite. It can likewise be said in another way, that there is a state [i.e. a point is reached] in the augmentation of form that must give some act so intense in respect of an infinite object.

2. Now, therefore, I say to the second instance that habit can not make a difficulty for the will, because if it were thus, it would be because of some productive or destructive action neither of which can be asserted in the question proposed; nevertheless the will, as is commonly the case, follows the passion freely without any compulsion, and the saints call this a difficulty of the will in genus.

If you say that then it would be no more culpable for the will to follow a small passion than a great one, I reply and I say that it can well be said that it is no more culpable because of the difficulty which is brought to the will, but it is more laudable because it wills to undergo more evil or sorrowful passions for God, and it is more culpable because it does not will patiently to bear fewer adversities or it is more laudable because it flees more and greater delights, and more vituperable because it does not flee fewer and small delights, but acquiesces in them.

It can likewise be said in another way, namely, that habit brings difficulty to the will. And I concede that habit can be so intense that it inclines the will sufficiently to action in conformity with the sensitive appetite, so that it can in no manner act in the contrary, unless perchance there be a state [i.e. a point beyond which it can not go] in the increase of passion, and then will can conquer the supreme passion, and consequently any more remiss passion. And perhaps the sensitive appetite is not capable of such habit or passion beyond a certain grade which the will can conquer. And according to the first way, if the habit can increase so much that it necessitates the will, one must say that the will in such an act could not sin. Whence it would then have no hope of liberty; yet not absolutely, because in respect of other objects it could sin, and likewise in respect of that object it could sin if the habit or the passion be relaxed.

To the other preceding argument answer can be made in another way, that some act in respect of a finite thing can be more perfect than some act which is in respect of an infinite.

QUODLIBET IV.

QUESTION XVIII.[10]

Whether the wayfarer has any simple and proper concept of God before [discursive knowledge by] composition and division or after.

PRINCIPAL ARGUMENT. And it seems that he has, because the concept is simple of which are sought such composite concepts as the following: *Whether God is an infinite being: whether he is the first actuality.* But such questions are raised concerning the concept of God: therefore etc. The major premiss is clear because such questions are not raised concerning the proper composite concept of God, because then the same thing would be asked concerning itself; which is false.

To THE CONTRARY, no creature contains a proper and simple concept of God essentially nor virtually: therefore, no creature can cause it.

[10] This question is numbered XVII in the 1487 edition.

CONCLUSION. 1. To this question I say that the wayfarer can not have from pure natural things any knowledge of God which is absolute not connotative, affirmative not negative, simple not composite, proper not common, before composition and division. The reason of this is that otherwise no one would be able to deny that God is, because if it is supposed that no proper knowledge of any impossible thing is caused by sensation of the thing before composition and division; then since sensation has no relation to the impossible that it may cause proper knowledge of it; then since for the same reason sensation would cause proper notions of infinite impossible things, because it has the same relation to all impossibles; then I argue thus, that you concede that proper knowledge of God is caused before composition and division, and not from faith because we agree in faith, and yet do not affirm this: therefore, it is known evidently that proper knowledge of God is caused by sensation, and consequently it is evident to every unbeliever that God is by the fact that he sees that whiteness is. For he could argue evidently that the concept caused by sensation mediating is not of anything impossible, but possible; wherefore, by the sensation of whiteness mediating for the thing, there is proper knowledge of God before composition; and this knowledge is not of anything impossible; it is possible therefore that any unbeliever be able to know God evidently. And since in perpetual things being does not differ from being able, any unbeliever can know evidently that God is; which is false. Therefore I say that before composition and division, the wayfarer has no such concept nor can he have it.

Moreover, it is not of the nature of complex knowledge of one thing to cause first incomplex, simple, and proper knowledge of another thing, because it is not intuitive, for such knowledge is caused immediately by the thing, speaking naturally. Nor again is it abstractive, because if such knowledge were simple proper knowledge, it necessarily presupposes intuitive knowledge. Since therefore the wayfarer can not see God intuitively in this state he can have no such knowledge of God.

2. To the second I say that the wayfarer can not have such a simple and proper concept after composition and definition. The reason of this is that discourse is properly among complexes: therefore, by discourse alone only complex knowledge can be acquired, and not incomplex knowledge which is presupposed in composition and division: therefore etc.

BUT TO THE CONTRARY. 1. Because if this were granted we would then understand God by understanding nothing else; this is proved because these common concepts, *being, first, three and one*, follow each other in the same order of time in mind as in word. But when the first concept is in mind, God is no more understood than creature, nor when the second is in mind, nor when the third: therefore, God is never understood by a proper concept, unless these concepts formed successively contain the simple and proper concept.

2. Moreover, to understand God otherwise it is necessary to begin with being and descend by composition and definition; and thus it will be a long time before one could again understand God.

3. Moreover, the definition of a created substance can cause a simple concept proper to the thing defined: therefore, the description of God can cause a simple concept of God. The consequence holds, because otherwise a definition and a simple concept of the thing defined would not be distinguished in the predicamental line, nor would there be three terms in demonstration

because there would not be in demonstration a simple concept of the thing defined.

4. Moreover, otherwise there would not be a relative concept in us, because neither extreme can cause a concept of the other, nor is the extreme concept caused before composition and division, because experience teaches that understanding does not have a relative concept before it compares one thing to another by composition and division, as when the understanding forms the following complex: *this whiteness is such as that is.*

5. The concept of the likeness of a chimera is caused. Moreover, then, we would not be able to have an act of understanding in one instant, for the parts of the composite concept follow each other in mind as in word, as has already been said.

6. Moreover, when the understanding forms the following complex, *God is distinguished from anything else which is not he,* either the subject of that proposition in the mind is a simple concept of God, and the proposition is had; or else it is not, and then I shall make the proposition by demonstrating the thing which God is thus: this thing which is signified by this complex is distinguished from every other which is not it; and then I demonstrate God by one actuality, and the proposition is had. Or else by composition from many acts, and there will be a process *in infinitum.*

1. To the first of these I concede that the wayfarer can not naturally understand God, understanding nothing else, because although by the total concept alone I understand only the being which is God, nevertheless by any partial concept of that composite I understand something other than God, because any such concept is common to God and others. But further I say that the proof is incomplete because although it is possible in some case that common concepts follow each other in the

same order in mind as in word, yet it is necessary that one can form some proposition in which many common concepts are predicated or subjected at the same time, and consequently in such a composite concept God can be understood.

2. To the second I say that it is not necessary to begin from being, because one can begin from the first being or from the ass. Nor is such a descent or discourse by composition and division required for understanding God again, nor is a great amount of time required, because when God is understood first by any composite concept, he can be understood again in an instant by an interior habit inclining to a consimilar notion, just as in an instant a whole proposition can be formed.

3. As regards the third I deny the assumption, that the concept of the thing defined is presupposed by a common law in the definition. For knowledge of the thing defined by definition properly so called is caused because of the mediating of intuitive knowledge of one individual, because the concept of the species can be abstracted from one individual. Division, however, can not be caused with respect to every part of it except by knowledge of many individuals. For proof of this I say that neither of these impossibles follows, for the concept of the thing defined is not distinguished from definition because of the fact that it is caused by it, because it is in no manner caused by it. But they are distinguished from each other and causally from their causes because they are diverse.

4. To the fourth I say that the argument is to the contrary because the relative concept is compounded and distinguished positively at the same time from both extremes. I prove this because the subject and predicate of a proposition precede the composition at least

in order of nature. Now the understanding however
in the very formation of the following complex, *this
whiteness is similar or equal to another*, asserts the relative concepts from the part of the predicate: therefore,
these concepts precede the proposition. There is this
one order, therefore, because when two whitenesses have
been seen, a specious concept [i.e. a concept of the
species] of whiteness is caused in the mind, and I say
this immediately from the whitenesses themselves or
from the ideas of them, and the proposition is formed
later, at least according to the order of nature. To the
proof of this I say that experience teaches that one
does not judge by an act of assenting that those whitenesses are similar before the understanding compares
one to the other by composition and division; and this is
so because such assent presupposes composition and
division, as has been said above. But experience does
not teach that one does not have a relative concept
before composition and division.

5. To the fifth I say that we can understand a chimera
in one instant by a composite concept involving a contradiction, but in no wise by a simple proper conception.
And further I say that the proof makes a false assumption, namely, that the parts of a composite concept
follow each other in the mind as in the word, because
the concepts exist together in the indivisible subject, but
in the word they do not.

6. To the last I say that the subject of this proposition: *God is distinguished* etc., is not a simple concept
but a composite one. In the same way I say that in
forming the following proposition: *this thing signified by
this composite concept is distinguished* etc., the subject
of this second proposition is composite of the concept of
God and the demonstrative pronoun. And further, in
forming the proposition which states the following: *this*

thing signified by this second composite concept is distinguished etc., the subject is still a composite concept. And therefore I concede a process *in infinitum* in forming such propositions distinct at least in number, and the subject in each proposition is always a composite and not a simple concept.

To THE PRINCIPAL ARGUMENT I say that such composite concepts as *infinite being, pure act,* are sought and demonstrated of the concept of being taken particularly, as when it is asked whether there is in the universe *any infinite being* and pure act. The subject of this proposition, however, is a concept compounded from the concept of *being in common* and of this syncategorematic, *any,* and thus it is not improper that one composite concept be sought and proved of another composite concept.

QUODLIBET V.

QUESTION VII.

Whether several proper concepts can be had of God.

PRINCIPAL ARGUMENT. And it is argued that they can not, because either absolutely the same thing corresponds to these concepts or not. If it does, then the concepts are synonymous. If not then there is some real distinction in the divine beings besides the distinction of persons.

To THE CONTRARY, the supreme good, infinite being, pure act, which are several concepts proper to God, are predicated of God: therefore etc.

CONCLUSION. To this question I say that concerning God there can not be had several concepts proper and convertible with him, all of which are absolute not

connotative, affirmative not negative, simple not composite. By the first are excluded such concepts as first
cause, creative, governing, glorifying. By the second
are excluded such concepts as incorporeal, immortal,
infinite. By the third are excluded such concepts as
infinite being, being intensively, supreme good, pure
act. But when these conditions are circumscribed no
one can have two proper quidditative concepts of God,
nor one quidditative and another denotative. And I
speak of the concept which is abstractive knowledge.

1. The first is proved because if it is thus, then for
the same reason an infinite number of quidditative concepts can be had of God, because no cause can be given
wherefore they may be reduced to a certain number
if two can be had, since argument is impossible from
the simplicity of an object, for notwithstanding the
simplicity you posit two proper quidditative concepts,
and thus another for the same reason would posit an
infinite number.

Moreover, a thing is not otherwise perceptible by
abstractive concepts than by intuitive concepts; but
only intuitively is the thing which is visible by a single
vision, distinct and clear by a single conception which
is the proper idea: therefore, only one such proper
concept is possible of God.

Moreover, if the understanding is the same and the
object the same, and there is no diversity, then the
concept which is the effect will be the same and only
one: otherwise every way of proving the unity of the
effect would disappear.

2. The second is proved because such distinct concepts of different[11] kinds [*ratio*] can not be had of the
same thing of which one concept is quidditative and

[11] The 1491 edition has *the same kind.*

another connotative without any distinction in the thing, and without any extrinsic connotation, and without any grammatical and logical mode. Wherefore, if all these are set aside, whatever is signified by the one is signified by the rest and in the same mode of signifying, and thus both will be quidditative or neither.

3. Moreover, of the same simple there are not two proper abstractive likenesses of which neither is like the other. But the concept is like that of which it is [the concept]: therefore, there could not be two such concepts, one quidditative, another denominative.

4. Moreover, by each concept the whole quiddity is expressed and nothing else: therefore, each is quidditative, because it is this for a concept to be quidditative.

[1. No reply to the first argument is given in either edition, doubtless because the argument is in accordance with the conclusion.]

2. To the second I say that one such proper concept of God can not be had naturally, neither before composition nor after, together with all the aforesaid conditions, as has been shown in another quodlibet.

3. To the third I say that the blessed, seeing God for the first time, has only one such proper concept of God after such a vision, because he has one abstractive notion which is the proper concept of God, absolute, affirmative, and simple, which can not correspond to any other.

4. To the fourth I say that our understanding can have no such simple, proper concept of any creature without sight of the creature, nor can it with any sight whatever, and this is because any such notion or concept is equally a likeness and represents all very similar individuals, and thus it is no longer the concept of one more properly than of the other.

1. But to the contrary, the negative concept is not

predicated affirmatively of the thing of which it is [the concept]. This is proved because the affirmative and the negative concepts of the same thing are contradictory concepts, such as white and not-white, and clearly they signify the same thing, otherwise they would not be contradictory, and consequently these two concepts are not predicated affirmatively of the same thing; but infinite is predicated affirmatively of the divine wisdom, wherefore the following is true: *the divine wisdom is infinite*: therefore etc.

2. Moreover, although infinite, which is part of the complex concept, is negative, yet the whole complex concept is affirmative, because it is equivalent to an affirmative proposition such as the following: *the divine wisdom is infinite*.

1. To the first of these I say that the negative concept signifies something negatively, something affirmatively. For example, not-white signifies whitenesses negatively, of which it is not verified, nor does it stand for them. Affirmatively, however, it signifies all things other than whiteness, and concerning these it is predicated affirmatively, and it stands for them because, whatsoever else may have been demonstrated from whiteness, this is true, *this is not-whiteness*.

2. And by this [distinction] I say to the argument, that the negative concept is not predicated affirmatively of the thing which it signifies negatively, yet it is truly predicated affirmatively of the thing which it signifies affirmatively; and therefore infinite is predicated affirmatively of no finite thing, because infinite signifies all finite things negatively; but it signifies all infinite things affirmatively; and therefore I say that it is predicated truly of all these, and it stands for them truly.

To the proof I say that although affirmative and negative concepts are contradictory, yet obviously they do not signify the same thing, except this contradiction, *being and non-being,* because whatever being signifies affirmatively, non-being signifies negatively; and it signifies nothing else affirmatively.[12]   In other contradictories the negative concept signifies many things affirmatively, which the affirmative concept does not signify, as not-white signifies many things affirmatively which white does not signify.   But such concepts are said to be contradictory, because that which one signifies affirmatively, the other signifies negatively.

To THE QUESTION PROPOSED I say that finite and infinite are opposed: therefore, infinite is predicated affirmatively of nothing of which finite is predicated affirmatively, and this is because infinite signifies all finite things negatively, but of those things which are not finite, of which sort God is, infinite is predicated affirmatively.   By this the answer to the second is clear.

To THE PRINCIPAL ARGUMENT I say that several composite concepts can be had of God formally and equivalently, but not simple in the stated way.

[12] The edition of 1491 has *negatively.*

GLOSSARY[1]

LATIN—ENGLISH

A

ABLATIO, *denial*.

ABSOLUTE, *absolutely*, in a variety of senses: an attribute is predicated absolutely (as opposed to accommodatively)

[1] The glossary which follows does not, of course, pretend to completeness. Its purpose is to clarify the terms and distinctions used in the preceding translations. The words discussed are, therefore, for the most part those proper to the problems of knowledge and the distinctions of logic; terms from the ethical and political sciences have been omitted almost entirely; theological, metaphysical, physical terms have in some cases been defined. The principal need for such a glossary is in the circumstance that writers in the middle ages had constantly in mind detailed distinctions and precise usages, which latter-day writers in the platonic and aristotelian traditions frequently ignore. There may be some question concerning whether Plato and Aristotle are correctly interpreted in the distinctions which had become current; but usually the medieval commentator, if read carefully, can make a good case for the relevance of his distinctions. In any case the commentator himself can not be understood if the distinctions are not kept in mind; and in many cases, whether they are good or bad platonism and aristotelianism, they are good philosophic distinctions and such as might well be recalled from their oblivion into present-day usage. But the glossary is designed to fill a second need as well. The tendency recently in translations from greek and latin philosophers, has been to seek out anglo-saxon terms, and to avoid latin derivatives. Words as clear and as definitely fixed in a long tradition of usage as privation, accident, and even substance, have been replaced by barbarous compound terms, which awaken no echo

when it applies to all the individuals of a given species; it is predicated absolutely or simply (as opposed to comparatively) when it applies to its subject, not as compared to something else, but as it is in itself; words differ absolutely when they signify different things, connotatively when they signify the same thing, but one involves a relation not expressed in the other; in still different senses absolutely is contrasted with dependently, hypothetically, modally, totally, in space and time.

ABSTRACTIO, *abstraction*, the separation of one thing from another; a thing which is taken separately from those things with which it is joined is taken abstractly; particularly the process of deriving the universal from the species of par-

---

in the mind of one familiar with the tradition, and afford no entrance into the tradition to one unfamiliar with it. In the translations above an attempt has been made to return to the terminology of the classical english tradition, not of some constructed anglo-saxon model, but of the english philosophers of the seventeenth century. Most of the latin derivatives which are used, and the senses in which they are used, have justification in the works of Hobbes, Kenelm Digby, Cudworth, Culverwell, More, even Bacon, and scores of writers contemporary with them. It was only with the nineteenth century that the word *cause* became restricted to efficient cause and *accident* came to be associated only with unforeseen occurrences; there is no reason why they should not be intelligible in their original broader meanings. On the contrary two further reasons enforce the wisdom of preserving the older usages: first, that the mass of commentary on Aristotle will be rendered more difficult, if not impossible, of understanding if the terms of the discussion are changed arbitrarily after two thousand years; second, that as latin became a supple philosophic medium only after expressions had been constructed in it on the model of greek distinctions, so too, english is a richer philosophic language if the expressions which were constructed in it on the model of the latin are preserved.

The paragraph numbers of the Taurini edition of Thomas Aquinas's *Commentary on the Metaphysics of Aristotle* (Taurini: Marietti, 1915) and *Commentary on Aristotle's on the Soul* (Taurini: Marietti, 1925) are given in reference to those works.

ticular things. Abstraction may be *total* (by which a superior or more universal nature is considered without the properties which are related to the individual or the species, as a given man may be considered as rational mortal animal) or *formal* (by which a nature is taken in its essence alone, apart from the subject in which it subsists, as humanity, square). According to Thomas (*Sum. Theol.* I, q. 40, a. 3 concl.), "Abstraction by the understanding is of two sorts: one by which the universal is abstracted from the particular, as animal from man, another by which form is abstracted from matter, as the form of circle is abstracted by the understanding from all sensible matter."

ABSTRACTIVUM, *abstractive*, according to the nominalists, particularly Ockham, abstractive knowledge is knowledge by which the thing is apprehended not as it is in itself, but through the species of some other thing, as opposed to intuitive knowledge by which the thing is known immediately as it is in itself.

ACCIDENS, *accident*, that which (unlike substance) is not in itself, but inheres in some subject, as figure or any mode. Logically accident is a quality which is understood to advene on a subject or "happen" (*accidere*) to it in such wise that it does not constitute the essence of the subject nor flow necessarily from its essence. It is commonly defined, therefore, as that which is present or absent without the corruption of the subject; white and learned are accidents of man. According to the pseudo-Grosseteste (see above, vol. I, p. 295), it is that "the being of which consists only in inhering in something else." Aristotle describes accident (*Top.* 1, 5, 102^b 4–14), as that which is not definition, property, or genus, yet belongs to the thing, or as something which may possibly either belong or not belong to any one and same thing, as for example sitting posture. Compare PRAEDICABILIS, SUBSTANTIA, PER SE.

ACCIDENTALITER, *accidentally*; things differ accidentally when they are individuals belonging to the same species, as Socrates and Plato. A substance advenes on another accidentally when it advenes by contact, as clothing on a man, or when it advenes as mover of a mobile, as an angel to a body which he assumes. Contrasted with *essentially, substantially*.

ACCIDERE, *to happen*, in the sense that accidental qualities advene on substances without corrupting or generating them.

ACCIPERE, *to receive or undertake*, particularly (as Anselm) to receive from God; therefore, to be determined by that from which one has one's being.

ACTIO, *action*, properly the actuality of a power, as being is the actuality of a substance or essence. Contrasted therefore to passion. According to Thomas (*Sum. Theol.* I, q. 41, a. 1 ad 2; compare also ibid. ad 3; and I, q. 42, a. 2 concl.), "Action according to the first imposition of the name, indicates the origin of motion. For just as motion, according as it is in the mobile from some mover, is called a *passion*, so the origin of that motion, as it begins from something else and is terminated in that which is moved, is called *action*. Therefore if the motion is taken away, action means nothing else than the order of origin, according to which it proceeds from some cause or principle into that which is from that principle." Sometimes action is distinguished into two sorts, one which goes forth into an exterior matter, as heating and drying, the other which remains in the agent, as understanding, feeling, wishing, the difference between the two being that the former is not the perfection of the agent which moves, but of the thing moved, the latter is the perfection of the agent. Properly, however, the latter variety alone, that which is the perfection of the agent, is called ACTIO, the former is FACTIO, and the two are kinds of OPERATIONES. Compare therefore, FACTIO, OPERATIO.

ACTUS, *act, actuality*, either an operation (in the sense of *actio*), as an act of the understanding or a creditive act (Ockham); act in this sense is a second act as contrasted to the power or faculty which is its proximate principle and in virtue of which the operation is produced: or else that which determines the thing or perfects it, as the soul is the actuality, perfection, and entelechy of the body; in this sense the formal actuality. Thence it is sometimes taken as the entity or existence of the thing; in this sense whatever is not nothing, but exists, is an entitative act.

AD ALIQUID, *relative to something*, thence *relativity*, the fourth of the ten categories, *relation* ($\pi\rho\delta\varsigma\ \tau\iota$). Aristotle defines relation (*Cat.* 7, 6ᵃ36), "Those things are said to be

relative, which are said to be that which they are *of*
something else or are said to be otherwise in any manner
whatever as *related to* something else, as the greater is
said to be greater because it is so related to something
else." Examples of relatives are disposition, double,
slave, son. Aristotle distinguishes three kinds of relative
terms (*Met.* V, c. 15, 1020ᵇ25–31), "(1) as half to double
and treble to a third, and in general that which contains
something else many times to that which is contained
many times in something else, and that which exceeds to
that which is exceeded; (2) as that which can heat to
that which can be heated, and that which can cut to that
which can be cut, and in general the active to the passive;
(3) as the measurable to the measure and the knowable to
knowledge and the sensible to sense." According to
Thomas (?) (*Sum. Log.* V, c. 1), "It must be noted that
since relation [*relatio*] has little of entity, therefore the
Philosopher does not treat of it but only of relatives
[*relativum*], which because of their greater concretion can
be known to us, for he calls the relative that [relative] to
something [*ad aliquid*], and he defines it thus: those things
are said to be relative [*ad aliquid*] which are said to be
that very thing which they are *of* another, or are said to
be otherwise in any manner whatever *to* something else.
To understand this definition it must be known that certain things are relative according to statement, certain
things according to being; certain things are real relatives, but others are relatives according to reason. Those
are called relatives according to statement, which state,
as that which is signified by them principally, a thing of
one of the other categories, but state secondarily a relation or state a respect: as knowledge states, as that which
is signified by it principally, a condition of the mind, and
thus it is in the first species of quality; but secondarily
it states a relation to the knowable, and of sense to the
sensible, which is a certain power in the second species of
quality, and such relatives are relatives according to statement. But relatives according to being are those which
signify, as that which is signified principally by them, a
respect to something else. Real relatives are those which
hold really when all act of understanding has been circumscribed, as father and son; for having circumscribed
all act of understanding, father is referred to son and

son to father because the father really gave birth to the son and the son was born of the father." According to Thomas, Avicenna is responsible for a fourfold division of relatives according to reason; see above, Thomas Aquinas, *Quaest. disp. de Ver.* q. 1, a. 5 ad 16, pp. 199-200.

ADAEQUATIO, *adequation, commensuration,* the identity of two quantities or the motion and approach to identity of quantity, as the commensuration of space and the thing in space; thence any approach to equality, as opposed to assimilation or approach to likeness; thus truth is the adequation of thing and understanding.

ADAEQUABILITAS, *adequability.*

AEQUALITAS, *equality*; things are equal when they agree in quantity: that can be in two ways, dimensively or virtually, as quantity is of two sorts, modal and virtual. According to Thomas (*In lib. I Sent.* d. 19, q. 1, a. 1 sol.), "Since equality is founded on unity of quantity, it is the same for a thing to be equal to something else, as to have its quantity, and it is the same for it to be like something else, as for it to have its quality." The equality of things may be quantitative (as in commutative justice) or proportional equality (as in distributive justice). Since proportionality is equality of proportions the principle of these two usages is the strict usage by which those things are equal which are one in quantity; equality is a species of proportion, since equality is the proportion of any things which have a single quantity. Compare SIMILITUDO, QUANTITAS, ANALOGIA, PROPORTIO, AEQUIPARANTIA.

AEQUIPARANTIA, *comparison, equiparance, equivalence*; includes all symmetrical relations, that is, relations in which both extremes are denominated in the same way, as the relations of likeness and equality; contrasted to RELATIO DISPARANTIAE, all asymmetrical relations in which the extremes are diversely denominated, as the relation of father and son, greater and less.

AEQUALITAS AEQUIPARANTIAE, *comparative equality,* equality according to absolute quantity: that which exists between two quantities of the same measure, as the equality of two yards to two yards, as opposed to AEQUALITAS PROPORTIONIS, *proportional equality,* such as the equality of the fingers of the hand, "which are not equal according to absolute quantity, since one, when superposed on another exceeds it, yet they are equal according to proportion, since, as the quantity of one finger suffices to its office, so the quantity of another suffices to its" (Thomas, *In lib. III Sent.* d. 36, q. 1, a. 4 sol.; compare also *In lib. IV Sent.* d. 32, q. 1, a. 3 sol.).

AEQUIVOCUM, *equivocal* (ὁμώνυμος); "Things are said to be named equivocally when, though they have a common name, the definition corresponding to the name differs for each, as a man and that which is painted in a picture are animals, for they have only the name in common" (Aristotle, *Cat.* 1, 1ª); thus the bear is a constellation and an animal. Compare UNIVOCA.

AEQUIVOCATIO, *equivocation*; "Where there is pure equivocation there is no likeness in the thing, but only a unity of name" (Thomas, *Cont. Gent.* I, c. 33.).

AESTIMATIO, *estimation*, the faculty of the sensitive soul which judges of the advantageous and agreeable, the hurtful and contrary, by perception of the constitutional qualities of the thing, which are unperceived by the other faculties of sense; in rational beings this function is exercised by the cogitative faculty or particular reason.

AETERNITAS, *eternity*; the principle (*ratio*) of eternity consists in having its entire being altogether, and therefore lacking beginning and end; proper only to God in an absolute sense; "the perfect and completely simultaneous possession of interminable life" (Boethius, *Consol. Phil.* V, prosa 6).

AEVUM, *aeon*, permanent duration, immutable in its nature, having a beginning, but lacking an end (Simplicius, *Phys.* IV, 154). According to Thomas (*Quaest. Quodl.* V, q. 4, a. 7 concl.), "Aeon will be nothing other than the participation of eternity, so that essential eternity is attributed to God himself, but aeon, as it were, participated eternity, to spiritual substances, which are above time." Aeon is medium between time and eternity. Thomas says (*Sum. Theol.* I, q. 10, a. 5 concl.), "Since eternity is the measure of permanent being, in the respect in which anything recedes from permanence of being, in that respect it recedes from eternity. Certain things recede from permanence of being in such wise that their being is the subject of change and consists in change, and things of this sort are measured by time, as all motion and likewise the being of all corruptible things. Certain things on the other hand recede less from permanence of being, because their being neither consists in change nor is it the subject of change, yet they have change adjoined, either in actuality or in potentiality. This is clear in the case of celestial bodies, the substantial being of which is immutable; yet they have immutable being together with mutability with respect to place. And in the same way it is clear in the case of angels, because they have immutable being together with mutability with respect to election, in so far as that pertains to their nature, and together with mutability of intelligences and affections and places in their mode. And therefore things of this sort are measured by aeon, which is medium between eternity and time. The being, however, which eternity measures, is neither mutable nor adjoined to mutability. Thus, therefore, time has prior and posterior; aeon does not have in itself prior and posterior, but they can be conjoined to it; eternity, however, does not have prior and posterior, nor is it compatible with them."

AFFECTIO, *affection* (in the sense of modification), *condition, affect*; the inclination of the soul to something; AFFECTIO and AFFECTUS are related to the final cause as EFFECTIO and EFFECTUS (*effection* and *effect!*) to the efficient cause; affection is, in other words, the inclination of any thing considered in terms of its end as opposed to its antecedent conditions.

AFFECTUS, *affect*, state of body or mind, the state to which *affection* is process or inclination, *love*; sometimes used to denote specifically the emotional faculty of the soul.

AGERE, *to do, to work, to act*; to act is nothing other than to do something actually; this is accomplished through form; it is the communication of that which the agent is actually according to that which is possible. Usually distinguished from FACERE in that it does not go forth into an exterior matter; but often used synonymously with it. Compare FACERE, ACTIO.

AGENS, *agent*, active cause. Compare INTELLECTUS AGENS.

ALIQUID, *something*, defined by Thomas Aquinas as the division of one thing from another. Compare RES.

ALTERATIO, *alteration*, (ἀλλοίωσις), motion or change in the category of quality. Compare MOTUS, PASSIO.

AMPHIBOLIA, *amphibology*, a phrase or proposition susceptible of more than one interpretation.

ANALOGIA, *analogy*, contrasted by Bonaventura to *univoca-tion*. A name is used analogically when it is taken according to different significations, yet not without a principle on which what is common to them depends, as healthy is spoken of analogically relative to animal, medicine, pulse, because of their relation to health. Derived from the greek, ἀναλογία, *proportion*. Compare AEQUIVOCA, UNIVOCA.

ANALOGIA ATTRIBUTIONIS, *attributive analogy*, an analogy in which the terms are derived from something to which that which is signified by the name is proper and to which the terms are referred for an identical reason, as food, medicine, and pulse are called healthy by attributive analogy, because the word healthy is derived from health which is proper to animal.

ANALOGIA PROPORTIONIS, *proportional analogy*, an analogy in which the terms arise from a common name, because that which is signified by the name, although it is absolutely different in the various terms, can none the less be in accord through a likeness or order which obtains between the terms, as animal and food, or animal and pulse are called healthy by a proportional analogy, not because of some relation to a given principal thing, but because health (although different in the various terms) presents in them a signification in some respect the same.

ANIMAL, *animal*, that is, a corporeal creature with a soul; a sensitive animated substance; in the animal man, the intellective soul is superadded to the sensitive. The two principal characteristics of animal life are sensibility and movement. According to Albert the Great (see above, vol. I, p. 341), "The soul is intellectual because it operates without using the body, and animal because it uses the organic body."

APPARENTIA, *evidence*, that is, apparentness, in the logical sense of the apparentness or evidence of a proposition; also in the sense of *appearance*, as phenomenal.

APPETITUS, *appetite*, natural appetite, the power or inclination of a thing by which it tends naturally to its own good and end, as matter tends to form; *elicited appetite*, on the contrary, arises from knowledge. Compare APPREHENSIO.

APPREHENSIO, *apprehension*, the simple act of the understanding conceiving a thing without affirmation or denial; all animal activities are either *apprehensive* or *appetitive*.

APPROPRIATUM, *appropriated quality or aspect*, as the Trinity of God has in creatures qualities appropriated to each of the persons, thus, unity, truth, and goodness.

APTITUDO, *aptitude,* natural inclination, ability, or order toward something.

APTITUDINALIS, *aptitudinal*.

ARGUMENTUM, *argument*, the process of reason from the known to making manifest the unknown; according to Boethius, the reason of the doubtful thing making for faith; by argument the intellect is induced to adhere in a given truth; the etymology is sometimes given from arguing the mind (*arguere mentem*) to assenting to something; broadly of any discourse of reason from principles to conclusions; inference by which a conclusion is demonstrated from premisses; one of the two ways of knowing according to Bacon, experience being the other.

ARGUMENTUM A PRIORI, *a priori argument*, inference from cause to effect (Ockham). Equivalent to *propter quid* in older usage.

ARGUMENTUM A POSTERIORI, *a posteriori argument*, inference from effect to cause (Ockham). Equivalent to *quia* in older usage.

ARS, *art*, defined by Thomas (*Sum. Theol.* Ia IIae, q. 57, a. 3 concl.) as nothing other than the right reason of any works to be done; the right reason of things which are to be made (*factibilis*); from art proceed the things the forms of which are in the soul of the artist. As opposed to the virtues or powers, the arts are factive; they are prepared by *experience* (*experientia, peritia*) and are therefore possible without knowledge on the part of the artisan, though they involve knowledge (*scientia*). Aristotle states the principles of the distinction (*An. Post.* II, 19, 100^{a}3–9), "So out of sense-perception comes to be what we call memory, and out of frequently repeated memories of the same thing develops experience; for a number of memories constitute a single experience. From experience again—i.e. from the universal now stabilized in its entirety within the soul, the one besides the many as if it is constituted a single identity within them all,— originate art [τέχνη=ars] and knowledge or science [ἐπιστήμη = *scientia*], art in the sphere of coming to be or generation and science in the sphere of being." According to Albert the Great (see above, vol. I, p. 312), "There seems to be this difference between science and art, that science contemplates and examines principally certain causes of its truth, but art considers rather the manner of operating according to the truth transmitted and proposed." According to Aristotle, the human race lives by art and reasonings, in counterdistinction from animals other than man who have little connected experience, but live by appearances and memories. (*Met.* I, c. 1, 980^{b}27-981^{a}7). "From memory experience is produced in men; for many memories of the same thing produce finally the capacity for a single experience. And it seems almost that experience is like science and art; but really science and art come to me *through* experience; for 'experience made art', as Polus says, and rightly, 'but inexperience luck'. And art arises, when from many notions gained by experience [that is, from many 'experimental concepts'] one universal judgment concerning similar things is formed." According to Thomas (*In lib. I An. Post.* lect. 1) logic is the art of arts. "For art seems to be nothing other than a certain ordination of reason by which human acts arrive by determined means at their proper end. But reason can direct not only the acts of inferior parts, but is directive also of its own acts. . . . And this is the art of logic, that is, rational science. It is not only rational from the fact that it is according to reason, but it is common to all the arts. And therefore it seems to be the art of arts, because it directs us in the act of reason, from which all the arts proceed." Compare FACTIO, NATURA, DISCIPLINA, QUADRIVIUM, TRIVIUM.

ARTIFICIALIS, *artificial*, that which is the product of art as opposed to natural things, which are the product of nature; the forms of artificial things are accidents, whereas the forms of natural things are genera of substance.

ARTIFICIOSE, *artificially*; that is made artificially which requires the art or industry of some one, as opposed to that which is made naturally.

ASSIMILARI, *to be assimilated*; the likeness of two qualities or the motion of approach to such likeness. According to Thomas (*In lib, I Sent.* d. 19, q. 1, a. 2 sol.), "To be assimilated posits, in addition to that which is involved in being like, a certain motion and access to unity of quality, and in like manner to be adequated is related to quantity."

AUGMENTATIO, *augmentation, increase* (αὔξησις), motion or change in the category of quantity. Compare MOTUS.

B

BEATITUDO, *beatitude, blessedness, happiness*; defined by Boethius as the state perfect by the aggregation of all goods; its principle (*ratio*) is stability of confirmation in the good; it consists in the most perfect operation of one possessed of reason and intellect; considered from the part of the object, God alone is beatitude, since one is blessed only from understanding him, but from the part of the act of understanding, beatitude is something created in blessed creatures, as it is something uncreated in God; either in the sense of the supreme good which is the ultimate end or the acquisition and fruition of that good; also in the sense of the beatitudes enumerated in the Gospels, which according to Bacon, are the fourth of the seven grades of inner experience.

BEATUS, *blessed*, particularly in the sense of those who, having gone to their reward, see God perspicuously. Compare VIATOR.

BONUM, *good* (ἀγαθόν), the conformity of that which is to the appetite; according to Thomas Aquinas this is the good *relatively*, that is, in its order to those whom it perfects and by whom it is desired. That is good *absolutely* which is good considered according to its nature; that which in itself is good absolutely can be good relative to one person and evil relative to another. God's essential actuality is life most good and eternal. Compare TRANSCENDENTALES.

C

CATEGOREMATICE, *categorematically*; a thing is affirmed categorematically to be such or such because it is actually such, as God is said categorematically to be infinite. Compare SYNCATEGOREMATICE.

CATHEGREUMA, CATEGOREMA, *categorematic term*, one which is significative in itself and can therefore be subject or predicate of a proposition without addition of any other

term; one which makes perfect sense combined with the
verb is, as, *Isaiah is.* Compare SYNCATHEGREUMA.

CATEGORIA, *category,* the real order and disposition of categorematic terms. Compare PRAEDICAMENTA.

CAUSA, *cause, reason,* that from which a thing has its origin
in such wise that it is produced properly from it and
therefore depends on it in being and action. Thomas says
(*Sum. Theol.* I, q. 33, a. 1 ad 1.), "The word cause seems
to import a diversity of substance and a dependence of
one on the other, which the word principle does not import." Compare, therefore, PRINCIPIUM. In the aristotelian tradition, causes (αἰτία) were classified under four
heads, efficient, final, formal, material, and each included
a great diversity of kinds. According to Aristotle (Phys.
II, c. 3, 195ª15-26), "But all the causes we have enumerated
full into four most manifest modes. For letters are the
causes of syllables, and the material is the cause of manu-
factured articles, and fire and other [elements] of this
sort are causes of bodies, and the parts are causes of the
whole, and the premisses are causes of the conclusion, in
the sense that they are the causes *out of which* these
things respectively are. But some of them are causes in
the sense of *subject,* for example the parts, and others
are causes in the sense of *essence,* as whole, and composition, and species. And again fertilizing sperm, and
the physician, and the one who takes counsel, and in
general the *agent* is a cause in the sense of that from
which the beginning of the change is, whether of coming
to rest or of motion. And finally some are causes in the
sense of the *end* and the good of the others. But it is
in the sense of end of the others that cause is used in its
fullest and most important sense, and the end of the other
causes has sought to be [that is, each cause desires its
own good or end], although it is the same to say 'its
good' as 'what seems to be good.' " Compare PRINCIPIUM,
ELEMENTUM.

CAUSA EFFICIENS, *efficient cause,* that which initiates the
process of change or brings about its cessation when the
process is completed, as the action of a voluntary agent,
e.g. a smith, or any agent.

CAUSA FINALIS, *final cause,* the end or purpose for the sake of
which the process is initiated, as when a man takes exercise for the sake of his health.

Causa formalis, *formal cause*, the form or characteristics of the type, which matter receives, by which it is brought within the definition of the thing it is said to be, whether specifically or generically, as the ratio of two notes by which they are said to be an octave; that which determines matter and in a sense perfects it.

Causa materialis, *material cause*, that from which the generative process starts, as the bronze or marble of a statue.

Causa accidentalis, *accidental cause*, a cause considered, not in itself but associated with irrelevant accidents, thus Polycleitus (instead of the sculptor) is the cause accidentally of the statue.

Causa propria, *proper cause*, the agent considered qua agent, not according to his accidental characteristics, thus the sculptor is the proper cause of the statue.

Causativum, *causative*; the practical intellect (unlike the speculative) is not only apprehensive, but also causative.

Certitudo, *certitude*; according to Thomas Aquinas (*Quaest. disp. de Ver.* q. 6, a. 3 concl.), "Certitude of knowledge is when knowledge does not depart in any respect from that which is found in the thing, but estimates concerning the thing as the thing is. And because certain estimation concerning the thing is had most of all through the cause of the thing, therefore the name certitude is treated in the order of cause to effect, so that the order of cause to effect is said to be certain, when the cause infallibly produces the effect"; the well-educated man seeks only so much certitude as the matter into which he is inquiring permits: certitude in contingent and variable things can not be so great as certitude in necessary things; certitude is the firmness of adhesion of the cognoscitive faculty in its cognoscible, and it therefore consists in the firmness with which the mind adheres to any given proposition.

Coaptatio, *connection*.

Cogitare, *to think, to judge, to cogitate*; according to Thomas, quoting Augustine (*In lib. I Sent.* d. 3, q. 4 sol.), "To cogitate is to consider a thing according to its parts and properties."

Cogitatio, *thought, judgment, cogitation*, consists properly in the inquisition of truth.

Virtus cogitativa, *the cogitative faculty*, the highest faculty of the sensitive soul, directive of all the others, taking the place of reason in brutes (according to some philosophers, as Bacon); by means of it the spider weaves its web, the swallow builds its nest, and so forth; by means of it too man dreams. According to other philosophers, as Thomas Aquinas, this highest sensitive power is properly called cogitation only in men, in whom the rational soul is superposed on the sensitive, whereas in brute animals, its functions are taken over by a natural "estimation"; he distinguishes the two (*In lib. II de An.* lect. 1, 398): "The cogitative faculty apprehends the individual as existing under a common nature; this happens to it, in so far as it is united to the intellective faculty in the same subject, therefore it knows this man as he is this man, and this wood as it is this wood. The estimative, however, does not apprehend any individual as it is under a common nature, but only as it is the term or the principle of some action or passion, as a sheep knows this lamb, not in so far as it is this lamb, but in so far as it is milkable by it, and this grass in so far as it is its food. Whence other individuals to which its action or passion does not extend, it in no manner apprehends by its natural estimative faculty. For natural estimation is given to animals in order that they might be ordered by it to pursuing or avoiding the proper actions or passions." Compare AESTIMATIO.

COGNITIO, *knowledge, cognition, acquaintance, consideration, conception, notion, idea.* Cognition is divided by Bonaventura into knowledge by apprehension and by comprehension.

COGNITIO ABSTRACTIVA, *abstractive knowledge.* Compare ABSTRACTIVUM.

COGNITIO INTUITIVA, *intuitive knowledge*; (Ockham finds it difficult to state how intuitive and abstractive knowledge differ, but he finds two marks of their difference (see selection above, *Quodl.* V, q. 5): "In one way in that, by intuitive knowledge assent is first given to the contingent, and by abstractive knowledge it is not. In another way through the fact that by intuitive knowledge I not only judge that a thing is when it is, but also that is is not when it is not; by abstractive knowledge I judge in neither of these manners." Compare INTUITUS.

COGNITIO NATURALIS, *natural knowledge*, such as is common to all the human species, that is, the knowledge of first principles, such as that the whole is greater than its part (Bacon).

COGNOSCENS, *knower.*

COGNOSCERE, *to learn, to perceive, to know.*

COGNOSCIBILE, *cognoscible, knowable*; according to Thomas (*In lib. I Phys.* lect. 1), "Those things are better known in themselves [as contrasted to those better known to us] which have more entity, for each thing is cognoscible in so far as it is that which is (*ens*)."

COGNOSCIBILITAS, *knowability.*

COLLECTIO, *inference.*

COLLIGO, *to gather, to bring together, to bring out, to infer.*

COMMUNICARE, *to be common.*

COMMUNE, *common*; something may be common to many things by participation or by predication; individual things are common by participation, in the proper sense of participation, and this involves either that the common thing be shared by parts, or pass at different times from one to the other of the things that share it, or be shared at the same time, like a spectacle viewed by many; a genus is common to its species by predication, that is, unlike participation, it is in each of the individuals to which it is common, wholly and at one and the same time, and its name is predicated of all of them. Broadly participation is used to include both predication and participation in their proper senses. Compare PARTICIPATIO.

COMPLEXIO, *combination* (of premisses in syllogism), *inference, constitution* (of things in virtue of which they possess their individual peculiarities and also their kinship to other members of their species and genus).

COMPLEXUM, *complex*; Albert the Great describes the distinction between complex and incomplex (*de Praedicab.*, tract. I, c. 5.), "The ancient peripatetics, defining the incomplex, said that a speech significative at will is incomplex if its parts signify nothing concerning the intention of the whole, as when *man* [*homo*] is said, the one part of it, *ho*, and the other part, *mo*, signify nothing concerning the intention of *homo*. But even if the name of a simple thing be composite, like *Adeodatus* [*Godgiven*], none the less in so far as it is the name of one simple thing, the speech is incomplex. And the part *adeo* [*by God*] and the part *datus* [*given*] signify nothing concerning the intention of the whole named by the name *Adeodatus*. A speech is complex, however, the parts of which signify something concerning the intention of the whole, as when we say, *the man walks*; and the speech *man* and the speech *walks* signify something concerning the intention of the complex, *the man walks*." True and false are not in the incomplex, but only in the complex.

COMPONERE, *to compound*; the logical process of asserting one simple or incomplex term of another; composition and division are affirmation and negation; the physical process of uniting substance and accident or even form and matter.

COMPOSITIO, *composition*; logical composition (as distinguished from physical and metaphysical) is the relation between terms when one is predicated of the other in a proposition.

COMPOSITUM, *composite*, a whole of parts such that the composite is proper to none of the parts; a *substantial composite* is one which arises from two incomplete substances, as *man* from form and matter; an *accidental composite* is one which is formed from complete substances, as a *pile* of stones.

COMPREHENSOR, *one who comprehends*.

CONCEPTUS, *concept*; according to Thomas (*Con. Graec.* 3), "Whenever [the intellect] understands actually, it forms a certain intelligible, which is a kind of offspring of it, and is therefore called a concept of the mind;" the concept may be based on properties or on common predicates.

CONCRETUM, *concrete*, a composite of subject and form by which some denomination is attributed to the subject. Thus *omnipotent God* is a metaphysical concrete, because in him omnipotence is not distinguished really from the subject, that is, God; a *figured body* is a physical concrete, since figure is distinguished from body and at the same time inheres in it; a *seen tower* is a logical concrete, for vision is distinguished from the tower but does not inhere in it.

CONDITIO, *condition, creation*; in the sense of condition Bonaventura speaks of the three conditions of the image in the soul, trinity, unity, equality; Matthew of Aquasparta speaks of the three conditions of *that which is through itself*, or substance, namely, the one, the true, the good. Compare TRANSCENDENTALES.

ᴄᴏɴɪᴜɴɢᴇʀᴇ, *to conjoin*; the logical process of asserting a relation between two terms; the physical process of relating things, either by likeness, as two men in that they are men or grammarians are conjoined, or by aggregation, as wine and water, form and matter are conjoined (see Abailard above, vol. I, p. 247).

ᴄᴏɴᴛᴇᴍᴘʟᴀᴛɪᴏ, *contemplation*, taken either strictly for the act of the intellect meditating divine things, and thus contemplation is the act of the wise man, or in another way commonly for every act by which any one sequestrated from exterior affairs considers God, and this can come about in two ways, either as man hears God speaking in the Scriptures (and this is done by reading), or as he speaks to God (and this is done by prayer). By contemplation one considers God as he is in himself, by speculation as he is imaged in created things as in a mirror (*speculatio* from *speculum*). Compare ꜱᴘᴇᴄᴜʟᴀᴛɪᴏ.

ᴄᴏɴᴛɪɴɢᴇɴꜱ, *contingent*, that which can be and not be; distinguished from the necessary by the manner in which it is in its cause: the contingent is so in its cause that it can be or not be from it, but the necessary can not not be from its cause. In respect to that which each of them is in itself, they do not differ in being, on which the true is based, because in the contingent, in respect to that which it is in itself, there is not being and non-being, but only being, although in the future it is possible for it not to be.

ᴄᴏɴᴛɪɴᴜᴜᴍ, *continuum*; according to Aristotle, continuum (συνεχές) is in the genus of state, a kind of coherence (ἐχόμενον). Coherence is defined as that which when it is in sequence touches. Continuum is a species of coherence, such that both terms by which it is contained are one and the same, and, as its name signifies, they are contained; but this can not be when there are two terms. Commenting on this passage of Aristotle Thomas says (*In lib. V Phys.* lect. 5), "It is manifest what a continuum is; and Aristotle says that the continuum is a species of state. For when the ends of two things which touch are made one and the same, that is said to be a continuum. Continuum is derived from containing (*continendum*). When therefore many parts are contained in one, that is. hold together as it were at the same time, then there is a continuum. But this can not be when there are two end terms, but only when there is one. From this it follows further that there can not be continuation except in those things, from which a unity is made naturally by contact. For any whole is one and continuous according to itself, for the same reason as one continuum is made from many: either by some joining of them together, or some indwelling of them within, or by some mode of conjoining, such that one end is made of both, or even by this device, that something is naturally born of something else, as fruit is born to a tree and in a manner continues it." A continuum therefore has identical terms, and only a single motion which can not be other, as the periphery of a circle is continuous, or a line indefinitely generated by the movement of a point; it is infinitely divisible. Therefore (*In lib. III Phys.* lect. 1), "A continuum is that which is divisible *in infinitum*. And it is called a manifold (*multoties*) because there is also another definition of the continuum which is stated in the *Categories* (c. 6, 5ᵃ1ff.): *a continuum is that the parts of which are joined to one common end.* These two definitions differ however. For the continuum, since it is a certain whole, must be defined by its parts. But the parts are compared to the whole in two ways, namely, according to composition as the whole is compounded out of the parts, and according to resolution as the whole is divided into the parts. This definition of the continuum, therefore, is made according to the way of resolution, but it is stated in the *Categories* according to the way of composition." The definition of the continuum by its parts joined to one common term is its formal definition, for the unity of the continuum is its form. The definition according to its parts, that it is ever further divisible, is its material definition. According to Albert (see above, vol. I, p. 346), the continuous is perceived by the imagination.

CONTRADICTORIA, *contradictories*: an affirmation is the contradictory of a denial when, the subject remaining the same, the one is universal, the other not, as *every man is white* is contradictory of *not every man is white*; and *no man is white* is contradictory of *some men are white*. There is no intermediate between contradictories, but of any subject any predicate can be affirmed or denied; yet no predicate can be affirmed and denied of the same subject at the same time and in the same respect: the former is the law of the excluded middle, the latter the law of contradiction. Compare OPPOSITIO.

CONTRAHERE, *to contract*, particularly to contract genus or species, that is, to determine and as it were apply the genus to some species, or the species to some individual, as man contracts the genus of animality, and Peter contracts the species of humanity.

CONTRARIA, *contraries*; propositions are contraries when both the affirmative and the denial are universal, as *every man is white, no man is white*. According to Aristotle (*Cat.* 6, 6ª 15–19), "Things which, within the same genus, are separated by the greatest possible distance," and which expel each other from the same subject as heat and cold. It is defined in a broader sense (*Met.* V, c. 10, 1018ª25–31): "Those things are said to be contraries (1) which, differing in genus, can not be present in the same thing at the same time; (2) the most different of the things in the same genus; (3) the most different of the things in the same susceptive material; (4) the most different of the things that fall under the same faculty; (5) the things whose difference is greatest either absolutely or in genus or in species." Contraries, unlike contradictories, admit of intermediates or media. Qualities have contraries, but quantity does not strictly admit of contraries. Motion is from contrary to contrary; or the extremes of mutation are contraries, as motion from black to white. Aristotle defines contraries in space as those points which are most distant in a straight line. Compare OPPOSITIO.

CONTUERI, *to behold, to see*, either with the eyes (bodies or sensibles) or with the mind (forms or intelligibles).

CONVENIENTIA, *agreement, relation*; as in the ratio, one to two, the *convenientia* is "double"; the relation of ratios in proportions is a *convenientia*.

CONVERTI, *to be converted*; terms are said to be converted or to be convertible, if one can be affirmed of the other and the second in turn of the first. Definition and property are converted with their subject, as *man* and *rational animal*, or *man* and *capable of learning grammar*. Likewise the transcendentals are converted, as *good* and *that which is* (*bonum* and *ens*).

CORRUPTIO, *corruption*; change in the category of substance, the contrary to generation; corruption occurs when a form, which had been connected with matter, ceases to be;

corruption is of two sorts: it may remove the first perfection by which a thing has its first being; such corruption involves mutation of species. The other corruption
may remove a second perfection by which the thing is
perfected in complete second being; such corruption does
not vary the species but only removes a complement of
species. Compare MUTATIO, GENERATIO.

CORRUPTUM, *the corrupted.*

CREATURA, *creature, creation.*

D

DEFECTUS, *defect,* the negation of some good. Evil, however,
is privation, that is, the defect of an entity in a thing
which should naturally possess it. Thus lack of life is a
defect in a stone; in a man death is a defect and an evil.

DEFINITIO, *definition;* according to Aristotle one of the four
essentials to logic (and particularly to the topics) which
were later called predicables; medieval philosophers substituted for it species and differentia. First in the sense
of delimitation or implication: the "definition" of a proposition would be all that the proposition involves, not only
implied meanings, but grammatical structure; it would
not, however, include external references. More particularly Aristotle defines definition (*Top.* I, 5, 101^b37), "A
definition is a phrase signifying a thing's essense; it is
assigned either as a phrase for a name or a phrase for a
phrase." Strictly and primarily, however, only substance
is definable (*Met.* VII, c. 5, 1031^a1). Definition by division
is through genus and differentia. Boethius says of definition (see above, vol. I, p. 86), "Definition reveals substance, joins genus to differentia, and, reducing to one
species, which it defines, those things which are essentially
common and of many, it makes them equal." *Definitio* and
terminus [definition and term], because of their similar
etymological significances, were both used as translations
for ὅρος, and were used equivalently. Compare PRAEDICA-
BILE.

DEFINITIO NOMINIS, *definition of name, nominal definition,* a
phrase by which the significance of the name by which a
thing is called is explicated. (Compare Aristotle, *An.
Post.* II, c. 10, 93^b29–37.)

DEFINITIO REI, *definition of the thing, real definition,* a phrase by which the essence of the thing defined is stated; according to Thomas (*Quaest. disp. de Ver.* q. II, a. 1 ad 9) such definition is possible "when the understanding conceives some form of the thing which corresponds to the thing itself in all respects."

DEIFORMIS, *deiform*, like to God.

DEIFORMITAS, *deiformity*; the soul in glory is deiformed or takes on the form of God.

DELIBERATIO, *deliberation*; deliberation imports two things, that is and the perception of a reason together with certitude of judgment concerning that of which the deliberation is made, and thus deliberation can be in an instant in him in whom there is no doubt concerning the things of which it is question. It can likewise involve discussion or inquisition, and thus it imports a certain discourse, in which sense it can not be instantaneously.

DEMONSTRATIO, *demonstration*; demonstration is a kind of argumentation; certain knowledge or science is the effect of demonstration: therefore, it is concerning only those things which are present essentially in things; it is from necessary things and concerning necessary things, because it is scientific, that is, leading to knowledge; it is therefore a syllogism showing cause and that because of which, for it is that to know; it is from first and proper principles. Boethius speaks of demonstration as "a sure inference of reason concerning anything inquired about," and says (see above, vol. I, p. 89) that it "is made from things known prior naturally, from agreements, from first principles, from causes, from necessary things, from things subsisting through themselves."

DEMONSTRATIO PROPTER QUID, *demonstration based on the nature of the thing investigated*; it investigates the proper cause because of which that truth must be admitted. Demonstration *propter quid* gives the proximate and adequate cause; demonstration *quia* proceeds either from effects or from causes which are not immediate and proximate, but remote, on which the demonstration of the truth depends. Equivalent to *a priori*.

DEMONSTRATIO QUIA, *demonstration based on the effect*, or on the grounds of some one thing; it proves only that some truth must be admitted to be. Equivalent to *a posteriori*.

DENOMINATIVE, *denominatively*, that is, derivatively; a name is predicated denominatively of a substance if it is formed from the accidents which are present in the substance, as, if wisdom is present in Socrates, the name of wise, formed from the word *wisdom*, must be proper to him. Aristotle defined denominative words, παρώνυμα (*Cat.* 1, 1a11), "Things are said to be named denominatively which derive their name from another name with only a difference of termination, as grammarian is derived from grammar, and strong from strength."

DESCRIPTIO, *description*; names a characteristic or property of a thing (unlike definition which names its genus and differentia); description may, therefore, demarcate the species unambiguously, but it can not state its essence.

DETERMINATE, *determinately* (or disjunctively); a word is used disjunctively when any individual which falls under it is separately to be taken as predicate in respect of a given subject, that is, in the proposition, *Man is white*, *man* is used determinately or disjunctively, because it signifies not this or that man in particular, but any man.

DIALECTICA, *dialectic*; contrasted by Aristotle to demonstrative reasoning, which is based on premises which are primary and self-evidently true, whereas dialectic proceeds from premises generally accepted, and depends therefore not on the assertion of one of two contradictory propositions, but rather on an adversary's choice between two contradictories (when one proceeds by questioning) or the assertion of that which is apparent and generally accepted (when one proceeds by syllogizing); there are according to Aristotle two sorts of dialectical reasoning, syllogistic and inductive. Boethius, however, following Cicero (see above, vol. I, p. 74) contrasts dialectic as the art of judging with topic or the art of discovering; in his *Commentary on the Topics of Cicero*, on the other hand, he treats dialectic as a single science, composed of two parts, a science of discovery and a science of judgment. Thomas returns to the aristotelian usage (*In lib. I An. Post. lect.* 1), "In the process of reasoning, which is not with absolute certitude, some grade is found, according to which one comes more or less to perfect certitude. For through this process sometimes, although science is not set up, faith or opinion or probability is established because of the probability of the propositions, from which one proceeds, for reason declines totally from one part of the contradiction, although with fear of the other:

and topic or dialectic is ordered to this, for the dialectical syllogism is from probable premisses."

DIFFERENS, *differing*; things differ which have something in common in such wise that that in common is determined in diverse manner in the things, as man and brute are said to *differ* with respect to animality, in that animality is determined by rationality in the former and irrationality in the latter; according to the pseudo-Grosseteste (see above, vol. I, p. 293), "things which are different differ in that they are divided by the specific difference of some genus, and they agree in something common which is prior by nature to the things which are different and even to the differences themselves." Thomas distinguishes *difference* from *diversity*, in that things which differ agree in something and differ in something superadded to that, whereas in things which are diverse, it is not absolutely necessary that they agree in anything. (*Sum. Theol.* I, q. 3, a. 8 ad 3; also q. 90, a. 1 ad 3). Compare DISTINCTUM, DIVERSUM.

DIFFERENS NUMERO, *differing in number*, that is, as members of the same species differ from each other.

DIFFERENTIA, *differentia, difference*; that which in a genus separates one species from another; according to the middle ages one of the five predicables; genus and differentia constitute the definition of the species. Porphyry is responsible for a threefold division of differentiae:

DIFFERENTIA COMMUNIS, *common difference*, one which accidentally separates one thing from another (as that one person is standing, another seated), which difference indicates nothing permanent in the thing.

DIFFERENTIA PROPRIA, *proper difference*, one which makes the distinction accidentally, but by means of something inseparable from the thing, as a crow is distinguished from a swan in that the former is black, the latter white.

DIFFERENTIA MAXIME PROPRIA, *most proper difference*, one based on some property which indicates the essence of the thing, as *rational* is the differentia of man.

DIFFINITIO, *definition*. Compare DEFINITIO.

DIFFINITIO SUBSTANTIALIS, *substantial definition*.

DIFFINITIO QUID NOMINIS, *nominal definition*. Compare DEFINITIO NOMINIS.

DIFFINITIO QUID REI, *definition of the thing, real definition*. Compare DEFINITIO REI.

DESCENSUS PER DEFINITIONEM, *descent by definition*, to resolve a common word into the various significances embraced in it (Ockham).

DILECTIO, *love, choice*; every appetitive act is derived from love or choice; election precedes love; *dilectio* is an act not of the concupiscible nature, but of will and the rational nature; it is, however, unlike *caritas* in that *caritas* adds a certain perfection of love.

DIRECTE, *directly*; a direct act is one affirmed of the thing as it is part of the thing; thus a thing is known *directly* when our knowledge is turned to the thing itself. Compare REFLEXE.

DISCERNERE, *to discern, to distinguish*; according to Thomas, quoting Augustine (*In lib. I Sent.* d. 3, q. 4 sol.), "To discern is to know a thing through its difference from other things."

DISCIPLINA, *discipline, art*; the acquisition of understanding of a science; an external aid to the acquiring of knowledge; every doctrine and every discipline is formed from preexisting knowledge. Compare PERITIA.

DISCIPLINATUS, *disciplined*, that is, well-instructed.

DISCRETIO, *discretion, discreteness*.

DISCRETIO PERSONALIS, *personal discretion* or distinctness. Compare PERSONA.

DISCURSUS, *discourse*, the motion or progress of the understanding from one notion to another, as in the syllogism; opposed to immediate or intuitive apprehension. There are two kinds of discourse: one according to succession only, as when, after we understand something actually, we turn ourselves to understanding something else; the other according to causality, as when through principles we attain to knowledge of conclusions.

DISIUNGERE, *to disjoin*, the logical process of distinguishing and separating terms or ideas which are joined together.

DISPOSITIO, *disposition*; disposition always imports an order of something which has parts: this occurs in three ways, according to place, or according to power, or according to species; all dispositions are included in these three, but there is another triple division in which dispositions are frequently classified: the disposition of matter to receiving form, as heat is the disposition to the form of fire; the disposition by which an agent is disposed to acting, as velocity is the disposition to running; finally the or-

dination of things to each other. An inclination such
that it is true to say that disposition is made into habit
(*dispositio fit habitum*); both habit or condition (*habitus*)
and disposition (*dispositio*) are qualities which inhere in a
subject and bring about that it is well or ill constituted
in itself or its operations. The distinction between them
is that a habitus is a quality fixed in the thing by immobile
principles, whereas a disposition is a quality mobile by
nature, and therefore inhering lightly in its subject.

DISPONENS (MEDIUM), *disposing medium.*

DISPUTATIO, *disputation, investigation, discussion,* a syllogistic
act between an opponent and a respondent to establish a
point or proposition.

DISTINCTIO, *distinction,* the resolution of an equivocal word
into its various significances; the separation of things that
are distinct, that is, such that one is not another; opposite
differences are distinguished from each other.

DISTINCTUM, *distinct,* a distinct thing; things are distinct
which are numerically not one and the same; the negation
of identity.

DIVERSUM, *diverse;* things are diverse if the essence of one is
not the essence of the other, as man is diverse from brute,
in so far as man is not that which is brute, and brute is
not that which is man; two things which are diverse need
not be diverse through anything, but may be diverse
through themselves alone, whereas things which are different must differ in genus or species; *diverse* is contrasted to *the same,* as *different* is contrasted to *like.*
Diverse things are those the substance of which is not one;
unlike things, those which do not have one quality; unequal things, those which do not have one quantity. Compare IDEM.

NON DIFFERENTES PROPRIE SED TANTUM DIVERSAE, *not differing
in the proper sense of the word but only diverse,* that is,
possessed of nothing in common; the ten categories are
diverse from each other and not properly different.

DIVERSIFICATIO, *diversification.*

DIVIDERE, *to divide, to separate,* particularly the logical process
of separating genus into its species or of denying the
relation between two terms.

DIVISIO, *division, resolution,* properly the distribution of genus
into species by opposed difference, as, of animals, some
are rational, others irrational. Boethius divides division

broadly into two kinds, substantial and accidental, each of which has three subdivisions (see above, vol. I, p. 87): substantial division, (1) of genus into species (as color into white, black, and medium), (2) of the various significations of a word (as dog into barking, fourlegged animal, celestial constellation, and marine beast), (3) of whole into its proper parts (as house into foundations, walls, and roof); accidental division (1) of accident into subjects (as goods into goods of body and of mind), (2) of subject into accidents (as bodies into white, black, and medium color), (3) of accidents into accidents (as liquids into white, black, and medium color, or white things into hard, soft, and medium). In substantial division, the division of genus into species differs from division of a whole into parts in that the name of the genus applies to every species (man and horse are both animals), but the name of the whole does not apply to the parts (walls and foundations are not houses). All negative propositions are instances of division, as affirmative propositions are instances of composition. Compare DISTINCTIO.

DONUM, *gift*, as contrasted to DATUM, the grace of God shown to man above what is granted to other creatures. *Gift* is contrasted to *datum*, according to Bonaventura (*In lib. I Sent.*, d. 18, a. 1, q. 3 resp.), in two respects: that the latter (*datum*) being the participle of a verb, time is involved in it, and it is therefore less proper to apply to God; and *gift* adds over and above it a liberality which is the mark of great nobility.

SEPTEM DONA SPIRITUS SANCTI, *the seven gifts of the Holy Spirit*, as enumerated by Isaiah, according to Bacon the third of the seven grades of interior experience.

E

EFFECTIVE, *effectively, in effect.*

EFFECTUS, *effect*; that which follows from an efficient cause; something may be the effect of something else either essentially or accidentally: it is essentially the effect of something when it is produced by it as ordered to that end, as a house is the effect essentially of a builder; it is an effect accidentally when it is joined to that which is the effect essentially or through itself, as if the habitation of the house were said to be the effect of the builder.

Accidental effects, in turn, are of two sorts: that at which
the action of a cause can be terminated, although it was
beyond the intention of the agent, as the discovery of a
treasure chest, and such an effect although it is in this
sense the effect of an accidental cause, can be of an
essential cause; another accidental effect is one at which
no action of any agent is terminated, but because it happens to an effect, it can be called an accidental effect,
as the accident white can be said to be the accidental
effect of the builder. Effects are proportional to their
causes; every effect is convertible with the principle or
cause from which it proceeds. Compare EMINENTER,
FORMALITER (for univocal and equivocal causes), CAUSA,
AFFECTUS.

EFFICIENS (MEDIUM), *efficient medium.*

ELEMENTUM, *element*; according to Thomas (*In lib. V Met.*
lect. 4, 795-798), "There are four things to be considered
in the definition of element. The first of these is that it
is the cause, as it were, from which [*causa sicut ex quo*]
[the thing is]; wherefore it is clear that *element* is placed
in the genus of material cause. The second is that it is
the principle from which anything is made first, for cop-
per is that from which the statue is made, yet it is not
an element, because it has some other matter from which
it is made. The third is that it is inexistent or intrinsic,
in which respect an element differs from all that from
which something is made as from something transeunt,
whether it be privation, or contrary, or matter to contrariety, or subject to privation, which is transient matter.
As when we say that the musical man is made from the
non-musical man, or the musical from the non-musical.
For elements must remain in the things of which they
are the elements. The fourth is that it have some species,
which is not divided into diverse species, by which the
element differs from first matter, which has no species,
and likewise from all matters which can be resolved into
diverse species, such as blood and others of this sort.
Because of this it is said that *an element is* (with respect
to the first) *that from which something is composed*;
(with respect to the second) *first*; (with respect to the
third) *inexistent*; (with respect to the fourth) *indivisible
in species into another species*." Element is distinguished
from principle and cause. According to Thomas (*In lib.*

I Phys. lect. 1), "Cause is more inclusive than element. For an element is that from which a thing is composed first and the element is in it, as is stated in the Vth book of the *Metaphysics* [c. 3, 1014ª 26 ff], as letters are the elements of speech, but syllables are not. Those things are called causes on which anything depends with respect to its being or its becoming, whence those things which are outside the thing or those likewise which are in the thing, from which the thing is not first compounded, can be called causes, but not elements. Principle, however, imports a certain order of some process, whence something can be a principle which is not a cause, as that from which a motion begins is the principle of the motion, but not the cause, and the point is the principle of the line, but not the cause. Thus, therefore, by principles, Aristotle seems to mean moving and active causes, in which the order of a certain process is considered. By causes he seems to understand formal and final causes, from which, most of all, things depend in their being and coming to be. By elements, finally, he means material causes properly." Compare CAUSA, PRINCIPIUM.

ELENCHUS, *elenchus*, a syllogism in which the contradictory of the conceded conclusion is inferred.

EMINENTER, *eminently*; a thing is contained eminently in something else more excellently than in itself, as the vegetative and sensitive souls are contained in the intellective soul, and as the perfection of effects are found in analogical or equivocal causes (if the cause is univocal the perfection of the effect is found in it formally); in this analogical sense the perfections of creatures are to be found in God, and God is the eminent cause of things.

ENS, *that which is, the thing which is, a being* (ὄντος); according to Thomas (see selection above, *Quaest. disp. de Ver.* q. 1, a. 1 concl.), "*Ens* [that which is] expresses the act of being, but the name of *thing* expresses the quiddity or essence of that which is." That which is of two sorts: the essence of things (in which sense it is divided into the ten categories) and the conception formed by the mind; in the latter sense it is not essence. According to Thomas (*De Ente et Ess.* c. I), "It must be known that as the Philosopher says in book V of the *Metaphysics* that that which is through itself is spoken of in two ways: in one way as it is divided into the ten genera, in another way as it signifies the truth of propositions. The difference between these, however, is that in the second way all that concerning which an affirmative proposition can be formed, although it posits nothing in fact, can be said to be *that which is*; in this way privations and negations are called things which are, for we say that affirmation is the opposite to negation, and that blindness is in the eye. But in the first way something can not be said to be that which is, unless it posits something in fact; whence in the first way, blindness and others of this sort are not things which are. The name of essence is not derived from that which is (*ens*) in the second sense, for some things which have no essence, are said to be things which are, as is clear in the case of privations; but essence is derived from that which is in the first sense." That which is is the first concept of the understanding; it is therefore beyond the categories, one of the transcendentals. The first division of that which is, is by potentiality and actuality; the second is into the ten categories. Compare RES, ESSENTIA, ENTITAS, ESSE, ESSENDI, TRANSCENDENTALES.

ENS NATURAE, *thing of nature, that which is in nature, natural thing*, that which actually or potentially exists outside the mind; *ens* in the first sense. Similarly ENS PER SE, *that which is through itself, that which is essentially*; this expression is most usually given as the definition of substance. Or ENS IN SE PER MODUM SUBSTANTIAE, *that which is in itself according to the mode of substance.*

ENS RATIONIS, *that which is in reason, a thing of reason*; according to Scotus, it is that which has being in the understanding which considers it, and which can have no being outside the understanding; it posits nothing in the actual thing and it is not itself an actual thing, but it is none the less formed or apprehended by reason. Thomas (*Sum. Theol.* I, q. 16, a. 3 ad 2) speaks of the true as founded in that which is not (*non-ens*), "in so far as that which is not is a certain thing of reason, that is, apprehended by reason." The same consideration holds for the good. Again he says (*In lib. IV Met.* lect. 4, 574), "Thing of reason is properly spoken of relative to those intentions, which reason devises in the things considered, such as the intention of genus, species, and others like these, which are not discovered in the nature of things, but follow from the consideration of reason. And of this sort, that is, a thing of reason, is the subject of logic. Intelligible intentions of this sort, however, are equivalent [*aequiparantur*] to natural things in that all natural things fall under the consideration of reason. And therefore the subject of logic extends itself to all things concerning which *natural thing* is predicated. Whence it is concluded that the subject of logic is equivalent to the subject of philosophy which is the thing of nature." A thing of reason may have a foundation in the thing (as man, considered not in himself, but as man is a species) or no foundation (as a chimera).

ENTHYMEMA, *enthymeme*, a truncated syllogism.

ENTITAS, *entity*, the character or property of being.

ENUNTIATIO, *statement*, an affirmative or negative *proposition*; speech in which there is true or false; it is the sign of composition or division in the understanding.

  VERITAS ENUNTIATIONIS, *truth of statement*. Compare VERITAS.

ERROR, *error*, consists in approving the false as true; it adds over ignorance a certain act, for there can be ignorance without the bearing of judgment concerning the things ignored, and a person ignorant in that sense is not in error. (Compare Thomas, *Quaest. disp. de Malo* q. 3, a. 7 concl.) Compare IGNORANTIA, FALSUM.

ESSE, *being*; according to Thomas (*In lib. I Sent.* d. 33, q. 1, a. 1 ad 1), "Being is spoken of in three ways. In one way being is said to be the very quiddity or nature of the thing, as it is said that definition is speech signifying what it is to be [i.e. essence], for definition signifies the quiddity of the thing. In another way being is said to be the very act of the essence, as living (which is being to living things) is the act of the soul, not the second act which is operation, but the first act. In a third way being is said to be that which signifies the truth of composition in propositions, according to which *is* is called a copula, and in this way it is in the understanding compounding and dividing so far as its complement is concerned, but it is founded in the being of the thing, which is the act of the essence." Being is the actuality of all things and even of forms.

ESSENDI, *of being*, concerned with the act of being.

ESSENTIA, *essence*, that through which the thing is constituted in its species and distinguished from other things, and therefore it is something primary in the thing and the root of all its properties; that which is conceived first in the thing without which the thing cannot be, and the foundation and cause of whatever other things are in that thing; the essence is conceived in the concept of the thing and stated in its *definition*, as rational mortal animal is the essence of man. Essence, therefore, is something common to all natures by which diverse entities are collocated in diverse genera and species, as humanity is the essence of man; according to Thomas (*Sum. Theol.* I, q. 3, a. 3 concl.), "Essence or nature comprehends in itself only those things which fall in the definition of the species, as humanity comprehends in itself those things which fall in the definition of man; for by them man is man, and humanity signifies this, namely, that by which man is man"; and again (ibid. q. 29, a. 2 ad 3), "Essence properly is that which is signified by definition; definition, however, embraces the principles of the species, but not the individual principles; wherefore in things compounded from matter and form, the essence signifies not only the form, nor only the matter, but the composite from matter and the common form, as they are the principles of the species." The greek expressions in which the problems related to essence are discussed, τὸ τί ἦν εἶναι, τὸ τί ἐστι, become in latin *quod quid erat esse*, and *quid est*. Compare QUIDDITAS, NATURA.

ESSENTIALITER, *essentially*; things differ essentially which either are diverse in every genus and in accord in no genus (as God and creature) or which, although they agree in some genus, still differ in other proximate genera (as man and tree) or at least in species (as man and horse). A substance advenes on another substance essentially when it forms a single complete being with it, such as is formed by the conjunction of body and soul in man.

EVIDENTER, *evidently*, that is, with evidence or clarity, and consequently, *certainly* and *self-evidently*.

EVIDENTIA, *evidence*, the type of certitude which is had of first principles known immediately or of a syllogistic inference, which according to Duns Scotus is based on the form of the syllogism known self-evidently. Thomas had said that evidence adds, over the firmness of adhesion of certitude, a quietude of the understanding in the thing known (*Quaest. disp. de Ver.* q. 10, a. 12 ad 6).

EXEMPLAR, *exemplar*; that according to which something else is made in such wise that it imitates the exemplar; according to Thomas, only the intellectual reasons in God, in imitation of which things are produced in being, can properly be called exemplars.

EXISTIMATIO, *estimation*, the highest faculty of the sensitive soul, by which the brute distinguishes good from evil. Compare AESTIMATIO.

EXPERIENTIA, *experience, experiment*; experience is formed from many memories, as memory is formed from sensations; it is knowledge of singulars, but the active intellect operating on its data abstracts universals; one of the two ways of knowing according to Bacon, argumentation being the other, but certainty can come only from experience; according to him experience is of two sorts, exterior and interior.

EXPERIMENTUM, *experience, experiment*, synonymous with EXPERIENTIA, formed from the collection of many singulars received in memory; reason is based on it. Compare SCIENTIA EXPERIMENTALIS.

F

FACERE, *to do, action*, the ninth of the ten categories. Action and passion admit of variation in degree. Compare FACTIO, PASSIO.

FACTIO, *making*; usually contrasted to action (or in particular that action which is called intelligence, which begins with the species of the thing to be made or the end of the art); making is an act which goes forth to an exterior matter, such as building, drying, and so forth. According to Thomas (*In lib. VII Met.* lect. 6, 1394), "For although we can use the name *making*, which in greek is *praxis*, concerning natural things, as when we say that heat and an actual thing *makes* such an actual being, still we use it more properly concerning those things which are made by the understanding, in which the understanding of the agent has dominion over what it makes so that it can make it thus or otherwise, which does not happen in natural things, but they act to some effect in a way determined by something superior set above them." Compare PRAXIS, ACTIO.

FACULTAS, *faculty*; according to Thomas (*Sum. Theol.* I. q. 83, a. 2 ob. 2), "Faculty names a facility of power which is through habit"; and again (ibid. ad 2), "Faculty sometimes names an expedited power for operating." Elsewhere (*In lib. II Sent.* d. 24, q. 1, a. 1 ad 2) he defines it, "Faculty signifies according to the common usage of speech the power by which something is had at will, and therefore faculties are also called possessions, because they are in the dominion of the one possessing."

FALSIGRAFIS, *falsigraphic*; a proposition or argument which is incorrectly expressed or written is falsigraphic.

FALSUM, *false*; a thing is false according to Thomas (*Sum. Theol.* I, q. 17, a. 4 concl.; compare Aristotle, *Met.* IV, c. 7, 1011^b 27) "by the fact that what is said is seen either to be something which is not, or not to be that which is." Compare ERROR.

FIGURA, *figure*; according to Thomas (*Sum Theol.* I, q. 7, a. 1 ad 2), "Figure, which consists in the termination of quantity, is a certain form with respect to quantity." Compare IMAGO.

FINIS, *end*; according to Thomas (*In lib. II Met.*, lect. 4, 316), "The end is that which is not because of other things, but other things are because of it." Moreover (*In lib. X Met.*, lect. 5, 2028), "The end is that which is ultimate in each thing, and that which contains the thing, wherefore nothing is without end."

FINIS OPERIS, *end of the operation*, often distinguished from—
FINIS OPERANTIS, *end of the one who performs the operation*, since the latter, although the intention of the operator, does not always coincide with the actual end.

FORMA, *form*; by its form each thing is constituted in its species; form is one of the three principles of natural change, matter and privation being the other two; together with matter it makes up the material composite; it is the actuality which determines matter, the latter being potentiality, that is, indifferent to any species of being. Thomas (?) distinguishes three kinds of forms (*De Nat. Mat.* c. 3), "For there is a form which is its own being, and is not received from anything prior, nor communicated to anything posterior; and such a form is God. And therefore he alone is absolutely infinite. There are other forms which although they are not received in matter, nevertheless are not their own being, since a composition of essence and being falls in them; and therefore from one part they are finite and from another infinite, for they are limited according to their being, terminated from above, but not from below, since they are not received in anything inferior. And this is the doctrine of the Commentator in the book *on Causes*. There are other forms which are finite from all sides and which have being otherwise than is common to every creature; nevertheless they are received in some matter. Yet among these there is a great difference, for the less they are immersed in matter, the less they are limited, and therefore the human mind is in a certain manner all." Compare MATERIA, PRIVATIO.

FORMA SEPARATA, *separated form*, one which is not ordered to matter, consequently not only is it not dependent on matter, but it can not be united to matter, as the Angel according to Thomas.

FORMABILIS, *apt to be formed or fashioned, subject to form, formable.*

FORMALITER, *formally*; a thing is formally such or such in so far as it is so specified by its definition. One thing is formally contained in another when it is found in it according to its concept and definition; thus heat is formally contained in fire and any effect in its univocal cause. Various meanings of formally are determined by its use in opposition to a number of concepts such as causally, concomitantly, eminently and virtually, identically, materially, objectively, really, in reason.

FRUCTUS, *fruit*; among the fruits which, according to Bacon, constitute the sixth of the seven grades of interior experience, is the peace of the Lord.

G

GENERATIO, *generation* (γένεσις); change in the category of substance by which natural things begin to be by the inducing anew of form in matter, as opposed to creation which is their production *ex nihilo*. Generation is change (*mutatio*) or sudden change (*mutatio subita*) not motion (*motus*), since it is accomplished, not in time, but instantaneously; generation and its opposite, corruption, do not affect matter nor form directly, but only the composite. Thomas defines generation (*Con. Gent.* I, c. 26), "Generation is the way to being, and corruption the way to non-being"; Ockham defines it (*Sum. Phys.* III, c. 8), "Generation is when a substantial form is induced anew into matter. Corruption is when a substantial form ceases to be in matter." Compare MUTATIO.

GENUS, *genus*; according to Aristotle and the medieval philosophers, one of the five predicables. Genus took on a variety of meanings which are summed up by Thomas (*Met.* V, lect. 22, 1119–1123), "Genus is used in four ways. In the first way as the *continuous generation* of any things have the same species (as it is said, *so long as the genus of men will be*, that is, so long as the continuous generation of men will endure). This is the first way stated in Porphyry, namely, a multitude of things having a relation to each other and to a single principle. In the second way genus is used as that from which as a *first mover to being*, that is, a generator, any things proceed, as some men are called Hellenes in genus [kind] because they descend from a certain Hellen by name, and some men are called Ionians, because they descend from a certain Ion as first generator. Men are denominated however rather from the father, who is the generator, than from the mother, who supplies the matter in generation; and none the less some are denominated in genus from the mother, as certain Pleiades are so called from a woman by the name Pleione. And this is the second manner of genus stated by Porphyry. In the third way genus is used in the sense in which superfice [surface] is said to be the genus of superficial figures, and solid, that is, body, is said to be the genus of solid figures, that is, of bodily figures. Genus in this sense, however, is not that which signifies the essence of a species, as animal is the genus of man, but that which is the proper subject of accidents different in species; for the superfice is the subject of all superficial figures. . . . In the fourth way genus is used as that which is stated first in definition and is predicated of first substance [*quod quid*]; and the differentia are qualities of it, as in the definition of man *animal* is stated first, and next *biped* or *rational* which are certain substantial qualities of man. It is clear then that genus is used in all these ways. In one way according to a continuous generation in the same species, which pertains to the first way. In another way according to the first mover, which pertains to the second way. In another way as matter, which pertains to the third and fourth ways. For in this way genus is related to differentia as subject to quality, and therefore it is clear that genus as predicable and genus as subject are comprehended as under a single mode, and both are constituted in the mode of matter. For although genus as predicable is not matter, nevertheless it is derived from matter, as differentia is from form. For any animal is so called by the fact that he has a sensitive nature; he is called rational by the fact that he has a rational nature, which is related to the sensitive as form to matter." Genus is defined by Boethius (see above, vol. I, p. 97) as the thought collected from the substantial likeness of species; according to his doctrine genera subsist in sensibles, but are understood beyond bodies.

GENERALISSIMUM, *generalissimum, most general genus*. Compare PRAEDICAMENTA.

H

HABERE, *to have, condition, state*; as shod or armed; the eighth of the ten categories. Compare HABITUS.

HABITUDO, *condition, aptitude, relation, respect, capacity for something*. A distinction is made between the possession of a quality *quoad entitatem* and *quoad habitudinem*, with respect to entity and with respect to aptitude.

HABITUS, *condition, habit, character* (ἕξις), the quality which supervenes on potentiality and adheres permanently, aiding in the operation to which it is proper. More broadly Thomas (*In lib. V Met.* lect. 20, 1062–1064) speaks of two kinds of "having": "The first of these is something medium between that which has and that which is had. For habit [or having], although it is not an action, signifies nevertheless according to the mode of action. And therefore habit is understood to be medium between that having and that had and as it were a kind of action, just as heating is understood to be medium between that heated and that heating, whether that medium be taken as an act, as when the heating is taken actively, or as a motion, as when the heating is taken passively. For when one thing makes, and another is made, the medium is making [*factio*] . . . In the second way habit means a disposition according to which something is disposed well or ill, as by health one is disposed well, by sickness ill." In the first sense, the eighth category is to be explained, for medium between a man having shoes and the shoes which are had, is the having of the shoes; shod is therefore a state or habit. Habit differs from *disposition* in being more permanent; according to Aristotle (*Cat.* 8, 8ᵇ 27), "Habit differs from disposition in being more lasting and more firmly established." The various kinds of knowledge and of virtue are habits. Knowledge and virtue are conditions or habits, because of their firm fixity, the former being established on principles necessarily true, the latter on the good and honorable which are immutable; suspicion, doubt, opinion, and so on are dispositions, as are illness and health. Habits may be entitative or operative. By habit, potentiality is more easily brought into actuality, and consequently it has been called another nature. Compare POSTPRAEDICAMEN-TUM.

HAECCEITAS, *hecceity*; according to Duns Scotus, the principle of individuation is not matter but a formal distinction; each thing is distinctive by its "thisness."

I

IDEA, *idea*; according to Thomas (*Sum. Theol.* I, q. 15, a. 1 concl.), "*Idea* in greek is translated by *form* in latin; wherefore by ideas are understood the forms of things existing without the things themselves. But the form of any thing existing without the thing itself, can be in two ways, either as the exemplar of that of which it is said to be the form, or as the principle of cognition of it, according to which the forms of knowable things are said to be in the knower."

IDEM, *the same*; a thing may be the same in species with another, or in the case of identity, the same in number, but as Thomas says (*In lib. V Met.* lect. 17, 1022), "Things are the same of which the substance is one"; as things are like of which the quality is one; and things equal of which the quantity is one. Everything which is or is one is the same as or diverse from everything;

same and diverse do not apply to non-being, however, for, "the same and the diverse are not opposed as contradictories of which one or the other must be true of anything that is or is not, but they are opposed as contraries which are verified only of that which is" (Thomas, *In lib. X Met.* lect. 4, 2015).

IDENTITAS, *identity*; Thomas says (*In lib. X Met.* lect. 4, 2007), "Where there is unity of substance there is not said to be likeness or equality but only identity." Where there are no differences there is identity.

IDOLUM SEU FANTASMA, *idol or phantasm*, the image which is present to the sensitive soul by which present things are known to the senses and absent things to the imagination.

ID QUOD EST, *that which is*, the definition, or more properly the description, of ENS.

IGNORANTIA, *ignorance*; according to Thomas a distinction must be made between two kinds of ignorance (*In lib. I An. Post.* lect. 26): "Ignorance, as a negation, is when a man knows absolutely nothing concerning a thing. And this is ignorance in not attaining, as the Philosopher says in book IX of the *Metaphysics*. As is clear in the case of the rustic who knows nothing of the triangle, as to whether it has three angles equal to two right angles. But ignorance, as a disposition, is when one has some disposition to knowing, but a corrupt disposition, when, namely, one estimates that some one is running, but falsely, or when one estimates either that that is which is not, or that that is not which is. And this ignorance is the same as error. The first ignorance is not made by syllogism; the second can be made by syllogism." Compare ERROR.

ILLUMINATION, *illumination*, the interior light of God by which the augustinians taught that knowledge is obtained.

  ILLUMINATIO SCIENTIALIS, *scientific illumination*, the first of the seven grades of interior experience according to Bacon.

IMAGINATIO, *imagination*, the faculty of the sensitive soul which preserves species received from the particular senses; called by Avicenna the treasury and repository of common sense. Compare MEMORIA.

IMAGINARI, *to be imaged*.

IMAGO, *image*; according to Thomas image means the expressed representation of the thing; the principle of the image is likeness, not any likeness, but a likeness which is in the species or at least in some sign of the species. In corporeal things figure is particularly the sign of the species, for animals diverse in species are of diverse figures, not of diverse colors, and therefore if the color of anything were painted on a wall, it would not be said to be the image of the thing unless the figure were painted too. But the likeness of the species and figure does not suffice, for its origin too is required for the principle of the image. Thomas concludes therefore (*Sum. Theol.* I, q. 35, a. 1 concl.), "For anything to be truly an image, it is required that it proceed from something else like to it in species or at least in the sign of the species." According to Bonaventura, image is one of the three ways (compare VESTIGIUM, UMBRA) in which God is represented in his creatures; a creature is an image in so far as God is not only his cause, but the object of the operations of his faculties, in so far, that is, as the creature is memory, understanding, will; man alone, therefore, of temporal things is made in God's image by virtue of the intellectual soul (see Eriugena above, vol. I, pp. 193–197).

INCOMPLEXUM, *incomplex.* Compare COMPLEXUS.

INCOMPOSSIBILE, *incompossible.* Compare INCONTINGENS.

INCONTINGENS, *incontingent*; according to Thomas (*In lib. III Sent.* d. 3, q. 5, a. 3 ad 3), "It is not necessary that everything which is made be made from a contrary, but only that which is made by way of generation and alteration; it is necessary, however, that everything that is made be made from the incontingent, that is, that which does not happen [*contingit*] to be at one and the same time."

INDIFFERENTER, *indifferently*; it was taken as axiom, that from a thing which is indifferent, in the respect in which it is indifferent, nothing determinate can arise.

INDIFFERENTIA, *indifference*; distinguished into physical (capacity of acting or not acting) or moral (capacity of acting well or ill).

INDISTANTIA, *proximity, indistance*; it is of two sorts, indistance of penetration or indistance of continuity or contiguity.

INDIVIDUARI, *to be individuated.*

INDIVIDUATIO, *individuation*; according to Thomas (*In lib. II de An.* lect. 12, 377), "The individuation of a common nature in corporeal and material things is by corporeal matter contained under determined dimensions"; matter, moreover, was the principle of individuation, not only in singular sensibles but also in mathematical things, for there is a sensible matter, like wood or bronze by which individual sensibles are individuated, and an intelligible matter which is in sensible things, not in so far as they are sensible things, but as they are mathematical things; as the form of man is in such a sensible matter, which is the organic body, so the form of the circle or the triangle is in such an intelligible matter which is the continuum or the surface or the body (see Thomas, *In lib. VII Met.* lect. 10, 1496); the principle of individuation can not be the collection of accidents of the individual thing. According to Duns, the principle of individuation is always the hecceity of the thing individuated.

INDIVIDUUM, *individual*; an individual is that which is indistinct in itself, but distinct from others. An individual (or a singular) is a being so determined and restricted that it can not be further divided by differences into parts the same as itself, and therefore exists undivided in itself and divided from other things which are or can be in the same species. Individual (or singular) may therefore be defined as that which is undivided in itself and divided from others by an ultimate division; Aristotle defines it as "that which is not predicated of many" (*De Interp.* 6, 17ᵃ 37), and Porphyry says (see above, vol. I, p. 223), "Individuals are defined as follows, that each one of them consists of properties the collection of which is not in another." Individual and singular are the same in fact, but the significances of the two can be distinguished: a thing is said to be singular in so far as it underlies a universal and in so far as it is none the less diverse from other things; it is said to be individual in so far as it is undivided and is not further divisible into other individuals. On the other hand the material principle enters to differentiate the *particular* from the *individual*: according to Thomas (*In lib. X Met.* lect. 11, 2132), just as the diversity of forms makes a difference of species, so a diversity of individual matter makes a difference of individuals; therefore a *particular* something, as Callias, is not only form, but form together with individuated matter. Compare SINGULARIS, SPECIES INFIMA.

INDIVISIO, *indivision*; unity does not, according to Thomas, import the principle of perfection, but only of indivision; division causes multitude, but indivision, unity.

INFINITUM, *infinite* (ἄπειρον); infinite is that which has no end but is unlimited or limitless; the infinite is the open possibility of more. Except for God there are no existent infinite things; God alone is actually infinite; the infinite does not exist in sensible things, or apart from sensible things, but only for thought—it is unlimited as potentiality, there is never an infinite actuality (see Aristotle, *Phys.* III, 5–8). Bonaventura makes a distinction (*In lib. I Sent.* d, 3, p. 1, a. 1, q. 1 ad 3; see selection above): "It must be said that infinity is to be taken in two senses; one which is constituted by opposition to the simple; and such an infinite is not encompassed by the finite, such as infinite mass; there is another which has infinity together with simplicity, such as God; and such an infinite, because it is *simple*, is everywhere whole; because it is *infinite*, it is in nothing in such wise that it is not outside it." Matthew of Aquasparta distinguishes (see selection above, q. 2 ad 18) between the infinite in actuality (as God) and the infinite in duration (as the movers of the orbs). Compare CATEGOREMATICE, SYNCATEGOREMATICE.

INFORMARE, *to inform*, said of the form, which, when united to matter or to any subject, constitutes it in a given determinate species of things; similarly, sense is informed by the likeness of sensible things.

INFORMATIO, *information*, that is, endowment with form.

INHAERENTIA, *inherence*; accidents inhere in subjects, whereas second substances are predicated properly of first substances.

INTELLECTUALE, *the intellectual (thing)*, perceived by the intellect as the sensible (thing) is perceived by sense.

INTELLECTUS, *intellect, understanding, meaning, conception, idea*; particularly the cognoscitive faculty which is concerned with that which is (*ens*) and which therefore perceives the true. According to the pseudo-Grosseteste (see above, vol. I, p. 304), "The understanding is a spiritual mirror bringing into actuality by an innate light the idol or the phantasm in the human imagination where it is in potentiality, just as light brings color into actuality. The phantasm itself however, once it has been brought into actuality, perfects the understanding by its own property and makes of the possible intellect the acquired intellect or the intellect in condition, just as the species of color moves and perfects the sense by its own property." According to Albert (see above, vol. I, p. 350), "The intellect is joined to man in three ways. In one way as a nature which gives being, and in this way it is individual. In another way as the power by which there is the operation of understanding, and in this way it is a universal power. In a third way as the form acquired from many intelligibles, as has been stated more clearly with reference to the active intellect which is not joined to contemplatives as agent only, but as it is their beatitude when they arrive at that which is in them as form. And the said intellect is not present in the second and third manners, as prudence and wisdom, equally in all men, but in some more and in others less, and in some perhaps there is present nothing of intellect."

INTELLECTUS ADEPTUS, *acquired intellect.*

INTELLECTUS AGENS, *active intellect*, the intellect in so far as it itself reflects the impressed species by which it is helped to effect the express species, thus actualizing the possible intellect and making it the acquired intellect. According to Bacon God is the active intellect of all mankind.

INTELLECTUS FORMALIS, *formal intellect*; according to Albert (see above, vol. I, pp. 373-374), "There is a third [intellect, that is, besides the possible and active], moreover, which is the formal intellect, namely when the form of that known or operating by the light of the intellect is in the soul; and this is divided into the practical and speculative."

INTELLECTUS POSSIBILIS, *possible intellect*, the intellect in so far as it is able to receive the species of all things, therefore called by Grosseteste the possible or *material intellect*. According to Bacon the human soul is the possible intellect.

INTELLECTUS PRACTICUS, *practical intellect*, contrasted to the speculative in that it extends to operation; ethics and politics are its proper sciences. Compare SCIENTIA.

INTELLECTUS SPECULATIVUS, *speculative intellect*, the function of the intellect which comes to rest in the object of its contemplation.

INTELLEGERE, *to perceive, to understand,* according to Thomas (*Sum. Theol.* I, q. 34, a. 1 ad 3), "To understand imports only a relation [*habitudo*] of the one understanding to the thing understood, in which no principle [*ratio*] of origin is imported, but only a certain information in our understanding, as our understanding is made in actuality by the form of the thing understood." The etymology is frequently given of *intellegere* from *intus legere,* to read within. Compare RATIO.

INTELLIGENTIA, *understanding, intelligence,* as when first principles are assented to from the *understanding* of the terms in which they are stated; or as the sense and application of a proposition, for example, the *understanding* of the meaning of these words. Used also either as intellect or intellection.

INTELLIGENTIA SEPARATA, *separated intelligence,* spiritual substance without body or matter, as the angels or the intelligences that rule the spheres.

INTENDERE, *to intend,* as the understanding or will intends, or *to intensify,* as opposed to remit.

INTENSIVE, *intensively,* as opposed to extensively or to remissly.

INTENTIO, *intention, knowledge, meaning;* the cognoscitive power never knows anything actually, unless there is some intention present; the mind in knowledge may intend the thing known, it may intend the thing which is, or that which is true of the thing which is. Bonaventura says (*In lib. II Sent.* d. 38, a. 2, q. 2 ad 2), "Although intention sometimes means the very *power* intending, sometimes means the *condition* according to which it intends, sometimes means the *act* of intending, sometimes the *thing intended* itself, nevertheless the name of intention is imposed principally upon the act itself; although, notwithstanding this, it happens that it is sometimes required in the other acceptations. For when it is said that the intention is the *eye,* intention is taken as *power.* When it is said that the intention is *light,* intention is taken as the *condition directing.* When it is said that the intention is the *end itself* . . . intention is taken as *that which is intended.* But when it is said that a certain intention is *right,* another *oblique,* intention is taken as the *act.*" According to Albert (see above, vol. I, p. 349), "In the soul, being is rather the intention of the thing than the thing."

Esse intentionale, *intentional being*, is therefore that being which the thing has in the intellect which knows, either as that being is in the understanding itself or as it represents the thing understood objectively.   According to Thomas (*In lib. I Sent.* d. 33, q. 1, a. 1 ad 3), "Intentions are not in things, but only in the mind, yet there is something corresponding to them in the thing, namely, the nature to which the understanding attributes the intentions of this sort, as the intention of genus is not in the ass, but in the nature of animal, to which the intention is attributed by the understanding."

Intentio prima, *first intention*; a thing is considered according to the first intention when it is considered according to that which is proper to it as a thing; this may be by a simple act of the understanding by which it is known that the thing is, or by a complex act by which some truth may be known of it, as that man is an animal. Ockham defines concepts of the first intention as mental names which naturally signify individual external things (which are not signs) and which can be the subject or predicate of propositions.

Intentio secunda, *second intention*, when the thing is considered according to extrinsic denominations, derived not from the thing, but from the act of understanding, as that man is species, or animal is genus. Ockham defines concepts of the second intention as mental names which signify intentions naturally significative, that is, first intentions.

Intentio generalis, *general intention*, an intention possessed by all things, in virtue of the fact simply that they are; that which is and that which is true are among the general intentions. Compare transcendentales.

Intentionis res, *a thing of intention*, that which exists only in mind; the same as ens rationis.

Intuitus, *intuition, intuitive knowledge*, that by which something is known immediately, without ratiocination; thus, first principles known through themselves are known intuitively, as that *the whole is greater than its part*, and so too the existence or non-existence of things is known. More generally even ratiocination is reduced to intuitive knowledge, as Thomas (following Augustine) points out

(*In lib. I Sent.* d. 3, q. 4, a. 5 sol.), "To understand means nothing other than intuition, which is nothing other than the presence of the intelligible to the understanding in some way."

INVENTIO, *invention, discovery*, the process of reasoning by which something is concluded to be true in a great many cases or in a majority of cases; it does not therefore have necessity, and discovery is not always with certitude; in the aristotelian tradition it is a process properly studied in the part of logic called dialectic or topic, in rhetoric, and in poetic.

IUDICUM, *judgment*, right determination in moral or logical sense; according to Thomas (*Sum. Theol.* IIa IIae, q. 60, a. 1 ad 1), "The name judgment, which according to its first imposition signifies the right determination of just men, is broadened to signify right determination concerning anything whatsoever, whether speculative or practical." According to the thomist psychology judgment follows upon and concludes the counseling of the mind concerning a problem, and leads to or constitutes election or choice of one of the parts.

L

LOCUS, *place* (τόπος); Aristotle points out (*Phys.* IV, c. 2, 209ᵃ 33–35) that "since there is a distinction between that which is relative to itself and that which is relative to something else, so too a distinction must be made between the place which is common, in which all bodies are, and the place which is proper in which each body is primarily." The proper place is the limit of the immediate envelope or the first container of an object; that which contains the object and nothing but the object. Place is the measure of the mobile, as time is the measure of motion (see Thomas, *In lib. IV Phys.* lect. 4).

LUMEN, *illumination*, the reflection or corporeal counterpart of *light*, as the illumination issuing from a physical body or even a celestial orb; in which illumination, things are seen.

LUMEN COMPLANATUM, *complanted light*, the light which the eye gives forth when it sees, in virtue of which owls and bats see in the dark.

Lux, *light*, especially the light of the divine understanding, in the augustinian tradition, by means of which truths are perceived; by it truth is impressed in the heart of man as an image is impressed in wax by a seal.

M

Malum, *evil*; Thomas says (*Quaest. disp. de Malo*, q. 16, a. 2 concl.), "A thing is said to be evil in two ways. In one way because it is evil in itself, as robbery or homicide, and this is evil absolutely. In another way a thing is said to be evil to someone, and there is nothing to prevent that that be good absolutely, but evil in some respect, as justice, which is good in itself and absolutely, is turned to evil for the robber who is punished by it." Compare DEFECTUS, BONUM.

Maneries, *manner.*

Manuductio, *manuduction*; as the type of proof which exemplifies and leads to, but does not present perfect knowledge.

Materia, *matter*; matter and form are the inseparable constitutive elements of all first substance; matter, form, and privation are the three principles of change. "I mean by matter," Aristotle writes (*Phys.* I, c. 9, 192ª32-34), "that first subject of each thing, from which each thing is generated, and it is present in the thing, not accidentally, [but as a substantive constituent]." Matter may be either sensible or intelligible. Compare INDIVIDUATIO.

Materialis, *material*; whatever is subject to any form is material to it; the formal always exceeds the material; thus the bodily transmutation is material to sensitive appetite; and the sensitive nature by which man has animality is material in him to the intellective nature, from which he has the specific differentia of man, rationality. Compare CAUSA MATERIALIS.

Materialiter, *materially*; a predicate accords with a subject materially when it accords by reason of matter or by reason of the subject itself; formally when it accords by reason of form, as fire is materially heavy, formally hot.

Mathematica, *mathematics*, includes the subject matter of the quadrivium, arithmetic, geometry, music, astronomy; it is a certain, not a probable, science, and its subject matter is therefore not the shifting changing things of experience.

There is some difference, however, concerning what its
subject matter is actually: in the augustinian tradition
numbers are eternal entities situated above the soul,
related to wisdom, to which the soul turns in contemplation; in the aristotelian tradition, there are no separate
eternal entities, but the changeless entities of mathematics
are arrived at by abstraction from the things of experience. According to Thomas Aquinas (*Sum. Theol.*
I, q. 5, a. 3 ad 4), "Mathematical things do not subsist
separated with respect to being . . . but mathematical
things are separated only according to reason, as they
are abstracted from motion and matter." They are
abstracted, however, only from sensible matter, and in
this they differ from metaphysical things; according to
Thomas (*In. lib. III de An.* lect. 8, 708), "Mathematical
things are abstracted from sensible matter, but not from
intelligible matter, in so far as continuous quantity remains in the understanding abstracted from sensible quality." Compare SCIENTIA.

MEDIUM, *middle, medium, mean*; according to Thomas two
things are to be considered in a medium, namely, the
reason why it is called a medium, and the act of the
medium. A thing is called medium from the fact that
it is between extremes; the act of the medium is to join
the extremes. Means may be physical, as in motion and
change; or logical, as when extremes are proved of each
other syllogistically by a mean; or moral, as virtue is
mean between extremes of vice.

MEMORIA, *memory* (MEMORATIVA VIRTUS, *memorative faculty*),
the faculty of the sensitive soul which is the treasury and
repository in which the species of the estimative faculty
are preserved, as the species of common sense are preserved in imagination; then used broadly to include all
faculties for retaining species. Man possesses not only
memory, or the sudden recollection of past things, which
all animals possess, but also reminiscence. As memory
is derived from perceptions, so from many memories
comes experience (*experimentum* or *experientia*), and
thence art (in the realm of generation or coming to be)
and science (in the realm of being).

MODUS, *mode*; mode means a certain determination of measure; broadly mode is an "adjacent" determination of
the thing, which is accomplished by the "adjection" of

an adjective name which determines the substantive, as when it is said the man is white, or by an adverb which determines the verb, as when it is said that the man runs well. It is taken as axiom that the mode of operating, of knowing, and of predicating follow the mode of being.

MOTUS, *motion, movement,* (κίνησις); the actualization of the potentially active and the potentially passive as such; it is of four sorts: substantial (which is not properly motion although it is mutation or change), quantitative, qualitative, local. Motion proper, in the last three senses, is change or mutation which is discernible in sensible things; it follows the conditions of the body; it is a continuum and requires the passage of time. Aristotle defines motion (*Phys.* III, c. 1, 201ª9-19), "And since each one of these kinds [of motion] is divided into that which is in actuality and that which is in potentiality, therefore motion will be the actuality of that which is in potentiality in the respect in which it is in potentiality. For example, the actuality [or perfection] of that which is alterable [that is, of that which can be changed in quality], in the respect in which it is alterable is alteration; and the actuality of that which is susceptible of augmentation and of its contrary, that is, that which is susceptible of diminution [that is, that which can be changed in quantity], for we do not have a single word common to the two, is augmentation and diminution; and the actuality of that which is generable and corruptible [that is, that which can be changed in substance] is generation and corruption; and the actuality of that which is susceptible of translation [that is, that which is mobile in place] is translation or locomotion. It is manifest that this is what motion is actually, since we say that that which is constructible, in the respect in which it is constructible, is in actuality as it is constructed, and this is construction or building; and in the same way too with learning, healing, rotation, jumping, adolescence, age." When something is moved, it has something actually and it is mobile, that is, it is in potentiality to having something immediately; for that reason motion has an indefinite character. According to Aristotle (*Phys.* III, c. 2, 201ᵇ28-32), "Now the reason why we think that motion is indeterminate is that it is impossible to place it either in the potentiality or in the actuality of any kind of thing as such; for there is no necessity that any thing change or be moved in quantity, either because it is potentially or because it is actually of this or that specified quantity. And motion, therefore, is seen to be an actuality, but an imperfect one." Motion is the actuality of a potentiality; the actuality can be effected only when a body which has the potentiality of being in motion receives the impact of a body which is in actual motion, in any of the senses of motion; it therefore becomes active by entering into motion, and at the same time is passive to the impact that keeps it in motion; these, however, are accidental aspects, for primarily motion is the actuality of the thing's potentiality. In the proper sense of passion, moreover, not every motion is a passion, but only alteration (or change of quality). According to Thomas (*In lib. III Sent.* d. 15, q. 2, a. 1 sol 1), "Because passion is a motion from one thing to another, not any motion is a passion, but only alteration properly speaking, because in that motion alone is something cast out from the thing and something impressed upon it, which is the definition of passion. For local motion is according to that which is outside the thing, that is, place; motion of augmentation, moreover, is according to this, that from that which is already, namely, from nutriment, that which is augmented is produced to greater quantity. That there be alteration, however, it is required on the part of the thing altered that it be a thing subsisting through itself, for otherwise it could not be the subject of motion, and that it be body, because only body is moved . . . and moreover that it have a nature subject to contrariety, because alteration is motion between contrary qualities." Compare PERFECTIO, PASSIO.

MOTUS NATURALIS, *natural motion*, which proceeds from a principle intrinsic to the thing, or extrinsic but according to its own natural inclination, as the growth of plants or the fall of bodies.

MOTUS VIOLENTUS, *violent motion*, which is from an extrinsic principle and contrary to the inclination of the thing, as a stone thrown upward or thrown downward with greater force than it would naturally fall.

MUTATIO, *mutation, change* ($\mu\epsilon\tau\alpha\beta o\lambda\dot{\eta}$); the principle of change is that something is constituted otherwise now than it was previously; there are four kinds of change: the three kinds of motion and substantial change, which is

instantaneous and therefore not properly motion although
it is sometimes called instantaneous motion. Ockham defines change (*Sum. Phys.* III, c. 3) in a nominal definition:
"That is changed which preexisting has some form or place
which previously it did not have, or which lacks a form
or place which previously it had." Compare MOTUS,
OPPOSITUM.

N

NATURA, *nature*; derived from *nasci* (compare φύσις) it signifies primarily the generation of living things; thence the
intrinsic principle of motion of a thing; nature is defined
therefore as the principle of motion in that which is
through itself and not accidentally; the intrinsic principle
of any motion or the intrinsic principle from which the
operations of the thing derive; nature is thus contrasted
to art as the principle and cause of motion which inheres
intrinsically and primarily as opposed to extrinsically and
accidentally. Therefore Thomas (*In lib. I Phys.* lect. 1)
defines nature as "the principle of motion and rest in that
in which it is. Natural science is concerning those things,
therefore, which have in themselves the principle of motion." Anything consequently which has in itself such a
principle of motion (or change) and rest may be said to
possess a nature of its own. The two meanings—Nature,
the principle, and all things which have natures—are
therefore usually found together properly without differentiation. Moreover all behavior, in either sense, accord·
ing to an intrinsic principle is "natural," for example, for
fire to rise, as distinct from having a tendency to rise is
natural (although fire neither is a nature nor has a nature). Aristotle's "revised" definition of nature is "the
form or species of such things as have within themselves
a principle of motion, such form or characteristic not being
separable from the things themselves save by reason."
(*Phys.* II, c. 1, 193ᵇ4-6). Finally, since the essence of
a thing is perfected through change by its form, the essence itself of the thing comes to be called its nature.
Thomas orders the various meaning according to generality
(*In lib. II Sent.* d. 37, q. 1, a. 1 sol.), "The name of nature
is used in many ways. For in the first way, nature is
used as that which is related commonly to all things that

are, as nature is defined as all that which can be seized in any manner by the understanding. In the second way, it is proper only to substances; and thus nature is said to be that which can act or suffer. In the third way, nature is spoken of as that which is the principle of motion or rest in those things in which it is essentially and not accidentally. In the fourth way, each thing informing with a specific difference is called a nature." Compare VIS, RATIO.

NECESSARIUM, *necessary*; that is necessary whose nature is such that it is impossible for it not to be.

NEGATIO, *negation*, division in so far as it signifies the separation of things.

NOMEN, *word, significative word, noun, name* (the latter in the sense in which Hobbes and a long line of english logicians used the term), that is, the grammatical logical unit as opposed to the spoken word (vox). Boethius defined name as a significative word, and Thomas pointed out that five things are asserted in the definition of *name* or *noun*: first the genus, *word* (*vox*) as it is distinguished from other sounds; second, the first differentia, *significative*; third, the second differentia, *at will* (that is the signification of the name is by human institution at will); fourth, the third differentia *without time* (the noun differs from the verb in that the latter involves time); fifth, the fourth differentia, *of which no part is significative apart from the noun as a whole.*

NOMINATIO, *nomination*, the imposition of a name.

NOTIO, *notion, conception*; according to Thomas (*Sum. Theol.* I, q. 87, a. 4 ob. 3; cp. ibid. ad 3), "It does not seem that there can be other notions of things in the soul except either the essences of the things known or their likenesses."

NOTITIA, *knowledge, cognition, idea*; four senses of *notitia* are enumerated (Thomas, *Quaest. Quodl.* VII, q. 1, a. 4 concl.): the cognoscitive nature itself, the cognoscitive power of that nature, the cognoscitive state, and finally the act of cognition itself. In the first sense, knowledge is not in the substance of the mind, like an accident in a subject, but essentially and consubstantially, as it is said that rational is in living, and living is in being. In the other three senses, knowledge can be considered either as compared to the knower (and thus it is present in the knower like an accident in a subject and it does not ex-

ceed the subject because it is never found to be present in
any thing except a mind) or as it is compared to the
knowable (and from this point of view it does not have
something in which it is but something of which it is).

NUMERUS, *number,* number is multitude measured by one; an
aggregation of unities. Division of the continuous is accomplished by number; the continuous, therefore, (such
as the line) is capable of division indefinitely and is, in
this sense, unlimited or infinite, that is, not by virtue of
that which is numbered or that which is numerable, but
by virtue of that by which it is numbered. Members of
the same species have no proper differentiae from each
other, but are distinguishable as *different only in number;*
properties moreover may be shown to belong not only to
individuals the same in species, but also to a single individual, one in number. In the augustinian tradition
numbers were associated in their eternity and immutability
with the objects of wisdom (compare above, vol. I, pp.
46-49).

O

OBIECTIVUM, *objective* (in the mind), *formal.*

OBIECTUM, *object,* that concerning which any power or discipline is exercised; it is related as matter to action;
according to Thomas (*Sum. Theol.* I, q. 1, a. 7 concl.),
"That it is properly said to be the object of any power
or condition, under the reason of which all things are
referred to the power or the condition, as man and stone
are referred to sight in so far as they are colored, wherefore that which is colored is the proper object of sight";
to be distinguished into material and formal object, as in
the case above, man or stone are the material objects of
sight, but colored is its formal object, since man and stone
are referred to sight in so far as they are colored.

OPERATIO, *operation,* any act of a thing even though it does
not proceed outside the thing, as to understand, is an
operation of the intellect. Compare ACTIO, FACTIO.

OPINIO, *opinion,* the assent of the understanding to any proposition, whether from the terms themselves or from a
probable middle term, together with a fear of the opposed
positions. Opinion is infirm knowledge (*cognitio*) because
it judges that a thing can be other than it is, since it

knows the thing by a reason situated outside the thing itself.

OPPOSITIO, *opposition, contradictory*, consists in the presence and absence, or the affirmation and negation of the same thing; Aristotle says (*An. Pri.* I, c. 5, 27ª29-30), "By *an opposite manner* I mean, if the universal statement is negative [or privative] the particular is affirmative [or predicative], or if the universal is affirmative, the particular is negative." This, however, is properly contradictory opposition. "By contradictory opposition," Aristotle says (*An. Pri.* II, c. 8, 59ᵇ9-11), "I mean the opposition of *to all* to *not to all*, and of *to some* to *to none*; by contrary opposition the opposition of *to all* to *to none*, and of *to some* to *not to some*." More broadly it is customary to distinguish (see Aristotle, *Met.* V, c. 10, 1018ª20-1018ᵇ19) four types of opposition: the *contradictory* (the opposition of a being to its negation, as white and not-white), the *privative* and *possessive* (the opposition of a being to its privation, as sight and blindness), the *contrary* (the opposition of two beings as absolute, as sweet and bitter), the *relative* (the opposition of two beings respective to each other, as father and son). The extremes from which generation and dissolution take place are opposites. Aristotle states the relations between the kinds of opposition (*Met.* X, c. 4, 1055ᵇ1-29), "Now if the kinds of opposition are contradiction and privation and contrariety and relation, and of these the first is contradiction, and contradiction admits of no intermediate, while contraries admit of one, clearly contradiction and contrariety are not the same. But privation is a kind of contradiction: for what suffers privation, either in general or in some determinate way, is either that which is quite incapable of having some attribute or that which, being of such a nature as to have it, has it not; for we speak of it in many senses, which have been distinguished elsewhere. Privation, therefore, is a kind of contradiction, either in a determinate power or in some power conceived together with the receptive material. This is the reason why, while contradiction does not admit of an intermediate, privation sometimes does; for everything is equal or not equal, but not everything is equal or unequal, save only in that which is receptive of equality. If, then, the generations of matter itself start from contraries, and proceed either from a species and the possession of a species or from some privation of the species and form, clearly all contrariety will be a kind of privation. But perhaps not all privation is contrariety, the reason being that that which suffers privation may suffer it in many ways. For the extremes from which changes proceed are contraries. And this is obvious also by induction. For every contrariety involves the privation of one of the contraries. But not all cases are alike; inequality is the privation of equality, and unlikeness of likeness, and vice of virtue. But the cases differ as has been said; for in the one case the thing only suffers privation, in another case it does so at a certain time or in a certain part, as at a certain age or in the principal part, or throughout. This is why in some cases there is a mean (there are men who are neither good nor bad), and in others there is not (a number must be either odd or even). Further, some contraries have their subject defined, other have not.— Therefore it is evident that one of the contraries is always stated according to privation; but it is enough if this is true of the first—that is, the generic—contraries, that is, the one and the many; for the others can be reduced to these."

OPPOSITUM, *opposite*; attributes which cannot be present at the same time in that which is susceptive of both are said to be opposed or opposite.

ORATIO, *discourse*; the derivation is frequently given from *oris ratio*, reason of mouth; signifies therefore the expression of any act of reason by any effect of speech. Since it is the property of reason to compound and divide, and to proceed discursively from one thing to another taking note of their causes, discourse expresses these processes in words; the syllogism is discourse which results from the latter property of reason.

P

PARS, *part*; that into which the whole is divided and which is related to the whole as matter; distinguished into quantitative parts (those into which numbers or quantity is divided) and essential parts (as matter and form from which the natural whole is constituted, or genus and differentia from which the species of the thing exists).

PARTICIPATIO, *participation*; to take part in, in the various sense of part, as, for example, that which has fire but is not fire is fiery by participation. According to Thomas (*In lib. Boet. de Hebd.* c. 2), "To participate is, as it were, to take part, and so when something receives particularly that which pertains to something else, it is said universally to participate in it, as man is said to participate in animal because man does not have the reason of animality according to its entire community; and for the same reason Socrates participates in man; and similarly too a subject participates in an accident and matter participates in form, because the substantial or accidental form, which is common with respect to its reason, is determined to this or that subject; and similarly an effect is said to participate in its cause, especially when it is not adequated to the power of its cause, as if we were to say that air participates in the light of the sun, because it does not receive it with the clarity with which it is in the sun." According to Aristotle (*Top.* IV, c. 1, 121ª12), "*To partake* is defined as *to take on the definition* of that which is partaken." According to Anselm (see above, vol. I, p. 153) nothing is true except by participation in truth; Eriugena holds (see above, vol. I, p. 134) that since man is the image of God, whatever is predicated of God essentially can be predicated of man by participation. Compare DIVISIO.

PARTICULARE, *particular*; so called because the common nature is "particulated" in it, since the common nature can be in many and be the reason of each, as man is a particular in the species humanity. Compare INDIVIDUUM.

PASSIO, *passion*; strictly the undergoing or reception of a destructive quality, as excessive heat. As a category (compare PATI) it is the act of the patient in virtue of which it is patient, or the receiving of the effects from the agent, as the receiving of the form of fire in the matter of wood, or of heat in the hand. The emotions are passions of the appetite, that is, the emotion of the sensitive appetite caused by the apprehension of good or evil together with some mutation which is not natural to the body, such as love and hatred. According to Thomas (*In lib. III Sent.* d. 15, q. 2, a. 1 sol. 1), "It is required by the nature of passion that the quality introduced be extraneous and the quality forced out be connatural, and

this is so because passion imports a certain victory of the
agent over the patient; but all that which is conquered is
as it were drawn beyond its proper bounds to alien
bounds; and therefore alterations which occur beyond the
nature of the thing altered are most properly called passions, as sicknesses more properly than states of health."
Aristotle says (de An. II, 5, 417^{a}14-417^{b}16), "In the first
place, then, we speak as if to be passive and to be moved
is the same as to act and to move. For motion is a certain act, though imperfect, as is stated elsewhere. But
all things are passive and are moved by an active and
actual being. Whence it is that that which is passive is
passive to that which is like it; but on the other hand it
is passive to that which is unlike it, as we have stated.
For that is passive which is unlike, but after the passion
it is like that which has acted on it. . . . To be passive
or to suffer, however, is not simple in significance. Sometimes it means a kind of corruption by a contrary; sometimes it is rather the preservation of that which is in
potentiality by that which is in actuality and like it, being
constituted as potentiality is constituted in relation to
actuality. For one who speculates becomes one possessed
of knowledge, which clearly either is not alteration [that
is, change in quality] (for the addition is in the one himself and in actuality) or else it is another sort of alteration. Wherefore it is not good usage to say that the wise
man, when he is wise, is altered, just as the builder,
when he builds is not altered. It is not right, therefore,
to give that the name of teaching, which leads to actuality
from that which is in potentiality in respect to knowing
and being wise, but it should have some other name. But
he who, beginning from that which is in potentiality,
learns and accepts knowledge from him who is actually
and is learned and teaches, either must not be said to
suffer or be passive, or else there are two kinds of alteration, one a mutation which is into privative dispositions
and one which is into conditions (or habits) and nature."
Compare ALTERATIO, MOTUS.

PATI, to suffer, to undergo, to receive, as opposed to facere,
to make or do; to be passive, passion, the tenth of the
categories. Compare PASSIO.

PATIENS, patient in the sense of that which is passive to or
undergoes an action.

PERFECTIO, *perfection*; Matthew of Aquasparta, on the authority of Aristotle (see selection above, q. 2 ad 20),
states the order of perfections and of motions to perfection, "Some things are whole in goodness; and these
acquire their perfection with no movement, such as God.
Others are very close to integral goodness; and those
acquire their perfection with very few movements. There
are others which are ordered to great goodness, but are
none the less removed from that perfection: therefore,
they acquire their perfection with many movements.
There are some, which are ordered to slight perfection;
and those of this sort arrive at it with few movements.
Some to no perfection; and they are immobile, because
motion is for the acquiring of some perfection. The first
is God; the second is the order of Angels; the third is
the order of rational creatures, such as men; the fourth
is the order of brute animals; the fifth is the order of
higher elements; in the last and lowest place is earth."

PERFECTIVUM, *perfective*; the habit of any power is perfective.

PER SE, *essentially, substantially, through itself*; that exists *per
se* which does not have its being in anything else as in a
subject, therefore any substance exists *per se*. *A se*, on
the other hand, means that which requires no cause that
it exist: God alone is *a se*. From these expressions derive
the terms *perseity* (denying any dependence on a subject)
and *aseity* (denying even dependence on any producing
cause, or *abaliety*). *Per se* is therefore contrasted to *per
accidens, accidentally*. According to Thomas (*Quaest.
disp. de Pot.* q. 10, a. 4 concl.), "Whatever is present *per
se* in a thing either is from its essence or follows from
essential principles, from which principles is the first root
of the distinction of things . . . Everything which is present *per accidens*, since it is extraneous to its nature, must
accord with it because of some exterior cause." Therefore
essentially refers to that which agrees with the thing from
the nature of the thing itself or from the intrinsic principles of the thing, thus the attributes which accord essentially with man are his essential predicates, as rational,
free, and those which follow necessarily from the nature
of man, as being biped. On the contrary *per accidens*
indicates that which accords with the thing accidentally
and not necessarily, or that which accords with the thing

as if by chance, thus man is accidentally white, noble, pious.

PERITIA, *expertness, learning, experience.*

PERSONA, *person;* according to Boethius (*Con. Eut.* c. 3), derived from *persona,* mask in a theatrical performance, and used to translate the greek ὑπόστασις; however, since it seems to have been used first by Tertullian, it is probably derived first from *persona* in its legal sense. Boethius defines it as "the individual substance of a rational nature"; Anselm (*Monol.* c. 78) restates the definition reserving substance for contrast to person: "Person is spoken of only in respect of an individual rational nature; and substance is spoken of in respect of individuals, which subsist most of all in plurality." Person is individual since it must be a completed substance, existing through itself, whereas an essence may be common to many; it must be rational to distinguish it from subject or *suppositum;* thus there is a divine, an angelic, and a human person, but no person of horse or stone, *persona* adding over and above *suppositum* a dignity and excellence derived from the intellectual nature.

PERSUASIO, *persuasion,* rhetorical device, operating by enthymeme or example.

PHANTASIA, *phantasy,* the internal sense perceptive of objects, when they are absent, which have previously been perceived by the external senses; made up of common sense and imagination; thence properly imagination alone; and finally the *impressions* of the internal sense as opposed to the *species* or images of the external sense.

PONERE, *to affirm, to posit.*

POSITIO, *affirmation, position, thesis,* a proposition which, although it is evident once the terms have been explained, none the less requires some explication and is proper to some science. A *positio,* therefore, is taken as the opinion or the hypothesis which is adduced as the middle to an argument, and which is agitated in discussion; in this sense a *premiss* or *supposition.* According to Thomas (*In lib. I An. Post.* lect. 4) one of the two immediate principles of the syllogism: a thesis "cannot be demonstrated, and therefore is said to be immediate, nor is it necessary that any one who is to be taught, that is, who should be taught in demonstrative science, have it, that is, perceive it with the mind, or assent to it." Compare the other immediate principle of the syllogism, PROPOSITIO PER SE NOTA.

POSSE, *to be able*, that is, to have potentially as opposed to having actually.

POSSIBILITAS, *possibility*; the principle and cause of mutation is the possibility of the thing; in God there is no admixture of possibility. Possibility and impossibility were suggested by Eriugena as additions to the ten categories of Aristotle. Frequently, however, *possibilitas* was used instead of *potentia* as a translation for the aristotelian δύναμις. Compare POTENTIA.

POSTPRAEDICAMENTUM, *postpredicament, postcategory*, categories which are consequences of the ten categories properly so called; they are five: opposition, priority and posteriority, simultaneity, motion, and condition (i.e. *habitus* in the sense that all nine of the categories involve condition or state, rather than the special meaning of the eighth category).

POTENTIA, *power, potency, potentiality*; means primarily the principle of an action; but secondarily is transferred so that that too which receives the action of an agent is said to have power. According to Aristotle (*Met.* IX c. 1, 1046ª10-19) the various kinds of potentialities are "principles or starting points and they can all be reduced to one primary kind, that is, the principle of change in another thing, in so far as it is other. For one kind of potentiality is of suffering, which in the thing itself which is passive is the principle of passive change by something else in so far as it is something else. Another kind is the condition of impassibility to change which is for the worse or toward destruction by something else in so far as it is something else, i.e. by the principle of change. In all these definitions there is present the principle of the first potentiality. But further these potentialities are referred either only to doing or to suffering, or to doing and suffering well. Wherefore in the principles of these there are present in some manner the prior principles of potentialities." Potency simply (*potentia*) signifies the non-existence of a thing and its indifference to being or non-being; its power or faculty (*potestas* or *facultas*) denotes that which already has its being and has through itself an order to action. Therefore, the potential in no manner is, but power lacks being only by a second actuality, which signifies action, because it can be and be understood without the action of which it is itself the principle, but it is by the first actuality which signifies being (for it cannot be understood not to be) which is the principle of the power itself. Yet it is proper to list, as Bonaventura does, the powers or potencies of the soul as memory, understanding, will. Power or potentiality moreover, is distinguished from *habitus* (*habit* or *condition*) in that the latter is not naturally implanted, like potentiality, though based on natural principles. Power, furthermore, gives the operation (as intellect gives understanding); habit gives better operation (as logic leads to better understanding). According to Bonaventura (*In lib. I Sent.*, d. 3, q. 2, a. 2, q. 1 ad arg.), "Habit is that by which power is in actuality." According to Aristotle potentiality is of two sorts (*de An.* II, c. 5, 417ᵃ21-417ᵇ2): "A distinction must be drawn with respect to potentiality and actuality, for we are using them at present absolutely [that is, without qualification]. For it is thus in the case of knowing anything, as if we say that a man is learned because he is of the number of those who know and have knowledge. But it is also as we say that he is already learned who knows grammar. These two men, however, are not in potentiality in the same way: the former is in potentiality because he is a genus of a certain sort and because he is matter [that is, related as matter to form]; the latter, because if he wishes he is able to consider [that which he knows], unless something external interfere. He, however, who is at the present moment considering is in actuality and is learned in the proper sense of the term, that is, learned, as of this letter A. The first two therefore are potentially learned. But the former is altered [that is, changed qualitatively] by teaching, and often he is changed from the contrary condition; the latter, however, because he has sense or grammar, does not act [that is, does not pass into actuality] because of the fact that he is excited to acting, but in another manner and because he had not yet acquired that which was previously a condition."

POTESTAS, *power*. Compare POTENTIA.

PRAEDICABILE, *predicable*, the five (or according to Aristotle, four) common notions through which, when known, it is shown how anything is predicated of anything else.

Aristotle lists the four, definition, property, genus, accident, which the middle ages expanded, following Porphyry, to species, differentia, genus, property, accident.

PRAEDICABILIS ET SUBIICIBILIS, *predicable and subjectible*; a species is subjectible as it is considered with respect to the higher genus under which it is contained; predicable as it is considered with respect to the inferior individuals of which it is predicated.

PRAEDICAMENTA, *the categories*, defined by Thomas (?) (*Sum. Log.* II, c. 1) as "certain predicables ordered in the predicamental order"; taken in the middle ages as the ten categories of Aristotle, substance, quantity, quality, relation, place, time, position, state (or habit), action, passion. The ten categories indicate the most universal classes to which all things can be reduced, and therefore show all the attributes that can be predicated properly of a subject. There are ten because there are ten, and no more, questions which can be raised concerning any given individual. The categories, of course, cannot be defined (although they may be described by induction), since definition requires a genus, and the categories fall under no genus.

PRAEDICAMENTALE, *predicamental, categorical*.

PRAEDICARE, *to predicate*; for one thing to be predicated of another is for that thing to be affirmed of that other; in its strict sense only second substances are predicated of first substances, whereas the accidents *inhere* or are present in substance.

PRAEDICATIO, *predication*; according to Thomas (*de Ente et Essentia* c. 4), "Predication is that which is completed by the action of the understanding compounding and dividing, having none the less as foundation in fact the very unity of those things which are affirmed one of the other."

PRAXIS, *praxis*, actions or operations considered in their bearing on good and evil, *practical* activities.

PRINCIPIUM, *principle* (ἀρχή), that from which a thing proceeds and has its origin in any way whatever, whether with dependence or not. Thomas says, contrasting cause and principle (*Sum. Theol.* I, q. 33, a. 1 ad 1), "Principle is more common than cause, as cause is more common than element; for the first term or even the first part of a thing is said to be a principle, but not a cause. . . . The word cause seems to import a diversity of substance and

a dependence of one on the other, which the word principle does not seem to import. For in all kinds of cause
there is always found a distance between the cause and
that of which it is the cause, according to some perfection
or power; but we use the word principle also of those
things which have no difference of this sort, but only
according to a certain order, as when we say, the point
is the principle of the line, or even when we say the first
part of the line is the principle of the line." Elements
differ from the principles which constitute natural bodies,
furthermore, in that principles are not given prior to the
composite and no body is constituted of them, whereas
elements flow from the principles, form and matter, and
therefore they are constituted bodies, but they are such
that they cannot be divided or resolved into other bodies,
but other bodies are resolved into them. Form, matter,
and privation are the three principles of the natural composite, by which change is explained.

PRIVATIO, *privation*, a determinate incapacity; absence in a
subject of that which naturally belongs to it then, there,
and under those conditions, as blindness in man; contrasted with negation, absence from a subject of that
which the subject is unable to receive, as absence of sight
in a stone. One of the three principles of the natural
composite; form and matter being the other two. According to Aristotle (*Met.* IX, c. 1, 1046ª32-36), "Privation is spoken of in many ways: for it means that which
does not have something and that which is naturally apt
to have it, if it does not have it, either absolutely or when
it is naturally apt to have it, and either in some particular way, e.g. perfectly, or only in some certain mode.
And in certain cases if things which are by nature apt
to have something, by violence do not have it, we say
that they suffer privation." Compare OPPOSITIO.

PROPORTIO, *proportion* (in modern usage *ratio*), a certain order
between two terms, as a proportion between arithmetical
quantities is called a relation (*habitudo*) or order between
equal or unequal numbers.

PROPORTIONALITAS, *proportionality* (in modern usage *proportion*), a certain order or likeness between two proportions,
that is, proportionality is a proportion of proportions.

PROPOSITIO, *proposition*, a proposition is the "subjective" part
of a statement (*enuntiatio*), in which one thing is

predicated of another; that is, it is called a proposition in relation to argumentation. The proposition is the principle of the syllogism; likewise propositions may be called the matter of the conclusion as terms are the matter of the proposition.

PROPOSITIO PER SE NOTA, *proposition known through itself*, one to which the intellect assents from an understanding of the terms alone, first principle, axiom. Also called PROPOSITIO IMMEDIATA, *immediate proposition*; defined by Aristotle as a proposition to which another is not prior. The *thesis* and the immediate proposition are the two first immediate principles of the syllogism, but whereas the thesis cannot be demonstrated and need not be assented to, the immediate proposition (according to Thomas, *In lib. I An. Post.* lect. 4) "must be had in mind and must be assented to by any one who is to be taught. And it is manifest that there are certain principles which are of such sort (as is proved in Book IV of the *Metaphysics* with respect to the principle that *an affirmation and its negation are not true at the same time*) the contrary of which no one can believe with his mind although he may state it with his mouth." The certitude of other propositions must be based on propositions of this sort. "Any proposition the predicate of which is in the reason of the subject, is immediate and known through itself, so far as it is of itself. But the terms of some propositions are such that they are in the knowledge of all, as that which is and one [*ens et unum*] and others which are of that which is as that which is. For that which is is the first concept of the understanding. Wherefore it is necessary that such propositions, not only in themselves, but also with respect to us, be held as known through themselves, as that *it is impossible that the same thing be and not be*, and that *the whole is greater than its part*, and like propositions. Wherefore all principles of science of this sort are taken from the *Metaphysics* the study of which is to consider that which is absolutely and those things which are of that which is. But certain propositions are immediate, the terms of which are not known to all. Wherefore although the predicate is in the reason of the subject, nevertheless since the definition of the subject is not known to all, it is not necessary that such propositions be conceded by all. As the proposition, *all right angles are equal*, as it is in itself, is known through itself or immediate, because equality falls in the definition of right angle. For a right angle is one which a right line makes falling on another right line, so that from either part of the angle equals are returned. And therefore principles of this sort are accepted with some thesis or position. And there is another manner, in which some propositions are called suppositions. For there are certain propositions which can be proved only by the principle of another science, and therefore it is necessary that they be supposed in this science, although they are proved by the principles of another science, as geometry supposes that the drawing of a straight line is from point to point, and natural philosophy proves it, showing that between any two points there is a straight line medium." Immediate propositions sometimes consist in first and common terms, as that which is and that which is not, equal and unequal, whole and part; these are first and immediate propositions, as *the same thing cannot both be and not be, things equal to one and the same thing are equal to each other*. Immediate propositions which are concerning posterior and less common terms, are second with respect to these first, as that *the triangle is a figure*, and that *man is an animal*.

PROPRIETAS, *property*, that which follows from the essence of a thing, as heat from fire, and which is distinguished from the essence only by mind.

PROPRIUM, *proper to, peculiar to, property*, one of the five universal attributes or predicables. That is proper to anything which accords with it alone, though it does not necessarily pertain to its essence, as risible is a property of man; a universal notion which follows necessarily from the nature once constituted in a species, and by the nature is predicated of many things different in number. A property accords with the given species alone and always, though in a given situation and at a given time there may be accidental properties. Property is unlike differentia, in that it is not completive of substance nor a part of substance, but only an aptitude of it, and therefore unsuited to divide species from species in a given genus.

PROVIDENTIA, *providence, foresight*.

Q

QUADRIVIUM, *quadrivium*, the mathematical portion of the seven arts; the four arts or disciplines, arithmetic, geometry, music, astronomy. Compare MATHEMATICA.

QUALITAS, *quality*; broadly, quality may be described (categories cannot be defined) as that according to which we answer the question *how?*; whatever perfects or determines substance in any way, and thus any mode, such as union, and any accident, such as paternity, can be called a quality. The third of the ten categories, as whiteness; it is the differentia of substance and the principle of knowing the thing. It is customary to distinguish four species of quality: disposition, natural power or impotence, passion, form. Quality is based on quantity as color is based on surface and figure on line or surface. Quality admits of degree in having; change in quality is called alteration; quality alone admits of likeness and unlikeness. Compare, therefore, ALTERATIO, SIMILITUDO, ASSIMILARI.

QUANDO, *when, time*, the sixth of the aristotelian categories. Compare TEMPUS.

QUANTITAS, *quantity*; quantity is the measure of substance; that according to which we answer the question *how much?*; it consists in a certain multiplication of parts; that by which a corporeal thing is capable of dimensions and can be increased or diminished; it is however not susceptible of degrees in having. Quantity may be continuous (as line or any magnitude) or discrete (as number or any multitude). Quantity alone admits of equality and inequality; change in quantity is augmentation or diminution. The second of the aristotelian categories, that nearest to substance. Compare AEQUALITAS, ADAEQUATIO.

QUIDDITAS, *quiddity*, the very entity of the thing, considered in relation to the definition explaining *what* (*quid*) the thing is. As Thomas says (*de Ente et Essentia* c. 1), "Since that by which a thing is constituted in its proper genus or species is what we signify by the definition indicating *what* the thing is, therefore it is that the name of essence is changed by philosophers to the name of quiddity."

Quies, *rest*; defined by Aristotle (*Phys.* III, c. 2, 202ª 4) as "absence of motion in that to which motion is possible."

R

Raptus, *rapture*; defined in its general sense as motion of anything beyond its natural or voluntary inclination by an extrinsic principle; particularly the direct vision of God and of divine things, the highest of the seven grades of interior experience according to Bacon. St. Paul experienced raptus according to Bonaventura, and in that was possibly (according to Bonaventura), unique among men after the fall, Moses and St. Francis being the only exceptions that suggest themselves. Augustine distinguished two kinds of raptus, one in which the mind is drawn away (*rapitur*) from sensible things to an imaginary vision, another in which the mind is drawn away from sense and imagination at the same time to an intellectual vision, through the intellect understanding God by some intelligible immissions or through the intellect seeing God in essence.

Ratio, *reason, nature, relation, principle, ground, argument, definition, criterion*, (λόγος). Sometimes used as identical with *intellectus*, then divided into speculative and practical reason; sometimes taken for the action of the understanding, most of all for the discursive act of understanding. According to Thomas (*In lib. I Sent.* d. 33, q. 1, a. 1 ad 3), "Reason is taken in two senses, for sometimes that is called reason which is in the reasoner, namely, the act itself of reason, or the power or faculty which is reason; but sometimes reason is the name of an intention, whether that according to which it signifies the definition of a thing, as reason is a definition, or as reason is called argumentation." There are according to Thomas (*In lib. I An. Post.* lect. 1) three acts of reason; the first two are acts of reason in the respect that reason is a kind of understanding: (1) the action of the intellect understanding indivisibles or incomplexes according to which action it understands what the thing is or its quiddity; in this there can be no error, truth, or falsity (this is called *information of the understanding*; this act of reason is the subject matter of the *Categories*), (2) the operation of the intellect

compounding and dividing, from which operation true
and false proceed (this is the subject matter of the
on Interpretation), (3) the act of reason according to
which it is reason proper, that is, the proceeding from
one thing to another that through what is known one may
come to knowledge of the unknown (this is the subject
matter of the remaining books of logic). Reason, as
an intention, may therefore mean the definition of the
thing, as, for example, in the *Categories* (1, 1ᵃ), "Things
are said to be univocal the names of which are the same
and also the *definitions* of the subjects accommodated
to the name are the same." Since it may mean definition,
reason is used also for final cause, or for formal cause,
or finally for any other kind of cause. Reason, as a
faculty of the soul, is the third power of the soul (compare Boethius, *In Isag. Por.*, 2 ed.; see above, vol. I,
pp. 71–72); it uses the vegetative and sensitive powers
as its servants, and is "occupied in the very firm conception of present things, or in the understanding of
absent things, or in the investigation of unknown things";
according to Boethius there are two parts to the logical
discipline or art of reasoning: dialectic or the art of
judging and topic or the art of discovering.

RATIO REI, *the essence of the thing*; the *formal reason of
the thing* consists in the definition of it or in the essential
attributes as they are conceived by us, that is, as they
are abstracted from particular conditions; the *objective
reason of the thing* is that being which the thing has
in the mode of object known.

RATIO SEMINALIS, *seminal reason*; the reasons, implanted by
God in the beginning, from which the things of the
world are, at their appropriate time and under appropriate
circumstances, generated.

RATIO AETERNA, *eternal reason*; according to Augustine,
the eternal reasons are the sempiternal truths of God,
in accordance with which things are made and by which,
above our minds, we are guided in thought.

RATIONABILITER, *reasonably*.

RATIOCINATIO, *reasoning, ratiocination*, knowledge mediately
by proceeding from the understanding of one thing to
another, to the end of understanding intelligible truth;
the inquisition of reason, the investigation of cause in
the thing caused. According to Albert (*de Intellectu*

et Intelligibili I, tract. 3, c. 2; see above, vol. I, p. 372),
"The condition of the principles is said to be *under-*
standing and the condition of the conclusion *knowledge,*
and the process from principles to conclusion is called
reasoning." Contrasted with *intellection,* which is the
immediate apprehension of intelligible truth.

RATIONALE, *the rational;* in two senses: everything intellectual
(proper to God and the angels) and knowing by discourse (the differentia of man).

RATIONALITER, *rationally.*

RECIPERE, *to receive,* to undergo any accident or transmutation; the term or end of receiving is *having* or *habitus.*

RECTIFICATUM, *rectified.*

REFLEXE, *reflexively;* an act is affirmed of a thing reflexively
when affirmed of the thing as conceived by us, as we
know reflexively when our knowledge is turned on the
knowledge of the thing already had. Thus one would
know directly that iron is heavy, reflexively that it is
true that iron is heavy. According to Ockham (see
selection above, *Quodl.* II, q. 12 concl.), "That act is
called direct by which the understanding understands
an object outside the soul, and that act reflex by which
this direct act is understood."

RELATIO, *relation,* the order of one thing to another; the
fourth of the ten categories. Compare AD ALIQUID.

REMINISCENTIA, *reminiscence;* the inquisition of something
which has fallen from memory; in addition to memory,
which man shares with other animals (that is, the sudden
recollection of past things) reminiscence is, as it were,
the syllogistic inquiry into the memory of past things
according to their individual intentions; the faculty by
which the intentions and phantasms of hidden and re-
condite things are educed for the understanding of sensible things.

REMITTI, *to remit,* to decrease in grades as to intensify is to
increase.

REMOTIO, *denial.*

REMOVERE, *to remove, to deny.*

RES, *thing,* according to Avicenna, the quiddity or essence
of that which is (*ens*). According to Thomas (*In lib.*
I Sent. d. 25, q. 1, a. 4 sol.), "There are two points
to be considered in a thing, namely, the quiddity and

reason of it and also the being of it, and the name thing
is taken from the quiddity. And since the quiddity can
have being both in the singular which is external to the
mind and as it is apprehended in the mind by the intellect,
therefore the name thing applies to both, to that which
is in the mind, as thing [*res*] is derived from knowing
[*reor*], and to that which is outside the mind, as thing
is spoken of as something known [*ratum*] and firm in
nature." Again (*In lib. II Sent.* d. 37, q. 1, a. 1 sol.),
"The name thing is taken in two senses. For that is
called a thing absolutely which has a known and firm
being in nature; *thing* is used in this way, taking the
name thing to indicate it as it has a certain quiddity
or essence; but it is called *that which is* [*ens*], as it
has being. But because a thing is cognoscible through its
essence, the name of thing is transsumed to all that
which can fall in cognition or understanding, in the sense
that thing [*res*] is derived from knowing [*reor*], and
in this manner things of reason [*res rationis*] are spoken
of, which do not have a known being in nature, according to which mode negations and privations can be called
things too, as likewise they are called things of the
reason [*entia rationis*]."

RESPECTUS, *in respect to*, the relation of thing to the principle
from which it derives, as of creature to creator; *relation.*

RESOLVERE, *to resolve*, the logical process of separating terms
previously conjoined and joining terms previously separated; the physical process of separating the elements
of a compound.

S

SAPIENTIA, *wisdom*, (σοφία) knowledge of eternal things.
According to Thomas (*Sum. Theol.* Ia IIae, q. 57, a. 2
concl.), "Wisdom pertains to the understanding of eternal
things"; according to Aristotle (*Met.* I, c. 1, 981^b 29) it
is concerned with first causes and principles. Wisdom
considers the most lofty causes, and therefore properly it
judges and orders all things, because perfect and universal judgment can not be had save by resolution to
first causes. Boethius defines it (see above, vol. I, p.
119) as "the comprehension of the truth of things which
are and which draw as by lot their immutable substance."

Scibile, *knowable*, that which can be known or be the object of science.

Scientia, *knowledge, scientific knowledge, science,* (ἐπιστήμη) any true and certain knowledge derived from certain but not demonstrable principles, or any certain and evident knowledge of things through their proper causes; understood broadly, all the arts may be called sciences. Strictly it is discourse from principles to conclusions, involving a firm inhesion and intellectual vision, for it has a certitude which proceeds from the understanding of principles. According to Aristotle and his followers, science in itself is to be considered in the category of relation, knowledge being a correlative of that which is known, with this peculiarity, that one of the correlatives (the thing) can exist without the other (knowledge), but there can be no knowledge without the thing; this notwithstanding that correlatives ordinarily come into existence simultaneously (see Aristotle *Cat.* 7, 7ᵇ 22–34). Strictly then (as, for example, according to the pseudo-Grosseteste, above, vol. I, p. 304), knowledge is a passion or a perfection resulting from the union of something intelligible and an intellectual power; that is the fashion in which its coming into being or generation in the understanding is to be considered; in terms of its actuality, it is a condition (*habitus*) by which the true is distinguished from the false, and one of them judged to be true. The pseudo-Grosseteste distinguishes the manners and kinds of condition (see above, vol. I, 307): "Knowledge is either the name of the condition by which the understanding speculates easily what is true, and what false, and understands actually—and thus it is properly called *knowledge*—for condition is midway between potentiality and actuality, by which potentiality passes easily into actuality; or else it is that act of speculating or understanding—and thus it is properly called *consideration*; or it is the disposition to the act of knowing or the condition in learning, whether the learner begins to know by his own exercise, and that is called *investigation*, or instructed by some one else, which is properly called in the person teaching, *doctrine*, in the person learning, *discipline*." According to the same writer, following in the distinctions of Aristotle, knowledge may be simple or complex: simple if it apprehends the unity or quiddity of the thing immediately, complex if it handles the quiddity by definition and proceeds discursively by propositions. There is also an apparently complex knowledge, which is our reconstruction of the uncreated understanding or God, and which is in reality most simple. Knowledge can be either through the cause (knowledge *propter quid*) or through the effect (knowledge *quia*); the first proceeds from principles known first and in themselves; the second is dialectical and concerned with joining the particulars of experience to universals, to the end of informing knowledge and action: it is called particular knowledge. There are, in most of the philosophers since Aristotle, three speculative sciences, which are capable of absolute certainty: metaphysics (which deals with things wholly abstracted from matter and motion) mathematics (which deals with things abstracted from motion but not abstracted from all kinds of matter) and physics (which deals with matter and motion). The particular sciences deal with the intentions of things (dialectic and demonstrative science) or of speech (grammar, rhetoric); these include those sciences of the particular which are most usually called practical sciences: ethics and politics. Compare ARS, PROPOSITIO PER SE NOTA.

SCIENTIA EXPERIMENTALIS, *experimental science*; according to Bacon the one way to certainty. Compare EXPERIMENTUM.

SCIENTIA PRACTICA, *practical science*, that is, *operative*; ethics according to Bacon is the practical science; he restricts practical to that having to do with moral and civil science, (for him) concerned with the relation of man to God and to his neighbor.

SCIENTIA SPECULATIVA, *speculative science*; sciences which consider the truths of things, not operations; and relative, therefore, to the speculative, not the practical intellect. Compare VERUM.

SCIRE, *to know, to understand, to perceive*; a thing is said to be known when its cause has been learned, and it is not known unless there is the certainty that it is impossible that it be other than it is. Knowledge is dependent on demonstration; according to Thomas (*In I lib. An. Post.* lect. 4), "To know seems to be nothing other than to understand the truth of any conclusion by demonstration."

SENSIBILE, *the sensible*, that which is perceived by the senses, as the intellectual is that which is perceived by the intellect.

SENSIBILE PROPRIUM, *proper sensible*, that which through itself or through its proper species can be perceived by only one external sense without error, as light (or color) by the eyes, sound by the ears; Bacon enumerates nine proper sensibles.

SENSIBILE COMMUNE, *common sensible*, that which is perceived by several external senses through modified species of the proper sensibles, as quantity, distance, motion, rest, figure; Bacon enumerates twenty common sensibles and adds to these, combinations of the twenty with each other.

SENSIBILE PER ACCIDENS, *accidental sensible*, that which falls under the external senses neither through its own species nor the modified species of something else, but only by means of something else with which is conjoined, as material substance.

SENSUS, *sense*, the faculty of the soul cognoscitive of material and singular objects.

SENSUS EXTERNI, *external senses*, those possessed of outward bodily organs, as sight, hearing, and so forth.

SENSUS INTERNI, *internal senses* (or SENSUS INTERIOR, *interior sense*), those whose organ is located within the head in the substance of the brain itself, that is, fantasy or imagination, common sense, memory, estimation, cogitation.

SENSUS COMMUNIS, *common sense*, the internal sense which perceives the objects of all the external senses and judges concerning their effects and concerning their operations.

SENSUS CORPOREUS, *corporeal sense*, the five external senses.

SENSUS SPIRITUALIS, *spiritual sense*, the fifth of the seven grades of interior experience according to Bacon.

SENTENTIA, *sentence*, a definitive, distinct, and most certain concept of one pole of a contradiction; assent to a sentence therefore is the determined acceptance of one part of a contradiction.

SIGNIFICATIO, *signification, meaning*.

VERITAS SIGNIFICATIONIS, *truth of signification*. Compare VERITAS.

SIGNUM, *sign*, something manifest to us by which we are led to a knowledge of something not manifest; that which represents something other than itself to a cognoscitive power.

Similitudo, *likeness, similitude*, the relation of two *qualities* of the same species and grade (as equality is the agreement of two quantities); the relation of cause and effect involves the relation of likeness, and in this sense all things are likenesses of God. Thomas defines likeness (*In lib. I Sent.* d. 2 q. 1 exp. text.), "Likeness signifies a relation caused by a unity of quality, which relation requires distinct subjects, for the likeness of different things is the same quality; wherefore the nature of that which causes likeness reveals a unity of essence, which is the same goodness and wisdom or whatever else is signified by the mode of quality." He says elsewhere (*Sum. Theol.* I, q. 93, a. 9 concl.), "Likeness is a certain unity, for the one in quality causes likeness." In the sense of likeness to God, there are distant likenesses (*similitudo longinqua*) and close likenesses (*similitudo propinqua sive expressa*) according to Bonaventura; the latter are images (*imago*) and are found only in the rational soul of man.

Simpliciter, *simply, absolutely*, (ἁπλῶς); indicates that the thing is as pronounced, and nothing of its determination is removed. According to Thomas (*Sum. Theol.* III, q. 50, a. 5 concl.), "Simply can be taken in two ways. In one way as simply is the same as absolutely, as 'that is spoken of simply which is spoken of without the addition of something else,' as the Philosopher says (*Top.* II, c. 11, 115ᵇ 34–35) . . . In another way it is the same as completely or totally." In both senses it is contrasted to *in some respect* (*secundum quid*). God exists simply; creatures, since God's will must be supposed, exist in some respect. Compare ABSOLUTE.

Singulare, *singular, individual*; that which is not apt naturally to be predicated of many, but only of one; this or that singular can not be defined. Compare INDIVIDUUM.

Situs, *position, situation, disposition*; the seventh of the ten categories; as a category it imports an order of parts in place; it may, however, be a differentia of quantity too, in which case it imports only an order of parts in a whole; it applies only to body; as sitting or lying.

Spatium, *space*; the middle ages early mingled platonic notions in its aristotelian discussion of space (χώρα). Thomas suggests the reason for departure from pure aristotelianism (which is in large part responsible for the discussions leading to the confusions of the doctrines of

space and time in the seventeenth and eighteenth centuries) by repeating the aristotelian dictum (*Phys.* IV,
c. 2, 209ᵇ 16–17), that whereas many would say that place
is something, Plato alone attempted to state what place is
(*In lib. IV Phys.* lect. 3).   "The ancients thought that
place is space, which is that between the limits of the
containing thing, which has the dimensions of length,
breadth, and thickness; but its space does not seem to
be the same as any body of sensible things, for space
remains the same when diverse sensible bodies have re-
ceded and advened. According to this therefore it follows
that place is separated dimensions. And Plato wanted
to prove from this by syllogism that place was matter.
And this is what he says, that as place seems to some
to be a distance of magnitude of space, separated from
any sensible body, it seemed that place was matter. For
the distance itself and dimension of magnitude is other
than magnitude, for magnitude signifies something determined by some species, as a line is determined from
points, and a surface by a line, and a body by a surface,
which are species of magnitude; but the dimension of
space is contained and determined under form, as body
is determined by the plane (that is, the surface) as by a
certain limit. That however which is contained under
limits, seems not to be determined in itself. But that
which is not determined in itself, but is determined by
form and limit, is matter, which has the nature of the
infinite, for if from any spherical body the sensible passions are removed and the limits by which the dimensions
of magnitude are figured, nothing remains but matter;
whence it follows that these dimensions, indeterminate of
themselves, which are determined by something else, are
matter itself. And this clearly followed from the roots
[i.e. the fundamental principles] of Plato, who posited
that numbers and quantities are the substances of things.
Since therefore place is dimensions, and dimensions are
matter, Plato said in the Timaeus, that place and matter
are the same, for anything receptive of anything was said
to be place, not distinguishing between the reception of
place and of matter; whence, since matter is receptive of
forms, it follows that matter is place." Thomas goes
on to repeat the aristotelian refutation of this position,
the aristotelian position being that place is a receptacle or

a vessel, a vessel being a place that can itself be moved about, and therefore place may be regarded as an immovable vessel, or vessel as a movable place (Aristotle, *Phys.* IV, c. 2, 209^b 28–30; and IV, c. 4, 212^a 15–16). The platonic position was however revived and laid the foundations of the doctrine that place is the interval, space, or distance occupied by a thing (not the limit of the containing body or vessel), that there can therefore be place without the thing in place; the introduction of the doctrine of the vacuum then is not improper (whereas for Aristotle there is no place without a body contained in place, for no otherwise is there a surrounding equal and separate limit, and a vacuum is therefore impossible and inconceivable); finally all bodies are in a real and existent space, and space itself becomes boundless and infinite (whereas for Aristotle every body in the universe is in place, but the universe is not itself in place, since it has no surrounding limit, and the universe is therefore finite). Compare LOCUS.

SPECIES INTENTIONALIS, *intentional species*; a certain image of the object, through which the object is joined with the cognitive faculty and is attained by it. Bonaventura says (*In lib. I Sent.* d. 31, p. 2, a. 1, q. 3 concl.), "Species imports likeness, the relation of knowing, and beauty."

SPECIES CORPOREA, *corporeal species*.

SPECIES INTELLIGIBILIS, *intelligible species*.

SPECIES EXPRESSA, *express species*, the idea itself which the object causes to appear, that is, the perception and presentation of the object; that which is formed by the possible intellect from the species which are derived by the active intellect, that it may know the object represented by it actually. It is, as it were, the principle which determines the understanding to knowledge and represents the object as intelligible. It is the concept of the thing which the mind forms when it knows the object, and it is said to be the term of knowledge or the verb of the mind.

SPECIES IMPRESSA, *impressed species*, the quality sent forth by the object as a kind of vicarious power of the object, which is impressed in the knowing faculty and aids it in eliciting the knowledge of the object or the express species; the intelligible species which is elaborated by the active intellect and received by the possible intellect; the image of the thing by which the mind is determined to knowing that thing, and therefore it is said to be the principle of knowledge.

SPECIES SENSIBILIS, *sensible species.*

SPECIES LOGICA, *logical species,* the notion which exhibits the common essence of many individuals; subclass of genus; species is defined by Boethius (see above, vol. I, p. 97) as "the thought collected from the substantial likeness of individuals unlike in number"; he speaks of species as caused by genus and differentia (ibid. p. 90); according to his doctrine species are sensible in individuals, but are thought universals and as universals are intelligible; one of the five universal attributes or predicables.

SPECIES PRAEDICABILIS, *predicable species,* one apt to be predicated of many things differing only in number, not in essence, as man may be predicated of Peter and Socrates.

SPECIES SUBIICIBILIS, *subjectible species,* the particular species which is collocated immediately under the genus and of which the genus is predicated immediately, as animal in respect to the living.

SPECIES INFIMA, (or SPECIES SPECIALISSIMA), *the lowest species, the most special species,* a species which has under itself only individuals, as horse has only this or that horse. According to Thomas (*In lib. X Met.* lect. 10, 2123), "These (i.e. *species specialissimae*) are called individuals, in so far as they are not further divisible formally. Individuals however are called particulars in so far as they are not further divisible neither materially nor formally." Compare INDIVIDUUM.

SPECIFICARE, *to specify, to specificate,* to collocate under this or that species, in this or that order, as potentiality is specificated by act.

SPECIFICATIO, *specification.*

SPECIFICATIVUM, *specificative,* that attribute or those attributes which distinguish a thing from other things and place it in a given species, as rationality is specificative of man.

SPECULATIO, *speculation;* according to Aristotle (*Met.* XII, c. 7, 1072[b] 21-24), "The intellect, however, [as contrasted to the intelligence of God, which in accordance with itself is of that which is best in itself] understands itself by the transumption of the intelligible [i.e. by taking or the nature of the object of thought], for it becomes ai intelligible [i.e. an object of thought] by coming into contact with and understanding [its objects], so that intellect and intelligible are the same. For the intellect is that which is susceptive of the intelligible and of essence; but intellect is actualized when it possesses [its object]. Therefore the latter [possession] rather than the former [receptivity] is the divine element which intellect seems to have, and the act of speculation is what is most pleasant and best." Compare CONTEMPLATIO.

SPIRITUS, *spirit*, as opposed to body, is simple, complete, immaterial, and intellective substance.

SUBIECTIVUM, *subjective*; particularly in knowledge the aspect to be attributed to the thing as contrasted to objective.

SUBIECTUM, *subject*, that subject to or underlying, particularly that subject to change (thus susceptive of contraries) and that subject to an idea or to the understanding, that is, the things themselves without; finally, that of which anything else is said.

SUBIICI ALIQUIBUS PRAEDICATIS, *to be a subject having certain predicates*.

SUBIICIBILIS, *subjectible*, that which can be the subject in any proposition, or that which can have a certain predicate, as water is subjectible to the predicates of heat or cold.

SUBSTANTIA, *substance*, (οὐσία) the first category, that which subsists through itself (*per se ens*). That however is not to be taken as its definition, for substance (like the other nine categories) can not be defined. According to Thomas (*Con. Gen.* I, 25), "*That which is through itself* is not the definition of substance. For from what has been said of *that which is* [*ens*] it could not be a genus, for it has already been proved that that which is does not have the nature of genus [because no proper differentia could be found to divide it into species]. In the same way from what has been said of *through itself* [*per se*], it could not be a genus, for it seems to import only a negation; for it is called that which is through itself because it is not in another, which is a pure negation, which can not constitute the nature or reason of a genus, for then the genus would not state what the thing is, but what it is not. The nature [*ratio*] of substance, therefore, must be understood in this way, that substance is a thing to which being is proper without being in a subject, (but the name *thing* is imposed from quiddity, as the name *that which is* is imposed from being) and thus it is understood in the nature of substance, that it has a quiddity (to which being is proper) not in something else." It is the property of substance that, remaining the same in number itself, it may undergo contraries; it is not itself susceptible of a contrary, nor of more or less, although it is the subject of both in change or mutation. Thomas distinguishes the meanings of substance (*In lib. II Sent.* d. 37, q. 1, a. 1 sol.), "Substance is spoken of in two ways. For in one way substance is spoken of as it signifies the nature [*ratio*] of the first category: and this is either form, or matter, or the composite which is through itself in genus. In another way, that is said to be substance which signifies the essence in all things, as we say that definition signifies the substance of a thing, and in this manner whatsoever is said positively in any genus whatever is substance or has substance."

SUBSTANTIA PRIMA, *first substance*, that which is neither in a subject nor predicated of a subject; individual existent things, as Socrates.

SUBSTANTIA SECUNDA, *second substance*, that which is in no subject, but may be predicated of a subject, that is, genera and species, or universals, as man may be predicated of Peter.

SUBSTANTIA SEPARATA, *separated substance*, as angels or intelligences.

SUBSTANTIA CONIUNCTA, *conjunct substance*, formed by the union of form and matter.

SUBSTITUTIO, *determination*.

SUBSTARE, *to underlie*; to underlie an act is to be the object of it as when I perceive the moon, the moon underlies my perception.

SUPPONERE, *to suppose, to hypothesize, to stand for*; according to Thomas (*In lib. III Sent.* d. 6, q. 1, a. 3 sol.), "In any name there are two things to consider, namely, that because of which the name is imposed (which is called the quality of the name), and that on which the name is imposed (which is called the substance of the name). The name properly speaking is said to *signify* the form or quality because of which the name is imposed; but it is said to *stand for* that on which it is imposed." Thus the name of animal signifies sensible animated substance; it stands for (for example) man, because man falls under

the definition of animal as determinate under indeterminate.

SUPPOSITIO, *supposition, premiss*, that which underlies intellectually; that is, that which is prerequisite intellectually;
thus, according to Bonaventura, there is a fourfold supposition of knowledge: proportion, union, judgment, and
information. supposition is the usurpation of a word for
the things signified by the word: as numbers are used for
money in counting money, so terms are used in the place
of things signified by terms. Supposition for something
is therefore to signify it or stand for it (compare SUP-
PONERE); therefore, there is a material supposition (when
the reference is to the term and not to the thing signified),
as when it is said *Man is a word*; and a formal supposition
(when the thing signified is considered), as when it is
said, *Man is endowed with reason*.

SUPPOSITIO TERMINI, *supposition of the term*, embraces therefore that which the term stands for and its own characteristics and its functions in proposition.

SUPPOSITUM, *subject, subordinate, suppositum*; singular or
completed substances (which exist through themselves) are
supposita if they lack understanding; in virtue of the
same peculiarities they are *persons* if they possess understanding; *suppositum* is used also in the more general
sense to include persons, as when Bonaventura holds that
in the Trinity there is a plurality of supposita and a unity
of essence. Compare PERSONA.

SUSCEPTIO, *a taking on, susception, assumption*; in respect to
extraneous accidents, a substance is susceptive only.

SUSCIPERE, *to assume, to take on*.

SYLLOGISMUS, *syllogism*, defined by Aristotle (*Top.* I ,1, 100ª
25-27), "The syllogism is discourse in which certain things
being posited and conceded, something else follows necessarily from those things which have been posited and
conceded." It is the concourse of three propositions,
major and minor premisses and a conclusion, in which
three terms occur: the efficient cause of the syllogism is
the rational soul forming it, the material cause is the
three terms (as remote matter) and the two propositions
(as near matter), the final cause is to lead to faith in or
knowledge of the unknown conclusion, the formal cause is
the faculty or power of inferring the conclusion from the
premisses.

SYNCATEGOREMA, SINCATHEGREUMA, *syncategoremtatic term*, a term which must be joined to another term in the nominative case in order to enter into a proposition, as *this book is John's*, or such words as *all, each, every*, all adjectives and verbs. Compare CATEGOREMA.

SYNCATEGOREMATICE, *syncategorematically*, a thing is said to be such and such syncategorematically because it is potentially such, as mathematical quantity which can be understood without any other term is said syncategorematically to be infinite.

T

TEMPUS, *time*; according to Aristotle time (χρόνος) is the number of motion according to prior and posterior; thence the measure of duration of a variable thing; opposed to *eternity*, the measure of a thing invariable both according to substance and duration; and to *aeon* (*aevum*), a medium measure of an invariable being, which none the less admits of some variation with respect to operation, as the heavenly spheres which undergo only local motion; time is sometimes used broadly to include aeon.

TENERE, *to hold, to know.*

THEOSOPHIA, *theosophy, the science and love of God.*

TOLLERE, *to deny.*

TOPICA, *topic*; the places (τόποι) of argumentation; contrasted by Boethius (see above, vol. I, p. 74), as the art of discovering arguments, to dialectic, the art of judging arguments; used by Aristotle and the medieval aristotelians as synonymous with dialectic, the distinction being made between induction and reasoning, or inductive and syllogistic dialectic. The problems of the two are the same though their directions are opposite: both are concerned with the means of becoming well supplied with reasonings: the means are four, the securing of propositions, the distinguishing of the various senses of an expression, the discovery of differences of things, the investigation of likeness.

TRANSCENDENTALES, *the transcendentals*, terms or properties which accord with all things of every genus whatsoever; they are therefore transcendentals as opposed to the categorials or predicamentals (compare too the POSTPREDICAMENTA). The scholastics usually list three such terms: the true, the one, the good; but more ancient writers enumerated six: *res, ens, verum, bonum, aliquid, unum*, and then taking the initial letter of each word, referred to the six by the term *Reubau*. Nothing can be found in the nature of things of which they can not be predicated. The nature of the transcendentals is well illustrated by Boethius (above, vol. I, p. 93), who in order to prove that genera and species are not, demonstrates that they can not be one, and since they are not one, they can not be. Compare CONVERTI.

TRIVIUM, *trivium*, the linguistic portion of the seven arts (which constituted for a part of the middle ages the major portion of primary education); the three arts or disciplines, grammar, rhetoric, dialectic (or logic).

U

UBI, *where, place*, the fifth of the ten aristotelian categories.

UMBRA, *shadow*, according to Bonaventura, one of the three ways (compare VESTIGIUM, IMAGO) in which God is represented in his creatures; a creature is a shadow of God in so far as he has any property which looks to God in an undetermined relation.

UNIO, *union*, the conjunction of things into one.

UNITAS, *unity*, according to Aristotle the indivision of a thing in itself and its division from every other thing.

UNIVERSALE, *universal*, that which is one although it is extended to many; that which is naturally apt to be present in many and to be predicated of many. (Compare Aristotle, *de Interp.* 6, 17ᵃ 37). Therefore Albert says (*de Praed.* tract II, c. 1), "A universal is that which, although it is in one, is naturally apt to be in many; . . . and therefore, since it is in many by aptitude, it is predicable of them. And thus the universal is that which is in many and of many because of its aptitude."

UNIVERSITAS, *whole (of things)*.

UNIVOCA (or UNIVOCALIS), *univocal*, (συνώνυμος) those things to which the same predicate is proper in the same sense; a name which is attributed commonly to many under the same definition, in such wise that they are reduced to a single superior nature, is predicated univocally of them, as animal is predicated of lion and sheep univocally. Equivocal, on the other hand, refers to those things to which the same predicate is proper but in different senses, as dog is predicated of the dog-fish, the dog-star, and the canine animal. ANALOGA, *analogous* is referred to those things to one of which the predicate accords in the proper sense, to the other in an improper sense, as man in the case of a living man and a man painted in a portrait; the analogous is medium between equivocal and univocal.

UNIVOCATIO, *univocation*, denominating by the same name in the same sense.

UNUM, *one*, the indivision of the thing that is. Compare TRANSCENDENTALES.

USIADIS, *substantial*; derived from οὐσία.

V

VERITAS, *truth*, a relation (*habitudo*) between thing and under-standing. There is (1) a *truth in being*, which is the agreement of the thing with the understanding on which it depends as on a cause (that is, the divine understanding), and thus natural things are called true, and truth, in this sense, is the essence of all things which are, because they are that which they are in the supreme truth or God (see Anselm, above vol. I, p. 163); there is (2) a *truth in knowing*, which is the agreement of the thing with the understanding to which things are referred accidentally (that is, our ideas are the effects, not the causes of things), and thus our ideas are said to be true; finally there is (3) a *truth in signifying*, which is the agreement of signs with things or with that which is in the mind; truth, in this sense, is the saying that that which is is and that that which is not, is not (Aristotle, *Met.* IV, 7, 1011^{b} 27). The pseudo-Grosseteste distinguishes these three kinds of truth as incomplex, complex, and medium truths (see above, vol. I, pp. 294–296): "the incomplex truth is the very entity of any thing, that is, the indivision of the thing that is and its being; . . . the complex truth . . . is the adequation of the thing and the understanding joining the intention of the predicate with the intention of the subject or disjoining the latter from the former; . . . the medium truth is in signs, which the understanding uses to express complex truth, and in things themselves, for truth is in these as if in its material principle without the ade-quation necessary for the understanding." The augustinian tradition is concerned with proving the eternity of truth in its primary incomplex sense; as the pseudo-Grosseteste says (above, vol. I, p. 294), "Truth will therefore be an eternal uncreated substance, wholly unique, and whose being of necessity must be and can not but be." In view of these three meanings, truth is variously defined: it was first defined as the adequation of thing and understanding by Isaac Israeli; according to Grosseteste (see above vol. I, p. 269) it is being in the thing signified, as the speech signifies; according to Anselm it is rightness perceptible to the mind alone (see above, vol. I, p. 172); according to Augustine it is that by which that which is, is shown; according to Hilary it is manifestive and declarative being.

VERITAS COMPOSITIONIS, *truth of composition,* according to Duns Scotus, the propriety, discoverable in terms themselves of the relation of the terms to each other which makes the proposition stating such a relation selfevidently and necessarily true.

VERUM, *the true,* a disposition (*dispositio*) of the thing which is (*ens*): the conformity of the thing that is to the understanding, according to Thomas Aquinas; it is defined by Augustine as that which is. The true is the object of contemplation of the speculative intellect. According to Thomas (*Sum. Theol.* Ia IIae, q. 57, a. 2 concl.), "The intellectual speculative power is that by which the speculative intellect is perfected for considering the true, for that is its good work. The true, however, is considerable in two ways: in one way as known through itself, in another way as known through something else. That which is known through itself, however, is constituted as principle and is perceived immediately by the understanding; and therefore the habit perfecting the understanding for the consideration of the true of this sort is called the understanding which is the having (or habit) of principles. But the true which is known through something else, is not perceived immediately by the understanding, but through the inquisition of reason. This can be in two ways: in one way as it is the ultimate in any genus; in another manner as it is ultimate in respect of the whole of human knowledge. And because *those things which are known posterior with respect to us, are prior and more known according to nature,* as it is said [by Aristotle, as in

Phys. I, c. 1, 184ª 17–22, or *Met.* VII, c. 3, 1029ᵇ 4],
therefore that which is ultimate with respect to the whole
of human knowledge is that which is first and most of all
cognoscible. And with the true of this sort wisdom is
concerned, which *considers the highest causes*, as it is said
[by Aristotle, *Met.* I, c. 1, 981ᵇ 28], whence properly it
judges of and orders all things, because perfect and universal judgment can be had only through resolution to
first causes."

VESTIGIUM, *footprint, vestige, trace*, according to Bonaventura
one of the three ways (compare IMAGO, UMBRA) in which
God is represented in his creatures; Bonaventura's division is a systematic statement of the traditional augustinian doctrine. A creature is a trace in so far as he is one,
true, and good, dependent thus on God as efficient, formal,
and final causes; see Lombard above, vol. I, pp. 188–193.

VIATOR, *wayfarer, one on the way*, one who is in the present
world, whose life is a peregrination to another world.
Compare BEATUS.

VIRTUALITER, *virtually*; one thing is contained in another virtually when there is present a power to produce such an
effect; as every effect is contained virtually in its cause.

VIRTUS, *power, virtue*, a perfection or strength for performing
something rightly; it has been called the disposition of the
perfect to the best, in that it is a disposition enabling
a potentiality to elicit an actual good. Virtue is also
taken as power, thus contrasted to essence; this is the
use that appears in the adverb *virtually*. In its ethical
sense, virtue was held to be a prerequisite to intellectual
as well as moral perfection; thus Bacon makes it the
second of the grades of interior experience.

VIRTUS AFFECTIVA, *affective power*.

VIRTUS APPREHENSIVA, *apprehensive power*.

VIS, *power, faculty, strength*; according to Boethius (*In Isag.*
2nd ed. I; above, vol. I, p. 70), there is a threefold power
of the soul, vegetative, sensitive, and intellectual.

VOX, *word, spoken word*; name (*nomen*) is *vox significativa*.

ENGLISH—LATIN[1]

A

ABLE (TO BE), *posse.*

ABSOLUTELY, *absolute, simpliciter.*

ABSTRACTIVE, *abstractivum.*

ABSTRACTIVE KNOWLEDGE, *cognitio abstractiva.*

ABSTRACTION, *abstractio.*

ACCIDENT, *accidens.*

ACCIDENTAL CAUSE, *causa accidentalis.*

ACCIDENTAL SENSIBLE, *sensibile per accidens.*

ACCIDENTALLY, *accidentaliter, per accidens.*

ACQUAINTANCE, *cognitio.*

ACQUIRED INTELLECT, *intellectus adeptus.*

ACT (TO), *agere.*

ACT, *actus.*

ACTION, *facere, actio.*

ACTIVE, *agens.*

ACTIVE INTELLECT, *intellectus agens.*

ACTUALITY, *actus.*

ADEQUABILITY, *adaequabilitas.*

ADEQUATION, *adaèquatio.*

AEON, *aevum.*

AFFECT, *affectio, affectus.*

AFFECTION, *affectio.*

AFFECTIVE POWER, *virtus affectiva.*

AFFIRM (TO), *ponere.*

AFFIRMATION, *positio.*

AGENT, *agens.*

AGREEMENT, *convenientia.*

ALTERATION, *alteratio.*

AMPHIBOLOGY, *amphibolia.*

ANALOGY, *analogia.*

ANIMAL, *animal.*

APPETITE, *appetitus.*

APPREHENSION, *apprehensio.*

APPREHENSIVE POWER, *virtus apprehensiva.*

APPROPRIATED QUALITY OR ASPECT, *appropriatum.*

APTITUDE, *aptitudo, habitudo.*

APTITUDINAL, *aptitudinalis.*

ARGUMENT, *argumentum, ratio.*

ART, *ars, disciplina.*

ARTIFICIALLY, *artificiose.*

ASSUME (TO), *suscipere.*

ASSIMILATED (TO BE), *assimilari.*

ATTRIBUTIVE ANALOGY, *analogia attributionis.*

AUGMENTATION, *augmentatio*

B

BEATITUDE, *beatitudo.*

BEHOLD (TO), *contuere.*

BEING (A), *ens.*

BEING, *esse.*

[1] The English-Latin Glossary is appended as a key, for those who read no latin, to the Latin-English Glossary.

BEING (OF), *essendi.*
BLESSED, *beatus.*
BLESSEDNESS, *beatitudo.*
BRING TOGETHER (TO), BRING OUT (TO), *colligo.*

C

CAPACITY FOR SOMETHING, *habitudo.*
CATEGOREMATIC TERM, *categorema.*
CATEGOREMATICALLY, *categorematice.*
CATEGORICAL, *praedicamentalis.*
CATEGORY, *praedicamentum, categoria.*
CAUSE, *causa.*
  CAUSATIVE, *causativum.*
CERTITUDE, *certitudo.*
CHANGE, *mutatio.*
CHARACTER, *habitus.*
CHOICE, *dilectio.*
COGITATE (TO), *cogitare.*
  COGITATION, *cogitatio.*
  COGITATIVE FACULTY, *virtus cogitativa.*
COGNITION, *cognitio, notitia.*
COMBINATION, *complexio.*
COMMENSURATION, *adequatio.*
COMMON, *commune.*
  COMMON DIFFERENCE, *differentia communis.*
  COMMON SENSE, *sensus communis.*
  COMMON SENSIBLE, *sensibile commune.*
  COMMON (TO BE), *communicare.*
COMPARATIVE EQUALITY, *aequalitas aequiparantiae.*
COMPARISON, *aequiparantia.*

COMPLANTED LIGHT, *lumen complanatum.*
COMPLEX, *complexum.*
COMPOUND (TO), *componere.*
  COMPOSITE, *compositum.*
  COMPOSITION, *compositio.*
COMPREHENDS (ONE WHO), *comprehensor.*
CONCEPTION, *cognitio, conceptus, intellectus, notio.*
CONCRETE, *concretum.*
CONDITION, *affectio, conditio, habere, habitudo, habitus.*
CONJOIN (TO), *coniungere.*
  CONJUNCT SUBSTANCE, *substantia coniuncta.*
CONNECTION, *coaptatio.*
CONSIDERATION, *cognitio.*
CONSTITUTION, *complexio.*
CONSUBSTANTIAL, *consubstantialis.*
CONTEMPLATION, *contemplatio.*
CONTINGENT, *contingens.*
CONTINUUM, *continuum.*
CONTRACT (TO), *contrahere.*
CONTRADICTORIES, *contradictoria.*
CONTRADICTORY, *oppositio.*
CONTRARIES, *contraria.*
CONVERTED (TO BE), *converti.*
CORPOREAL SENSE, *sensus corporeus.*
CORPOREAL SPECIES, *species corporea.*
CORRUPTED, *corruptum.*
CORRUPTION, *corruptio.*
CREATION, *conditio, creatura.*
CREATURE, *creatura.*
CRITERION, *ratio.*

D

DEFECT, *defectus.*

DEFINITION, *definitio, diffinitio, ratio.*

  DEFINITION OF NAME, *definitio nominis, diffinitio quid nominis.*

    DEFINITION OF THE THING, *definitio rei, diffinitio quid rei.*

DEIFORM, *deiformis.*

DEIFORMITY, *deiformitas.*

DELIBERATION, *deliberatio.*

DEMONSTRATION, *demonstratio.*

  DEMONSTRATION BASED ON THE EFFECT, *demonstratio quia.*

  DEMONSTRATION BASED ON THE NATURE OF THE THING INVESTIGATED, *demonstratio propter quid.*

DENIAL, *ablatio, remotio.*

DENOMINATIVELY, *denominative.*

DENY (TO), *removere, tollere.*

DESCENT BY DEFINITION, *descensus per definitionem.*

DESCRIPTION, *descriptio.*

DETERMINATELY, *determinate.*

DETERMINATION, *substitutio.*

DIALECTIC, *dialectica.*

DIFFERENCE, *differentia.*

DIFFERENTIA, *differentia.*

DIFFERING, *differens.*

DIMINUTION, *diminutio.*

DISCIPLINE, *disciplina.*

DISCOURSE, *discursus, oratio.*

DISCOVERY, *inventio.*

DISCRETENESS, *discretio.*

DISCRETION, *discretio.*

DISJOIN (TO), *disiungere.*

DISPOSING MEDIUM, *disponens medium.*

DISPOSITION, *dispositio, situs.*

DISTINCT, *distinctum.*

DISTINCTION, *distinctio.*

DISTINGUISH (TO), *discernere.*

DIVERSE, *diversum.*

DIVERSIFICATION, *diversificatio.*

DIVIDE (TO), *dividere.*

DIVISION, *divisio.*

DO (TO), *agere, facere.*

E

EFFECT, *effectus.*

EFFECTIVELY (IN EFFECT), *effective.*

EFFICIENT CAUSE, *causa efficiens.*

EFFICIENT MEDIUM, *efficiens medium.*

ELEMENT, *elementum.*

ELENCHUS, *elenchus.*

EMINENTLY, *eminenter.*

END, *finis.*

  END OF THE OPERATION, *finis operis.*

  END OF THE ONE PERFORMING THE OPERATION, *finis operantis.*

ENTHYMEME, *enthymema.*

ENTITY, *entitas.*

EQUALITY, *aequalitas.*

EQUIPARANCE, *aequiparantia.*

EQUIVALENCE, *aequiparantia.*

EQUIVOCAL, *aequivoca.*

ERROR, *error.*

ESSENCE, *essentia.*

  ESSENCE OF THE THING, *ratio rei.*

  ESSENTIALLY, *essentialiter, per se.*

ESTIMATION, *aestimatio, existimatio.*

ETERNITY, *aeternitas.*

EVIDENCE, *apparentia, evidentia.*

  EVIDENTLY, *evidenter.*

EVIL, *malum.*

EXEMPLAR, *exemplar.*

EXPERIENCE, *experientia, experimentum.*

EXPERIMENT, *experientia, experimentum.*

  EXPERIMENTAL SCIENCE, *scientia experimentalis.*

EXPRESS SPECIES, *species expressa.*

EXTERNAL SENSES, *sensus externi.*

F

FACULTY, *facultas, vis.*

FALSE, *falsum.*

FALSIGRAPHIC, *falsigrafis.*

FINAL CAUSE, *causa finalis.*

FIRST INTENTION, *intentio prima.*

FIRST SUBSTANCE, *substantia prima.*

FOOTPRINT, *vestigium.*

FORESIGHT, *providentia.*

FORM, *forma.*

  FORMABLE, *formabilis.*

  FORMAL CAUSE, *causa formalis.*

  FORMAL INTELLECT, *intellectus formalis.*

  FORMALLY, *formaliter.*

FRUIT, *fructus.*

G

GATHER (TO), *colligo.*

GENERAL INTENTION, *intentio generalis.*

GENERALISSIMUM, MOST GENERAL GENUS, *generalissimum.*

GENERATION, *generatio.*

GENUS, *genus.*

GIFT, *donum.*

GOOD, *bonum.*

GROUND, *ratio.*

H

HABIT, *habitus.*

HAPPEN (TO), *accidere.*

HAPPINESS, *beatitudo.*

HAVE (TO), *habere.*

HECCEITY, *haecceitas.*

HOLD (TO), *tenere.*

HYPOTHESIZE (TO), *supponere.*

I

IDEA, *cognito, idea, intellectus, notitia.*

IDENTITY, *identitas.*

IDOL, *idolum.*

IGNORANCE, *ignorantia.*

ILLUMINATION, *illuminatio, lumen.*

IMAGINATION, *imaginatio.*

IMAGE, *imago.*

IMPRESSED SPECIES, *species impressa.*

INCOMPLEX, *incomplexum.*

INCOMPOSSIBLE, *incompossibile.*

INCONTINGENT, *incontingens.*

INCREASE, *augmentatio.*

INDIFFERENCE, *indifferentia.*

  INDIFFERENTLY, *indifferenter.*

INDISTANCE, *indistantia.*

INDIVIDUAL, *individuum, singulare.*

ĪNDIVIDUATED (TO BE), *individuari.*

INDIVIDUATION, *individuatio.*

INDIVISION, *indivisio.*

INFER (TO), *colligo.*

INFERENCE, *collectio, complexio.*

INFINITE, *infinitum.*

INFORM (TO), *informare.*

INFORMATION, *informatio.*

INHERENCE, *inhaerentia.*

INTELLECT, *intellectus.*

INTELLECTUAL, *intellectuale*

INTELLIGENCE, *intelligentia.*

INTELLIGIBLE SPECIES, *species intelligibilis.*

INTEND (TO), *intendere.*

INTENSIVELY, *intensive.*

INTENTION, *intentio.*

INTENTIONAL BEING, *esse intentionale.*

INTENTIONAL SPECIES, *species intentionalis.*

INTERNAL SENSES, *sensus interni.*

INTUITIVE KNOWLEDGE, *cognitio intuitiva, intuitus.*

INVENTION, *inventio.*

J

JUDGE (TO), *cogitare.*

JUDGMENT, *cogitatio, iudicium.*

K

KNOW (TO), *cognoscere, scire, tenere.*

KNOWABILITY, *cognoscibilitas.*

KNOWABLE, *cognoscibile, scibile.*

KNOWER, *cognoscens.*

KNOWLEDGE, *cognitio, notitia, scientia.*

L

LEARN (TO), *cognoscere.*

LIGHT, *lux.*

LIKENESS, *similitudo.*

LOGICAL SPECIES, *species logica.*

LOVE, *affectus, dilectio.*

LOWEST SPECIES, *species infima, species specialissima.*

M

MAKING, *factio.*

MANNER, *maneries.*

MANUDUCTION, *manuductio.*

MATERIAL, *materialis.*

MATERIAL CAUSE, *causa materialis.*

MATERIALLY, *materialiter.*

MATHEMATICS, *mathematica.*

MATTER, *materia.*

MEAN, *medium.*

MEANING, *intellectus, intentio, significatio.*

MEDIUM, *medium.*

MEMORATIVE FACULTY, **virtus** *memorativa.*

MEMORY, *memoria.*

MIDDLE, *medium.*

MODE, *modus.*

MOTION, *motus.*

MOVEMENT, *motus.*

MUTATION, *mutatio.*

N

NAME, *nomen.*

NATURAL KNOWLEDGE, *cognitio naturalis.*

NATURAL MOTION, *motus naturalis.*

NATURE, *natura, ratio.*

NECESSARY, *necessarium.*

NEGATION, *negatio.*

NOMINAL DEFINITION, *definitio nominis, diffinitio quid nominis.*

NOMINATION, *nominatio.*

NOTION, *cognitio, notio.*

NOUN, *nomen.*

NUMBER, *numerus.*

O

OBJECT, *obiectum.*

OBJECTIVE, *obiectivum.*

ONE, *unum.*

OPERATION, *operatio.*

OPINION, *opinio.*

OPPOSITE, *oppositum.*

OPPOSITION, *oppositio.*

P

PART, *pars.*

PARTICIPATION, *participatio.*

PARTICULAR, *particulare.*

PASSION, *passio, pati.*

PATIENT, *patiens.*

PECULIAR TO, *proprium.*

PERCEIVE (TO), *cognoscere, intelligere, scire.*

PERFECTION, *perfectio.*

PERFECTIVE, *perfectivum.*

PERSON, *persona.*

PERSONAL DISCRETION, *discretio personalis.*

PERSUASION, *persuasio.*

PHANTASM, *fantasma.*

PHANTASY, *phantasia.*

PLACE, *locus, ubi.*

POSIT (TO), *ponere.*

POSITION, *positio, situs.*

POSSIBLE INTELLECT, *intellectus possibilis.*

POSSIBILITY, *possibilitas.*

POSTCATEGORY, *postpraedicamentum.*

POSTPREDICAMENT, *postpraedicamentum.*

POTENCY, *potentia.*

POTENTIALITY, *potentia.*

POWER, *potentia, potestas, virtus, vis.*

PRACTICAL INTELLECT, *intellectus practicus.*

PRAXIS, *praxis.*

PREDICABLE, *praedicabile.*

PREDICABLE SPECIES, *species praedicabilis.*

PREDICAMENTAL, *praedicamentale.*

PREDICATE (TO), *praedicare.*

PREDICATION, *praedicatio.*

PRINCIPLE, *principium, ratio.*

PRIVATION, *privatio.*

PROPER, *proprium.*

PROPER CAUSE, *causa propria.*

PROPER DIFFERENCE, *differentia propria.*

PROPER DIFFERENCE (MOST), *differentia maxime propria.*

PROPERTY, *proprietas, proprium.*

PROPORTION, *proportio.*

PROPORTIONAL EQUALITY, *aequalitas proportionis.*

PROPORTIONALITY, *proportionalitas.*

PROPOSITION, *propositio.*

PROVIDENCE, *providentia.*

PROXIMITY, *indistantia.*

Q

QUADRIVIUM, *quadrivium.*
QUALITY, *qualitas.*
QUANTITY, *quantitas.*
QUIDDITY, *quidditas.*

R

RAPTURE, *raptus.*
RATIOCINATION, *ratiocinatio.*
RATIONAL, *rationale.*
  RATIONALLY, *rationaliter.*
REAL DEFINITION, *definitio realis.*
REASON, *causa, ratio.*
REASONABLY, *rationabiliter.*
REASONING, *ratiocinatio.*
RECEIVE (TO), *accipere, recipere, pati.*
RECTIFIED, *rectificatum.*
REFLEXIVELY, *reflexe.*
RELATION, *ad aliquid, habitudo, ratio, relatio.*
RELATIVE TO, *ad aliquid.*
RELATIVITY, *ad aliquid.*
REMINISCENCE, *reminiscentia.*
REMIT (TO), *remitti.*
REMOVE (TO), *removere.*
RESOLUTION, *divisio.*
RESOLVE (TO), *resolvere.*
RESPECT, *habitudo, respectus.*

S

SAME, *idem.*
SCIENCE, *scientia.*
  SCIENTIFIC ILLUMINATION, *illuminatio scientialis.*
  SCIENTIFIC KNOWLEDGE, *scientia.*
SECOND INTENTION, *intentio secunda.*

SECOND SUBSTANCE, *substantia secunda.*
SEE (TO), *contuere.*
SEMINAL REASON, *ratio seminalis.*
SENSE, *sensus.*
SENSIBLE, *sensibile.*
  SENSIBLE SPECIES, *species sensibilis.*
SENTENCE, *sententia.*
SEPARATE (TO), *dividere.*
  SEPARATED FORM, *forma separata.*
  SEPARATED INTELLIGENCE, *intelligentia separata.*
  SEPARATED SUBSTANCE, *substantia separata.*
SHADOW, *umbra.*
SIGN, *signum.*
SIGNIFICATION, *significatio.*
  SIGNIFICATIVE WORD, *nomen.*
SIMILITUDE, *similitudo.*
SIMPLY, *simpliciter.*
SINGULAR, *singulare.*
SITUATION, *situs.*
SOMETHING, *aliquid.*
SPACE, *spatium.*
SPECIFICATE (TO), *specificare.*
SPECIFICATION, *specificatio.*
  SPECIFICATIVE, *specificativum.*
  SPECIFY (TO), *specificare.*
SPECULATION, *speculatio.*
  SPECULATIVE INTELLECT, *intellectus speculativus.*
  SPECULATIVE SCIENCE, *scientia speculativa.*
SPIRIT, *spiritus.*
  SPIRITUAL SENSE, *sensus spiritualis.*
SPOKEN WORD, *vox.*
STAND FOR (TO), *supponere.*
STATE, *habere.*

STATEMENT, *enuntiatio.*

STRENGTH, *vis.*

SUBJECT, *subiectum, suppositum.*

  SUBJECTIBLE, *subiicibilis.*

  SUBJECTIBLE SPECIES, *species subiicibilis.*

SUBJECTIVE, *subiectivum.*

SUBORDINATE, *suppositum.*

SUBSTANCE, *substantia.*

  SUBSTANTIAL, *usiadis.*

  SUBSTANTIAL DEFINITION, *diffinitio substantialis.*

  SUBSTANTIALLY, *per se.*

SUFFER (TO), *pati.*

SUPPOSE (TO), *supponere.*

SUPPOSITION, *suppositio.*

  SUPPOSITION OF THE TERM, *suppositio termini.*

  SUPPOSITUM, *suppositum.*

SUSCEPTION, *susceptio.*

SYLLOGISM, *syllogismus.*

SYNCATEGOREMATIC TERM, *syncategorema, sincathegreuma.*

SYNCATEGOREMATICALLY, *syncategorematice.*

THEOSOPHY, *theosophia.*

THESIS, *positio.*

THING, *res.*

THING WHICH IS, *ens.*

  THING OF INTENTION, *intentionis res.*

  THING OF NATURE, *ens naturae.*

  THING OF REASON, *ens rationis.*

THINK (TO), *cogitare.*

THOUGHT, *cogitatio.*

THROUGH ITSELF, *per se.*

TIME, *quando, tempus.*

TOPIC, *topica.*

TRACE, *vestigium.*

TRANSCENDENTALS, *transcendentales.*

TRUE, *verum.*

TRUTH, *veritas.*

  TRUTH OF COMPOSITION, *veritas compositionis.*

  TRUTH OF SIGNIFICATION, *veritas significationis.*

  TRUTH OF STATEMENT, *veritas enuntiationis.*

T

TAKE ON (TO), *suscipere.*

  TAKING ON, *susceptio.*

THAT WHICH IS, *ens, id quod est.*

  THAT WHICH IS ESSENTIALLY, *ens per se.*

  THAT WHICH IS IN ITSELF ACCORDING TO THE MODE OF SUBSTANCE, *ens in se per modum substantiae.*

  THAT WHICH IS THROUGH ITSELF, *ens per se.*

U

UNDERGO (TO), *pati.*

UNDERLIE (TO), *substare.*

UNDERSTAND (TO), *intelligere, scire.*

UNDERSTANDING, *intellectus, intelligentia.*

UNDERTAKE (TO), *accipere.*

UNION, *unio.*

UNITY, *unitas.*

UNIVERSAL, *universale.*

UNIVOCAL, *univocalis, univoca.*

UNIVOCATION, *univocatio.*

W

V

WAYFARER, *viator.*
WHEN, *quando.*
VESTIGE, *vestigium.*
WHERE, *ubi.*
VIOLENT MOTION, *motus vio-*
WHOLE, *universitas.*
   lentus.
WISDOM, *sapientia.*
VIRTUALLY, *virtualiter.*
WORD, *nomen, vox.*
VIRTUE, *virtus.*
WORK (TO), *agere.*